ENGLISCH FÜR

BERUFLICHE SCHULEN

VON

TERRY MOSTON UND

LAURENCE HARGER

Work With English wurde geplant und entwickelt von der
Cornelsen & Oxford University Press GmbH, Berlin.

Das Lehrwerk wurde verfaßt von
Terry Moston, Fröndenberg und
Laurence Harger, Nürnberg
in Zusammenarbeit mit der Verlagsredaktion.

Beratende Mitwirkung erfolgte durch:
Studiendirektorin Dipl.-Hdl. Mary Fohrmann, Kempen;
Oberstudienrat Heiner Günster, Neuwied;
Studiendirektorin Gabriele Holtermann, Leonberg;
Studiendirektor Ulrich Kiewitz, Nürnberg;
Oberstudienrätin Alice Romberg, Bergisch Gladbach.

VERLAGSREDAKTION Michael Freyer (verantwortlicher Redakteur)
und James Abram

LAYOUT UND HERSTELLUNG Dirk Risch

Erhältlich sind auch
LEHRERHANDBUCH (Best.-Nr. 57461)
WORKBOOK (Best.-Nr. 57429)
WORKBOOK MIT VORKURS (Best.-Nr. 57445)
VORKURS (Best.-Nr. 57410)
TEXTCASSETTEN (Best.-Nr. 57470)
LISTENING COMPREHENSION CASSETTE (Best.-Nr. 57402)

1. Auflage
5.
93 92
Die letzten Ziffern bezeichnen
Zahl und Jahr des Druckes.

Alle Drucke dieser Auflage können, weil untereinander unverändert,
im Unterricht nebeneinander verwendet werden.

Bestellnummer 57 437

© Cornelsen & Oxford University Press GmbH, Berlin 1989

Das Werk und seine Teile sind urheberrechtlich geschützt.
Jede Verwertung in anderen als den gesetzlich zugelassenen Fällen bedarf deshalb
der vorherigen schriftlichen Einwilligung des Verlages.

SATZ dsd Demmer Satz + Daten GmbH, Berlin
REPRODUKTION OffsetReproTechnik Kirchner + Graser, Berlin
dsd Demmer Satz + Daten GmbH, Berlin
DRUCK Adolph Fürst & Sohn GmbH, Berlin
WEITERVERARBEITUNG Fritzsche/Ludwig, Berlin

ISBN 3-8109-5743-7

VERTRIEB Cornelsen Verlagsgesellschaft, Bielefeld

Vorwort

Was ist Work With English?
Ein Englischlehrwerk für berufliche Schulen, in denen der mittlere Bildungsabschluß in bis zu zwei Jahren erreicht wird.

An wen wendet sich Work With English?
An junge Erwachsene, die bereits über Vorkenntnisse in Englisch verfügen und erste Erfahrungen im Berufsleben gemacht haben oder auf persönliche Zielvorstellungen in z. B. einem kaufmännischen, gewerblich-technischen oder hauswirtschaftlichen Beruf hinarbeiten wollen.

Welches Ziel verfolgt Work With English?
Englisch ist heute Verkehrssprache Nr. 1. Insofern wird es immer wieder sowohl im beruflichen als auch im privaten Bereich Situationen geben, in denen man mit Menschen aus England, den USA, Kanada, Australien – um nur einige Länder zu nennen – zusammenkommt. Es gibt ferner eine Vielzahl von Ländern der Dritten Welt, in denen Englisch auch Verkehrssprache ist, wie z. B. Indien, Kenia, Nigeria. Tourismus und Handel sind wichtige Wirtschaftszweige, die uns mit diesen Ländern zunehmend verbinden.

Was ist im Schülerbuch enthalten?
Das Lehrwerk enthält 16 Units bzw. thematische Einheiten sowie einen Leseanhang mit sich daran anschließenden Fragen zur Überprüfung von Textverständnis, Grammatik und Wortschatz. Es sind ferner Übungen zum Übersetzen (E-D) sowie Anregungen zur eigenständigen Textproduktion vorhanden. (Diese Art von Übungen bereitet auf die Abschlußprüfung vor.) Das Durcharbeiten der Units und des Leseanhangs wird durch Vokabelanhänge und eine Grammatikzusammenfassung unterstützt.

Wie sind die Units im Schülerbuch von Work With English aufgebaut?
Jede Unit enthält genau zehn Seiten bzw. fünf Doppelseiten. Unit 1 fängt auf Seite 10, Unit 2 auf Seite 20, Unit 3 auf Seite 30 usw. an. Man weiß also anhand der Seitenzahl sofort in welcher Unit man sich befindet.

Der Aufbau einer Unit im Überblick:

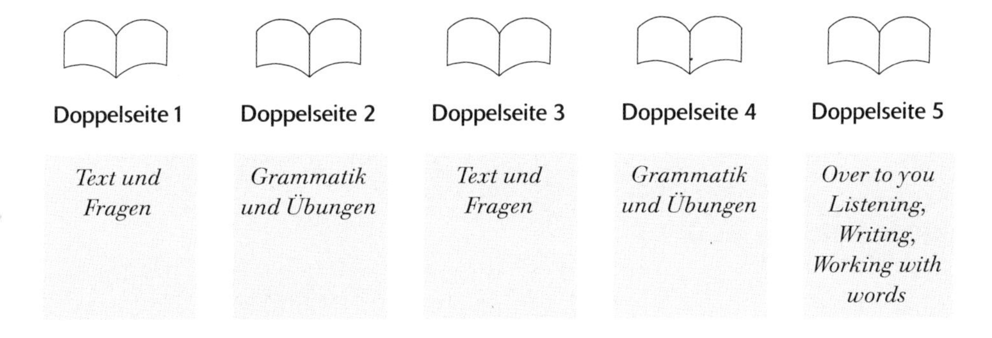

Mit den Texten und der Grammatik wird Stoff entweder wiederholt oder neu eingeführt und eingeübt. Die letzte Doppelseite jeder Unit (Over to you) bietet verschiedene Möglichkeiten an, das Gelernte produktiv mündlich oder schriftlich umzusetzen.

Inhaltsverzeichnis

1 SWITCHED ON

10	**Handbook for young visitors to Britain**	Listening to radio stations in Britain	*Simple present*
11	Did you follow? 1		*Adverbs 1*
12	Watch your grammar 1		*Question words*
13	Get it right 1		
14	**On the air**	Daily life of a radio presenter and a disc jockey	*Quantifiers 1*
15	Did you follow? 2		*Personal pronouns 1*
16	Watch your grammar 2		*Modals 1*
17	Get it right 2		
18	**Over to you** Listening, Mindfield, Working with words, Key words and phrases		

2 FAST FOOD

20	**Lunch break**	Working in a hamburger bar	*Modals 2*
21	Did you follow? 1		*Personal pronouns 2*
22	Watch your grammar 1		
23	Get it right 1		
24	**Feeding the world**	The growth of the American fast food business	*Simple past*
25	Did you follow? 2		*Comparison*
26	Watch your grammar 2		
27	Get it right 2		
28	**Over to you** Listening, Writing, Working with words, Key words and phrases		

3 A START IN LIFE

30	**Training for skills – YTS**	A training scheme for school leavers in Britain	*Verbs + infinitive*
31	Did you follow? 1		*Advice and warnings*
32	Watch your grammar 1		*One, ones*
33	Get it right 1		
34	**'Nothing like a real job'**	Letters about the YTS	*Present continuous 1*
35	Did you follow? 2		*Quantifiers 2*
36	Watch your grammar 2		
37	Get it right 2		
38	**Over to you** Listening, Writing, Working with words, Key words and phrases		

Travelling to Britain · Government in Britain

4 LOTS TO DO

40	**'When shall we meet?'**	Arranging a date	*Future forms*
41	Did you follow? 1		*Likes and dislikes*
42	Watch your grammar 1		*Agreeing*
43	Get it right 1		
44	**Something for everybody**	Different types of summer camp activities in Britain	*Adverbs 2 and adverbial clauses*
45	Did you follow? 2		
46	Watch your grammar 2		
47	Get it right 2		
48	**Over to you** Listening, Working with words, Key words and phrases		

5 A LOOK AT BRITAIN

50	**Mr and Mrs Average**	Facts about British society	*Present continuous 2*
51	Did you follow? 1		*Comparative of adverbs*
52	Watch your grammar 1		*Comparatives and superlatives of adjectives – Revision*
53	Get it right 1		*Irregular comparatives and superlatives – Revision*
54	**Leaving home**	Young people moving to London	*Present perfect*
55	Did you follow? 2		*Adverbs of time: already, yet, just, ever*
56	Watch your grammar 2		*Prepositions of time: since, for, ago*
57	Get it right 2		
58	**Over to you** Listening, Writing, Working with words, Mindfield, Key words and phrases		

6 THE SENSIBLE WAY TO TOWN?

60	**Think about it**	Going to work by motorcycle	*Relative clauses 1*
61	Did you follow? 1		*Possessive adjectives and pronouns*
62	Watch your grammar 1		
63	Get it right 1		
64	**Angel of mercy**	A motorcycle accident	*Relative clauses 2*
65	Did you follow? 2		*Relative clauses 3*
66	Watch your grammar 2		*Genitive: 's/s'/of-phrase*
67	Get it right 2		
68	**Over to you** Listening, Writing, Speaking, Working with words, Key words and phrases		

Travelling in the United States of America

	7 THE CHUNNEL		
70	**'The fast lane to Europe'**	The advantages of the Channel Tunnel project	*Defective modals can and must*
71	Did you follow? 1		*Numbers*
72	Watch your grammar 1		*Irregular verbs*
73	Get it right 1		*Word formation*
74	**Ghost towns and pollution**	The disadvantages of the Channel Tunnel project	*Conditional 1 if + present + will-future*
75	Did you follow? 2		*Question tags*
76	Watch your grammar 2		*Present continuous as future*
77	Get it right 2		*Conjunction although*
78	**Over to you** Speaking, Listening, Writing, Mindfield, Key words and phrases		

	8 AMERICAN WAYS OF LIFE		
80	**When a job's not a living**	Minimum wage jobs in the United States	*Past continuous*
81	Did you follow? 1		*Reflexive pronouns*
82	Watch your grammar 1		*Each other and one another*
83	Get it right 1		
84	**How we live**	Reports on daily life in two American towns	*Past perfect*
85	Did you follow? 2		*-ing form or infinitive with verbs of perception*
86	Watch your grammar 2		
87	Get it right 2		
88	**Over to you** Listening, Writing, Mindfield, Working with words, Key words and phrases		

	9 LONDON PRIDE		
90	**Covent Garden**	Renovating London's Covent Garden	*The passive 1*
91	Did you follow? 1		*Permission*
92	Watch your grammar 1		
93	Get it right 1		
94	**The train in the drain**	Facts about the London Underground	*The passive 2*
95	Did you follow? 2		
96	Watch your grammar 2		
97	Get it right 2		
98	**Over to you** Listening, Mindfield, Writing, Working with words, Key words and phrases		

Energy consumption in Britain · Cumbria: Industry and local government

10 WORK AND PLAY

Page	Section	Topic	Grammar
100	**Jobs with a difference**	Two types of jobs: a thatcher and a nurse	*-ing form 1*
101	Did you follow? 1		*Noun endings*
102	Watch your grammar 1		
102	Get it right 1		
104	**Play, play the U.S. way**	American sports in Britain and the U.S.A.	*-ing form 2*
105	Did you follow? 2		
106	Watch your grammar 2		
107	Get it right 2		
108	**Over to you** Listening, Writing, Working with words, Key words and phrases		

11 LEGEND

Page	Section	Topic	Grammar
110	**Give peace a chance**	John Lennon's life	*-ing form 3*
111	Did you follow? 1		*Definite and indefinite article*
112	Watch your grammar 1		
113	Get it right 1		
114	**The man who never died**	Joe Hill: The story of a union leader	*Infinitive construction to show intentions*
115	Did you follow? 2		*Participle construction to shorten sentences 1*
116	Watch your grammar 2		*Past tenses so far*
117	Get it right 2		*This, these, that, those*
118	**Over to you** Listening, Writing, Mindfield, Working with words, Key words and phrases		

12 HEAD IN THE CLOUDS

Page	Section	Topic	Grammar
120	**Space flying**	Travelling in the twenty-first century	*Conditional 2 if + simple past + would*
121	Did you follow? 1		*May and might*
122	Watch your grammar 1		*During/while*
123	Get it right 1		
124	**Metric mix-up downs jumbo jet**	A plane crash-lands in Canada	*Conditional 3 if + past perfect + would have*
125	Did you follow? 2		*Indefinite quantifiers – much, many, a few, a little*
126	Watch your grammar 2		
127	Get it right 2		
128	**Over to you** Writing, Listening, Mindfield, Working with words, Key words and phrases		

Arizona, U.S.A. · Washington, D.C.

13 DOWNTOWN AND UPTOWN

130	**Central City U.S.A.**	Different views of the future of America's central City areas	*Reported speech 1* *American English*
131	Did you follow? 1		
132	Watch your grammar 1		
133	Get it right 1		
134	**Twin City news**	Different housing areas in Minneapolis/St. Paul	*Adverbs 3* *American English*
135	Did you follow? 2		
136	Watch your grammar 2		
137	Get it right 2		
138	**Over to you** Listening, Writing, Working with words, Key words and phrases		

14 CAN YOU BELIEVE IT?

140	**In my beautiful balloon**	Newspaper reports of a balloon trip across the Atlantic	*Reported speech 2*
141	Did you follow? 1		
142	Watch your grammar 1		
143	Get it right 1		
144	**Farewell to Fleet Street**	New technology in newspaper publishing	*Reported speech 3*
145	Did you follow? 2		
146	Watch your grammar 2		
146	Get it right 2		
148	**Over to you** Listening, Mindfield, Working with words, Key words and phrases		

15 CLEANING UP

150	**An oily mess**	Pollution from a cargo ship	*Present perfect continuous* *Present perfect, simple present and present continuous – Revision* *Present perfect and simple past – Revision*
151	Did you follow? 1		
152	Watch your grammar 1		
153	Get it right 1		
154	**Stopping the rot**	Cleaning up Britain's industrial waste	*Future continuous* *Simple present and present continuous – Revision*
155	Did you follow? 2		
156	Watch your grammar 2		
157	Get it right 2		
158	**Over to you** Listening, Mindfield, Working with words, Key words and phrases		

16 PREJUDICE

160	**Bellefontaine Park**	A story of racial prejudice	*Participle construction to shorten sentences 2*
161	Did you follow? 1		
162	Watch your grammar 1		
163	Get it right 1		
164	**'Girl in a million'**	Overcoming job discrimination	*Prefixes and suffixes*
165	Did you follow? 2		
166	Watch your grammar 2		
167	Get it right 2		
168	**Over to you** Use your head, Speaking or writing, Mindfield, Key words and phrases		

READING TEXTS

Lesetexte mit Übungen

170 1 An English-speaking world
171 2 Where time has stood still
173 3 A sport made for the box
174 4 Motorway madness
176 5 Underground London that nobody knows
177 6 The electronic church
179 7 Hong Kong count-down
180 8 Pacific paradise?
182 9 Where does all the trash go?
183 10 Life in a greenhouse
185 11 Looking for millionaires
186 12 Silicon Valley – hi-tech and pollution

GRAMMAR

188 Grammatikübersicht mit Seitenverweisen

VOCABULARY

202 **Wörterverzeichnis** – in der Reihenfolge des Auftretens
220 **Wörterverzeichnis** – in alphabetischer Reihenfolge (Fundstelle, Englisch, Deutsch)
228 **Wörterverzeichnis** – Grundwortschatz (Englisch, Deutsch)
230 **Liste der unregelmäßigen Verben**

Im Lehrwerk verwendete Abkürzungen und Symbole

▸▸ synonym	**▸◂** opposite	**AE** American English	**conj** conjunction	**pron** pronoun
n noun	**v** verb	**adj** adjective	**adv** adverb	**prep** preposition

1 Switched on

HANDBOOK FOR YOUNG VISITORS TO BRITAIN

Welcome to Britain! Thousands of young people from Europe come to Britain every year. You stay with guest families or go camping and hitchhiking. You visit new places and make new friends. And many of you learn a lot of English during your stay.

But what do campers do in a tent in the rain? Or on the sand after a swim? Many of you listen to the radio, of course. An English-language radio station can be a great help to learners of English. But do you know the best stations for you?

THE MAIN RADIO STATIONS

There are four national BBC stations:

Radio 1 pop music
Radio 2 light music, sport and entertainment
Radio 3 classical music
Radio 4 news, radio plays, comedies, documentaries

In London you can hear two big commercial stations:

LBC **London Broadcasting Company** news, weather reports, traffic reports
Capital Radio pop music, news

and the BBC's local station

Radio London pop music, news

In other parts of Britain, you can still get the four national BBC stations but there are many different local stations. There are over fifty local commercial stations like Ocean Sound in Portsmouth or Radio Trent in Nottingham, and over 30 BBC local stations like Radio Oxford or Radio Jersey. These usually have a mixed programme like BBC Radio 2.

In Britain, people pay about £60 a year to the BBC for a TV and radio licence. There is no separate radio licence. The commercial stations do not get any of this money. They get their money from commercials.

Pop music fans often listen to one of the commercial stations. But maybe you don't like commercials between the records? Then BBC Radio 1 is the best station for you. The BBC does not have any commercials at all.

What's on today?

RADIO 3

There are two magazines for the television and radio programmes: the 'Radio Times' (BBC stations) and the 'TV Times' (commercial stations). Here is a part of the 'Radio Times':

THURSDAY RADIO 10 March

58

Records to be made, records to be played – Norris McWhirter joins Steve Wright at the Trocadero for a noisy afternoon
Radio 1, 3.00pm Steve Wright and Nicky Campbell

1 FM 88-90·2 MW 1053 + 1089 kHz 285 + 275 m

FM stereo between 10.00pm and 12 midnight except in the London area, where you can hear Radio 1 in stereo all day on FM 104.8
News on the half hour from 6.30am until 8.30pm, then 10.00 and 12 midnight

5.30am Adrian John

2 FM 88-90·2 MW 693+ 909 kHz 433 + 330 m

FM stereo except between 10.00pm and 12 midnight
News on the hour
Headlines 5.30am, 6.30, 7.30, 8.30
Major Bulletins 7.00am, 8.00, 1.00pm, 5.00 and 12 midnight
Sports Desks 6.31am, 7.31, 8.31, 12.02pm, 1.05, 2.02, 3.02, 4.02, 5.05, 6.02, 6.45 (MW), 9.55
Sports Round-up 8.50*am

10.00 The News Huddlines
A hip-hop spectacular starring MC **Rapping Roy Huddski June 'Rock Steady' Whitfield** and the original body-popper **Chris 'In Plaster' Emmett**
Mixmasters PETE MOSS and the HUDDLINERS
Joke crew: PETER HICKEY, TONY HARE, MARTIN BOOTH, ALAN WHITING, MIKE COLEMAN, PAUL B. DAVIES, STUART SILVER, MALCOLM WILLIAMSON and others
Songs by RICHARD QUICK and JEREMY BROWNE
Producer MARK ROBSON
(Re-broadcast next Saturday)

10.30 Star Sound Cinema
presented by **Nick Jackson**
Written and compiled by ROY PICKARD
Producer NEIL CARGILL

11.00 Brian Matthew
presents **Round Midnight**
12.00 FM rejoins Radio 2

1.00am Steve Madden
presents **Nightride**

3.00-4.00 A Little Night Music

3 FM 90·2-92·4 MW 1215 kHz 247 m

Music programmes and drama are in stereo except where indicated
News 7.30am, 8.30, 1.00pm, 7.00 and 12 midnight

6.35-6.55am *FM* **Open University**
The State and Economic Intervention

6.55 Weather
followed by **News Headlines**

10.05 Richard Markham and David Nettle
(piano duet)
Grainger Walking Tune; Let's Dance Gay in Green Meadow; Harvest Hymn
Bridge Two Old English Songs: Sally in Our Alley; Cherry Ripe
Kenneth Leighton Sonata, Op 92
BBC Pebble Mill (R)

10.50 Raphael Ensemble
James Clark (violin)
Elizabeth Wexler (violin)
Sally Beamish (viola)
Roger Tapping (viola)
Andrea Hess (cello)
Hummel Trio in E flat, for two violas and cello
Mendelssohn String Quintet in A, Op 18
BBC Wales (R)

11.50 NCOS Symphony Orchestra
conducted by GRAEME JENKINS
Britten American Overture
Shostakovich Symphony No 10

1.00pm News

1.05 Bristol Lunchtime Concert
direct from **St George's, Brandon Hill, Bristol**
DENNIS LEE (piano)
Debussy Images oubliées (1894)
Chopin Sonata No 3 in B minor, Op 58
Debussy L'Isle joyeuse
(Concert arranged by St George's Music Trust in association with John Player and Sons. Tickets available at the door) BBC Bristol

2.00 Wind Music
MEMBERS OF THE BBC SCOTTISH SYMPHONY ORCHESTRA
conducted by TIMOTHY REYNISH
Ernst Toch Spiel
(first broadcast)
Iain Hamilton The Chaining of Prometheus
Gustav Holst Hammersmith
BBC Scotland

2.35 Hans Hotter
(baritone)

7.30 EBU 20th Anniversary Season
Continuing the series of concerts given by the radio orchestras of the European Broadcasting Union.
BELGRADE RADIO AND TELEVISION CHOIR
BELGRADE RADIO AND TELEVISION SYMPHONY ORCHESTRA
conducted by EDWARD COLOMER
Stevan Mokranjac Requiem No 2 in F sharp minor
Stravinsky Les Noces
8.05* Interval Reading
8.10* C. P. E. Bach Magnificat
(Given on 22 February in the Kolaratz University Hall, Belgrade)
(Next concert on Monday)

9.00 The Sicilian Expedition
2: *The Syracusans Prepare, 415 BC*
with **Edward de Souza** as Thucydides
News of the expedition has reached Syracuse, the principal city-state in Sicily. Its leaders decide to resist Athenian aggression. The expeditionary force arrives at Rhegium, but Alcibiades is recalled to Athens to stand trial for allegedly conspiring to overthrow the democracy.
Readers STEPHEN THORNE, STUART ORGAN, ALAN DUDLEY and ERIC STOVELL
(Next programme on Wednesday)

9.25 Psalms of Penitence
The second of two programmes
Hear my prayer, O Lord, give ear to my supplications: in thy faithfulness answer me, and in thy righteousness.
Settings of Psalm 142 (Vulgate) by **Andrea Gabrieli, Melchior Franck** and **Giovanni Croce.**
CONSORT OF MUSICKE
directed by ANTHONY ROOLEY
9.50 Reading

9.55 Music in Our Time
from the International Festivals
The first of two editions from

4 FM 92·4-94·8 LW 198 kHz 1515 m

Programmes are in mono except where indicated
For news, weather and shipping forecast details see Monday

6.00am News Briefing

6.10 Farming Today
Farming, food and countryside news, market trends, weather

6.25 Prayer for the Day
with THE REV JIM COTTER
Stereo

6.30 Today
Presented by **Brian Redhead** and **Sue MacGregor**
6.30, 7.30, 8.30 News Summary
6.45* Business News with PETER DAY
7.00, 8.00 Today's News
Read by EUGENE FRASER
7.25*, 8.25* Sport with GARRY RICHARDSON
7.45* *Thought for the Day*
8.35* Yesterday in Parliament

9.00 News

9.05-10.45 *FM* **For Schools**
9.05 Preview
9.10 Together: An Assembly for Schools
The Search (3)
by GEOFFREY CURTIS
Presented by NICK PAGE
Stereo (e)
9.30 Living Language
Dream of Unicorns (2)
by BERLIE DOHERTY
Stereo (e)
9.50 First Steps in Drama
The Hall of Mirrors
3: Through the Clouds
by CATHY DRYSDALE

Did you follow? 1

1 Answer the questions on the text.
1 Who comes to Britain every year?
2 What are many of the visitors like? Say three things about them.
3 What do they do in Britain? Say two things they do.
4 How much English do they learn?
5 What do some campers often do when it is raining?
6 Why is it good to listen to the radio?
7 How much does a licence for television and radio cost?
8 Which station is best for classical music?

2 Put in the missing words. Find the information in the text.
commercial – commercials – licence – light music – local – national – pop music – records – stations
1 There are four national BBC ☐ in Britain.
2 On Radio One you can hear ☐.
3 LBC and Capital Radio are ☐ stations.
4 BBC Radio Oxford is a ☐ station.
5 BBC stations get their money from a ☐ but commercial stations get their money from ☐.
6 Radio 2 is good for ☐.
7 You can get the ☐ BBC stations in all parts of Britain.
8 Capital Radio has commercials between the ☐.

3 Find out from the text the English names for these sorts of radio programmes:

Wetterberichte	Nachrichtensendungen	Popmusik	klassische Musik
Sportberichte	Hörspiele	Unterhaltung	Verkehrsberichte
leichte Musik	Dokumentarberichte		

4 Complete the text. Use words from the text.
'I am a radio fan. I listen to the radio all day at home. I like ☐[1] so I often listen to Radio One. I live in Nottingham and we have Radio Trent here. That's a ☐[2] station. I listen to Radio Trent in the afternoons. They have a ☐[3] programme like Radio Two. But I don't like the ☐[4] between the records on Radio Trent. Radio Four is best in the evenings. I like a good radio ☐[5] and Radio Four has one every day.'

5 Key words
Put in the missing words. They are in the right order.
the – to – reports – during – to – music – get – like – between – go – great
'Some people like the music programmes on radio. I listen Radio London for the traffic in the mornings and the afternoons I listen Radio 1 for the pop. I can Capital Radio and LBC. I like them, too, but I don't commercials the records. In the summer I camping and I take my radio. A radio is in a tent in the rain.'

6 What sorts of radio programmes are in 'What's on today?'.

Watch your grammar 1

Simple present (Einfache Gegenwart/Präsens)

1 Statements and negatives (Aussagen und Verneinungen)

I **like** 'Dallas'. — Ich mag 'Dallas'.
My brother **doesn't like** it. — Mein Bruder mag es nicht.
He always **leaves** the room. — Er verläßt immer das Zimmer.
My parents always **watch** it. — Meine Eltern sehen es sich immer an.
I **don't go** every week. — Ich gehe nicht jede Woche.
S/he **doesn't go** without me. — Sie/Er geht nicht ohne mich.

Aussagesätze: Bilden der 3. Person Singular *(he, she, it)*.

REGELMÄSSIGE BILDUNG	AUSNAHMEN			
Grundform des Verbs + s	do does	go goes	reply replies	watch watches

2 Questions and short answers (Fragen und Kurzantworten)

Do you often **go** to the cinema? — Gehst Du oft ins Kino?
No, I **don't**. — Nein.
Does your friend **go** without you? — Geht dein/e Freund/in ohne dich?
No, s/he **doesn't**. — Nein.
When do you **go** to the cinema? — Wann gehst Du ins Kino?

Aussagen/Verneinungen

SUBJEKT	PRÄDIKAT		OBJEKT
	HILFSVERB (Verneinung)	VERB	
I/You/We/They	– don't (do not)	watch watch	television.
He/She/It	– doesn't (does not)	plays play	football.

Fragen

FRAGEWORT	HILFSVERB	SUBJEKT	VERB	OBJEKT
–	Do	I/you/we/ they	like	*Dallas?*
–	Does	he/she/it	listen to	pop music?
When/Why ...	do/does	I/you/he ...	go	out?

Kurzantworten

Yes, No,	I/you/ we/they	do. don't.
	he/she/ it	does. doesn't.

Wir benutzen das **simple present**, um auszudrücken, daß etwas allgemein wahr ist oder daß etwas häufiger geschieht.

Adverbs 1 (Adverbien 1)

Adverbs of frequency (Häufigkeitsadverbien)

Do you **often go** to the cinema? — Gehst Du oft ins Kino?
We **sometimes go** on Fridays. — Wir gehen manchmal freitags.

We **usually go** on Saturdays. — Wir gehen gewöhnlich samstags.
He **is usually** at the club. — Er ist gewöhnlich im Club.

Adverbien beschreiben ein Verb näher. Die Häufigkeitsadverbien zeigen an, wie oft etwas passiert. Sie stehen normalerweise vor dem Verb, bei Formen von *to be* nach dem Verb und Adjektiv.

Andere Häufigkeitsadverbien sind: *always, frequently, generally, never, normally, regularly, still.*

Question words (Fragewörter)

who	where	why	how	when	what	which
wer(n, m)	wo	warum	wie	wann	was	welche(r, s, n)

how often	how much	how many	what sort of/kind of
wie oft	wieviel	wieviele	was für
	nicht zählbar	*zählbar*	

Get it right 1

1 Simple present statements

Put the verbs into the right forms.

Example My sister *(like)* fast cars.
My sister **likes** fast cars.

1 I often *(listen)* to Capital Radio.
2 My friend *(like)* classical music.
3 Radio 1 *(play)* pop music.
4 You *(need)* a radio on holiday in Britain.
5 People often *(listen)* to the radio on holiday.
6 My girlfriend *(go)* to bed late.
7 My young brother always *(switch)* the TV on after school.

2 Simple present negative

These sentences are wrong. Put them right.

Example Most Americans live on farms.
Most Americans **don't** live on farms.

1 Most Americans ride horses to work.
2 Milk makes you fat.
3 Old cigarette smoke smells wonderful.
4 My sister sings very well.
5 I like 'Dallas'.
6 People speak English in all parts of Canada.
7 I drive a Jaguar.

3 Simple present questions

Ask questions about these people.

Example your best friend – read many books?
Does your best friend read many books?

1 you – watch sport on television?
2 your friend – play sport at the weekends?
3 you – get up late on Sundays?
4 your friends – like the same music as you?
5 Radio 2 – play a lot of pop music?
6 people – listen to Radio 3 much?
7 your sister – travel a lot?

4 Simple present questions with question words

Ask the speakers questions using the question words.

Example I watch television. *(when?)*
When do you **watch** television?

1 My father plays football. *(where?)*
2 I read a lot of books every week. *(how many?)*
3 Susie likes music. *(what sort of?)*
4 I like somebody in my class. *(who?)*
5 I get a lot of pocket money. *(how much?)*
6 I go camping. *(when?)*
7 I have two hobbies. *(which?)*
8 I like hitchhiking. *(why?)*

5 Adverbs of frequency

Put the adverbs of frequency in the right place.

Example I go to the cinema. *(often)*
I **often** go to the cinema.

1 I smoke American cigarettes. *(usually)*
2 I ride my bicycle to school. *(normally)*
3 My friends watch 'Dallas'. *(never)*
4 Do you go to France? *(often)*
5 Why do you play sport at school? *(always)*
6 Martin listens to his walkman in bed. *(generally)*
7 I am a fan of Elvis Presley. *(still)*
8 We go to Austria on holiday. *(regularly)*

ON THE AIR

Beacon Radio – 990 kHz and 97.2 VHF for the Wolverhampton area.

05.00 a.m. Gordon Astley, the presenter of the 'Breakfast Show', arrives at the studio with all the morning papers. He finds the best stories for his show and reads the latest information about the weather and the traffic.

07.15 a.m. The news editor, Peter Brookes, gets the latest news stories for the 'Breakfast Show'. The news is on every fifteen minutes between 6 a.m. and 9 a.m.

08.00 a.m.-09.00 a.m. Gordon Astley presents the 'Breakfast Show'.

08.30 a.m. Office staff arrive at the station.

09.00 a.m. Andy Wint presents Beacon Radio's morning show. It lasts for three hours. Andy plans the programme, organizes the interviews and writes a lot of letters.

09.15 a.m. Staff meet and talk about some of the programme plans for the next days and weeks.

10.45 a.m. Today's guest is Cliff Richard. He visits the station and talks to the audience.

11.30 a.m. The guests for the 12 o'clock magazine programme – a talk show with music – arrive at the studio and get ready for the programme.

12.15 p.m. In the studio Richard Caperon talks to his guests. They often answer questions from listeners.

02.30 p.m. News reporters from Beacon Radio are out in the area. Sometimes they do live interviews with local people. Sometimes they record the interviews and use them later.

05.30 p.m. 'Newsday' is a very complicated programme for the station because it needs a news editor, a sports editor and two presenters.

08.00 p.m. In the evenings, there are sometimes outside broadcasts.

10.30 p.m.-05.00 a.m. Most of the listeners go to bed for the night. But not everybody. For the others, Beacon Radio broadcasts pop music and light music all night, seven nights a week.

Listeners' Letters

A listener writes about her favourite disc jockey.

'My favourite DJ is Sally O'Keefe. She is really funny and plays all the latest records. I always listen to her in the afternoons. I need some music after a hard day at school. She usually tells funny stories and jokes. Sally O'Keefe is a reggae fan and so am I. Most of the DJs only play the Top 40, but there are a lot of really good bands around and she plays a lot of their music. I can hear new groups on her show. That's why I like her. And she doesn't talk over the records like some of the other DJs.'

Jan Burley

Sally O'Keefe replies:

'I'm glad you like the show, Jan. Some of the DJs have phone-ins and a quiz with a few prizes. I could do the same thing, but I don't. I think people want to hear music on a music

45 programme. Anyway, I have my own style and people needn't switch on. Thank you for your letter, Jan. Listen to the programme next Saturday and you
50 can hear a special record – just for you.'

Did you follow? 2

1 Answer the questions on the text 'On the air'.
1 What sort of station is Beacon Radio?
2 Who is the presenter of the 'Breakfast Show'?
3 How often can you hear the news early in the morning?
4 When do most of the staff arrive at the station?
5 Which programme can you hear at ten o'clock in the morning?
6 What sort of programme can you hear at twelve o'clock?
7 When do the reporters go out to find news stories?
8 Why is 'Newsday' a complicated programme?
9 Does Beacon Radio close at ten thirty in the evening?

2 Put the events in the right order. Start at 5 a.m.
Example 1 = **d**. At 5 a.m. Gordon Astley ...
a Beacon Radio plays music all night.
b The station broadcasts 'Newsday' every day.
c The planning meeting for the following days starts.
d Gordon Astley starts his Breakfast Show.
e Richard Caperon's magazine programme starts.
f The morning show starts.
g Reporters do interviews with people in the area.
h Office workers arrive for work at the station.

3 Which words do the sentences define *(definieren)*?
audience – interviews – morning papers – news editor – office – outside broadcasts – radio station – reporter
1 The people who make the programmes work here.
2 They do not make these programmes in the studio.
3 The stories for the Breakfast Show come from these.
4 This person collects news stories in the area.
5 The presenters plan their programmes here.
6 When reporters talk to people, they do these.
7 These people listen to the programmes.
8 This person plans the news stories.

4 Answer the questions on the text 'Listeners' Letters'.
1 When does Jan listen to Sally O'Keefe?
2 Why does she listen to her?
3 What sort of music do Jan and Sally O'Keefe like?
4 What doesn't Jan like about other DJs?
5 What do DJs often do in their programmes?
6 What could Sally O'Keefe do? Does she do it? Why or why not?
7 When can Jan hear her special record?

Watch your grammar 2

Quantifiers 1 (Mengenangaben 1)

all	most	a lot of (many)	some	a few

Most Americans in Frankfurt listen to AFN.
Die **meisten** Amerikaner in Frankfurt hören AFN.

Most of the Americans in Frankfurt listen to AFN.
Die **meisten** der Amerikaner in Frankfurt hören AFN.

There are **a lot of** really good pop stations in Europe.
Es gibt **viele** sehr gute Popmusiksender in Europa.

Some of the stations have phone-ins.
Einige Sender lassen sich anrufen.

They often have a quiz with **a few** prizes.
Sie machen oft ein Quiz mit **ein paar** Preisen.

Man kann die Mengenangaben *most, some, all* und *a lot of* direkt mit einem Substantiv verbinden: *most people, some friends, all Americans, a lot of Germans* usw. Wenn es sich aber um eine Auswahl dieser Dinge oder Personen handelt, so kann man sie auch mit *of the, of my* usw. verbinden: *most of my friends, some of the disc jockeys, all of the Americans in Frankfurt* usw.

Personal pronouns 1 (Persönliche Fürwörter 1/Personalpronomen)

ALS SUBJEKT	ALS OBJEKT
I have a friend in Portsmouth.	He sometimes visits **me**.
We usually go to Scotland for our holidays.	Our dog comes with **us**.
You smoke too much.	It isn't good for **you**.
He is a good friend.	I like **him**.
She is nice.	I like **her**.
That car is nice and **it** doesn't cost too much.	We like **it**.
My best friends don't live here. **They** live in Nottingham.	I sometimes visit **them**.

Modals 1 (Modal-/Hilfsverben 1)

I **can** hear new groups on her show.
Ich **kann** bei ihrer Sendung neue Gruppen hören.

I **could** do the same thing, but I don't.
Ich **könnte** das gleiche machen, aber das tue ich nicht.

Die Modalverben *can* und *could* haben folgende Bedeutung:

1. *Can (cannot, can't)* und *could (could not, couldn't)* sind unveränderlich, d. h. sie haben bei allen Personen die gleiche Form.
2. *Can* heißt, daß man die **Möglichkeit** oder die **Fähigkeit hat**, etwas jetzt zu machen/zu tun.
3. *Could* heißt, daß man die **Möglichkeit** oder die **Fähigkeit haben könnte**, etwas unter Umständen in der Zukunft zu machen/zu tun.

Get it right 2

1 Quantifiers

Put in the missing words.
all – most – a lot of – some – a few

1 She is really funny and plays ☐ the latest records.
2 There are ☐ really good bands around.
3 ☐ of the DJs only play the Top 40.
4 She doesn't 'talk over' the records like ☐ of the other DJs.
5 ☐ of the DJs often have phone-ins and a quiz with ☐ prizes.
6 In the morning the staff plan ☐ of the new programmes.
7 Gordon Astley brings ☐ the morning papers to the studio.
8 Andy Wint writes ☐ letters for the morning show.

2 Quantifiers

Translate these sentences into English.
Use the quantifiers from exercise 1.

1 Einige meiner Freunde sind Sportfans.
2 Alle Sendungen sind live.
3 Die meisten Sportsendungen sind lang.
4 Einige wenige Sendungen im Fernsehen sind interessant.
5 Einige der Unterhaltungssendungen sind schlecht.
6 Viele Leute sehen zu viel fern.

3 Personal pronouns – subject

Put pronouns in place of the nouns in brackets. Use *he*, *she*, *it*, *we* and *they*.

Example *(John)* is my best friend.
He is my best friend.

1 Mary is in my class at school. *(Mary)* lives in my street.
2 Mary and I are good friends. *(Mary and I)* go to school together.
3 Mary and Sally are in a sports club. *(Mary and Sally)* go there every week.
4 The club is very good. *(The club)* does not cost much.
5 David does not like sport. *(David)* is not in the club.
6 Susan and Danny are not sports fans. *(Susan and Danny)* are not in the club.
7 Jane does not often go out. *(Jane)* does not have a moped.

4 Personal pronouns – object

Put pronouns in place of the nouns in brackets. Use *her*, *him*, *it*, *them* and *us*.

Example I visit *(John)* on Saturdays.
I visit **him** on Saturdays.

1 My mother is learning French. She likes *(French)* very much.
2 I cannot help *(my mother)*.
3 My brother is learning French, too, so my mother helps *(my brother)*.
4 I cannot understand *(my mother and my brother)* when they speak French.
5 My brother says, 'Listen to *(mother and me)* and you can learn, too.'
6 French is a nice language but I do not learn *(French)* at school.
7 'Can you give *(Dad and me)* your French book?' I asked.
8 He said, 'I can show *(Dad)* the book, but I need *(the book)* for my homework.'

5 Personal pronouns – subject or object

Put in the missing pronouns. Say if you use subject or object pronouns.

Example Cliff Richard arrives at the studio.
Andy Wint interviews **him**.

1 Richard Caperon's guests arrive at the studio. He talks to ☐ before the show.
2 'Newsday' is a complicated programme. ☐ needs a lot of presenters.
3 Jan likes Sally O'Keefe. ☐ often listens to her after school.
4 Other DJs talk over the records. ☐ often have a quiz with a few prizes.
5 Sally is a reggae fan. Jan is, too. That's why she likes ☐.
6 Gordon Astley does the 'Breakfast Show'. Peter Brookes helps ☐ with the news.
7 Beacon Radio broadcasts seven days a week, twenty-four hours a day. You can hear ☐ on 990 kHz.
8 Cliff Richard is the guest today. ☐ talks to the audience about his music.
9 Sally O'Keefe wrote, '☐'ve got a letter from Jan Burley.'
10 'Jan says she likes ☐ and my show.'

OVER TO YOU

Listening *A mixed bag*

1 Listen to the tape. You can hear parts of radio programmes. Copy the table. Write down what you hear. Choose from this list.

a traffic report – a weather report – the news
a sports report – a documentary – a play

ITEM	SORT OF PROGRAMME
1	weather report

When you have finished, compare your list with other people's lists.
If you have written different answers, listen to the item again and find who has the correct answer.

2 Which radio programmes do you listen to in Germany? Copy the table.
Write down the sorts of programmes you listen to.

ALWAYS	OFTEN	REGULARLY	SOMETIMES	NEVER
		SPORTS		

Find out from other people in the class which programmes they listen to.
Ask like this: *Do you listen to (the news)?*
Answer like this: *Yes, I do. Often/Sometimes/etc.*
No, I don't.

3 Write down the answers from all your group in a table like this:

NAME	PROGRAMME	HOW OFTEN
Thomas	sports reports, news	often, never

4 Report what you know about your group to the class. Say what your group listens to and what they don't listen to.

Report like this: Thomas often listens to sports reports. He doesn't listen to the news. Most of the people in our group listen to music. A few people in our group listen to magazine programmes. The people in our group never listen to weather reports.

Mindfield

Odd man out

Which is the odd man out in each group? Can you say why?

green red great blue	listener reader hitchhiker reporter	car hicycle ship moped	radio television cassette recorder telephone

Opposites

Find the opposites of the words in box 1 from box 2. If you do not know them, look them up in a dictionary.

BOX 1

always	ask	bad	before
big	black	brother	buy
clean	dangerous	dark	long
sit	bring	hot	learn
pen	push	same	talk
tomorrow	laugh	walk	fast

BOX 2

after	answer	cold	cry
different	dirty	good	light
listen	never	paper	pull
run	safe	sell	short
sister	slow	small	stand
take	teach	white	yesterday

Working with words

1 Word formation

A person who camps is called a **camper**.
A person who visits is called a **visitor**.
A person who runs is called a **runner**.

What do we call a person who does these things? Check the spelling in your dictionary.
begins – collects – dances – edits – hitchhikes – organizes – plays – presents – reads – reports – sings – smokes – speaks – works – writes

2 Key words

Put the missing words in the gaps.
afternoons – around – because – capital – different – Europe – favourite – great – local – maybe – p.m. – still – welcome to

When visitors from ▭[1] arrive in Dover they see a sign '▭[2] Britain'. Many visitors go to the ▭[3]. London is the ▭[4] city for visitors ▭[5] there are so many interesting places ▭[6]. ▭[7] they walk in the parks in the ▭[8] or see a film in the West End in the evenings. After the film, they go to a ▭[9] pub. Many things are ▭[10] in Britain. For example, the pubs shut at 11 ▭[11]. But many visitors ▭[12] think they are ▭[13].

Key words and phrases

on holiday
Welcome **to** Britain!
afternoon ▶◀ morning
p.m. ▶◀ a.m.
in the morning
to talk **to**
to listen **to**
to last **for**
Thank you **for** your letter.
I always go camping, **of course**.
There are a lot of good teams **around**.
What's on?
I could watch TV, but I don't because I play sport **on** Saturdays.

I **still** have £5.
Maybe you don't like sport.
Anyway, I do.
capital
different ▶◀ same
Europe
latest ▶◀ oldest
local
outside (adj) ▶◀ inside
area
really
generally
regularly
usually
favourite
great

2 Fast food

LUNCH BREAK

At the counter in a hamburger bar.

Girl Yes, sir, what can I do for you?

Wilson Can you give me a cheeseburger and a shake, please?

Girl What sort of shake, sir?

Wilson Chocolate. Chocolate shake.

Girl One cheeseburger and one chocolate shake. Is that everything, sir?

Wilson Yeah, thanks.

Girl Here you are. That's three dollars twenty, please.

Wilson Right. Here.

Girl Thank you, sir. Here's your change. One dollar eighty cents. Enjoy your meal.

Wilson Thanks. Say, is Lora here?

Girl Lora Raines?

Wilson That's right.

Girl Sure. I believe she's on lunch break right now. Up those stairs.

Wilson Hey, Lora, that's a great uniform! I really love it!

Lora Oh, shut up. You needn't tell me that, Wilson. It's terrible. I know. I hate it.

Wilson Okay, okay. Do you have to wear it?

Lora Sure we do. Everyone does here. But nobody likes it.

Wilson What's the job like?

Lora It's pretty hard. This place is busy all day. And the boss talks and talks. 'You must serve the customers in just one minute. You mustn't ever stand around and do nothing. Keep the place clean.' That's him. All day long.

Wilson Well, it sure is busy now. What shift are you on?

Lora I'm on duty from 8 till 4.30 this week. That's okay. I don't mind that.

Wilson Is the pay okay, too?

Lora Well, it's better than nothing.

Wilson Not too good, eh? Is that what you mean?

Lora Right. And I don't like the late shift. That's 6 till 2 a.m.

Wilson 2 a.m.! Hey, when does this place close?

Lora 1 a.m. It's open from 5.30 in the morning till one. But you needn't work the late shift. Or at weekends.

Wilson Why do you do it then?

Lora The money's better after 8 p.m. And you don't have to work so hard. Not at night. Oh, no! 1.30 already. I have to start again.

Wilson I have to go soon, too. See you around, Lora.

Lora Sure. Enjoy your meal.

Did you follow? 1

1 Put in the missing words.

1 Wilson eats ▭ and drinks ▭ .
2 He pays three ▭ twenty ▭ for his food and drink.
3 He gives the counter girl ▭ .
4 He asks her if ▭ is there.

2 Are these sentences about the text right or wrong?

Example Wilson thinks Lora looks funny in her uniform.
Yes, that's right. He laughs at her.

1 Lora doesn't mind this.
2 She thinks that her job is not very hard.
3 Her pay is good.
4 She works the late shift because she gets more money.
5 She is on the late shift this week.
6 It is usually very busy at lunchtime.
7 She thinks her boss makes them work too hard.
8 She goes home when the restaurant closes.

3 Put in the missing words. Use the menu and the text to help you.

Charley Yes, please?
Paula I'll have a ▭1.
Charley One hamburger. Is that all?
Paula No, give me a banana shake, too, please.
Charley One ▭2. Right. Is that everything now?
Paula Yes, thanks. How much is that?
Charley ▭3.
Paula Here's five dollars.
Charley Thank you. ▭4. Here's ▭5.

Charley What would you like, sir?
Ray Can you give me two eggburgers and two fries, please?
Charley ▭6 fries?
Ray Just small.
Charley Right. Here ▭7.
Ray ▭8.
Charley ▭9.
Ray Five eighty. Here's six dollars.
Charley Thank you, sir, and here's ▭10.

4 Complete this text about Lora at her fast food restaurant. Use the words from this list.

busy – has to – hours – job – must (2x) *– needn't – pay* (2x) *– shift* (2x)

Lora says her ▭1 is okay but she's always very ▭2. She ▭3 serve the customers quickly. She ▭4 work eight ▭5 a day and ▭6 do a different ▭7 every week. This week she is on the early ▭8. She ▭9 work late at night but she does because then her ▭10 is better. It's not very good. But after six months her ▭11 goes up.

Watch your grammar 1

Modals 2 (Modal-/Hilfsverben 2)

1 You **must** serve the customers in just one minute.
I **have to** start again.
Do you **have to** wear that uniform? – Yes, I **do/have to**.
Must you work late? – Yes, I **must**.

Must hat in allen Personen die gleiche Form und wird nur im Präsens verwendet. *Have to* kann auch in anderen Zeiten verwendet werden. In der Frageform wird bei *have to* die Umschreibung mit *do* verwendet, z. B. '**Do** *you* **have to** ... ?'
Must und *have to* werden verwendet, um eine Notwendigkeit auszudrücken.

MODALVERBEN		ERSATZVERBEN	GEBRAUCH
PRESENT	*PAST*	*ANDERE ZEITEN*	
can	could	be able to	Bitte, Vorschlag, Erlaubnis
must	–	have to	eindringlicher Vorschlag/Ratschlag, Zwang
needn't (need not)	–	don't have to	Fehlen eines Zwangs/einer Notwendigkeit

2 You **don't have to** work so hard.
You **needn't** tell me that, Wilson.

Wenn man ausdrücken will, daß keine Notwendigkeit besteht, verwendet man die Verneinung von *have to* + die Umschreibung mit *do (don't/doesn't have to)* oder die Formen *needn't/need not.*

3 You **mustn't** ever stand around and do nothing.

Mustn't (must not) drückt aus, daß etwas **nicht erlaubt** ist. Es darf **nicht** mit 'muß nicht' verwechselt werden.

mustn't	needn't/don't have to
nicht dürfen	nicht müssen

4 Lora **has got to** wear a uniform.

In der Umgangssprache wird häufig *have/has got to (Have you got to ... ?/I haven't got to ...)* anstatt *have to* verwendet.

Personal pronouns 2 (Persönliche Fürwörter 2/Personalpronomen)

My boss doesn't like **me**.
Can you give **me** a cheeseburger and a shake?

Im Englischen verwendet man für das Dativobjekt und das Akkusativobjekt die gleiche Form, z. B. *me* = mich/mir, *you* = dich/dir, *it* = es/ihm usw. (Siehe auch Seite 16.)

Get it right 1

1 Simple present

Ask and answer five questions about this fast food cook.
Use these verbs: *be – get – live – work.*

Example Where does Wayne Molino work?
He works at …

PRIMECUT HAMBURGER COMPANY

Restaurant: Dover, Delaware
Wayne MOLINO
1492 Hopper St., Ridgewood, Delaware 07454
Phone: (302) 764412
Job: GRILL COOK: $4.25/hour

2 Modals

Say what Wayne Molino's duties are. Use *must, have to, mustn't* and *needn't.*

Example First Wayne must switch on the grill. Then he has to …

Grill Cook – Duties

1 Switch on grill.
2 Check temperature of grill.
3 Take orders.
4 Never touch hamburgers with hands.
5 Cook hamburgers on both sides.
6 Put cooked hamburgers into box.
7 Turn off grill at end of late shift. Clean top of grill.
8 **Saturday:** do not clean grill (cleaners will do this).

3 Modals

Put in the missing words. Use *mustn't* or *needn't.* The boss says:

'I want our restaurant to be the fastest and the cleanest in town. So you **mustn't** stand around talking when customers are waiting. You ☐[1] be quiet all the time, but the customers must come first. You ☐[2] clean the grills at night. We have cleaners. They do that job. But you ☐[3] forget to keep things clean during the day. I'll say it again: you ☐[4] ever cook hamburgers on a dirty grill and you ☐[5] ever take longer than a minute to serve a customer.'

4 Pronouns

Put in the missing pronouns. Use *he, him, it* (2x), *me, them, they* and *we.*

Example My boss is a very hard man. **He** makes **me** work so much.

1 I have to do the early shift. ☐ is not too bad.
2 I hate the late shift but ☐ pays better.
3 The customers like our restaurant and ☐ make it very busy.
4 The other counter girls are nice. I like ☐ a lot.
5 But nobody likes the boss. ☐ all hate him.
6 I don't like ☐ because ☐ tells ☐ what to do all day long.

5 Simple present statements

Talk about these people.

Example John: 'I play football on Saturdays.'
John **plays** football on Saturdays.

1 Susie: 'I ask a lot of questions at school.'
2 Martina: 'I like the new school better than the old one.'
3 Grant and Jilly: 'We know somebody with a Ferrari.'
4 Liz: 'I want a new stereo for Christmas.'
5 Ken and Lucy: 'We watch too much television.'
6 Ann: 'I often read a book in bed.'
7 Greg and Pat: 'We have too much work at school.'

FEEDING THE WORLD

by Annie Helmholtz

'Time is money,' say Americans, so they invented fast food. People just want to fill up with food. The same way that they fill up their cars with petrol. That was a way they could save time and money. Fast food companies have sales of about 90 billion dollars a year. They serve every sort of food you can think of, but hamburgers are the most popular. In fact, the hamburger companies are the biggest restaurant companies in the world. 5

1965	1970	1983	1985	1986
The largest hamburger chain became a public company. 100 shares cost $2,250.	For the first time a fast food restaurant reached sales of $1 million.	There were now over 70,000 fast food restaurants in the U.S.A. Their sales in that country reached $90,000,000,000.	The 100 shares from 1965 were now 4,131 shares and were worth about $275,000. The company sold its 55 billionth hamburger.	The sales of the largest fast food company reached over $11 billion. It had more than 9000 restaurants in the world.

This sort of hamburger restaurant only began about 30 years ago in America but now you can find them in many other parts of the world. We visited one last week. 'Why did you come here?' we asked some customers. 'You know what you're getting when you come here,' said one. 'The food is good, and it's quick,' another told us. People know what to expect and they feel at home because the restaurants look the same and serve the same food in Europe, Japan, or the U.S. 'The staff are faster 10 and more polite than in other restaurants,' a mother with two children said. 'And it's the cleanest place in town. That's important to me.' So clean restaurants and fast, polite staff are the 15 reasons for the success of the hamburger chains.

This success shows that millions of people like these restaurants. But a lot of the people who work there do not. 20 They say the work is hard and the pay is bad. They do not get much of the big profits. And a lot of companies do not like workers who are in a trade union. Other people are not happy about the 25 food. They say it does not have enough vitamins, minerals or natural fibre. Many people believe that there is nothing worse for you to eat. They call it junk food. Of course, everyone would like to eat better food, but fast food is cheaper. Do you choose healthier food when it is also more expensive? 30

Did you follow? 2

1 Choose one of these headings for each part of the text.
Fast food facts
Clean and fast
Not everyone likes fast food
Saving time and money

2 Answer these questions on the text.
1 Why did Americans invent fast food?
2 In what way are people and cars the same?
3 What is the most popular sort of fast food? Can you think of any other sorts?
4 What question did Annie Helmholtz ask the customers in the restaurant?
5 Why do people feel at home in fast food restaurants?
6 What do a lot of workers feel about the restaurant companies?
7 Why do some people believe fast food is not good for you?

3 Describe in your own words what the following words and phrases mean.
1 chain (box 1965) – profits (line 23) – public company (box 1965) – share (box 1965) – staff (line 10) – sales (box 1970)
2 Time is money. (line 1)
The food is good and it's quick. (line 8)

4 Complete these statements about the fast food industry. Use words from the text.
– The largest hamburger ☐[1] became a ☐[2] in 1965.
– ☐[3] worth $2,250 in 1965 rose to $275,000 by 1985.
– Two years earlier 70,000 ☐[4] had ☐[5] of over $90 billion.
– By 1986 the biggest company's sales ☐[6] over $11 billion.

5 Find three reasons in the text why people eat in fast food restaurants.
Why are fast food restaurants such a success? Write a short report about the restaurants, the staff and the food. You can begin like this:
Fast food restaurants are a success because people like …

Watch your grammar 2

Simple past (Einfache Vergangenheit/Präteritum)

1 Statements

So they **invented** fast food.
He **stopped** the car in front of the restaurant.

In Aussagesätzen wird das **simple past** von regelmäßigen Verben mit *-ed* gebildet. Das **simple past** hat bei allen Personen die gleiche Form. Bei manchen regelmäßigen Verben gibt es kleine Rechtschreibänderungen (z. B. *travel-travelled*).

2 Questions and negatives (Fragen und Verneinungen)

Why **did** you come here? Because I **didn't** want to spend a long time in a restaurant.
Were you at the restaurant yesterday? No, I **wasn't**.

Aussagen/Fragen

FRAGEWORT	HILFSVERB	SUBJEKT	HILFSVERB	VERB	OBJEKT
–	–	I/You/He ...	–	ate cooked	lunch.
–	–	We/You/They	didn't (did not)	eat cook	lunch.
–	Did	I/you/we/they	–	eat cook	lunch?
When	did	I/you/we	–	eat cook	lunch?

Kurzantworten

Yes, No,
I/you/we/they/
... did. ...didn't.

Verneinungen und Fragen mit dem Verb *to be* werden wie folgt gebildet:

–	I/He/She/...	wasn't	at the restaurant.
–	We/You/They	weren't	
Was	I/he/she/...	–	at the restaurant?
Were	we/you/they	–	

Das **simple past** wird verwendet, wenn man über abgeschlossene Ereignisse in der Vergangenheit spricht. Es kommt deshalb oft in Geschichten vor. Wörter wie *ago, last month/year, yesterday, in 1970* usw. zeigen, daß ein Zeitraum oder ein Ereignis abgeschlossen ist, so daß man zusammen mit solchen Ausdrücken das **simple past** verwenden muß.

Comparison (Vergleich, Steigerung)

1 Comparatives and superlatives of adjectives (Komparative und Superlative der Adjektive)

Bei kurzen Adjektiven werden die Steigerungsformen mit *-er/-est* gebildet. Bei manchen kurzen Adjektiven gibt es Rechtschreibänderungen.

GRUNDFORM	fast	big	healthy	happy	late	hot
KOMPARATIV *-ER*	faster	bigg**er**	health**ier**	happ**ier**	later	hott**er**
SUPERLATIV *-EST*	fastest	bigg**est**	health**iest**	happ**iest**	latest	hott**est**

Bei längeren Adjektiven, im allgemeinen mit mehr als zwei Silben wie z. B. *ex-pens-ive*, bildet man die Steigerungsformen wie folgt:

GRUNDFORM	expensive	popular
KOMPARATIV *MORE*	more expensive	more popular
SUPERLATIV *MOST*	most expensive	most popular

2 Irregular comparatives and superlatives (Unregelmäßige Komparative und Superlative)

GRUNDFORM	good	bad	little *(wenig)*	few*	much	many
KOMPARATIV	better	worse	less	fewer*	more	more
SUPERLATIV	best	worst	least	fewest*	most	most
			(nicht zählbar)	*(zählbar)*	*(nicht zählbar)*	*(zählbar)*

* *not irregular*

3 Comparison in sentences (Vergleich, Steigerung in Sätzen)

The staff are **faster than** in other restaurants.
And the food is **as good as** in other restaurants.
But it's **not as/so quiet as** in other restaurants.

GLEICHHEIT	UNGLEICHHEIT
as ... as	not as/so ... as
GRÖSSER USW. ALS	
than	

as ... as wird benutzt, um Gleichheit zwischen zwei Gegenständen, Personen usw. und *not as/so ... as*, um Ungleichheit festzustellen. *Than* wird benutzt, um auszudrücken, daß etwas größer, schneller, höher usw. als etwas anderes Vergleichbares ist.

Get it right 2

1 Simple past – statements and negatives

Put the verbs in the right form.

Jim Delgado **opened** his twentieth fast food restaurant in 1988. It *(be)*[1] a success right from the start. In its first year it *(sell)*[2] food worth more than $1.1 million. The restaurant *(have)*[3] a good position on a busy road, so thousands of customers *(come)*[4] every day. On good days at weekends they *(buy)*[5] more than $5,000 worth of food.
Delgado *(start)*[6] his first restaurant in the sixties. 'We *(serve)*[7] a meal for $0.45 – hamburger, French fries and a drink. I *(know)*[8] it would be a success, but I *(not think)*[9] it would be this good.'
Of course, the new restaurant *(be)*[10] a lot more expensive than the first one. That only *(cost)*[11] 'a few thousand'. Delgado *(have to)*[12] find $300,000 before he *(can)*[13] start the latest one. But sales *(be)*[14] high at his other restaurants and he *(not find)*[15] it difficult when he *(speak)*[16] to his bank.

2 Simple past – questions

Ask questions about the underlined words.

Example Jim Delgado started his first restaurant in Illinois.
Where **did** Jim Delgado **start** his first restaurant?

1 He built a second one in 1965.
2 He worked 16 hours a day.
3 He never went on holiday.
4 He became a millionaire in 1980.
5 His first hamburgers cost 30 cents.
6 One restaurant had sales of a million dollars.
7 His first restaurant in Europe was in Munich.
8 Last year he opened restaurants in three towns.

3 Comparatives and superlatives

Compare these three fast food companies. Write at least eight sentences. Use *more ...*, *most ...*, *-er*, *-est* and these adjectives:
big – cheap – expensive – few – little – old – popular – small – young

Example Bigburger is the biggest company.
It is bigger than Chicken'n Chips.

	Bigburger	Chicken 'n Chips	Frank's
No of restaurants	over 2500	over 2000	160
First restaurant	1975	1960	1981
Profit last year	$10 million	$11 million	$1 million
Customers last year	1.875 million	1.64 million	128,000
Price of hamburger	$1.20	$1.30	$1.15

OVER TO YOU

Listening

1 Listen to the tape. Where would you usually hear something like this? What is it?
2 Where are the man and woman? What are they doing there? What time of day is it?
3 Describe what you hear.
4 Listen to the tape again and write down what information it gives you about *Freddie's Famous Hamburgers*.
5 What's your opinion of the advert? Say why you liked it, or why not.
6 How would you describe the advert in your own words for someone who has not heard it? Write down what you would say.

1 Lora's restaurant is open from 5.30 a.m. to 1 a.m.
What are opening times like in Germany for e.g. a bank, supermarket, baker's shop, fast food restaurant you know.

In our	town area village	the baker's shop opens from ... till ... the baker is open from ... the opening times of ... are from ... to ...

2 Here is what some young Germans said about eating at a fast food restaurant:

Gerlinde, 19, Postangestellte: „So ein-, zweimal im Monat muß ich dahin. Ich brauche das ab und zu, Hamburger zu essen. Ich mag auch die Leute. Es kommen immer lustige Typen rein."

Jürgen, 17, Berufsschüler: „Am liebsten schauen wir nach dem Kino rein. Ich find' es halt super, daß die Bedienung immer so freundlich bleibt. Außerdem gibt es die besten Pommes frites."

Explain in English what their opinions are. Don't try to translate word for word. Here is some help.
Jürgen goes to the fast food restaurant after ...
He thinks the counter staff are ...
He also thinks ...
Gerlinde goes ... because ...
She likes ...

Do you agree with what they say? Give reasons.
I agree/don't agree because ... is right/wrong about ...

Writing

1 Answer these questions about a restaurant you have eaten in or write a report.

1 What sort of food does it sell? *(fast food, normal, Greek ...)*
2 Can you call it fast, polite, clean ... ?
3 Is it a success? Does it have a lot of customers?
4 Who goes to the restaurant?
5 What do you think of the food, the customers, the prices, the way the restaurant looks?
6 What other information do you have about it?
7 Would you take your girl-/boyfriend to this restaurant?

Working with words

1 Find words or phrases that mean the opposite of the underlined part of the sentences.

Example The staff of that restaurant are not doing very much.
They are **very busy**.

1 The boss hates it if the workers are slow.
2 I do not think that fast food is a good thing.
3 The shop opens at 8 o'clock.
4 He doesn't like the long hours at work.

2 Find other words or phrases which mean the same as the underlined part of the text.

What kind of restaurants can you see in most towns today? No one can stop the hamburger restaurants. That is what I think, and most people I know agree with me, too. When the first hamburger restaurant arrived in Europe, American eating was here to stay. And I can't tell you about all the different sorts of fast food restaurants there are now.

3 Put in the missing words.

company – industry – pay – profit – sales – workers

The report for the year 1986 shows that the □[1] of the □[2] went up from $17.2 million to $19.6 million. There was a □[3] of $2.7 million. That is $450,000 more than 1985. During the year the company gave 124 new □[4] a job. They also got 3.1% more □[5]. All of this together was the biggest success story in the □[6].

Key words and phrases

ago
also
because

busy
polite
quick(ly)

believe, close
describe, reach
wear

okay
sure

What sort of ... ?
What's ... like?
See you around.
What can I do for you?
Can you ... please?
Here you are.
Here's your ...
I don't mind that.

boss
company
industry
pay
profit
share
shift
trade union
sales
worker

3 A start in life

TRAINING FOR SKILLS – YTS

THE YOUTH TRAINING SCHEME
What school leavers should know

Leaving school?

When they leave school young people have to make some big decisions. Some want to stay in education. Some school leavers get jobs without any training.

Others would like to find jobs but cannot. But when you decide to leave school at 16 or 17, the first step is the most important. And the best one is YTS.

What does it offer?

Young workers should have the chance to show employers what they can do. And the chance to get work experience and learn modern skills. YTS can give them both.

Pay

Young people with a two-year training programme earn £27.30 a week in the first year and £35 a week in the second. Those with a one-year programme get £27.30 a week in the first 13 weeks and then £35 for the next nine months.

Hours and holidays

Your working hours are not usually more than 40 hours a week. You get 18 days holiday a year as well as all the public ones.

How do I join?

You don't need any qualifications to join but you may have some before you leave. At the end of their programme trainees get a YTS Certificate. It shows employers what you can now do. You usually have an interview before you join YTS. After the interview you can decide to take a YTS place or not.

How do I start?

When you decide to leave school, don't forget to find out about YTS programmes, especially the ones in your area. Remember to talk to your careers teacher. You also ought to visit your local Careers Office or Jobcentre.

Did you follow? 1

1 Answer these questions from the YTS brochure.

1 Name three things people can do in Great Britain when they leave school.
2 When do people on YTS get £27.30 a week?
3 How long is a working week on YTS?
4 What can you say about YTS holidays?
5 What qualifications must you have before you join YTS? What else happens before you join?
6 What do you get at the end of your programme?
7 Where can you find out more information about YTS?

2 Put in the missing words.

experience – interview – qualifications – training programme – working hours

Before you can join a YTS ▭[1] you must have an ▭[2]. You do not need any ▭[3] but your YTS training may give you some. As you usually have 40 ▭[4] a week YTS is a good chance to get some ▭[5] of working life.

3 Find words in the YTS brochure for the following.

1 Someone who gives other people a job.
2 A piece of paper that shows someone's qualifications.
3 The money you get when you work.
4 Someone who can help you when you want a job or some training.
5 Someone on a training programme.
6 Days when you do not have to work.
7 The things you learn on a training programme.

4 This is what one YTS trainee said about his experiences. Put his statements into the right order. The first one is already in the right place. (1 = a, 2 = ...)

a 'When I was 16 I decided to leave school.'
b 'I decided to look for a YTS place.'
c 'I didn't really like the job. So I went to the Careers Office again.'
d 'I read the YTS brochure at the Jobcentre.'
e 'Then they offered me a job at a shoe shop.'
f 'Then I went to the Careers Office for more information.'
g 'They helped me to find a different training programme.'
h 'I stayed at the second job for nearly two years. I liked it a lot.'
i 'I had to have an interview first.'

5 Compare a school leaver without a job and a YTS trainee. Write three pairs of sentences.

Example A YTS trainee earns some money.
A young person without a job doesn't earn any money.

Watch your grammar 1

Verbs + infinitive (Verben + Grundform des Verbs/Infinitiv)

Some **want to stay** in education.
Others **would like to get** jobs but cannot.
Then you can **decide to take** a YTS place or not.

Nach bestimmten Verben steht der Infinitiv, z. B. *decide*, *forget*, *promise*, *remember*, *try*, *want*, *would like*.

Advice and warnings (Ratschläge und Ermahnungen)

What school leavers **should** know.
Young workers **ought to** have the chance to learn modern skills.
They **shouldn't** forget to visit their local Careers Office.

Should, *shouldn't* und *ought to* können verwendet werden, um Ratschläge oder Ermahnungen zu erteilen. Sie haben in allen Personen die gleiche Form.
Ought to wird nicht so oft in verneinten Sätzen und Fragen verwendet. *Ought to* verleiht einem Ratschlag oder einer Ermahnung etwas mehr Nachdruck als *should*.

One, ones (Stützwort *one, ones*)

The first step is the most important. And the best **one** is YTS.
Find out about the YTS programmes, especially the **ones** in your area.

Wir verwenden *one* (Singular) und *ones* (Plural) anstelle eines Substantivs, wenn wir das Substantiv nicht wiederholen wollen.

Get it right 1

1 Verbs + infinitives

Translate the following brochure. Begin: *Would you like to learn to be a mechanic? Would you . . .*
Use the following verbs: *ask – decide – do – find – forget – help – know how to – learn – operate – remember – visit – work*

1 Möchten Sie lernen, ein Mechaniker zu sein?
2 Möchten Sie wissen, wie man einen Computer verwendet?
3 Wollen Sie mit Menschen arbeiten?
4 Dann vergessen Sie nicht, Ihr Jobcentre zu besuchen.
5 Wir können Ihnen helfen.
6 Denken Sie daran, nach den YTS-Programmen in Ihrer Stadt zu fragen.
7 Wenn Sie sich für ein Programm entscheiden, können wir helfen.
8 Sprechen Sie mit uns.
9 Wir wollen Ihnen helfen.
10 Wir versprechen, vor Weihnachten ein Trainingsprogramm für Sie zu finden.

2 Simple past

Write about the work experience of Sandra Burton, a school leaver. Put the verbs in brackets in the right tense.

Example When Sandra Burton **left** school she **tried** to get a job without any training.

1 She *(find)* it difficult because she *(not have)* any qualifications.
2 After six weeks she *(decide)* to go to the Jobcentre.
3 The people at the Jobcentre *(promise)* to help Sandra, but four weeks later she still *(not have)* a job.
4 Sandra *(tell)* the officer at the Jobcentre that she *(want)* to work in a garage.
5 She *(want)* to be a mechanic.
6 The officer *(tell)* her that she must have some training first.
7 Then Sandra *(remember)* to ask the officer about YTS.
8 He *(send)* Sandra to the Careers Office where they *(tell)* her about training programmes.
9 Sandra *(say)* she would like to go on a training programme for mechanics.
10 The Careers Office *(promise)* to find her a programme like this but they never *(do)*.
11 In the end she *(decide)* to take a YTS place in an office but she *(not like)* the job.

3 Should, ought to

What advice can you give to school leavers? Use *should, ought to* or *shouldn't*.

Example Before you leave school you should think about your career.

1 You ☐ make any decisions without help from other people.
2 You ☐ forget to visit your Jobcentre and Careers Office.
3 You ☐ also go and see your careers teacher.
4 It's difficult to find a job without training, so you ☐ think about YTS.
5 You ☐ find out about the training programmes from the Careers Office.

4 Modals

Put in the missing words.
could – don't have to – must – ought to – should (2x) *– shouldn't*

Sandra ☐[1] I try to get a place in an office then?
Officer Well, you ☐[2] . You ☐[3] wait a few months.
Sandra But I ☐[4] start soon because I need the money.
Officer Well, yes, you ☐[5] wait too long then. Try for the office place.
Sandra What ☐[6] I do first?
Officer Well, you ☐[7] write a letter to the company. Here's the address.

5 One, ones

Which nouns in the text can you replace with *one* or *ones*?

There are lots of very ordinary training programmes in the Youth Training Scheme but also some very interesting **ones** *(programmes)*. You could have a place in an office but also a more interesting place in a television studio. You could work in a very small company or in a big company that employs 10,000 people. You could start without any qualifications and have a very important qualification at the end of your two years. You may have to do the bad jobs at first but you could have very important jobs later.

'NOTHING LIKE A REAL JOB'

Readers' letters about last week's article on the YTS.

Letters to the Editor

Dear Sir,

Your article on the YTS did not give the whole story. I'm doing the first year of my YTS training programme at the moment. I'm working in a shoe shop. They promised to teach me everything. I wanted to sell shoes and use the till. But I'm painting walls and doing other jobs all the time. And I work harder than the ordinary employees but they get a lot more money. It's nothing like a real job on YTS. Nobody is teaching me anything. I'm not going anywhere. When I'm not painting, someone always says 'Make some coffee'. After three months on YTS I still don't know anything about shoes.

Alan Dodd, Liverpool.

Dear Sir,

My friend said to me: 'In my opinion YTS is slave labour. It's only good for the employers. They can get someone for a job and pay them much less than the real wages.' I agree with her. I like my YTS job but I only get £27.30 a week! I have to give my mother £12. Then there's £3 for a bus pass and £3.50 a week for lunch. That leaves me £8.80 for everything else. The YTS is a good programme but I may be unemployed after my training. Perhaps my employer will employ another YTS trainee for less money. The Government ought to do something about this soon. It's disgraceful.

Caroline Hirst, Salford.

Dear Sir,

I agree with most of your article on the YTS. My training programme is nearly finished now, but after 11 months I'm still enjoying it. I learn something new every day. Everybody here helps me a lot. I can type quite fast. In fact I'm typing this letter right now in my lunch break.

Janie Scott, Edinburgh.

Dear Sir,

My experience on YTS was very important. I'm sure of that. When I left school I didn't know anything about working life. Now I think I know quite a lot. I feel much more confident now and I can talk to people. Last week I had an interview for a real job and they offered it to me. At first, I wasn't sure about YTS. But I decided to stay in it and I'm very glad about that now.

Ronnie Sears, Chester.

Dear Sir,

YTS gives young people a good training and it's certainly better than a year on the dole! But there is something wrong with the scheme. I'm doing the same job as the other girls now but they earn about £50 more than I do. They didn't do any training, either. That's not right. They should give trainees more money after a few months.

Emma Bell, Manchester.

Did you follow? 2

1 Who is happy with YTS? Who is not happy? Who says there are good and bad aspects to YTS?

2 Answer these questions about the five trainees.

1 Where is Alan Dodd working?
2 What year of his scheme is he in?
3 What does he want to learn?
4 What is he really doing all the time?
5 Who does Caroline Hirst's friend think the YTS is good for?
6 Why does she think that?
7 Why can't she have a very good time with her wages?
8 What could happen at the end of her programme?
9 Why don't some employers give trainees jobs at the end of their programmes?
10 What month of her programme is Janie Scott in?
11 What can she now do because of her training?
12 What happened to Ronnie Sears last week?
13 What sort of person is he now?
14 What does Emma Bell think is good and bad about YTS?

3 Find words in the letters for the following:

1 the people who work in a company
2 what a person thinks or believes
3 people who have no work
4 happy
5 terrible
6 sure of yourself

4 In your own words, say what these words or phrases from the letters mean:

1 the whole story
2 ordinary employees
3 slave labour
4 a bus pass
5 lunch break
6 on the dole

5 The five trainees give their opinions about certain things. Write down what they say about the following. They do not all say the same thing.

Example **Alan Dodd:** The newspaper article does not give the whole story.

1 the newspaper article
2 what they are learning
3 their wages
4 the YTS employers

Watch your grammar 2

Present continuous 1 (Verlaufsform der Gegenwart 1)

1 Statements and negatives

I'm doing a YTS training programme at the moment.
It **is not helping** anyone.

2 Questions and short answers

Are you **looking** for a job at the moment? – Yes, I **am**.
Are they **learning** much on their training programme? – No, they **aren't**.

Das **present continuous** wird wie folgt gebildet:

Präsensform von *be* + *-ing* Form des Verbs

Besonderheiten in der Schreibweise der *-ing* Form

write	make	plan	begin	travel
writ**ing**	mak**ing**	plan**ning**	begin**ning**	travel**ling**

(siehe auch Grammatikanhang Seite 193)

Aussagen/Fragen

BE	SUBJEKT	*BE*	*-ING* FORM	SATZERGÄNZUNG
–	I	am ('m)	typing	this letter right now.
–	He/She/It	is ('s)	helping	someone.
–	You/We/They	are ('re)	doing	a YTS training programme.
Am	I	–	helping	someone?
Is	he/she/it	–	doing	a YTS programme?
Are	you/we/they	–	learning	to type?

Kurzantworten

Yes, you are.
No, he isn't.
Yes, we are.

PRESENT CONTINUOUS	SIMPLE PRESENT
Wir verwenden das **present continuous**, um auszudrücken, daß etwas **gerade jetzt** oder nur für eine **begrenzte Zeit** passiert. Man findet es deshalb öfters in Zusammenhang mit Ausdrücken wie *right now* oder *at the moment*.	Das **simple present** wird verwendet, um **Zustände**, **Gewohnheiten** und **häufig wiederkehrende Vorgänge**, **Meinungen**, **Gefühle** und **Sinneswahrnehmungen** auszudrücken.

Manche Verben, die gewöhnlich Zustände beschreiben, wie *be*, *live*, *know*, *have* (= besitzen) werden daher fast nie im **present continuous** verwendet. Verben der Sinneswahrnehmung wie *see*, *hear* stehen auch meist nur im **simple present**.

Quantifiers 2 (Mengenangaben 2)

1 Some and any

Make **some** coffee, please.
There isn't **any** time for lunch.
Did you bring **any** drinks?

BEJAHENDE SÄTZE	VERNEINENDE SÄTZE/FRAGEN
some	any

In der Regel verwenden wir *some* in bejahenden Sätzen und *any* in verneinenden Sätzen und in Fragen.

2 Some-, any-, every- and no-

There is **something** good about every job. Of course, not **everything** is good. **Nothing** is perfect. Is there **anything** you don't like about yours?
Everyone has to leave school at some time. **Nobody** can stay for ever. This company is looking for **someone** who likes office work.

Is **anyone** interested?
You could go **somewhere** else. But **everywhere** you go you'll find the same old things.
I've never been **anywhere** where things are different. No, **nowhere** is it different.

Folgende Endungen können alle mit *some-*, *any-*, *every-* und *no-* verwendet werden.

-thing	um über Sachen zu sprechen
-where	um über Orte zu sprechen
-body, -one	um über Personen zu sprechen

Get it right 2

1 Present continuous

Two school friends meet three months after they have left school. Put the verbs into the right forms. (Be careful. The word order may change.)

Les Hallo Sheila! How are you?
Sheila Hi, Les. Well, okay. But **I am not enjoying** life really.
Les Why's that? What *(do)*[1] you at the moment?
Sheila Well, I tried to get a job, but I couldn't. So I *(do)*[2] a YTS training programme.
Les Me, too. Where *(work)*[3] you?
Sheila I *(work)*[4] in a bank. I *(learn)*[5] how to serve people at the counter.
Les That's what Richard *(do)*[6], too. He *(work)*[7] at the one in Upper Street.
Sheila What about you? What job *(do)*[8] you? Something to do with cars?
Les Right. I *(train)*[9] to be a mechanic. It's great.

2 Simple present – present continuous

Put the verbs into the simple or continuous form.

He **is looking for** a job. He **goes** to the Jobcentre every day. He always *(look)*[1] at the adverts first. He just *(look)*[2] at them now. Other people *(stand)*[3] and *(look at)*[4] the adverts, too. Another person *(read)*[5] a newspaper. Two men *(sit)*[6] behind tables. An unemployed man *(talk)*[7] to one of them and a girl *(wait)*[8] to talk to the other. Some people *(come)*[9] to the Jobcentre every day. They usually *(come)*[10] in the morning. This man always *(get)*[11] up early to go to the Jobcentre because he very much *(want)*[12] to find another job. He sometimes *(see)*[13] a job that he *(like)*[14] and then he *(write)*[15] a letter.

3 Some and any

Ask and answer questions about the table.

Example Are there **any** training places as cooks in Croydon?
Yes, there are **some** in Croydon but there aren't **any** in Sutton.

TRAINING PLACES IN CROYDON AND SUTTON	CROYDON	SUTTON
office clerk	12	9
cook	4	–
shop staff	18	7
secretary	10	8
computer staff	–	9
metalworker	5	7
bank staff	–	4

4 Somebody, anybody …

Complete the sentences. Use *some-*, *any-* etc.

Example The YTS has some**thing** for every**body**.

1 No□ has to go on the dole after leaving school.
2 Most people will find some□ they like some□.
3 The trouble is that you don't learn □ on some programmes.
4 So when you finish you have no□ to help you later.
5 Some people don't want to learn □. They just want a job.
6 But later, when they want to change jobs, they can't find one □.
7 □ should think about the job they would like to have in five or ten years' time.
8 Of course, □ knows for certain what will happen in ten years' time.

OVER TO YOU

Listening *After School*

Raymond Wall takes another look at the Youth Training Scheme in today's programme. Trainees, careers officers and employers say what they really think of the scheme.

1 Listen to the tape. Are these statements right or wrong?

1 The radio programme is for school leavers.
2 Alison Hayes is a YTS trainee.
3 She thinks it was a bad idea to do the training programme.
4 She did not like her programme at first.
5 Things are different now.
6 She works in a shop.
7 She only works with other girls.
8 She knows she can keep the job at the end of her programme.
9 She is looking for another job.
10 She has already got another job.
11 The YTS certificate is her only qualification.
12 She thinks it will help her later.

2 Now listen to the tape again. Write down reasons why:

1 she liked her job at first.
2 she doesn't like it so much now.
3 the YTS programme was the right thing for her.

Writing

1

JOBCENTRE	
JOB	GARAGE MECHANIC
QUALIFICATIONS	1 year's training
HOURS	42 a week
PAY	£160 a week
HOLIDAY	4 weeks
SATURDAY	1 per month

JOBCENTRE	
JOB	SECRETARY
QUALIFICATIONS	1 year's training
HOURS	35 a week
PAY	£140 a week
HOLIDAY	3 weeks
SATURDAY	–

Look at these two Jobcentre adverts. Choose one and describe the job. These verbs will help you: *earn – get – have – work.*
Begin: *There is a job at the Jobcentre as a ... You ...*

2 Make notes on the job you would like most. Say what job it is and what the hours, pay, holidays etc. are like. Then use your notes to write about it.

Working with words

1 Put in the missing words.

1 Someone who gives you a job is your ▭ .
2 He or she ▭ you.
3 You are his or her ▭ .
4 People without a job are ▭ .
5 ▭ are people who are learning how to do a job.

2 Replace the underlined words and phrases with others which mean the same.

That is right, there are a lot of people <u>without work</u> in this country. The Government <u>should</u> do more for them. People without <u>special skills</u> find it very hard to get a job.

3 Put in the missing words:
after – chance – decide – decision – experience – forget – help

When they are looking for a job, school leavers need a lot of ▭[1] because they do not have any ▭[2] of the world of work. They often ▭[3] to ask the right people for help. ▭[4] a visit to their Careers Office they ▭[5] to take the first job they find. That's usually the wrong ▭[6] because they then often never have the ▭[7] to find a better one.

Key words and phrases

agree

decide – decision

employ
employer
employee
unemployed

anyone
anybody
anything
anywhere

experience
programme
qualification
trainee
training

decide to
forget to
ought to
promise to
remember to

certain ▶▶ sure
certainly

address
letter

chance
instead of
moment
nearly
ordinary

TRAVELLING TO BRITAIN

DUTY-FREE ALLOWANCES

Goods obtained duty-free on a ship or aircraft

TOBACCO PRODUCTS
200 cigarettes or 50 cigars or 250 grammes of tobacco

ALCOHOLIC DRINKS
1 litre of whisky, gin or vodka, or 2 litres of sherry or port, or 2 litres of sparkling wine plus 2 litres of red or white wine

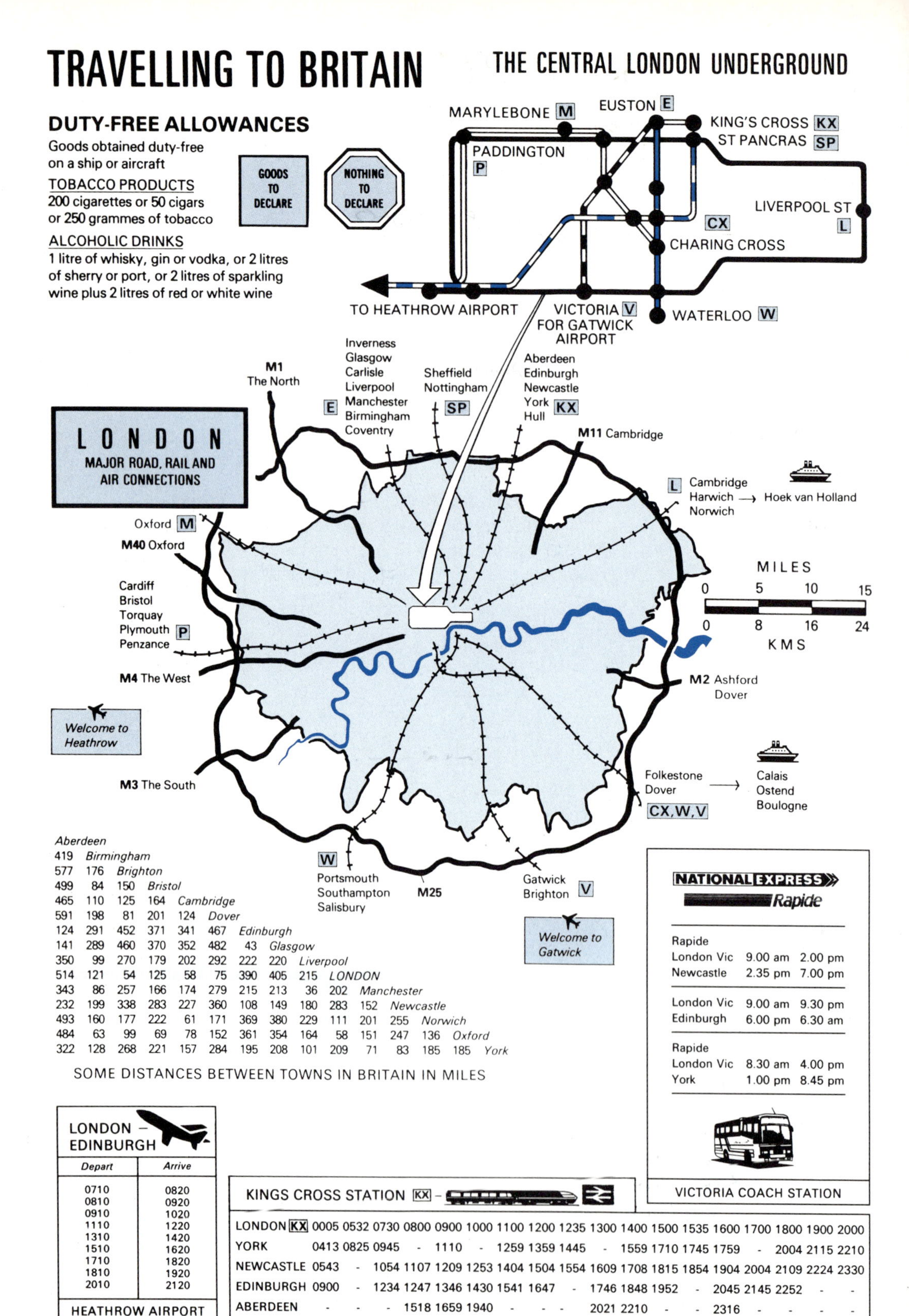

	Aberdeen	Birmingham	Brighton	Bristol	Cambridge	Dover	Edinburgh	Glasgow	Liverpool	LONDON	Manchester	Newcastle	Norwich	Oxford
Birmingham	419													
Brighton	577	176												
Bristol	499	84	150											
Cambridge	465	110	125	164										
Dover	591	198	81	201	124									
Edinburgh	124	291	452	371	341	467								
Glasgow	141	289	460	370	352	482	43							
Liverpool	350	99	270	179	202	292	222	220						
LONDON	514	121	54	125	58	75	390	405	215					
Manchester	343	86	257	166	174	279	215	213	36	202				
Newcastle	232	199	338	283	227	360	108	149	180	283	152			
Norwich	493	160	177	222	61	171	369	380	229	111	201	255		
Oxford	484	63	99	69	78	152	361	354	164	58	151	247	136	
York	322	128	268	221	157	284	195	208	101	209	71	83	185	185

SOME DISTANCES BETWEEN TOWNS IN BRITAIN IN MILES

NATIONAL EXPRESS Rapide

Rapide		
London Vic	9.00 am	2.00 pm
Newcastle	2.35 pm	7.00 pm
London Vic	9.00 am	9.30 pm
Edinburgh	6.00 pm	6.30 am
Rapide		
London Vic	8.30 am	4.00 pm
York	1.00 pm	8.45 pm

VICTORIA COACH STATION

LONDON – EDINBURGH

Depart	Arrive
0710	0820
0810	0920
0910	1020
1110	1220
1310	1420
1510	1620
1710	1820
1810	1920
2010	2120

HEATHROW AIRPORT

KINGS CROSS STATION KX

LONDON KX	0005	0532	0730	0800	0900	1000	1100	1200	1235	1300	1400	1500	1535	1600	1700	1800	1900	2000
YORK	0413	0825	0945	-	1110	-	1259	1359	1445	-	1559	1710	1745	1759	-	2004	2115	2210
NEWCASTLE	0543	-	1054	1107	1209	1253	1404	1504	1554	1609	1708	1815	1854	1904	2004	2109	2224	2330
EDINBURGH	0900	-	1234	1247	1346	1430	1541	1647	-	1746	1848	1952	-	2045	2145	2252	-	-
ABERDEEN	-	-	-	1518	1659	1940	-	-	-	2021	2210	-	-	2316	-	-	-	-

GOVERNMENT IN BRITAIN

VOTING IN BRITAIN

A General Election has to be held every five years, although they can be held sooner. Everyone over the age of 18 is allowed to vote. The candidate with the most votes in a constituency wins the right to sit in Parliament. Some small parties win a large % of the votes but only a few seats. Britain does not have Proportional Representation.

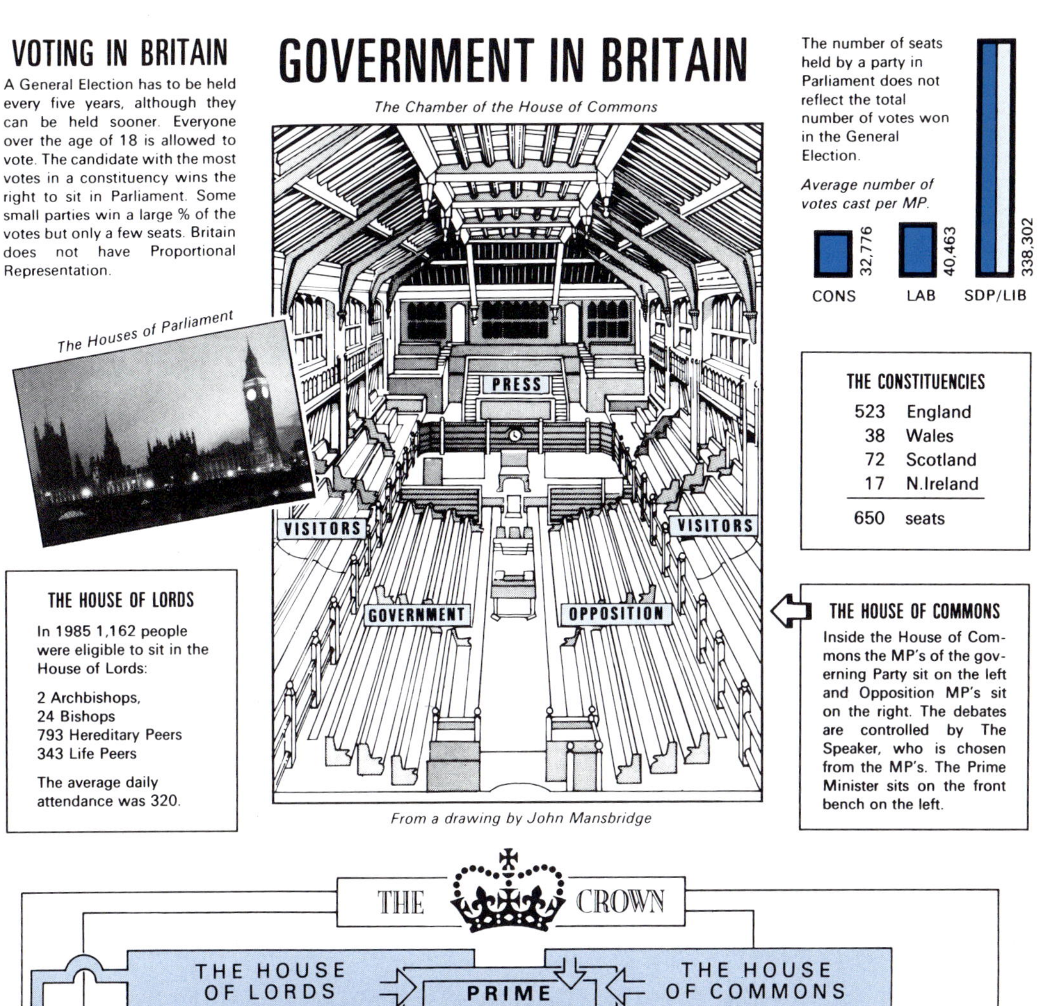

The Chamber of the House of Commons

From a drawing by John Mansbridge

The Houses of Parliament

The number of seats held by a party in Parliament does not reflect the total number of votes won in the General Election.

Average number of votes cast per MP.

CONS	LAB	SDP/LIB
32,776	40,463	338,302

THE CONSTITUENCIES

523	England
38	Wales
72	Scotland
17	N.Ireland
650	seats

THE HOUSE OF LORDS

In 1985 1,162 people were eligible to sit in the House of Lords:

2 Archbishops,
24 Bishops
793 Hereditary Peers
343 Life Peers

The average daily attendance was 320.

THE HOUSE OF COMMONS

Inside the House of Commons the MP's of the governing Party sit on the left and Opposition MP's sit on the right. The debates are controlled by The Speaker, who is chosen from the MP's. The Prime Minister sits on the front bench on the left.

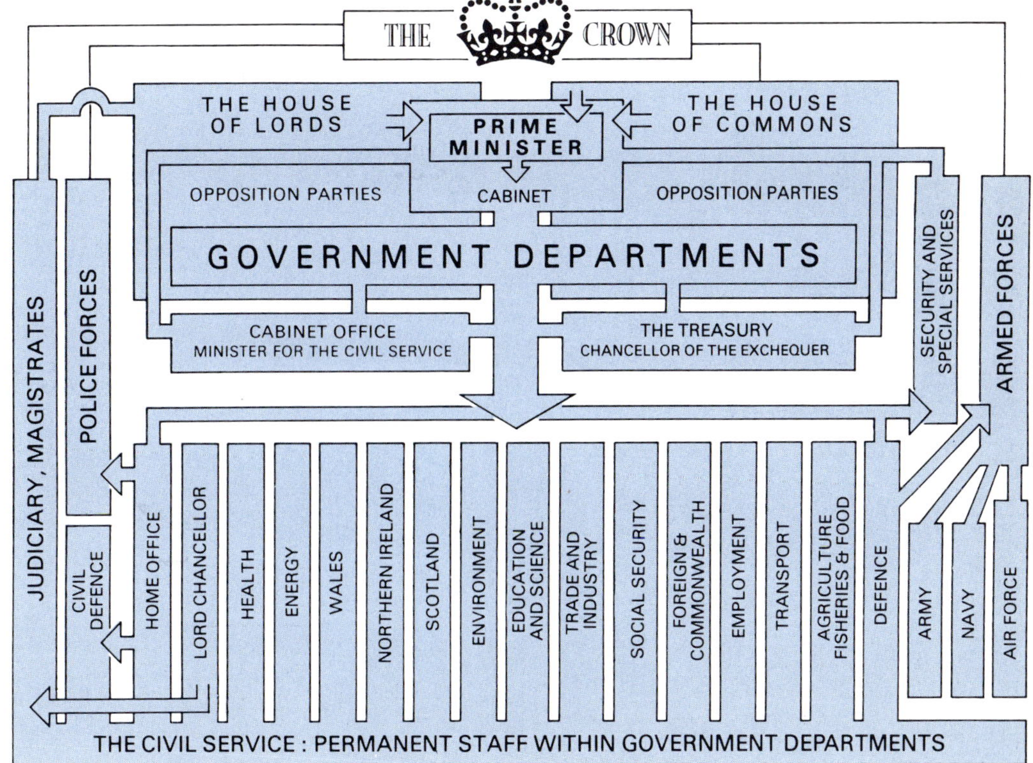

4 Lots to do

'WHEN SHALL WE MEET?'

Kevin Hello, Jenny?
Jenny Is that you, Kevin?
Kevin Yes. Are there any decent films on? I can't find a newspaper here.
Jenny I've got one. Oh, there's a good one on at the Plaza.
Kevin I like going to the Plaza.
Jenny So do I. I like the seats there. They're really comfortable.
Kevin Which film is on there?
Jenny *Love Story.*
Kevin Hmm. A love story. I'm not keen on seeing a love story. What else is on?
Jenny Let me see. There's *2001.*
Kevin That's quite good, isn't it? Science fiction.
Jenny I don't mind seeing a science fiction film, Kevin. But I prefer watching them at home on TV.
Kevin Is there anything else?
Jenny Not really. There's *Dirty Harry* at the Rank Cinema Centre.
Kevin *Dirty Harry*. That's with Clint Eastwood, isn't it?
Jenny I can't stand watching westerns. And I don't like him.
Kevin No, nor do I. But *Dirty Harry* isn't a western. It's a thriller, I think.
Jenny Well, I don't want to see a thriller this evening, thanks.
Kevin All right. What do you want to see?
Jenny I suggest *Love Story*. Don't you want to see it?
Kevin Well, I enjoy watching science fiction.
Jenny Can't we go to the Plaza? You'll enjoy it. I'm sure you will.
Kevin Oh, well. Maybe it will be all right. When does it start?
Jenny The last performance starts at half past seven.
Kevin All right. When shall we meet?
Jenny I'll meet you outside the Plaza at twenty-five past. Okay?
Kevin Yes, all right. Bye, then.
Jenny Bye, Kevin.

We've got a date

Mrs Underwood Who was that on the phone, Jenny?
Jenny That was Kevin Williams, mum.
Mrs Underwood Do I know him?
Jenny No, I don't think so. He goes to my college. He's going to be a cook.
Mrs Underwood What did he want?

in my mind: In meinen Gedanken

Jenny We've got a date.
Mrs Underwood That's nice. What are you going to do?
45 **Jenny** We're going to see a film.
Mrs Underwood What are you going to see?
Jenny *Love Story* at the Plaza.
Mrs Underwood Lovely. But take your coat. It's going to rain, I think. Look at the sky.
Jenny All right, mum.

YOUR LOCAL CINEMAS

PLAZA	Gaumont	Rank Cinema Centre
Love Story	**2001**	**Dirty Harry**
5.15 p.m.	5.30 p.m.	5.20 p.m.
LCP 7.30 p.m.	LCP 7.45 p.m.	LCP 7.30 p.m.

LCP Last complete performance

Did you follow? 1

1 Answer these questions about the first dialogue.
Give the correct name or say that the answer isn't in the text:
Jenny/Kevin/Not in the text
1 Who has got more money?
2 Who wants to go to the cinema?
3 Who has a newspaper?
4 Who made the phone call?
5 Who wanted to pay for the cinema tickets?
6 Who lives near the cinema?

2 Answer these questions about the first dialogue.
1 What do Jenny and Kevin think of the Plaza cinema?
2 What reason does Jenny give for her opinion?
3 What does Jenny think of Clint Eastwood?
4 What does Kevin think of Clint Eastwood?
5 Does Jenny like films like *2001*?
6 Does Kevin want to see *Love Story*?
7 Which film do they decide to see?
8 Where and when do they decide to meet?

3 Give reasons.
Here are some statements about the two dialogues. Say if you think they are right or wrong. Give reasons from the texts.
Example Jenny wants to see a good thriller. – No, that's wrong. She says, 'I don't want to see a thriller this evening, thanks.'
1 Kevin wants to see *2001*.
2 Jenny wants to see a science fiction film.
3 Kevin doesn't want to see *Love Story*.
4 Kevin and Jenny decide to meet ten minutes before the film starts.
5 Kevin wants to be a baker.
6 Jenny's mother does not like Kevin.
7 Jenny's mother wants her to stay at home.

Watch your grammar 1

Future forms (Zukunftsformen/zukünftiges Geschehen)

1 Simple present-future (Präsens Futur)

Kevin When **does** it start?
Jenny The last performance **starts** at half past seven.

Man verwendet das **simple present-future**, um zukünftiges Geschehen auszudrücken oder wenn es sich um feste Abläufe/Ereignisse in der Zukunft *(definite events)* wie Stunden-/Fahrpläne, Kino-/Theaterveranstaltungen usw. handelt.

2 Will-future (Will-Futur)

Jenny When **shall** we **meet**?
Kevin I'**ll meet** you outside the Plaza.

Jenny You'**ll enjoy** it.
Kevin Maybe it **will be** all right.

Man verwendet das **will-future**, um ...	
... Versprechen und gerade gefaßte Entschlüsse *(promises and decisions)* auszudrücken.	... bestimme Voraussagen *(predictions)* zu machen.

In der ersten Person Singular oder Plural *(I/we)* des Fragesatzes verwendet man *shall* statt *will/'ll.*

3 Going to-future (Going to-Futur)

What **are** you **going** to do?
We'**re going to** see a film.

I think it'**s going to** rain.
Look at the sky.

I'**m going to** be a cook.
She **is going to** visit Turkey.

Man verwendet das **going to-future**, ...		
... wenn man über feste Absichten *(intentions)* und Pläne redet.	... um über Dinge zu sprechen, die automatisch eintreten oder sich natürlich ergeben *(predictions about the near future)*.	... um über Dinge zu sprechen, die unmittelbar bevorstehen.

4 Present continuous as future (Verlaufsform der Gegenwart mit zukünftiger Bedeutung)

Das *present continuous* wird zusammen mit einer Zeitangabe wie z. B. *tonight, next Monday, on the fourth* verwendet, um etwas zukünftig Geplantes, Verabredetes oder Beschlossenes zu beschreiben (vgl. Seite 76).

Likes and dislikes (Vorlieben und Abneigungen)

Verben, die Gefühle ausdrücken wie z. B. *like, love, don't mind, be keen on, can't stand* und *hate* kann man entweder direkt mit einem **Substantiv** (the *seats, love stories*) oder mit einem **gerund** (*-ing* Form) verbinden *(going to the Plaza, seeing a love story)*.
(Siehe Grammatikanhang Seite 194)

Agreeing (Gleicher Meinung sein, zustimmen)

Kevin I like the Plaza.
Jenny **So do I.**

Jenny I don't like Clint Eastwood.
Kevin No, **nor do I.**

Mögliche Formen, um Zustimmung auszudrücken sind:

So/nor do I.	So/Nor am I.	So/Nor will I.

Get it right 1

1 Will future, future with simple present

Put the verbs into the correct forms.

Example When *(be)* your birthday?
Who *(be)* at your party?
When **is** your birthday?
Who **will be** at your party?

1 The bus *(stop)* at my house at seven p.m.
2 When *(be)* your birthday?
3 John *(be)* at the party this evening.
4 The train *(leave)* at 6 o'clock.
5 When *(start)* the film?
6 You *(like)* this film, I'm sure.
7 When *(you start)* school on Monday?
8 My father *(meet)* you at the station.
9 What time *(arrive)* your train?

2 Going to future and future with simple present

Put the verbs into the correct forms.

Example It *(be)* nice today.
It's **going to be** nice today.

1 I *(see)* a horror film this evening.
2 It *(rain)* this afternoon, I think.
3 The film *(start)* at 7 o'clock.
4 Jenny *(meet)* Kevin outside the cinema.
5 The English lesson *(end)* at 11.30.
6 My brother *(visit)* Florida soon.
7 The Western *(start)* at 9 p.m.
8 I *(be)* a doctor.
9 It *(be)* very cold tomorrow.

3 Future forms

Put the verbs into the correct forms.

1 It *(be)* my birthday on Tuesday.
2 My girlfriend and I *(go)* to a basketball match this evening.
3 Our team *(win)*, I think.
4 She *(come)* to my house and then we *(watch)* the match together.
5 The match *(begin)* at eight o'clock.
6 I think we *(enjoy)* it.
7 My girlfriend *(be)* a mechanic.
8 I *(start)* work in November.

4 Decisions and offers

Say what these people decide to do or offer to do. Use *will* in your answer and say which sentence is an offer and which is a decision.

Example This meat is terrible.
(go to a different shop next time)
I'll go to a different shop next time.

1 This sports programme is too long. *(turn off the television)*
2 It's very hot in here. *(open a window)*
3 Do you want some coffee? *(make some)*
4 Is that homework hard? *(help you)*
5 I'm bored. *(go to the cinema this evening)*
6 You look nice today. *(take a photo of you)*
7 It's mum's birthday tomorrow. *(buy her some flowers)*
8 Let's meet at 7 o'clock. *(meet you outside the cinema)*

5 Likes and dislikes

Say what these people feel about these things. Then say or write down what you feel about these things.

-- can't stand – doesn't like ? doesn't mind
+ likes ++ prefers

Example Max Versey can't stand fish and chips.
He likes cheese but prefers sweets.

MAX VERSEY	
fish and chips	--
hamburgers	–
apples	?
cheese	+
sweets	+ +

JOHN REDDISH	
love stories	--
animal films	–
westerns	?
thrillers	+
horror films	+ +

6 So/Nor (do) I

Here are some statements by Kevin's friend. Kevin agrees with them. He uses: *so (do) I* or *nor (do) I* and *do – will – can – be*.
How does he say it?

Example I like westerns. **So do I.**
I'm keen on westerns. **So am I.**
I don't like horror films. **Nor do I.**

1 I'm keen on science fiction films.
2 My mother likes baking cakes.
3 My father doesn't like very cold weather.
4 I don't like ketchup.
5 Some people don't like going to the cinema, but I do.
6 I will be at the party this evening.
7 I won't be at school tomorrow.
8 Most teenagers want to find an interesting job after school.

SOMETHING FOR EVERYBODY

Summer camps – more popular every year: a report on British camps for teenagers by *Crystal's* own reporter Shelley Starr.

It's a surprising fact, but American-style summer camps for teenagers are becoming more popular in Britain every year. *Crystal* made a sudden decision to send me to two camps this summer to find out what these camps offer. First of all, I went to *Camp Adventure* near Windermere in the Lake District. The camp offers a lot of outdoor activities. When I arrived, the camp was nearly empty. Most of the campers were out on an orienteering course. Orienteering means finding your way through woods and fields with a map and a set of directions. Other activities at *Camp Adventure* include judo, skiing (on grass in the summer) and mountain climbing. The camp wants campers to be happy and have fun but is careful about safety. Expert instructors organize all the courses and the cost of the holiday includes insurance.

The second camp I visited was *Pine View Summer Camp* near Invergordon in Scotland, which started in 1987. Most of the year, it is Harry Meadows' sheep farm. During the summer there are about 40 campers, six extra helpers and instructors. The Meadows, Harry and his wife Margaret, happily cook three meals a day for everybody! The morning I arrived, I saw a large sign: *'11 a.m. Eskimo Rolls on the Glass'.* I asked the organizers and they explained that the Glass was the fast river which flows through the camp. I saw a group of campers in canoes on the water. The instructor watched carefully and ten canoeists suddenly rolled over with their heads under water. That was an *Eskimo Roll!* I was really happy when they all came up again a few seconds later! The canoeing instructor told me, 'The canoe course is very hard but the campers really enjoy it. It's the most popular course here. The river here flows very fast and the campers have to work hard to control their canoes well. But they usually learn very quickly. Maybe because the water here is so cold!' *Pine View* is surprisingly keen on indoor workshops. There are workshops for all sorts of activities like music, video and computers. But the *Eskimo rolls* showed me that these campers did not only sit around all the time.

In general, the camps are not cheap but they all offer a lot of interesting activities and fun, something for everybody. Maybe some *Crystal* readers would like to try one next summer.

Wellow Farm near Chichester

A summer camp which concentrates on crafts. Three large workshop buildings. Local crafts - working with wool & wood. Outdoor activities: archery and riding. Camp fires with food and music every evening. The local beach is only a mile away with good, clean sand - great for swimming and barbecues.
Mr Ansell, **Wellow Farm,** *Wellow, Chichester. Tel: 34871*

Did you follow? 2

1 Answer the questions on the text.

1 What is *Crystal*?
2 Who is Shelley Starr?
3 Where did Shelley Starr go? Name the places.
4 Why did *Crystal* send her to these places?
5 What was her opinion of these places?

2 Which of these activities can you do at the three camps? Which activities can't you do? Use vocabulary lists or your dictionary to find any new words. Then write down which activities you can do in which camp.

cheese making	karate	sailing
computer workshop	mountain climbing	video workshop
grass skiing	music workshop	woodworking
judo	orienteering	

3 Find the information in the text and answer these questions about summer camps.

1 Where did the idea of summer camps come from?
2 Where were most of the campers at *Camp Adventure* when Shelley arrived?
3 Are the activities at *Camp Adventure* dangerous?
4 Which course do the campers at the camp in Scotland like best?
5 Is that course easy or difficult?
6 Are there only outdoor activities at *Pine View*?
7 What sort of place is *Pine View* most of the year?
8 How often do the campers eat a cooked meal at *Pine View*?
9 Are there more indoor or outdoor activities at *Wellow Farm*?

4 Which of the three camps is best for someone who likes ...

1 working with computers?
2 working with their hands?
3 water sports?
4 winter sports?
5 being with animals?
6 music?
7 hard outdoor activity?

5 Answer these questions.

1 Which of the three camps did you like best?
2 Which activities would you like to do?
3 Which other activities would you like to do?
4 Write a programme for an ideal summer camp for you and your friends.
Which activities would you include?
Where should the camp be? (near a beach/in the mountains/on a farm/...)
What should it have? (disco? club?)
Start like this: My ideal summer camp *should be/have ...*
shouldn't ...

Watch your grammar 2

Adverbs 2 and adverbial clauses (Adverbien 2 und adverbiale Nebensätze)

Adverbien und adverbiale Nebensätze sind Wörter oder Satzteile, die beschreiben, wie, wann und wo Ereignisse stattfinden. Adverbien bestimmen Verben, Adjektive, andere Adverbien oder ganze Sätze näher.

1 Adverbs: formation (Adverbien: Bildung)

Ten canoeists **suddenly** rolled over with their heads under water.
Instructors watch the canoeists **carefully**.
Canoeists learn **quickly**.

Adverbien werden im allgemeinen durch Anhängung von *-ly* an das Adjektiv gebildet.

REGELMÄSSIGE BILDUNG *(-LY)*			AUSNAHMEN				
sudden sudden**ly**	quick quick**ly**	bad bad**ly**	good well	fast fast	hard hard	straight straight	long long

Besonderheiten: Adjektive, die auf *-l* oder *-y* enden.

usual	careful	happy
usua**lly**	carefu**lly**	happ**ily**

2 Adverbs of place, time and frequency: position (Adverbien des Ortes, der Zeit und der Häufigkeit: Stellung im Satz)

There is a camp fire with food and music **every evening**.
Pine View Summer Camp near Invergordon started **in 1987**.
Campers **often** go to the beach together.

Häufigkeitsadverbien stehen bei **unbestimmter** Häufigkeit (*often, never*, etc.) **vor** dem Hauptverb, bei **bestimmter** Häufigkeit *(once, every evening)* **am Ende** des Satzes.

Abweichend vom Deutschen steht die adverbiale Bestimmung des Ortes vor der adverbialen Bestimmung der Zeit, d. h. die adverbiale Bestimmung der Zeit steht normalerweise am Ende des Satzes.

	ADVERB OF/ADVERBIALE BESTIMMUNG DER/DES		
	PLACE	TIME/ZEIT	ORTES
Crystal sent me	to two camps	this summer.	–
Crystal schickte mich	–	diesen Sommer	zu zwei Ferienlagern.

3 Adverbs of manner (Adverbiale Bestimmungen der Art und Weise)

The instructor watched **carefully**.

Adverbs of manner zeigen an, **wie** etwas geschieht. Zur Betonung können **adverbs of manner** vor das Hauptverb gestellt werden *(he carefully watched)*; im allgemeinen jedoch stehen sie am Ende des Satzes.

Get it right 2

1 Adverbs of frequency and adverbs of time

Put the adverbs of time and frequency in the correct position.

1 I go to London. *(often)*
2 Some people cook. *(every day)*
3 We have barbecues in the garden. *(sometimes)*
4 My father visited Berlin. *(in 1986)*
5 People are happy with their money. *(never)*
6 It rains in November. *(usually)*
7 Boris Becker won his match. *(yesterday)*

2 Adverbs

Put in the correct form – adjective or adverb?

1 It isn't *(surprising)* that summer camps are *(good)* fun.
2 *Crystal* magazine *(sudden)* sent their reporter to two camps.
3 The instructors watch campers *(careful)* when they are in the water.
4 There are three meals a day at *Pine View* on a *(normal)* day.
5 The canoeists learn *(quick)*. That's *(usual)*.
6 Instructors teach the campers *(different)* at *(different)* camps.

3 Adverbs regular and irregular

Change these adjectives into adverbs and put them in the right place.

1 The campers go to the barbecues on the beach. *(happy)*
2 They eat their food. *(hungry)*
3 The instructors train the campers. *(good)*
4 The river flows at *Pine View*. *(fast)*
5 The canoeists work on the river. *(hard)*
6 Some campers did the Orienteering. *(bad)*
7 Shelley made notes. *(careful)*
8 Shelley wrote her report. *(quick)*

4 Translate these sentences into English.

Use *like/don't mind* etc. + noun
or *like/don't mind* etc. + -ing
like – don't mind – can't stand – prefer

1 Ich gehe gerne ins Kino.
2 Ich kann Bud Spencer nicht ausstehen.
3 Ich kann Skilaufen nicht ausstehen.
4 Ich mag Hunde.
5 Ich sehe gerne fern.
6 Ich habe nichts gegen Sport.
7 Ich habe nichts dagegen, Sport zu treiben.
8 Meine Schwester mag lieber Musik.
9 Mein Bruder spielt lieber Musik.

5 Translate these sentences into English.

1 Mein Bruder spielt oft Fußball.
2 Er spielte Fußball gestern.
3 Unsere Klasse besuchte 1987 Berlin.
4 Ich fuhr letzte Woche nach Hannover.
5 Shelley Starr besuchte im August zwei Sommerlager.
6 Ich gehe oft ins Kino.

6 Which word fits which definition?

agree – canoe – college – date – Eskimo – popular – prefer – second

1 This describes something that a lot of people like.
2 One sixtieth of a minute.
3 Someone who lives in the north of Canada, Alaska or Greenland.
4 A light boat for one or two people.
5 To have the same opinion as another person.
6 To like something better.
7 A training school for older learners.
8 A time and a place to meet a person.

7 Put the correct words in the gaps.

around – away – by – for (2x) *– have – it's – its – on* (3x) *– over – out – up*

1 The *Sunny Days* camp concentrates ☐ outdoor activities.
2 The campers ☐ fun and learn a lot.
3 The camp is run ☐ Mr and Mrs Adams.
4 ☐ in Cornwall in the south-west of England.
5 My magazine wanted a report ☐ it.
6 I went there to find ☐ what the camp is like.
7 The camp is very modern. ☐ bedrooms are very clean.
8 The campers do not sit ☐ very long.
9 Mr Adams is keen ☐ canoe sports.
10 He is an instructor. He rolled ☐ in his canoe.
11 Then he came ☐ again.
12 There are workshops ☐ indoor activities, too.
13 The camp is ideal ☐ teenagers.
14 The beach is only half a mile ☐.

OVER TO YOU

Listening *'Where shall we meet?'*

Listen to the telephone conversation on the tape. You will hear a boy and a girl making a date.

1 Answer the questions about the conversation.

1 What are the names of the speakers?
2 Who phones whom?
3 What is the girl's phone number?
4 The boy knows what is on. What is on?
5 Does the girl know the group?
6 Can the girl go?
7 Who has the tickets?
8 Where will they meet?
9 When will they meet?
10 Who will pay for the tickets?

2 Make notes from the tape. Find out the following information.

1 How does Kim answer the phone? *(Phone number, name + 'speaking')*
2 How does John say who is phoning?
3 How does John tell Kim about what is on?
4 How does John ask Kim to go with him?
5 How does Kim agree?
6 How do John and Kim make a date?
7 How do they end the conversation?

3 Say what sorts of films you like watching and don't like watching.

I like		horror films
I love		westerns
I really like	–	thrillers
I don't mind	watching	love stories
I'm not keen on	seeing	mysteries
I don't like	going to	science fiction films
I dislike		action films
I can't stand		
I hate		

Working with words

1 Put the missing words in the gaps.
agree – college – comfortable – fire – fun – included – keen – lessons – lovely – questions – south – suggested – surprising – workshop

Hamilton House is a training ▭[1] for young nurses. It is in the ▭[2] of Birmingham and has a ▭[3] garden around it. The college is ▭[4] on safety. When I visited it, there was a ▭[5] practice. During the morning, there were the usual ▭[6] but after lunch there was an interesting ▭[7] on cigarette smoking. Some of the nurses asked ▭[8] and there were some ▭[9] answers. The bedrooms in the college are ▭[10] and modern. I ▭[11] that it was only hard work at the college, but the nurses did not ▭[12]. They have ▭[13], too. The evening activities ▭[14] a disco.

2 Here are some words which you know. Put in the missing vowels.
Remember that the letter y can be a vowel in English!

br★★kf★st	Br★t★sh	★★r★pl★n★	ch★c★l★t★s	c★n★m★
c★pb★★rd	★v★r★b★d★	f★★tb★ll	★nt★ll★g★nt	j★★ns
m★s★c	ph★t★gr★ph	p★l★c★m★n	q★★st★★n	q★★★t
r★d★★	s★p★rm★rk★t	t★x★s	t★l★v★s★★n	w★★k

3 *Opposites*

Find the opposites of the words in box 1 from box 2. Start with the ones you know.
If you do not know them, use a dictionary.

BOX 1

fast	start	popular
outdoor	clean	happy
careful		

BOX 2

careless	dirty	end
indoor	slow	
unhappy	unpopular	

4 Make a note of the different ways of making opposites in English; e.g. *happy* – *unhappy*
Use a dictionary and find the opposite of:
agree – definite – lucky – natural – practical – probably – regularly – safe
Look them up under: **dis- – un- – ir- – im- – in-**

5 What are they in English?

1 A fruit. Yellow. Needs hot sunshine. Long and thin.
2 An animal. Four legs. White. Gives us wool.
3 A vehicle. Uses petrol or diesel. No wheels. Travels on water.
4 Very high. You can sometimes ski on them. White in winter.
5 Made of paper. Has photos and texts. Comes out once a week or once a month.
6 Made of paper. Has photos and texts. Comes out once a day.
7 Made of water. Very cold. Hard. You can find it on lakes in the winter.
8 A place. Has many visitors. Lots of wild animals are inside.

Key words and phrases

When **shall** we meet?
I'll meet you at seven.
I'm going to be a cook.
We're going to see a film.
It starts at half past seven.

I'm not **keen on** learning about skiing.
I **can't stand** watching westerns.
I **enjoy** watching science fiction films.

The college **concentrates on** woodwork.
The beach is **great for** barbecues.
Shelley Starr wrote a **report on** summer camps for Crystal.

She liked the first camp best. **Its** name was Camp Adventure. **It's in** the Lake District.
The campers **have fun** there.
They have three meals **a day**.

like ▶◀ dislike
question ▶◀ answer
north ▶◀ south

map
lovely
decent

comfortable
building

insurance
fire
college

lesson

5 A look at Britain

MR AND MRS AVERAGE

Mr and Mrs Average live quietly in their own house with a garden, a dog and two children. They drive their own car, have a phone, a colour TV and a video-recorder and are planning to buy a home computer. They cut the grass carefully once a week in the summer and wash their family car punctually at 10 o'clock every Sunday morning. Mr and Mrs Average spend £135 a year on books, newspapers and magazines but less than £5 a year on the cinema. Both Mr and Mrs Average have to work to pay off the 25-year mortgage on their house. They enjoy a comfortable standard of living but sometimes worry about unemployment.

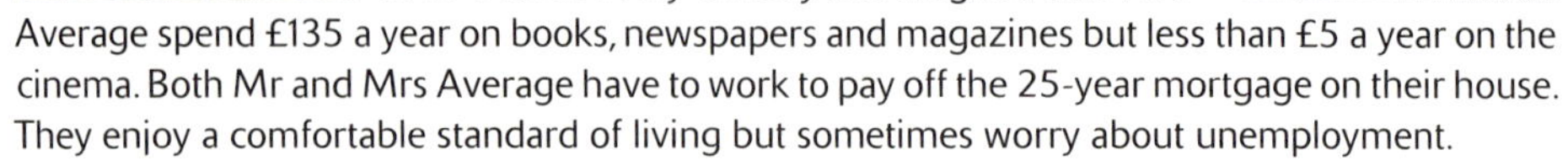

FACTS AND FIGURES

Average family
2 children, own house with mortgage garden, dog, own car, phone, colour TV, video-recorder

Man 71, **woman** 77 years
non-white population 2.5 m
members of churches
15 % of population
1987 56.5 m **2001** 59 m

Britain's wealth
1976 £140 bn **1984** £762 bn
Working hours
Men 44.3 hrs per week
Women 39.1 hrs per week

People

A boy born in 1984 can expect to live for 71 years, a girl for 77 years. Two and a half million Britons are non-white. A large minority (42 per cent) of the non-white population was born in the UK. The number of Christians is falling. Only 15 % of Britons are members of a church. The population of Britain is 56.5 million. By the year 2001 it will rise to 59 million.

Money and jobs

The richer half of the population receive 93 % of all the wealth. The poorer half share the other 7 %. In a survey, only 9 % of Britons said they wanted to 'get rich'. (In Japan, 38 % said this was the most important thing in life.) Working women work shorter hours (88 % of men's hours) but get much lower wages than men (66 % of men's wages). Generally, men's jobs are more qualified than women's jobs.

House and home

British families are living more comfortably today than ten years ago. In 1971 65 % of households still used coal or gas fires. But by 1984, 69 % of households had central heating. Today over 30 % of households have a video-recorder, 60 % own a car and 86 % have a colour television set. The number of households with telephones rose faster from 42 % in 1971 to 77 % in 1984 than in the ten years before. The majority of households (1984 57 %) are in privately owned houses, but 34 % of all housing belongs to local councils for rent.

Marriage and the family

Households are getting smaller (2.91 persons in 1971, 2.63 persons in 1984). In 1971 only 8 % of families with children were one-parent families. That number is rising fast and is now 13 %. Surprisingly, in 23 % of all households one person lives alone.

Education

Nearly all British schoolchildren go to comprehensive schools. But the number of pupils at private schools is rising (6.7 % in 1986).

Smoking

The British are giving up smoking. In 1971, 53 % of the adult population smoked. Nowadays, only 36 % are smoking cigarettes. On the other hand, the number of young women who smoke is rising.

Did you follow? 1

1 Which of these have Mr and Mrs Average got?
Say if it is right, wrong or not in the text.
a video-recorder/a home computer/central heating/a cat/children/a telephone/ a colour television set/a washing machine
If it is not in the text, do you think they probably have it? Give reasons.

2 Answer the questions on the text 'Mr and Mrs Average'.
1 In what type of home do Mr and Mrs Average live?
2 How big is their family?
3 Who has got a job – Mr Average/Mrs Average/Mr and Mrs Average/neither of them?
4 What else do you know about them?

3 Answer the questions on the text 'People'.
1 How old will the average boy born in 1984 be when he dies?
2 How old will the average girl born in 1984 be when she dies?
3 What does 'non-white' probably mean?
4 What is the 'UK'?
5 Were more British non-whites born in the UK or outside the UK?
6 How many more people will there be in Britain in 2001 than now?

4 Answer the questions on the text 'Money and jobs'.
1 What was the average wealth per person in 1976 and in 1984?
2 How many £ billion do the richer 50% of the population share?
3 What is the average wealth per person of the poorer half?
4 Where are more people interested in getting rich – in Japan or in Britain?
5 What can you say about men's working hours, wages and jobs?/What can you say about women's working hours, wages and jobs?

5 Answer the questions on the text 'House and home'.
1 How many per cent (%) of households had no central heating in 1971 and in 1985?
2 How many per cent of households have these? Put them in the right order starting with the lowest.
car – central heating – colour television set – house – rented flat – telephone – video-recorder

6 Find this information in the text 'Marriage and the family'.
Say if these statements are right or wrong. If the information is not in the text, say if you think it is probably right or wrong. Give reasons.
1 People are shorter now than in 1971.
2 People are having more babies than in 1971.
3 More children live with only one parent than in 1971.
4 People are getting married younger.
5 In nearly a quarter of all households there is only one person.
6 People who live alone are usually over 65.

7 Find this information in the texts 'Education' and 'Smoking'.
1 How many per cent of British schoolchildren do not go to private schools?
2 Will there be more or fewer children at private schools in future?
3 What is the usual school form in Britain?
4 Is the number of smokers rising or falling in Britain?
5 In which group of the population is there the opposite trend?

Watch your grammar 1

Present continuous 2 (Verlaufsform der Gegenwart 2)

The number of Christians **is falling**.
Households **are getting** smaller.

Das **present continuous** kann auch verwendet werden, um vorübergehende Zustände oder länger andauernde Prozesse zu beschreiben.

Comparative of adverbs (Steigerung von Adverbien)

The standard of living is rising **more slowly** than in the sixties.
British families are living **more comfortably** today than ten years ago.
The number of households with telephones rose **faster** between 1971 and 1984 than in the ten years before.

Regelmäßige Adverbien werden stets mit *more* oder *most* gesteigert, nie mit der *-er* Form. Unregelmäßige Adverbien (wie *fast*, *hard* usw.) werden mit der *-er* Form gesteigert.

Comparatives and superlatives of adjectives – Revision (Vergleiche, Komparativ- und Superlativformen von Adjektiven)

The **richer** half of the population share 93% of all the wealth. The **poorer** half share the other 7%.
Working women work **shorter** hours (88% of men's hours) but get much **lower** wages **than** men (66% of men's wages).
Generally, men's jobs need more qualifications than women's jobs.
The average number of unemployed in Britain is over 3,000,000, the **highest** number since the thirties.
In Japan, 38% said this was **the most important** thing in life.

Bei kurzen Adjektiven werden die Steigerungsformen mit *-er*, und *-est* gebildet.
Bei längeren Adjektiven bildet man die Steigerungsformen mit *more* und *most*.
Bei manchen kurzen Adjektiven gibt es Rechtschreibänderungen. (Siehe Grammatikanhang Seite 194.)

Irregular comparatives and superlatives – Revision (Unregelmäßige Komparativ- und Superlativformen)

good	bad	little *(wenig)*	much/many
better	worse	less	more
best	worst	least	most

Little in der Bedeutung von wenig wird nur bei **nicht** zählbaren Substantiven verwendet. Mit zählbaren Substantiven verwendet man *few – fewer – fewest*. Das gleiche gilt für *much* (**nicht** zählbar) und *many* (zählbar).

Get it right 1

1 Present continuous

Put the verbs into the present continuous.

1 The number of non-whites in Britain rose in the sixties, but it *(not rise)* now.
2 One hundred years ago, people had lots of children, but they *(not have)* so many children today.
3 In the past, people did not spend much money on entertainment, but they *(spend)* much more now.
4 Ten years ago, British families did not live very comfortably, but they *(live)* more comfortably today.
5 The number of Christians in Britain was a lot higher fifty years ago, but the numbers *(fall)*.
6 A majority of people over sixteen smoked twenty years ago, but now many *(give up)* smoking.
7 The number of men who smoke *(fall)* but the number of women smokers *(rise)*.
8 The standard of living rose very quickly in the sixties, but it *(not rise)* so fast in the eighties.

2 Adverbs of manner regular and irregular (revision)

Change the adjectives into adverbs and put them in the right place.

1 I wash my hair. *(careful)*
2 My brother asked me for help. *(polite)*
3 The climbers climbed the mountain. *(safe)*
4 My teacher drives her car. *(fast)*
5 The diving instructor jumped into the water. *(sudden)*
6 Our class answered the question. *(correct)*
7 I did the last test. *(bad)*
8 I cooked the dinner. *(quick)*

3 Comparative of adverbs

Change the adjectives into adverbs and put them in the comparative form.

1 People live *(comfortable)* than ten years ago.
2 Some sports players enjoy playing *(dangerous)* than others.
3 Some school leavers practise their answers for an interview and can talk *(confident)*.
4 An old machine often runs *(slow)* than a new one.
5 Only 4% of the British are non-white; *(surprising)*, nearly half were born in Britain.
6 Most people walk *(quick)* when it is raining.
7 Some people learn English from books; but you can learn it *(interesting)* in an English-speaking country.
8 A mile is about one and a half kilometres, or *(exact)* 1,609.3 metres.

4 Comparatives and superlatives (revision)

Put the correct words into either the comparative or the superlative and put them into the gaps.

early – interesting – popular – quiet – rich – strong – terrible – wet (spelling!)

1 Reggae music is ☐ with the West Indians than with the whites.
2 Older people like living in the country because it is ☐ than in the town.
3 Only the ☐ Americans can live in Beverley Hills.
4 Stone buildings are ☐ than buildings made of wood.
5 My first interview was the ☐ experience of my life!
6 The ☐ month of the year in Britain is usually November.
7 The ☐ date for a party is 6th July.
8 I always find other people's letters ☐ than mine.

LEAVING HOME

These three young people have done what thousands of other young people do every year: they have left home.

Josie

Josie is seventeen. She left home three months ago and found a job. She lives at her friend's flat in London. 'I have lived in London for nearly three months now. I have already found a job but it's not very interesting. But that's not my main problem, because I haven't found a proper room yet. I'm staying at my friend's flat at the moment. Her name is Kate. She has been very kind. She says she doesn't mind, but I'm in the way, really. I have to sleep on the sofa in the living-room. I'd like to get my own place, maybe a bedsitter or maybe share a small flat with someone from work. But it's very hard to find anywhere. The only flats which are available are very expensive. I can't afford much rent because I don't earn a lot. I haven't seen my parents since April. I have sent them my address and they have written, but I haven't replied yet. I don't want them to know that I'm living like this. They worry a lot.'

Frank

Frank is eighteen. He works at a large bread factory just outside London. He shares a flat with two other young men and pays about one-third of his wages in rent. Has he ever been sorry about leaving home? Frank: 'Well, yes and no. I don't enjoy cooking or shopping, but I can do it. We take turns in the flat. It's my turn this weekend. I've just cleaned the flat and cooked for everybody. I have shared this flat now for six months. My parents haven't visited me yet. They live in Birmingham, about a hundred miles away. They don't like the fact that I have left home. They don't think I'm old enough. But I am. I haven't been to Birmingham since last May and I don't want to go back. I have more freedom here.'

Rick

Rick, nineteen, has had a difficult time. He is from Newcastle and went to London to find a job, but he is on the dole. He lives in a young men's hostel. 'I've lived here since last July. It's better than nothing, better than sleeping on the streets. I share this room with four other men. It isn't very private. There's a sort of kitchen downstairs. We make our breakfast there and something to eat in the evenings. They close the doors at eleven o'clock in the evenings and the lights are out at eleven thirty. I've been out of work for twelve months. I've looked for a job, but I haven't found anything. Nothing. I think I'll try a seaside town in the summer.'

Did you follow? 2

1 Answer the questions on the part of the text about Josie.
1 Where does Josie live now?
2 Has she got her own room yet?
3 Where does she sleep?
4 What does she want to find?
5 Why hasn't she got a flat yet? Give two reasons.

2 Answer the questions on the part of the text about Frank.
1 Where does Frank work?
2 Does Frank live with his parents?
3 How do the three men organize the housework?
4 What are Frank's jobs this weekend?
5 Do Frank's parents come to the flat often?

3 Answer the questions on the part of the text about Rick.
1 Where does Rick live now?
2 Where did he live before?
3 Has he got a job?
4 Why isn't he working now?
5 Does he like living in the hostel?

4 Compare the three people. Copy this table on to a piece of paper. Take notes from the three texts. If you do not know, leave a gap.

	age?	comes from?	now living where?	happy?	job?	plans?
Josie						
Frank						
Rick						

Now talk about the three people and compare them. Who is the oldest? Who is the unhappiest? Who has got interesting plans?

5 Which definition fits which word?
afford – dole – earn – expensive – fact – factory – hostel – main – rent – wages – worry
1 You have to pay this for a room if you do not own it.
2 To find enough money for something.
3 Costing a lot of money.
4 The money you get for your work.
5 A place for people without a home.
6 To get money for your work.
7 The money you get when you cannot find a job.
8 Something which is true is a ▭ .
9 Most important.
10 To think about problems often.
11 A place where workers make things.

Watch your grammar 2

Present perfect (Das Perfekt)

These three young people **have done** what thousands of other young people do: **they have left** home.
She **has been** very kind.
I'**ve been** on the dole for twelve months. I'**ve looked** for a job. I **haven't found** anything.

SUBJEKT	HILFSVERB	VERB	OBJEKT
I/You/We/They	have haven't (have not)	phoned left	my parents. home.
He/She/It	has hasn't (has not)	cooked visited	the dinner. me.

Man benutzt das **present perfect**, um eine Handlung in der Vergangenheit zu beschreiben, deren Wirkung **heute noch** spürbar ist.
Das **present perfect** wird aus Formen von *to have* und dem **past participle** gebildet. Bei regelmäßigen Verben ist das **past participle** mit der Form des **simple past** identisch: *I looked, I have looked.* (Ausführliche Liste der unregelmäßigen Verben siehe Seite 225.)

Um zu beschreiben, **wie lange schon** oder **seit wann** ein Zustand anhält, wird **im Gegensatz zum Deutschen** nicht die Gegenwart, sondern das **present perfect** verwendet.

PRESENT PERFECT	GEGENWART
I **have shared** this flat now for six months.	Ich **teile** diese Wohnung schon seit sechs Monaten.
I **have lived** at my friend's flat for nearly three months now.	Ich **wohne** schon seit beinahe drei Monaten in der Wohnung meiner Freundin.

Adverbs of time: already, yet, just, ever (Adverbiale Zeitbestimmung)

I have **already** found a job.
I've **just** cleaned the flat and cooked for everybody.
My parents haven't visited me **yet**.
Has he **ever** been to America?

ALREADY, JUST, YET	EVER
zeigen an, **wann** (schon oder eben gerade) oder **ob** eine Handlung stattgefunden hat.	wird meist in Fragen benutzt.

Stellung der **adverbs of time** im Satz

SUBJEKT	HILFSVERB	ADVERB	PAST PARTICIPLE	OBJEKT	ADVERB
I/You ... He/She ... They	have(n't) has(n't)	already just –	found cleaned visited	a job. the flat. me	– – yet.
Have you		ever	been	to America?	–

Prepositions of time: since, for, ago (Präpositionen der Zeit)

I haven't seen my parents since April. *(Zeitpunkt)*
I have lived in London for nearly three months now. *(Zeitspanne)*

Die Präpositionen *since* und *for* zeigen an, seit wann (Zeitpunkt z. B. *April*) bzw. wie lange schon (Zeitspanne z. B. *three months*) ein Zustand anhält.

She left home three months ago. Sie ging vor drei Monaten von zu Hause weg.

Die Präposition *ago* („vor" mit Zeitangabe) steht im Gegensatz zum Deutschen nach der Zeitangabe.

ZEITPUNKT (SEIT WANN)	ZEITSPANNE (WIE LANGE SCHON)	„VOR" MIT ZEITANGABE
since	for	ago

Get it right 2

1 Present perfect statements

Put the verbs into the present perfect.

1 I *(live)* in London for three years.
2 I *(look)* for a job, but there aren't any.
3 My brother *(visit)* me.
4 I *(leave)* my first room in south London.
5 I *(find)* a nicer room in north London.
6 My friend *(go)* to the USA.
7 My parents *(write)* a letter to me.
8 They *(send)* me some money.

2 Present perfect questions and negative statements

Make questions and negative answers.

Example Your parents often send you money.
(send any money this week?)
Have they sent any money this week?
No, they haven't sent any money.

1 You live in London now. *(live in London long?)*
2 Your friend works in a car factory. *(work there long?)*
3 You often write a letter home. *(write a letter this week?)*
4 Your friend was unemployed *(find a job?)*
5 It's your turn with the cooking today. *(cook the dinner?)*
6 There's a good film on at the local cinema. *(see it?)*
7 Your father wanted to visit you in London. *(visit you?)*
8 There are two people in the flat down-stairs. *(be there long?)*

3 Adverbs of time – already, just, yet, ever

Put the adverbs of time in the right place.

1 My grandfather has come back from Africa. *(just)*
2 He has visited three African countries. *(already)*
3 He has been to Zambia, Mali and Kenya. *(already)*
4 He has given me a super present. *(just)*
5 He isn't here now. He has left. *(already)*
6 My grandfather sent us a postcard from Kenya, but it hasn't arrived. *(yet)*
7 But he wrote a letter, too, and that has arrived. *(just)*
8 Have you been there? *(ever)*
9 I haven't been to Africa. *(yet)*

4 Prepositions of time – since, ago, for

Put in the right preposition.

1 John has left home. He went two months ☐.
2 He hasn't written ☐ three weeks.
3 I haven't seen him ☐ January.
4 His mother phoned him a month ☐.
5 She hasn't heard from him ☐ then.
6 He hasn't phoned his girlfriend ☐ two weeks.
7 She hasn't spoken to him ☐ 7th March.
8 That's two weeks ☐.

OVER TO YOU

Listening *Metropolis*

1 Listen to the tape. Find out who is speaking, where they come from, where they are living now, why they are there, if they have jobs, how they like their new home, if they want to stay.

2 Compare the three young people on the tape with Josie, Frank and Rick. Who has been the luckiest/unluckiest? Who will probably stay in London/go back home?

3 Is it a good idea to leave home before you have a job/a new home? What do you think are the good/bad/interesting things about leaving home? Make a list and compare it with other people's lists. Could you do, for example, what Josie has done?

Writing

Write 30 to 40 words about how people live in West Germany today. Write it for somebody who does not know much about this country. Give this information:

1 where people live (flats and houses)
2 what people own and have in their homes (TV sets, videos, central heating)
3 the standard of living (rising, falling)
4 the number of members of churches (rising, falling)
5 non-Germans (where they are from)
6 marriage and the family (number of children, divorces)

Lifestyles

1 What is the best way to live for a young person? Say what you think of these lifestyles. Do you agree strongly(++), agree(+), disagree(–) or disagree strongly(––)? Or aren't you sure(?)?

1 living alone in your own bedsitter or your own flat
2 living with parents or one parent at home
3 living with grandparents
4 living with friends in your own flat
5 living with a boyfriend/girlfriend in your own flat
6 getting married and making your own home with your children

2 Some people buy things to impress (imponieren) their friends. What do you do when you want to impress

– a girl/boy you like?
– the people in the next house/flat?
– a teacher?
– a 9 year-old child?
– somebody you admire (bewundern)?

3 Not everybody wants to live like Mr and Mrs Average. Make notes and then speak about how you and your friends want to live. Remember the quantifiers from Unit Four (most of, a lot of, etc).

– Do you/they want to get married/have children/buy their own house?
– Do you/they want to buy a lot of things like video-recorders/cars/colour TV sets?
– Do you/they want to be rich/have a lot of friends/work hard?

Working with words

Find the opposites of these words in the texts. Discuss where the words can be used.
arrive – child – majority – non-white – richer – rise – slowly – unusual

Mindfield

English round the world

In these four countries most or many people speak English. Match the right map to the right name and the right text.

Australia – Canada – India – New Zealand

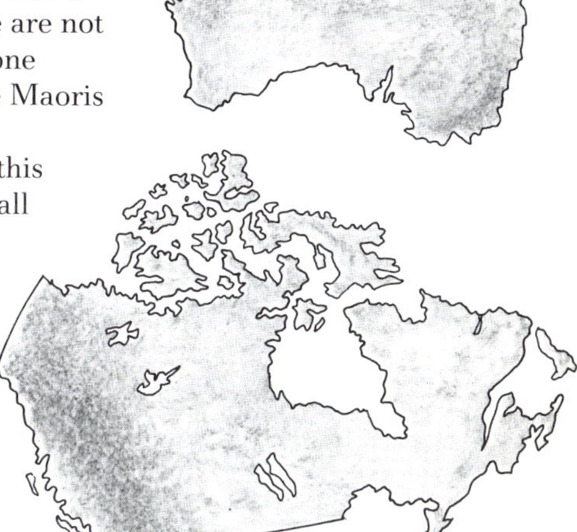

1 About 15% of the population of the whole world live in this country. Most people's first language is not English but they do not all have the same first language. In fact, there are 15 government languages. Until 1947 it was a colony of Britain.
2 This country is a little bigger than West Germany but has a much smaller population – just over 3 million. There are not many people there, but a lot of sheep – 20 for every one person. When Europeans discovered this country the Maoris already lived there.
3 Only one country in the world is bigger in area than this one. The people there – about 25 million of them – call their money 'dollars'. The winters are long and very cold in a lot of the country. In one part of the country most people's first language is French not English.
4 This country with a population of about 15 million is also the continent with the least water in the world. Most of the people live on or near the coast. Europeans discovered it more than 300 years ago but other people already lived there. There are now about 100,000 of these people left.

Key words and phrases

I **own** my **own** car. It **belongs to** me.
There is not much work **available**.
The number of car-owners is **rising**.
The number of Christians is **falling**.
I earn good wages. **I pay rent** for a flat. My friend has to **pay off a mortgage** on his house.
On average, people live longer now than before.
The majority of people live in houses. The minority live in flats.
house flat room bedsitter

6 The sensible way to town?

THINK ABOUT IT

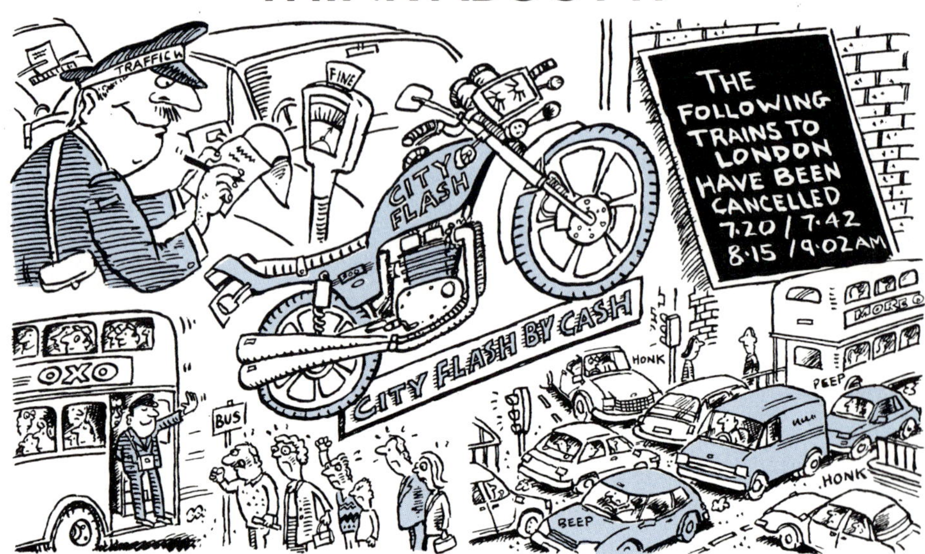

What's your situation? Do you have one of these problems? You can forget about all of them with *CITY FLASH,* our latest commuter bike. No more timetables. *CITY FLASH* takes you from door to door – faster than the bus or the train. And it can be cheaper than public transport, too.
Do you drive to work by car? And are you one of the people who cause traffic jams nearly every day? 5
Ride past them on your *CITY FLASH.* And forget parking problems and expensive car parks.
CITY FLASH – the **sensible** way to get to town. Think about it. And get yours today.
Ring 0602-727 7141 for brochures and prices.

City Flash By Cash

Salesman Hallo, can I help you? 10
Youth Yes, I was in here last week and ...
Salesman Oh, yes. I remember. You're the young man who was interested in one of our commuter bikes.
Youth Yes. Well, I've made up my mind now. I'd like to have the *City Flash.*
Salesman Oh, that's a very good choice, I must say. The *City Flash*, yes. Now do you want the old model? Or would you like the one which has just arrived? The new model. 15
Youth The new one. The new one, please.
Salesman Right. Would you come over here please and we can take down the information that we need? Now, how would you like to pay?
Youth By cash. 20
Salesman Cash. Good. And could you show me the colour that you'd like? Here, in this brochure.
Youth That one.
Salesman The dark blue. Yes, that's the one I like best, too. So the *City Flash* is your favourite? It's mine as well. Now, could I have your name and address, sir?
Youth Yes, it's Richard Hamilton. One nine four Trent Bridge Road, Nottingham. 25

Did you follow? 1

1 These sentences all fit one of the pictures in the advert. Which goes with which?
1 There are parking problems in town.
2 Trains are sometimes cancelled.
3 You can't always get on a bus when you want to.
4 Going into town by car could take hours.

2 The advert says the *City Flash* is better than public transport.
Find four reasons that it gives.
City Flash is ... than public transport.
It is also ...
You don't have to use a ...
It takes you ...

3 Why is the *City Flash* better than a car for commuters?
Find two reasons. Explain them in one sentence like this:
City Flash is better than a car because ...

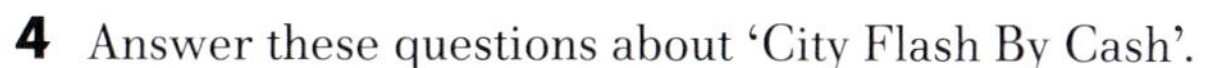

4 Answer these questions about 'City Flash By Cash'.
1 What is the youth's name?
2 Why was he at the shop last week?
3 What has he decided to do?
4 What does the salesman think of his decision?
5 Which model and what colour bike does the youth want?
6 How is he going to pay for the bike?

5 Which definition fits which word?
cancelled – car park – cheap – commuter – public transport – sensible – timetable – traffic jam
1 This is when all the traffic cannot move.
2 The system of buses and trains in a town or country.
3 A list of train, bus or plane times.
4 The opposite of expensive.
5 This is where you can leave your car.
6 The opposite of stupid.
7 Someone who goes to town to work every day.
8 A train that does not run.

6 What do you think? Is it better going to town by motorbike or by public transport? Give reasons.
Example **I think** it's better going into town by public transport because there's too much traffic.
Write down your reasons, then answer the question.

Watch your grammar 1

Relative clauses 1 (Relativsätze 1)

1 Defining relative clauses (Bestimmende Relativsätze mit Relativpronomen)

You were the young man **who was interested in one of our bikes.**
Would you like the one **which has just arrived**?
We can take down the information **that we need.**

Die Relativpronomen *who*, *which* und *that* beziehen sich auf ein vorausgehendes Wort:

who	which	that
auf Personen	auf Sachen	auf Personen/Sachen

Wir verwenden einen **defining relative clause**, um ein Wort genauer zu definieren. Die Information, die ein bestimmender Relativsatz enthält, ist notwendig, um den ganzen Satz zu verstehen.

Bestimmende Relativsätze **werden nicht durch Kommas** vom Hauptsatz getrennt.

2 Defining relative clauses without relative pronouns/contact clauses (Bestimmende Relativsätze ohne Relativpronomen)

RELATIVPRONOMEN ALS SUBJEKT	RELATIVPRONOMEN ALS OBJEKT
kann **nicht** weggelassen werden.	kann vor allem in der **Umgangssprache** weggelassen werden, da im Relativsatz ein neues Subjekt folgt.
Would you like the one **which** has just arrived?	That's the one **which/that** I like best. That's the one I like best.
We can take down the information **that** is necessary.	The man **who** Richard met was a salesman. The man Richard met was a salesman.

Possessive adjectives and pronouns (Possessivpronomen – adjektivisch und nominal gebraucht)

POSSESSIVE ADJECTIVES	POSSESSIVE PRONOUNS
That's **my** new motorbike. It's bigger than **your** one. Look, there's Gerry on **his** bike. Jane hasn't got **her** bike any more. **Our** motorbike club is smaller now. Are you sure that's not **their** bike?	It's all **mine**. **Yours** is smaller. No, that isn't **his**. It's Jane's. She sold **hers**. It's small, but it's still **ours**. Yes, it's not **theirs**, it's the club's.
Bei Körperteilen, Kleidungsstücken und abstrakten Substantiven (z. B. *life*, *death*, *mind)* muß – im Gegensatz zum Deutschen – das **possessive adjective** stehen.	Das **possessive pronoun** bezieht sich auf ein vorausgehendes Nomen. Es wird auch aus stilistischen Gründen verwendet, wenn man das Nomen nicht wiederholen will.

Get it right 1

1 Defining relative clauses

Put *who*, *which* or *that* into these sentences.

Example People **who** cause traffic jams are stupid.

1 The salesman spoke to the young man ___ was interested in commuter bikes.
2 He likes the bike ___ has just arrived.
3 He asked for one ___ does not need much petrol.
4 Two friends ___ work with him also have motorbikes.
5 Bikes ___ are small are easier to ride.
6 People ___ need to get to work quickly shouldn't go by car.
7 People ___ ride motorbikes have to be careful on the roads.
8 It's often difficult to find a car park ___ is not full.

2 Defining relative clauses

Make sentences with relative clauses from these phrases.

Example The Shinkansen/the Japanese train/travels at more than 200 kilometres per hour (kph).
The Shinkansen is the Japanese train which travels at more than 200 kph.

1 The Silver Shadow/the Rolls Royce car/ costs £50,000.
2 The jumbo jet/the plane/carries the most people.
3 The Queen Mary/the old ship/once made the fastest trip from Southampton to New York.
4 A bike tour/the cheapest holiday/travel companies offer.
5 The accidents/motorcyclists have/are often very bad.
6 Hundreds of people/lost their lives/died when the ship went down in bad weather.
7 We will never forget the bad weather/ caused the accident.

3 Contact clauses

Join the sentences together. Use a relative pronoun only if it is necessary. Remember, you can only leave out the relative pronoun if it is the object of the relative clause.

Example The car was red. The young man drove it.
The car the young man drove was red.

1 The bus is very full. I catch it every morning.
2 The train arrived at ten o'clock. It was late.
3 The traffic jam was two kilometres long. I passed it on my way to work.

4 The motorbike was a new model. She chose it.
5 The advert did not give any prices. It described the *City Flash*.
6 The colours are in the back of the brochure. The new models have them.
7 The bike has got blue wheels. She rides it to work.
8 The bike is a very popular model. She bought it yesterday.

4 Contact clauses

Write these adverts in a different way. Use contact clauses.

Example Sensible people buy the *City Flash* commuter bike.
The *City Flash* is the commuter bike sensible people buy.

1 Clever Londoners get a Travelcard ticket.
2 Most commuters prefer the train way.
3 The fastest people in town ride *Kabuki* bikes.
4 You'll find only full car parks in town. Why not take the train!
5 You'll see the oldest cars in the world in the London to Brighton Car Run.
6 Ride the big red buses. Londoners love them.

5 Possessive pronouns and adjectives

Put in the missing words. Use *my/mine*, *your/yours* etc.

At ___[1] last staff meeting we talked about ___[2] trips to work every morning. A lot of people were unhappy about ___[3] situation. One woman secretary who comes by car said ___[4] travel costs for the year were nearly £200. Another woman said ___[5] were the same. A lot of us come by bus. ___[6] trip of about five miles costs me £192 a year. The people who travel by train are unluckier. ___[7] costs are even higher. And if you come by motorbike you'll know that ___[8] costs for petrol and insurance are not very low. We think we should talk about this problem of ___[9] some more. If you're having ___[10] own problems like this and are interested come to ___[11] next meeting.

ANGEL OF MERCY saves boy's arm

STAFF NURSE ANNA SANDLE was the 'Angel of Mercy' after an accident in the centre of Nottingham yesterday morning. Her quick action saved a young motorcyclist's arm.

RICHARD HAMILTON lost control of his bike when the cars in front of him on a busy main road stopped suddenly. He swerved quickly and hit a car to his left, which was parked at the side of the road. He received serious cuts to his arm. Because of the traffic the ambulance took fifteen minutes to arrive. While other eyewitnesses just stood and watched, Nurse Sandle, who works at Nottingham General Hospital, gave the injured youth first aid. Her help saved Mr Hamilton from more serious injury.

Mr Hamilton, whose three-week-old commuter bike was a write-off, is now a patient in the hospital that Nurse Sandle works in.

More training necessary

CHIEF INSPECTOR ROYLE of the Nottingham police again criticized the poor training of young motorcyclists. 'The injured youth is a learner. He has had a provisional licence for only three weeks,' he said. 'He has had no training at all. We must change this law soon. A lot of young people's lives are in danger because of it.'

Motorcyclists' risk

Since last year there have been over forty-five serious injuries to motorcyclists on Nottingham's roads. Five have lost their lives. Young motorcyclists can ride bikes of up to 125 cc for two years without any training! That is two years too long. We agree with Chief Inspector Royle. The Government must change the law now. Motorcyclists must have proper training and take a test **before** they can ride in public. They are dangerous to themselves and to every road user.

IRA loses top gunman in Gibraltar shooting

David Hearst in Belfast

THE IRA has lost one of its most effective gunmen with the killing of Danny McCann, aged 31, by the SAS in Gibraltar on Sunday.

McCann, known as "the Butcher" by the Royal Ulster

Like many dedicated Republican fighters, McCann had a chequered relationship with the IRA leadership. After serving one year of a two-year sentence for possession of explosives in 1980, he lost favour by allying himself to Ivor Malachy Bell, the former commanding officer of the Belfast Brigade, who

forces, unleashed a new and deadly sense of confidence in the IRA.

He would have been the subject of 24-hour surveillance and sending such a high profile gunman out of the country would have been a risk.

Sean Savage, aged 24, from the Ardoyne was a noted ex-

Did you follow? 2

1 What does the title of the article mean?

2 Which parts of the article describe the following? Give the headings and make notes to support your statement.
1 A policeman's opinion about training for motorcyclists.
2 The accident.
3 The newspaper's opinion.

3 The police asked eyewitnesses these questions. How did they answer them?
1 What did the motorcyclist do when the cars in front of him stopped?
2 What happened then?
3 Who helped the injured man after the accident?
4 How long was it before the ambulance arrived?

4 Now answer these questions about the article.
1 What injuries did Richard Hamilton receive in the accident?
2 How did Nurse Sandle help him?
3 Where did the ambulance take Mr Hamilton?
4 What happened to Mr Hamilton's motorbike?
5 How long has he had his provisional licence?
6 How much training has he had?

5 Which of these statements about riding a motorbike in Britain are right and which are wrong? Correct the wrong ones.
1 Motorcyclists do not need a proper licence at first.
2 They must take a test for a provisional licence.
3 They can use their provisional licence for two years.
4 They can ride any motorbike with their provisional licence.

6 What does the article tell you about motorcyclists' accidents on Nottingham's roads?

7 What do the newspaper and the policeman think the Government should do about the problem with young motorcyclists?

8 Put in the missing words or phrases.
accident – cuts – first aid – injured – injuries – lost control – motorcyclist – nurse – provisional licence – received – swerved

Accident Report – Sergeant Miles
I arrived at 7.32 a.m. The □[1] happened ten minutes earlier. The □[2] person's name was Richard Hamilton, age 18. A □[3] gave the young □[4] □[5] . The □[6] he □[7] were □[8] to his arm. Eyewitnesses said the accident happened because Mr Hamilton □[9] . He □[10] of his bike. I checked Mr Hamilton's □[11] which was only three weeks old.

Watch your grammar 2

Relative clauses 2 (Relativsätze 2)

Non-defining relative clauses (Nicht-bestimmende Relativsätze)

He hit a car, **which was parked to his left**.

Nurse Sandle, **who works at Nottingham General Hospital**, gave the injured youth first aid.

In **nicht-bestimmenden** Relativsätzen werden die Relativpronomen *who* (für Personen) oder *which* (für Sachen) verwendet. *That* wird **nicht** verwendet. Ein nicht-bestimmender Relativsatz wird **immer** vom Hauptsatz durch Kommas getrennt.
Ein nicht-bestimmender Relativsatz enthält zusätzliche Informationen, die aber nicht unbedingt notwendig sind, um den Inhalt des ganzen Satzes zu verstehen. Er könnte weggelassen werden, ohne die Aussage des Hauptsatzes unklar zu machen.
Nicht-bestimmende Relativsätze kommen vor allem im formellem Englisch vor. In der Umgangssprache verbindet man zwei Sätze eher mit einer Konjunktion wie *and*, *but* oder *because*.

Relative clauses 3 (Relativsätze 3)

1 Relative clauses with prepositions (Relativsätze mit Präpositionen)

He is a patient in the hospital **that** Nurse Sandle works **in**.
The man **who** he spoke **to** was a salesman.

In einem Relativsatz wird eine Präposition meist an dieselbe Stelle gesetzt wie im Hauptsatz. Nur in sehr formellem Englisch kommt eine Präposition **vor** dem Relativpronomen.

2 Relative pronoun whose (Relativpronomen whose)

Mr Hamilton, **whose** two-week-old commuter bike was a write-off, is now in hospital.
The car **whose** window is broken was in an accident.

Das Relativpronomen *whose* (dessen/deren) wird bei **Personen** und oft bei **Dingen** verwendet. In der Umgangssprache werden oft andere Konstruktionen bevorzugt: *The car* **with the broken window** …

3 Relative pronoun whom (Relativpronomen whom)

The eyewitness **whom** the reporter interviewed saw everything.

Whom, die Objektform des Relativpronomens *who*, wird heutzutage nur noch in sehr formellem Englisch verwendet.

Genitive: 's/s'/of-phrase (Genitiv: *'s/s'/of*-Fügung)

SINGULAR ('s)	PLURAL (s')
'Angel of Mercy' saves man**'s** arm.	It's the motorcyclists**'** risk.

OF	IRREGULAR PLURAL ('s)
The colour **of** the bike was dark blue.	A lot of young people**'s** lives are in danger.

Mit dem Genitiv wird **Besitz** oder **Zugehörigkeit (Urheberschaft)** ausgedrückt (bei Personen und Tieren). Der Genitiv mit *of* wird eher bei **Sachen** selten mit Personen verwendet.

Get it right 2

1 Non-defining relative clauses

Make sentences with relative clauses. Use the notes and the phrases in brackets.

Example Richard Hamilton/buy/commuter bike – *(was 18 years old)*
Richard Hamilton, **who was 18 years old,** bought a commuter bike.

1 Salesman/sell/him/new model – *(didn't like his job)*
2 Mr Hamilton/have/accident/yesterday – *(only got his provisional licence three weeks ago)*
3 His bike/be/write-off – *(was one of the new models)*
4 Police/said/had no training – *(are worried about the law)*
5 One eyewitness/agree/with the police – *(also rides a motobike)*
6 City Flash Company/say/its motorbikes/ safe – *(has sold 7,000 machines this year)*

2 Relative clauses with prepositions

Make statements from these notes. Use relative clauses with prepositions.

Example Man – you – look at – is a salesman.
The man you are looking at is a salesman.

1 Bike – he – look for – was the *City Flash.*
2 Woman – reporter – speak to – was a nurse.
3 Policeman – we – listen to – was an inspector.
4 Problem – he – be unhappy about – is a serious one.
5 Driving school – I – go to – is a good one.
6 Lessons – I – pay for – have helped me a lot.

3 Relative clauses

Put in the right relative pronoun *who, whose, which, that* or use a *contact clause* in these sentences. Remember that non-defining relative clauses are separated from the main clauses by commas.

1 The woman ☐ saved him was a nurse.
2 The hospital ☐ she works at is in the centre of Nottingham.
3 She went there from another hospital in the town, ☐ she did not like much.
4 The job ☐ she does, ☐ is very hard work, gives her a lot of fun.
5 When she saw the boy ☐ caused the accident she helped him at once.
6 The boy, ☐ arm had serious cuts, was in the middle of the road.
7 A car ☐ window was broken stopped next to the injured boy.
8 The first aid ☐ she gave the boy saved his arm.

4 Simple past or present perfect

Alan Saunders wants a job with a local workshop. Give his answers at the interview. Use the information in the box.

> **ALAN SAUNDERS**
> *Training as mechanic:* 1983-6
> *Job:* mechanic – Fixit Garages. – since 1986 – service mechanic for Vega and Centaur cars
> *First Aid course:* last year
> *Passed driving test:* 1984

Interviewer You're a mechanic, Mr Saunders. When did you finish your training?
Alan ☐[1]
Interviewer I see. And have you worked as a mechanic since then?
Alan ☐[2]
Interviewer What cars have you worked on most?
Alan ☐[3]
Interviewer And what about first aid training? Have you had any?
Alan ☐[4]
Interviewer That's fine. Now tell me, when did you pass your driving test?
Alan ☐[5]
Interviewer Well, thank you Mr Saunders. I think that's all for now.

5 Simple past or present perfect

Put the verbs into the correct forms.
Jodie likes working at Green's, an office in the city centre. She *(work)*[1] there for two years now. She *(leave)*[2] college in 1986 and first *(apply)*[3] for a job with the police. The police *(not need)*[4] more recruits at that time, so Jodie *(look for)*[5] another job immediately. She *(find)*[6] the office job a week later. She *(be)*[7] happy at Green's for two years now and she *(not be)*[8] sorry up to now that the police *(not want)*[9] her in 1986.

OVER TO YOU

Listening

BRITISH RED CROSS First Aid on the Road

A course for people who have no first aid training

1 Listen to the tape. While you are listening decide what the right answers to these questions are.
1 How does the class begin?
2 What two things does the teacher ask them to remember from last week?
3 Do they learn anything new?

2 Now listen to the tape again and write down:
1 The two biggest dangers after a road accident.
2 Four things you should not do to injured people after an accident.
3 Why you should sometimes move an injured person.

3 What do you know about first aid? Make a list. Say what you think you should or shouldn't do for an injured person. Compare your list with other people's lists. Do you agree or disagree with them?
If you do not know anything about first aid make a list of three or four injuries. Ask other people in the class what you should do for people with these injuries.

Writing

Look at this part of a letter from Liz, an English girl, to a German friend. Make a note of the differences in Germany. Then write a reply to her. Tell her how people get a driving licence in Germany.

but I've been very busy. That's because I've been learning to drive. And last week I took my test and you'll never believe this. I passed first time!

My dad taught me in our Vega. I had about 25 hours driving with him. You can do it like that here. You just have to have someone in the car who has got a driving licence. A full one, I mean. Not just a provisional one. You have to get one of those before you can start driving. You need 'L' plates on the front and the back of the car, too. But you don't have to go to a driving school for lessons. I did have a couple of lessons with the local driving school before the test. They know just what you have to do in the test. The lessons are expensive but they helped me pass.

Have you got a driving licence yet? How old do you have to be? It's 17 years old here. Is the system the same in Germany? Tell me in your next letter. I'll have to stop now and take this to the post office.
Write soon,

Love,

Liz

Speaking

What is your opinion about the systems for learning to drive in Britain and Germany? Which system is better/worse? Give reasons.

I think ... In my opinion ...	is a	better/worse good/bad terrible/safe/dangerous expensive/cheap sensible/stupid	system because ...

Working with words

1 Put in the missing prepositions.
about (2x) – *by* (3x) – *from* – *in* – *of* (2x) – *to*

Every form ▭[1] transport has something good ▭[2] it. When you travel ▭[3] car you go ▭[4] door ▭[5] door and it is still quite cheap. If you travel ▭[6] train you don't have to worry ▭[7] the traffic but it's not as fast, of course. You can also relax better ▭[8] a bus, but traffic jams are still a problem. You usually get where you want to quickest ▭[9] plane, but it's also the most expensive form ▭[10] transport.

2 Find phrases in the text below which mean the same as these.
1 buses and trains
2 full of dangers
3 not as dangerous
4 lose your life
5 may not be as cheap
6 you are a driver

As a car driver, life can be very dangerous. Every time you go out in a car you could receive injuries or even die in an accident. Public transport is perhaps more expensive but it is also a lot safer.

3 Essay writing. Write at least 50 words.
– Describe a serious accident you have seen.
– Describe the traffic situation in the mornings and/or evenings in your town/village.

Key words and phrases

drive a car – driver
ride a bike/motorbike
motorcyclist
first aid
injured – injury
die – lose your/his/life

risk ▶▶ danger
cause
move receive

cheap ▶◀ expensive
safe ▶◀ dangerous
sensible ▶◀ stupid
lose ▶◀ take control
colour
public transport
situation
surprise

alone necessary
while

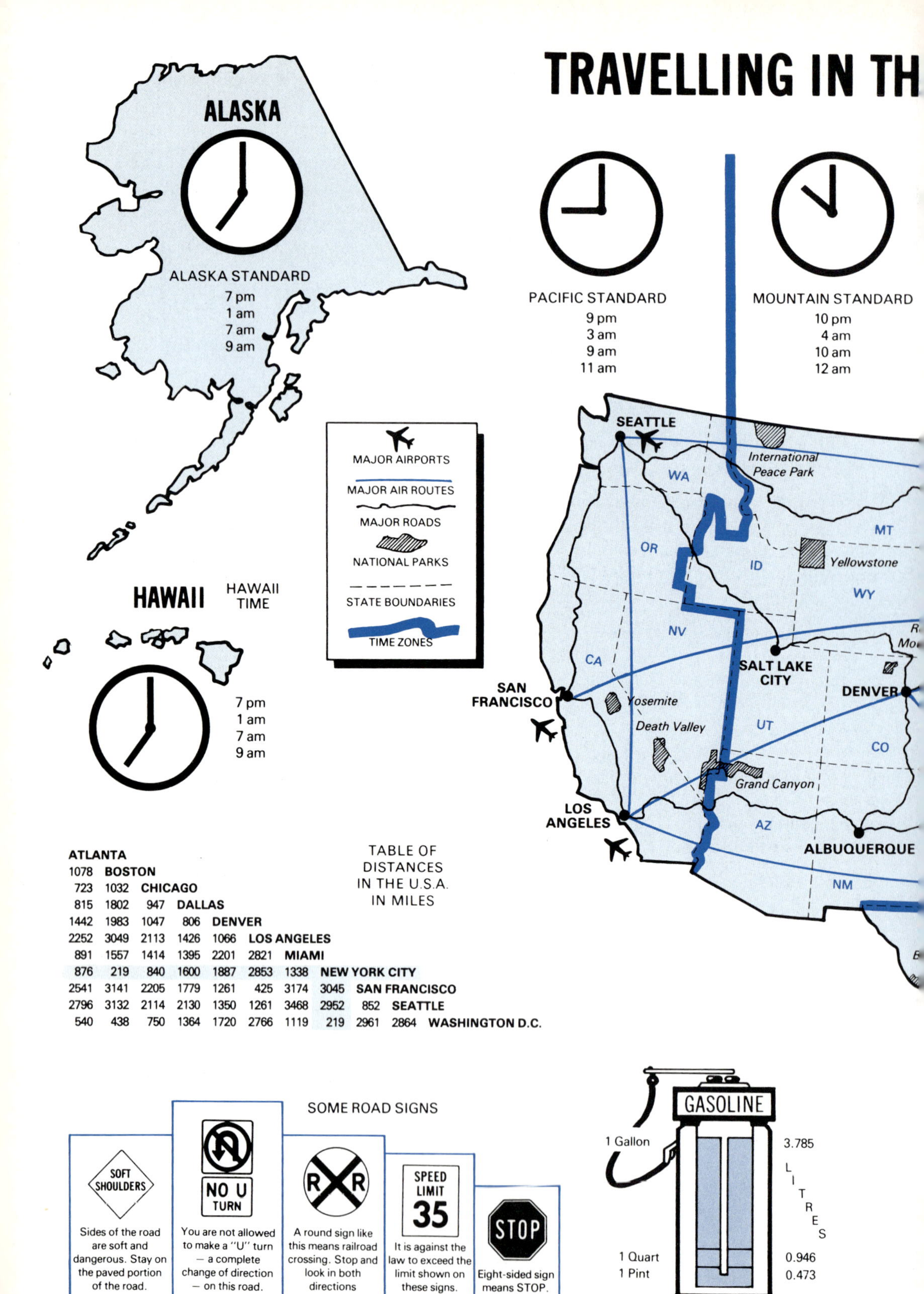

TABLE OF DISTANCES IN THE U.S.A. IN MILES

	ATLANTA	BOSTON	CHICAGO	DALLAS	DENVER	LOS ANGELES	MIAMI	NEW YORK CITY	SAN FRANCISCO	SEATTLE
BOSTON	1078									
CHICAGO	723	1032								
DALLAS	815	1802	947							
DENVER	1442	1983	1047	806						
LOS ANGELES	2252	3049	2113	1426	1066					
MIAMI	891	1557	1414	1395	2201	2821				
NEW YORK CITY	876	219	840	1600	1887	2853	1338			
SAN FRANCISCO	2541	3141	2205	1779	1261	425	3174	3045		
SEATTLE	2796	3132	2114	2130	1350	1261	3468	2952	852	
WASHINGTON D.C.	540	438	750	1364	1720	2766	1119	219	2961	2864

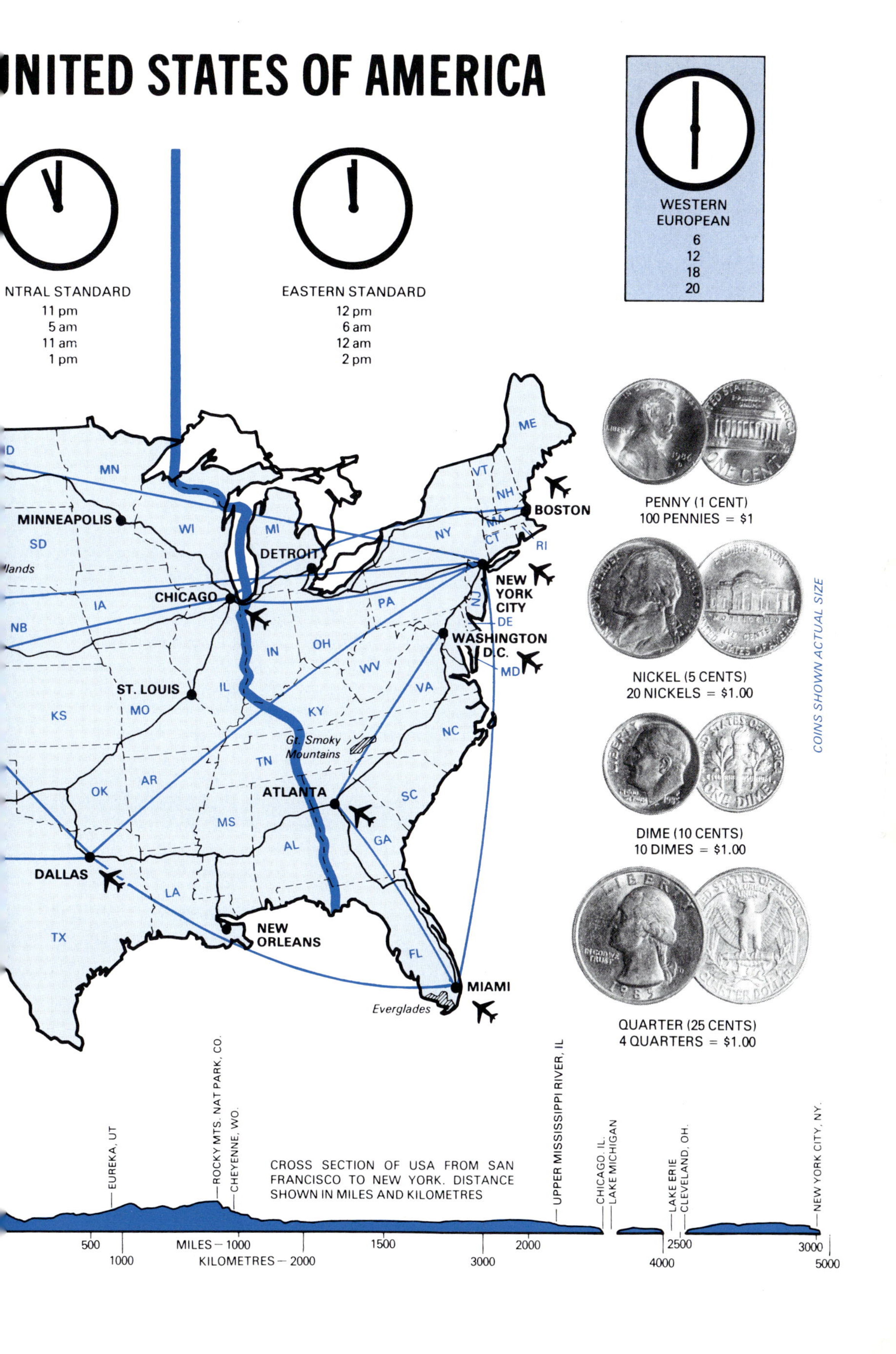

NITED STATES OF AMERICA
NTRAL STANDARD
11 pm
5 am
11 am
1 pm
EASTERN STANDARD
12 pm
6 am
12 am
2 pm
WESTERN EUROPEAN
6
12
18
20
MN
MINNEAPOLIS
SD
WI
MI
DETROIT
CHICAGO
IA
NB
ME
VT
NH
BOSTON
MA
NY
CT
RI
NEW YORK CITY
NJ
PA
DE
WASHINGTON D.C.
MD
OH
IN
WV
VA
IL
ST. LOUIS
MO
KS
KY
Gt. Smoky Mountains
NC
TN
OK
AR
ATLANTA
SC
MS
AL
GA
DALLAS
LA
TX
NEW ORLEANS
FL
MIAMI
Everglades
PENNY (1 CENT)
100 PENNIES = $1
NICKEL (5 CENTS)
20 NICKELS = $1.00
DIME (10 CENTS)
10 DIMES = $1.00
QUARTER (25 CENTS)
4 QUARTERS = $1.00
COINS SHOWN ACTUAL SIZE
EUREKA, UT
ROCKY MTS. NAT PARK, CO.
CHEYENNE, WO.
UPPER MISSISSIPPI RIVER, IL
CHICAGO, IL.
LAKE MICHIGAN
LAKE ERIE
CLEVELAND, OH.
NEW YORK CITY, NY.
CROSS SECTION OF USA FROM SAN FRANCISCO TO NEW YORK. DISTANCE SHOWN IN MILES AND KILOMETRES
MILES — 500 1000 1500 2000 2500 3000
KILOMETRES — 1000 2000 3000 4000 5000

7 The Chunnel

'THE FAST LANE TO EUROPE'

Traditionally, the white cliffs of Dover have always been the first parts of Britain visitors see from the deck of a ferry. In future, many will see a huge rail terminal for the Channel Tunnel at Cheriton, near Folkestone, 7 miles (11.2 km) from Dover. At the Cheriton terminal, travellers to France will be able to drive their cars into shuttle waggons, in which they and their cars will travel under the English Channel to Fréthun, near Calais. The new **Chunnel** (**Ch**annel T**unnel**) will be 31 miles (50 km) long and have two rail tunnels. They will carry fast passenger trains and freight trains; special shuttle trains will carry cars, lorries and buses. Travellers will be able to stay in their vehicles or walk about during the 30-minute crossing. The new tunnel should be ready by 1993. A tunnel will make possible direct rail links between London and Paris for the first time. It will decrease the present 6¼ hours' journey by 3 hours.

The present tunnel project is not the first. There was a scheme for a rail tunnel in 1856. Parliament, however, was afraid of a French invasion through a tunnel. It opposed the idea of a tunnel and the plan came to nothing. In 1880 Sir Edward Watkin suggested an electrically-lit rail tunnel through which fast trains could travel. After 14 years' work and nearly half a mile (800 metres) of tunnelling, Watkins gave up.

Parliament discussed plans for a Channel tunnel 38 times between 1802 and 1985. In 1985, the British and French Governments supported a private scheme for a fixed rail link. There will not be any public money for the new tunnel. It will have to pay its own way. Cross-channel traffic will increase from 24 million in 1985 to 50 million by the year 2000. This will cause problems for the ferries unless there is also a Channel tunnel, say *Chunnel* supporters. The *Chunnel* will not be the only way of crossing the channel, but they hope it will be a popular one. After all, they want to get back the £2.3 billion of their private money with which they are supporting the project.

THE CHANNEL TUNNEL

FACTS AND FIGURES

Cost of building work	£2.3 billion (bn)
Number of jobs after built	3,000 to 4,000
Cross-channel traffic in 1985	24 million passengers
in 2000	50 million passengers
Frequency of daytime service (hourly)	Tourist shuttles: 4-5
(night-time service = 50% of daytime)	Freight shuttles: 4
	Passenger trains: 4
	Freight trains: 2
Number of vehicles per shuttle waggon	191 cars or 25 lorries
Time in tunnel	28 minutes
Terminal to terminal time	35 minutes
Journey times from London to Brussels	2 hrs 55 mins
to Paris	3 hrs 15 mins

Did you follow? 1

1 Answer the questions on the first part of the text.
1 What do visitors to Britain usually see first?
2 What will many visitors to Britain see first in future?
3 Where will drivers put their cars?
4 Where will the *Chunnel* terminals be?
5 Will the *Chunnel* be a road tunnel?
6 Will drivers and passengers have to stay in their cars on the journey?
7 How long will the journey under the Channel take?
8 How long will the rail journey from London to Paris be?

2 Are these statements about the second part of the text right or wrong? Correct the wrong ones.
1 The 1856 plan was for a road tunnel.
2 Parliament liked the idea but did not have enough money.
3 Watkin suggested a new tunnel project in 1880.
4 He wanted to use electric trains.
5 Watkin never started work on the tunnel.
6 Britain stopped work in 1894 because it was afraid of a French invasion.

3 Answer the questions on the third part of the text.
1 How many times did the British Government discuss plans for a tunnel?
2 How much will the project cost?
3 Where will the money for the *Chunnel* come from?
4 What reason do supporters of the *Chunnel* give for the project?
5 What is their main reason for their support?
- They want to help travellers.
- They want to help the ferries.
- They want to earn a lot of money.
- They like building tunnels.

4 What are these?
bus – car – cross-channel traffic – ferry – lorry – train – waggon
1 A large vehicle which carries many passengers. It travels on roads.
2 A long vehicle which carries many passengers. It travels on rails.
3 A large vehicle which carries many passengers. It travels on water.
4 A small vehicle which carries 4 or 5 people.
5 A large road vehicle. It carries freight but no passengers.
6 Part of a train.
7 This describes all the passengers and freight which travel between France and Britain.

5 Find this information from the 'Facts and Figures' box.
1 How long will the trains be in the tunnel?
2 How often will the tourist shuttles run during the day?
3 How much will the tunnel cost?
4 How long will the journey be from *Cheriton* to *Fréthun*?
5 If a passenger leaves London at 1 p.m., when will s/he arrive in Paris?
6 How many people will cross the Channel yearly at the end of the century?
7 How many people will work for the *Chunnel*?

Watch your grammar 1

Defective modals can and must
(Unvollständige Hilfsverben *can* und *must*)

At the moment people can cross the Channel by plane or ferry.
In the past people could only cross the Channel by ferry.
In the past people were only able to cross the Channel by ferry.
In future people will be able to cross by tunnel.
At the moment drivers must drive their cars on to ferries.
In the past drivers had to leave their cars and go on deck.
The new tunnel will have to pay its own way.

Die Hilfsverben *can* und *must* können nicht in allen Zeiten gebildet werden (daher „unvollständig“). Um das **future** und das **past** zu bilden, benutzt man Formen von *be able to* und *have to*. Beim **past** von *can* kann man *could* anstelle von *was able to* benutzen (*could* ist aber gebräuchlicher).

PRESENT	PAST	OTHER TENSES
can	could/was able to	be able to
must	had to	have to

Numbers (Zahlen)

£2.3bn – two point three billion pounds (thousand million)

$18\frac{1}{2}$ – eighteen and a half

$5\frac{1}{4}$ – five and a quarter

$3\frac{3}{4}$ – three and three quarters

Bei Dezimalzahlen (Geldbeträge, Längenmaße usw.) wird im Gegensatz zum Deutschen statt eines Kommas ein Punkt zur Unterscheidung der Voll- und Teilsumme benutzt.

Irregular verbs (Unregelmäßige Verben)

PRESENT	see	make	break	come	get
PAST	saw	made	broke	came	got
PRESENT PERFECT	have seen	have made	have broken	have come	have got

(Ausführliche Liste der unregelmäßigen Verben siehe Seite 225.)

Word formation (Wortbildung)

VERB	suggest	cross	agree	plan
NOUN	sugges**tion**	cross**ing**	agree**ment**	plan

VERB	support	oppose	invade	travel
NOUN (person)	support**er**	oppo**nent**	invad**er**	travell**er**
NOUN (action)	support	oppo**sition**	inva**sion**	travel

Get it right 1

1 Defective modals can, must

Put the verbs in the right form in the future or the past.

Example He cannot come to Germany now. *(next week – yes)*
He **will be able to** come to Germany next week.

1. I must work hard this week. *(next week – no)*
2. A lot of people cannot find jobs. *(in future – no)*
3. I must get up early for my new job. *(when I was at college – no)*
4. You must work on Saturdays now. *(when you were at school – no)*
5. I cannot afford a new cassette player. *(when I find a better job – yes)*
6. My father can cook well now. *(when he was younger – no)*
7. The ferries cannot leave Dover at the moment. *(if the weather is better tomorrow – yes)*
8. You do not have to wear nice clothes now. *(when you start work in an office – yes)*

2 Irregular verbs – past tense or present perfect

Put in the right form of the verb.

1. A lot of pupils in my class *(already go)* to the new swimming-pool in Cologne.
2. I *(not see)* the pool yet.
3. Last year I *(make)* a model village.
4. A week later my brother *(break)* the model.
5. I *(never drive)* a car.
6. I *(meet)* a nice person on holiday last summer.
7. I *(write)* her a letter, but she *(not write)* yet.

3 Prepositions

Put in the right prepositons.

at – during – for – in – into – near – to – under

1. The *Chunnel* is called the 'fast lane ☐ Europe'.
2. The rail terminal will be ☐ Cheriton.
3. Cheriton is ☐ Folkestone.
4. Drivers will drive their cars ☐ waggons.
5. The journey ☐ the Channel will take half an hour.
6. There will be trains ☐ cars, buses and lorries.
7. Passengers will be able to stay ☐ their cars.
8. ☐ the journey they will be able to walk about.

4 Conjunction of condition – unless

Join the two sentences with *unless.*

Example I cannot go to the sports ground. My parents must agree.
I cannot go to the sports ground **unless** my parents agree.

1. This radio will not work. You must take it to the shop.
2. Dogs usually make a lot of noise. You must train them when they are young.
3. My car does not start in the mornings. I have to push it.
4. You cannot use the train. You must have a ticket.
5. There will be an accident. People must be more careful.
6. You cannot get that job. You must have good qualifications.
7. That computer will not work. It must have the right programs.
8. You cannot have your own flat. You must earn a lot of money.

5 What are these? Define these words. Use a complete sentence.

Example *a tunnel* – A tunnel is a hole under the ground through which vehicles or people can travel.

a deck – a ferry – a freight train – a passenger train – a rail terminal – a shuttle waggon

GHOST TOWNS AND POLLUTION

Although most people in Britain and in France welcome the plans for a new Channel tunnel, the project is unpopular in the area around Dover. Most local councils in Kent are against the tunnel. They have organized the *Flexilink* group to oppose the plan. Unless they can stop the tunnel, it will destroy around 40,000 jobs in Kent, they say. It will hit the ferries hard and those who depend on them – shops, garages, hotels and local companies. Mr Jonathan Slogget of *Flexilink* says, 'Dover will become a ghost town if the scheme goes through.'

The tunnel will directly affect many small communities. There will be a motorway and high-speed trains near the village of Newington (population 300) just north of Folkestone. The village hall will disappear and local sports grounds will become a rail yard. Work is starting soon but the villagers cannot find exact information about the *Chunnel* plans for their area. Many people in Kent like Harry Berman are angry with the Government. 'It will destroy our homes and our jobs. They call it 'progress'. It isn't funny, is it?' he says.

Flexilink claims that the tunnel will not be as safe as the ferries. A *Chunnel* shuttle will carry 250 cars, 2,500 gallons of petrol and 1,000 passengers at 100 mph. Experts say if there is an accident, there will be a fire. Mr Bob Blackburn, a Chief Fire Officer, is worried about safety. He warns, 'Even if there is a 'No smoking' rule, people will still smoke. If passengers are allowed to stay in their cars during the crossing a fire is certain to happen. The question is not **if** a fire will happen but **when** the fire will happen. That will mean a disaster.' On the French side, too, some people oppose the scheme. One opponent from Calais, Henri Ravisse says, 'Instead of spending an hour on a boat in the fresh air, millions of people will have to cross the Channel through a dark and polluted hole.'

Did you follow? 2

1 Answer the questions on the first part of the text.
1 Who likes the idea of a Channel tunnel?
2 Who does not like the idea?
3 What action have Kent councils taken?
4 What must the councils do to save 40,000 jobs?
5 Which jobs will the tunnel destroy?
6 What will happen to Dover if there is a tunnel?

2 Are these statements about the second part of the text right or wrong?
1 The tunnel will only affect towns like Dover.
2 Newington is a small village.
3 The village will disappear.
4 The sports grounds will disappear.
5 The village will need a new village hall.
6 The villagers are angry because they have seen the plans.
7 Most people in Kent support the Government.
8 Harry Berman thinks the plans are very funny.

3 Look at the last part of the text. Complete these statements.
although – danger – fast – fresh – opponent – polluted – safer – thousands – worried
1 *Flexilink* thinks that ferries are ▭ than the tunnel.
2 In the tunnel, the shuttles will travel very ▭ and carry ▭ of people and cars.
3 Mr Blackburn is very ▭ about the ▭ of a fire.
4 He says that people will smoke ▭ there will be a 'No Smoking' rule.
5 Henri Ravisse is an ▭ of the tunnel.
6 He thinks people on ferries enjoy ▭ air and that the air in a tunnel will be ▭.

4 Make notes about the last part of the text.
Make notes about the arguments **against** the tunnel, like this:
not as safe as the ferries
Then look back at the first text 'The fast lane to Europe'. Make notes about the arguments **for** the tunnel.
Write a short report (ca. 50 words) and give the main arguments for and against the Channel tunnel.
Use: *better – faster – oppose – safer – worse*
Say or write what you think are the good and bad sides of the project.

Watch your grammar 2

Conditional 1 if + present + will-future (Bedingungssätze 1)

If there **is** an accident, there **will** be a fire.
Dover **will** become a ghost town **if** the scheme **goes** through.
The question **is** not **if** a fire **will** happen but when the fire will happen.
When winter **is** over, the ice **will** disappear.

Mit *if* werden Bedingungssätze gebildet. Wenn man von einer gegenwärtigen Möglichkeit ausgeht, die sich bewahrheiten kann, werden die darausfolgenden Voraussagen mit dem **will-future** gebildet.

Die Verneinungsform *if ... not* kann durch *unless* ersetzt werden.

When benutzt man, wenn es keine Zweifel gibt, daß etwas passieren wird.

Die Übersetzung von *if* und *when*:

IF	WHEN
wenn, gesetzt den Fall, falls	wann, sobald (Vergangenheit: als, wenn, immer) Nicht mit „gesetzt den Fall" übersetzen!

Question tags (Bestätigende Rückfragen)

They call it 'progress'. 'It isn't funny, **is it**?' he says.
They have destroyed our town, **haven't they**?
The Minister can't do that, **can he**?
The new tunnel costs a lot of money, **doesn't it**?
It will be a lot faster, **won't it**?
Parliament didn't want a tunnel, **did it**?
Queen Victoria liked the idea of a tunnel, **didn't she**?

Question tags sind ein Mittel, meinen Gesprächspartner zu veranlassen, **meine** Aussagen zu bestätigen.
Sie werden mit dem Verb bzw. Hilfsverb gebildet, das im Hauptsatz benutzt wird, wobei Verbteil und Pronomen umgedreht werden. Falls der Hauptsatz kein Hilfsverb enthält, wird das **question tag** mit *do/does/did* gebildet. Ferner kann das **question tag** auch benutzt werden, um Ungläubigkeit oder Überraschung auszudrücken.

POSITIVE SATZAUSSAGE	NEGATIVE SATZAUSSAGE
negative *question tag*	positive *question tag*

Present continuous as future (Verlaufsform der Gegenwart mit zukünftiger Bedeutung)

Work **is starting** soon but the villagers cannot find exact information about the Channel plans for their area.

Ereignisse, die in der unmittelbaren Zukunft geschehen, werden mit dem **present continuous** und einer Zeitangabe beschrieben (vgl. Seite 42).

Conjunction although (Bindewort obwohl)

Although a lot of people in Britain and in France support the plans for a new Channel tunnel, the project is unpopular in the area around Dover.

Although drückt eine Einschränkung aus, z. B. obgleich, obwohl.

Get it right 2

1 Conjunction of condition – if

Say what this person will do.
Make conditional sentences. Use *if* + *present, will-Future.*

Example go to the beach – the weather is nice.
I **will** go to the beach **if** the weather is nice.

1 watch TV – there are good programmes on
2 visit my friends – there is nothing on TV
3 play some music – my friends are at home
4 do my homework – my friends are out
5 phone my friend for help – my homework is too difficult
6 read a book – my friend can't help me
7 go into town – the book isn't interesting
8 go to bed – it's raining

2 Conjunctions – although, if, unless, when

Translate these sentences into English. Use the correct conjunction.

1 Wenn das Wetter zu kalt ist, gehe ich nicht schwimmen.
2 Ich war nicht überrascht, als das geschehen ist.
3 Wenn Sie nicht aufhören zu rauchen, werden Sie krank.
4 Wenn der Tunnel fertig ist, wird er Tausende von Arbeitsplätzen zerstören.
5 Falls die Regierung den Tunnel baut, wird Dover zu einer Geisterstadt.
6 Obwohl London viele Busse hat, gibt es oft Staus.
7 Es wird aber mehr Verkehrsstaus geben, wenn es in der Großstadt nicht mehr Busse gibt.
8 Ich rufe dich an, wenn du zu Hause angekommen bist.

3 Word formation

Use a dictionary to find the nouns for these words from the text.
to affect – angry – to claim – to destroy – to disappear – safe – to worry

4 Question tags

Find the right question tags for these statements.
am I – did you – does she – doesn't he – don't you – do you – have you – have we – isn't it

Example He hasn't got a motorbike, ☐ ?
He hasn't got a motorbike, **has he**?

1 You haven't seen that film yet, ☐ ?
2 I'm not making you angry, ☐ ?
3 She doesn't look well today, ☐ ?
4 He looks nice today, ☐ ?
5 You didn't phone me yesterday, ☐ ?
6 We haven't done that exercise yet, ☐ ?
7 Your new car is faster than your old one, ☐ ?
8 You don't want to leave college yet, ☐ ?
9 You hate fast food, ☐ ?

5 Complete these sentences with the correct form of the word in brackets.

1 I *(go)* to Scotland next summer.
2 The bus *(go)*, I'm afraid. It *(go)* five minutes ago.
3 At weekends, I *(enjoy)* playing the guitar.
4 These apples are much *(sweet)* than the ones you bought last week.
5 *(want)* you to see the film with me?
6 *(look for)* a job at the moment?
7 This TV set *(cost)* £300 a year ago.
8 Do you know the person *(who/which/that)* was at the door this morning?

6 Prepositions

Put in the right prepositions.
between – by (3x) *– for* (2x) *– from – of* (3x) *– through – to*

1 The tunnel will be ready ☐ 1993.
2 When it is ready, there will be a direct rail link ☐ London and Paris ☐ the first time.
3 The journey will be quicker ☐ three hours.
4 The British Parliament was afraid ☐ a French invasion ☐ a tunnel.
5 In the 1980s both Governments accepted a scheme ☐ a fixed rail link.
6 Cross-channel traffic will increase ☐ 24 million ☐ 50 million ☐ the year 2000.
7 Supporters ☐ the tunnel say it will not be the only way ☐ crossing the Channel.

OVER TO YOU

Imagine this story happened to somebody you know last week. Tell the story in the pictures. Say what he wanted to do, what happened, where they took him, how long he was there, what his plans were. Use the past and future tenses of *can* and *must*. These words will help you:
ambulance – break – carry – cut – face – fall – run for the bus – skates – start – stay

Metric measures

IMPERIAL SYSTEM	METRIC SYSTEM
DISTANCE	
1 inch (in/″) –	2.54 centimetres (cm)
1 foot (ft/′) –	30.479 cm
1 ft = 12 inches (in) –	0.3048 metres (m)
1 yard (yd) = 3 feet (ft) –	0.9144 m
1 mile = 1,760 yd –	1.6093 kilometres (km)
0.3937 in –	1 cm
1.094 yd –	1 m
0.6214 miles –	1 km
WEIGHT	
1 ounce (oz) –	28.35 grams (g)
1 pound (lb) –	454 g
1 lb = 16 ounces (oz) –	0.454 kilograms (kg)
1 stone = 14 pounds (lb) –	6.356 kg
1 hundredweight (cwt) = 112 lb –	50.8 kg
1 ton – 20 cwt = 2,240 lb –	1,016.04 kg
0.0353 oz –	1 g
2.2046 lb –	1 kg
2,204.6 lb –	1 tonne (metric ton)

For hundreds of years Britain has used its own system of measurements, the Imperial system. In the last ten years, the Government has tried to change to the European metric system. At the moment, both systems are used. In general, older people prefer the old system; younger people are quite happy with the metric system. But for everyday things everybody uses the old system: for example – I'm five **foot** (or **feet**) eight. I weigh twelve **stone**. I have to travel two **miles** to school every day.

Now answer these questions about yourself using imperial measurements.

1. If someone says s/he is 6′ 2″, is s/he taller/shorter than you?
2. If someone says s/he weighs 14 stone, is s/he heavier/lighter than you?
3. The speed limit in British towns is 30 miles per hour (mph). Is that faster/slower than in German towns?
4. How tall are you? Answer in feet and inches.

5 How much do you weigh? Answer in stones and pounds.
6 How far do you travel to school/college each day? (or how far do you have to walk?) Answer in miles or hundreds of yards.

Listening

Listen to the radio interviews on the tape. You will hear people who live near the Channel tunnel project. Some people support the project, others oppose it.
Answer these questions about the tape:
1 What are the jobs of the three people Janeen Loxley interviews?
2 Are they for or against the tunnel? Give their reasons.

Writing

New ideas, better ideas?

New projects like the *Chunnel* are not always popular. Sometimes many people are opposed to a scheme, sometimes only a few people in one area are against it. Can you think of a scheme in your area or your country, to which many people are opposed? Describe the scheme for somebody who cannot speak German.
Say what it is for, where it is, who supports it and why, who opposes it and why.
Make notes first and then write a personal letter to somebody who uses English.

Start off with: *Dear (Susanne)*
Continue like this: *There has been a lot of discussion about a new project here in the last few months. There are plans to build ... .*
Finish it like this: *Yours, (Manfred)*

Mindfield

Imagine

You must leave your home and your family. You must spend a year on an island in the South Seas. You can take with you some tools, three books and one other thing. There are trees and fresh water on the island and a few animals, but they are quite small.
Make a list of the following:

the things you will take with you
the things which you will have to do first
all the good things which you won't be able to do
all the bad things which you won't have to do
all the good things which you will be able to do
all the bad things which you will have to do

Compare your list with that of a partner. Make one list together with him/her. Report to the class.

Key words and phrases

for ▶◀ against
increase ▶◀ decrease
fresh ▶◀ polluted
spend time and money
The only way of crossing the Channel
14 years' work
support ▶◀ oppose
agree ▶◀ disagree
popular ▶◀ unpopular
danger ▶◀ safety

8 American ways of life

WHEN A JOB'S NOT A LIVING

Dwight D. Weisskopf

I visited a friend the other day. We were discussing the 40 million jobs that the American economy has created in the last 15 years. I was explaining what a good thing this was when her son came in. He listened for a while and then stopped me: 'I have one of those jobs,' 5 he said. 'It's a dead-end job. I only get the minimum wage. Most of those jobs are like that.' His mother carried on the attack: 'It's harder living on the minimum wage now than it was 10 years ago. America should stop congratulating itself about new jobs and start helping its poor workers.' 10

They sounded bitter. That made me want to find out more.

The minimum wage

The minimum wage has not changed for six years. It's still at $3.35 per hour. 8.5% of the 58 million hourly workers receive the minimum wage. You get it for those dirty jobs that nobody 15 really wants to do: messenger, storeroom clerk, cook in a fast food restaurant. You need few skills for these jobs and there is no chance of improving yourself.

Liberal and labor

Liberal politicians and labor* leaders agree with each other. 'The minimum wage is not a living wage,' they say, 'and it is not a decent society in which a full-time job means a life in poverty.' 20 They would like the minimum wage to be half of the average hourly wage. At the moment it is only 38%.

Opponents

Of course, a lot of people oppose an increase. They say it will lead to higher unemployment and inflation. 'When you put up somebody's wages by a dollar,' says the U.S. Chamber of Commerce, 25 'then those people who are making a dollar more also have to have an increase.' Higher labor costs will lead to higher prices and employers will fire laborers to cut costs.

Black youths

My friend's son wants to stop work altogether anyway. 'Why work for low wages', he asks, 'if I can earn more in welfare or on the streets?' The problem is worse for him. He is an inner-city black 30 youth. He thinks that an increase in the minimum wage will help. 'If you can earn more from working, people will find themselves jobs and get off welfare.'

While I was thinking about these ideas I visited my lady friend again. 'I myself am in favor* of a minimum wage increase,' she said. 'But that's not enough. We need better job-education and an aggressive retraining program. That would help a lot more.' Opponents and those in 35 favor of an increase agree with one another on this. The Government in Washington is thinking about an $800 million training program for youths on welfare. Without the skills to build a career, workers on the minimum wage cannot help themselves, even if there is an increase.

** AE spelling*

Did you follow? 1

1 Find out the following information from the text.
1 How many new jobs have been created in the U.S. in the last 15 years?
2 What pay do many of these jobs offer?
3 How many workers receive the minimum wage?
4 Give two examples of the sort of jobs which only pay the minimum wage.
5 What qualifications do you need for these sorts of jobs?
6 Do these sorts of jobs help you find a better one in future?

2 Look at these opinions about the minimum wage. Find the parts of the text which give the same opinions. Whose opinions are they?
1 It is more difficult to live on the minimum wage than it used to be.
2 Life in a country where people who work full-time are still poor is unfair.
3 It is not possible to live properly on the minimum wage.
4 If you can get more money from the Government on welfare there is no reason to work for the minimum wage.
5 If the minimum wage goes up more people will lose their jobs and the cost of living will get higher.

3 Find the parts of the text where people make suggestions for the future of the minimum wage.
1 Say what these suggestions are in your own words.
2 Who makes what suggestion?
3 Opponents of an increase in the minimum wage and those in favour of one agree about one suggestion. Which suggestion is it?

4 What does the U.S. Chamber of Commerce think will happen if the minimum wage rises? Describe in your own words the reasons they give for this opinion.

5 What does the son of the writer's friend call the sort of jobs which pay the minimum wage? What does this mean?

6 Find words from the text which fit these definitions.
1 The money poor people in America get from the Government.
2 The rise in prices and wages.
3 Learning to do a new job.
4 To end the employment of someone.
5 The least you have to pay someone for work.

7 Put in the missing words from this list.
careers – employers – increase – labor – poverty – skills – society – unemployment

☐[1] is bad for any ☐[2] because it also leads to ☐[3]. One big problem is that a lot of workers do not have the right ☐[4] for good ☐[5]. That's why ☐[6] leaders and ☐[7] both think there should be more job education. If things do not change then the numbers of people out of work will ☐[8] even more.

8 Is there a minimum wage system in your country? What do you think of the idea? How high is it or how high should it be? Give reasons.

Watch your grammar 1

Past continuous (Verlaufsform der Vergangenheit)

1 Statements and negatives

We **were discussing** the 40 million jobs that the American economy has created.
I **was explaining** what a good thing this was.

2 Questions and short answers

Was the reporter **explaining** something when the lady stopped him? – **Yes, he was.**
Were they **talking** about unemployment when someone said something about the minimum wage? – **No, they weren't.**

Das **past continuous** wird mit der Vergangenheit von *be* + *-ing* Form des Verbs gebildet. (Besonderheiten in der Schreibweise der *-ing* Form im Grammatikanhang S. 193)

BE	SUBJEKT	*BE*	*-ING* FORM	SATZERGÄNZUNG
–	I/he/she/it	was wasn't (was not)	listening	to Barry.
–	You/we/they	were weren't (were not)	watching	television.
Was Were	I/she/he/it you/we/they	– –	following cooking	the car in front? the dinner?

Das **past continuous** drückt aus, daß eine Handlung in der Vergangenheit zu einem bestimmten Zeitpunkt **noch im Verlauf war**. Es kommt häufig zusammen mit dem **simple past** vor und beschreibt dabei die Handlung, die bereits andauerte, während das **simple past** für die **neue, abgeschlossene Handlung** verwendet wird.
Das **past continuous** wird außerdem oft in den **beschreibenden Teilen** von **Erzählungen** oder **Berichten** verwendet.

Reflexive pronouns (Reflexivpronomen)

1 'I **myself** am in favor of a minimum wage increase.'
2 'People will find **themselves** jobs.'

Diese Pronomen können zwei verschiedene Funktionen haben:
1 **Hervorhebung** – wenn ein Substantiv oder Pronomen hervorgehoben werden soll;
2 **reflexiv** – wenn sich die Aussage eines Satzes auf das Subjekt bezieht.

SINGULAR: *-SELF*	PLURAL: *-SELVES*
myself yourself herself/himself/itself	ourselves yourselves themselves

Im Englischen verwendet man die Reflexivpronomen viel seltener als im Deutschen, z. B. sich treffen = *meet*, sich bewegen = *move*, sich erinnern = *remember*.

Each other and one another

They looked at **each other**.	Sie sahen einander an.
They loved **one another**.	Sie liebten sich.
They looked at **themselves** in the mirror.	Sie sahen sich selbst im Spiegel an.

Each other und *one another* drücken eine **wechselseitige** Beziehung aus, während Reflexivpronomen wie z. B. *themselves* nur rückbezüglich sein können.

Get it right 1

1 Past continuous statements, questions

Use these notes and ask and answer questions about blacks in the U.S.

Example Q. What/Martin Luther King/do somebody shot him
A. stand on a balcony
What was Martin Luther King doing when somebody shot him? – He was standing on a balcony.

NOTES		
1	**Q.**	What/take place/the murder happened
	A.	public meeting/take place
2	**Q.**	What/speak about/they killed him
	A.	speak about civil rights for Black Americans
3	**Q.**	What town/speak in/he died
	A.	speak/Memphis
4	**Q.**	How much/blacks/earn/1977
	A.	earn 62% of an average white
5	**Q**	What/earn/ten years later
	A.	earn only 56%.
6	**Q.**	What happen/situation/blacks/during that time
	A.	not get better

2 Past continuous statements, negatives

Use the notes to make sentences.

Example Martin Luther King/not talk to politician/make a speech at a meeting.
Martin Luther King was not talking to politicians. He was making a speech at a meeting.

1 In 1987/most blacks/not live in same places as white/live in black areas.
2 Blacks/get better education and jobs/but not find houses in white neighbourhoods.
3 In 1984/30% of blacks in New York/live in poverty/their situation not get better.
4 More and more Hispanics/come to New York/but not earn as much as blacks.
5 New York/lose a lot of factory jobs/not create new jobs for workers without skills.
6 Office workers/learn skills/find new jobs there/poor blacks/Hispanics not find work easily.

3 Past continuous or simple past

Put the verbs in brackets into the right tense. (This is the first of four exercises in this unit which tell a murder story.)

Who murdered Lord Ritz?

Somebody *(kill)*[1] **killed** Lord Ritz this afternoon but nobody else *(be)*[2] with him when it *(happen)*[3]. All of them *(do)*[4] **were doing** something somewhere else. Most of them have good alibis. For example, Lady Ritz and Alan Love *(play)*[5] tennis when the murder *(happen)*[6]. Unless, of course, they *(not tell)*[7] the sergeant the truth. The butler *(look for)*[8] his master and Mrs White *(see)*[9] him just before she *(hear)*[10] the shot. So he can't be the murderer. And Mr Love and Lady Ritz *(can)*[11] see the gardener while they *(play)*[12] tennis. He *(cut)*[13] the grass so he *(not kill)*[14] Lord Ritz either. And what about the chauffeur, Adams? Well, he *(work)*[15] in the garage, because everybody *(can)*[16] hear the noise he *(make)*[17] while he *(repair)*[18] the Rolls Royce. It's all very difficult. Of course, Alf, the gardener, *(not say)*[19] that he *(can)*[20] see Mr Love and Lady Ritz. Perhaps that's it.

4 Reflexive pronouns

Put in the right reflexive pronouns.

The inspector was talking to **himself**. 'Lord Ritz didn't kill ☐[1]. That's certain. Somebody shot him in the back. The butler hated his master. He says so ☐[2]. And Mrs White said the same. She was always telling him: 'Keep ☐[3] under control, Johnson. We won't make things better for ☐[4] like that.' Of course, she didn't like Lord Ritz ☐[5]. In fact nobody did. But they have all found ☐[6] very good alibis.'

5 Reflexive pronouns – each other/one another

Translate these sentences into German.

1 It is not surprising that blacks and whites often hate each other.
2 When I was a child blacks and whites never saw one another in the same part of town.
3 I remember that well.
4 No whites lived in our neighbourhood. So we could never talk to one another.
5 We did not even see each other at school.
6 Since then things have got better but blacks and whites still do not understand each other well enough.

HOW WE LIVE

This week **How we live** hears what a couple of overseas visitors have to say about American lifestyles.

Venice, California

Before I arrived in Los Angeles to start a job with a new firm, I had expected to live in the smog of a huge, dirty city. But my apartment is in a super beach resort where a non-stop carnival goes on. And it's only 20 minutes from L.A. by car. That's Venice. Of, course, it's hard to imagine a place as different from Venice, Italy, as Venice, California. But I love it here.

Every day you can watch the street vendors on Ocean Front Walk selling everything from the cheapest T-shirts in the world (three for $5.95) to expensive jewellery and strange works of art. But the main attraction is the people themselves. From my window I can see the young muscle men working out on Muscle Beach. Every weekend I can hear the man play Beethoven on the piano he rolls on to the seafront. Crowds come to see the 60-year-old *Skateboard mama* put on a show with the other skateboard riders and roller skaters. It's a non-stop seafront show. The whole place is full of artists of every kind. There are great restaurants and cafés where you can eat and drink in the warm Californian sun. To go with all this there is one of the most beautiful beaches of golden sand that you'll ever see. So it's not too hard to understand why Venice, California is a wonderful place to live.

Las Cruces, New Mexico

I had heard of Las Cruces before I got there because it is so close to the famous White Sands Missile Range. In fact, the missile range is the town's biggest employer. Now that I know it better, I cannot understand why Las Crucians are so proud of their desert town.

A couple of days after I had arrived I was sure that Las Crucians would rather have four wheels than two legs. I haven't changed my mind since. It is impossible to live here without a car. Public facilities are very bad. There is no public transport system. Finding a launderette is hard work, but there are car washes on every corner. With drive-in fast foods, drive-in banks, drive-in movies, there's very little reason ever to leave your automobile. And with most of the city taken up by parking lots, why should you want to? Walking about town is nearly impossible, too, because there are so few sidewalks. And taking the kids to the park means an hour's drive first.

Las Crucian's conversation is just like their town. The only thing they are really interested in is cars. They won't listen to anyone talk about politics and their idea of a good night out is drinking beer in the *Diamond J Bar* with the motorcyclists and a country and western band. A new survey on places to live in America says that Las Cruces is one of the fifty best towns. I'd hate to see the other 49 if they're anything like this one.

Did you follow? 2

1 Which part of the text is positive and which negative?

2 Answer these questions about Venice, California.
1 Where is the town?
2 What sort of town is it?
3 Why did the writer go there?
4 What sort of people can you see there?
5 What sort of music can you hear there every weekend?
6 What happens on Muscle Beach?
7 Who is *Skateboard Mama* and what does she do?
8 What other things, apart from the people, make Venice a good place to live?

3 Answer these questions about Las Cruces, New Mexico.
1 What is the climate like in Las Cruces?
2 Where do many Las Crucians work?
3 Why do you need a car in Las Cruces?
4 Why is it hard to walk about town?
5 What things show you that the town is made for people with cars?
6 What do Las Crucians like doing and talking about?

4 Look at these words and phrases in the text and say what they mean in your own words. Use a dictionary if necessary.
1 overseas visitor
2 beach resort
3 public facilities
4 launderette

5 What words would people from Britain use for these ones from the text? If you do not know, use a dictionary.
apartment – movies – parking lot – sidewalk

6 What things do you find strange, good, bad, funny, interesting about these two American towns?
Do you agree with the writers' opinions? Give reasons.
Would you like to live in one of these places? What could you do there that you cannot do where you live now?

Watch your grammar 2

Past perfect (Vollendete Vergangenheit/Plusquamperfekt)

Statements and negatives

I **had heard** of Las Cruces before I got there.

No, I certainly **had not lived** in such a terrible place.

When I **had noticed** (I noticed) it I asked my firm for a job somewhere else.

Questions

Had you **lived** in a town like it before?

Das **past perfect** wird mit *had ('d)* und dem **past participle** gebildet.

HAD	SUBJEKT	*HAD*	PAST PARTICIPLE	SATZERGÄNZUNG
–	I/You/We/...	had ('d) had not (hadn't)	talked spoken	to an Australian before. to an American before.
Had	I/you/we/...	–	seen	a film in English before then?

Wenn wir über die Vergangenheit reden und ausdrücken wollen, daß ein Ereignis **vor** einem anderen geschah, verwenden wir das **past perfect** für das Ereignis, das zuerst geschah, das **simple past** für das sich später ereignende.
Das **past perfect** tritt deshalb oft mit Zeitangaben wie *after* oder *before* auf. Mit *when* kann auch das **simple past** verwendet werden, wenn die Reihenfolge der zwei Handlungen klar ist.

-ing form or infinitive with verbs of perception (-ing Form oder Infinitiv bei Verben der Sinneswahrnehmung)

From my window I can **see** the young muscle men **working out** on Muscle Beach.

Every weekend I can **hear** the man **play** Beethoven on the piano.

Nach Verben der Sinneswahrnehmung wie z.B. *feel, hear, listen to, look at, notice, see* und *watch* findet man oft folgende Konstruktionen:

OBJEKT + *-ING* FORM	OBJEKT + INFINITIV (OHNE *TO*)
Der **Ablauf** einer Handlung wird betont, aber nicht notwendigerweise von Anfang bis Ende.	Es soll betont werden, daß diese Handlung **beendet** wurde.

Get it right 2

1 Past perfect and simple past

Make sentences from the notes.

Example After the war end/the economy of the South begin to grow.
After the war **had ended** the economy of the South **began** to grow.

1 Before this happen/people in the South always be poorer.
2 After things in the South start to improve/someone invent the name Sunbelt for the southern states.
3 After they create this word/people also begin to talk of the rest of the U.S. as the Snowbelt.
4 When the Sunbelt economy start growing/people already see signs of trouble for the Snowbelt.
5 After the situation change/a lot of people moved to the Sunbelt states.
6 Before they get there/firms create a great many new jobs.

2 Past perfect and simple past

Back to our love and crime story. Remember what happened to Lord Ritz? Before they killed him, Alan Love and Lady Ritz made these notes. Say what they did on the day of the murder like this:
After they had met in front of the house, they got the gun from Alan's room. When they had ...

Meet in front of the house.
Get the gun from Alan's room.
Put the gun in the little cupboard near the stairs.
Have lunch.
Put on tennis clothes.
Play tennis till four.
Go back to house.
Take gun from cupboard.
Wait for Lord Ritz on stairs.

3 -ing form or infinitive with verbs of perception

Complete these sentences with the right form of the verbs in brackets.

Example The gardener saw Lady Ritz and Mr Love *(play)* **playing** tennis at 3.30 p.m.

1 Half an hour later he saw them *(talk)* in front of the house.
2 After that he watched them *(go)* into the house and saw them *(walk)* towards the stairs.
3 Mrs White saw the butler *(walk)* past the kitchen.
4 A minute later he went back and watched her *(make)* a cake.
5 They could hear the gardener *(cut)* the grass outside and the chauffeur *(repair)* the car in the garage.
6 After the butler had left to look for his employer everyone heard someone *(shoot)* Lord Ritz.

4 Simple past or present perfect

Put the verbs in brackets into the right form.
In the 1970's when people *(talk)*[1] of 'two Americas', they *(mean)*[2] the Sunbelt and the Snowbelt. Since the early seventies, in the Sunbelt the economy *(grow)*[3] and the industries of the Snowbelt *(face)*[4] huge problems. By 1986, the situation *(change)*[5]. Some experts still *(talk)*[6] of 'two Americas' but these *(be)*[7] different. Now the coasts *(become)*[8] much richer than the rest of the country. From 1981 to 1985 incomes in California and 15 states on the Atlantic coast *(increase)*[9] by 4%, while in the rest of the country this increase *(be)*[10] only 1.4% during that time. Of course, other experts *(not share)*[11] these ideas and *(state)*[12] that the differences would not last long. But the differences *(last)*[13] for many more years since then.
The Sunbelt and the coastal states *(become)*[14] even richer than in the mid-eighties; many high-tech industries *(move)*[15] south, west and south-east and *(take)*[16] their jobs with them and they are staying in the sun.

5 If-clauses I

Join the sentence halves. Use *if* or *unless* in the if-clause.

Example ☐ you buy a car – find life in Las Cruces impossible
Unless you buy a car, you **will** find life in Las Cruces impossible.

1 ☐ you go to the U.S. – see a lot of different lifestyles.
2 ☐ the situation of blacks improve – Americans never be able to live together in peace.
3 ☐ you want to understand Americans – have to learn a lot about their country.
4 ☐ you know something about American lifestyles – your visit be much more interesting.
5 ☐ you visit different regions of the country – not have a true picture of the U.S.
6 ☐ Europeans want to understand American politics – must have a better idea of the way Americans think.

OVER TO YOU

Listening

1 What town and state is the radio station from?
2 What big American cities are the subject of the report?
3 The people talk about the fashions in the following areas: *food and drink*, *clothes*, *hobbies and sports*, *vacations*, *cars*. Listen to the tape again. For which town or towns are the following things in or out?
Example Aerobics is in in Los Angeles.
Food & drink: meat, vegetarian, vitamin pills, white wine
Clothes: black, bright colours, grey clothes, sneakers, suits
Hobbies & sport: computers, country & western music, jogging, squash, walking fast
Vacations: Acapulco, Caribbean islands, Las Vegas, Mexico
Cars: big, small
Write your answers in a table like this:

	IN	OUT
town 1 (name) town 2	aerobics	

Compare your answers with the rest of the class.

4 What things are in and out for you? Write down a list for food, clothes, holidays and hobbies. Check your list with other people's. What are the most popular things in your class?

Writing

1 Liberal and labour leaders in the U.S. think that putting up the minimum wage is one way of cutting unemployment. If people can earn more they will look harder for a job. Here are some other suggestions for cutting unemployment.

- Cut the number of hours people have to work in a week.
- Let people stop work at the age of 55.
- Start a big government building programme.
- Cut the tax that companies have to pay.
- Make sure that people get better job training and qualifications.

For each suggestion write down **how** it could cut unemployment.
Example 'If people have to work fewer hours a week then companies ...'

2 Write about your town or the area you live in. Say what things make it
1 a good place to live in. 2 a bad place to live in.
Finish by saying where you would like to live when you start work. Give reasons for this choice.

Mindfield

The trip to America

Write down the names of the places on your 'trip to America'.
1 You fly from Frankfurt to the biggest city on the West Coast.
2 You rent a car and drive to the famous Casino town in the state of Nevada.
3 You go west, back into the state you arrived in.

4 You give back your car and take the plane to the state whose largest city is Seattle.
5 From there you fly to the big town with an old French Quarter in Louisiana.
6 Your next flight takes you to the city with the busiest airport in the U.S.A.
7 You next visit the largest city in the U.S.A.
8 After a few days there you take a trip to the smallest U.S. state.
9 You fly back to America's busiest airport and take a trip on the lake the city is on.
10 Your next stop is the state that is closest to Cuba.
11 You fly to the capital of Massachusetts.
12 You leave the U.S. from the biggest airport in the biggest city.

Write your answers in a list. Then take these letters from the answers to make up the name of the capital of an American state.

1 = 3rd letter	2 = 7th letter	3 = 3rd letter	4 = 8th letter
5 = 6th letter	6 = 5th letter	7 = 7th letter	8 = 5th letter
9 = 3rd letter	10 = 5th letter	11 = 4th letter	12 = last letter

What is the name of the state?

Working with words

1 Replace the underlined parts of the sentences with words that mean the opposite.
1 Since last year the situation of the economy has got worse.
2 There has been a big rise in the unemployment figures.
3 A lot of things play a part when jobs are destroyed.
4 There are people in this country who live lives of great wealth.
5 The numbers of poor families is decreasing.

2 Replace the underlined parts of the sentences with words or phrases which mean the same.
1 A lot of big companies in the U.S. have their main offices in the Sunbelt.
2 American trade union leaders would like to improve the lives of their members.
3 The public services in many American towns are not very good.
4 The wages that some Americans receive are not enough to put them above the poverty line.

Key words and phrases

airport
climate
crowd
suggestion

create
fight
grow
improve
lead

dead-end
strange

society and economy
Chamber of Commerce
civil rights

economy
employment
facility
firm

labor *(AE spelling)*
in favor of *(AE spelling)*

income
politician
politics
poverty
society

9 London pride

COVENT GARDEN

What do you do with a 140-year-old fruit and vegetable market in the middle of an important city when it isn't needed any more? Easy, isn't it? You pull it down and build something clean and new and modern instead. You could build offices, or maybe luxury flats. It's a good way to make money and improve the area at the same time. – At least, that's what the owners of the land thought when London's fruit and vegetable market left Covent Garden in 1971.

The local people had other ideas. They didn't want their area to change. They liked the atmosphere, and they wanted to keep the old houses and pubs in the streets around the market. As one of them said: 'If people are allowed to build offices here, it will destroy the whole area. Everything will get more expensive. No one will be able to afford to live here any more and Covent Garden will die.'

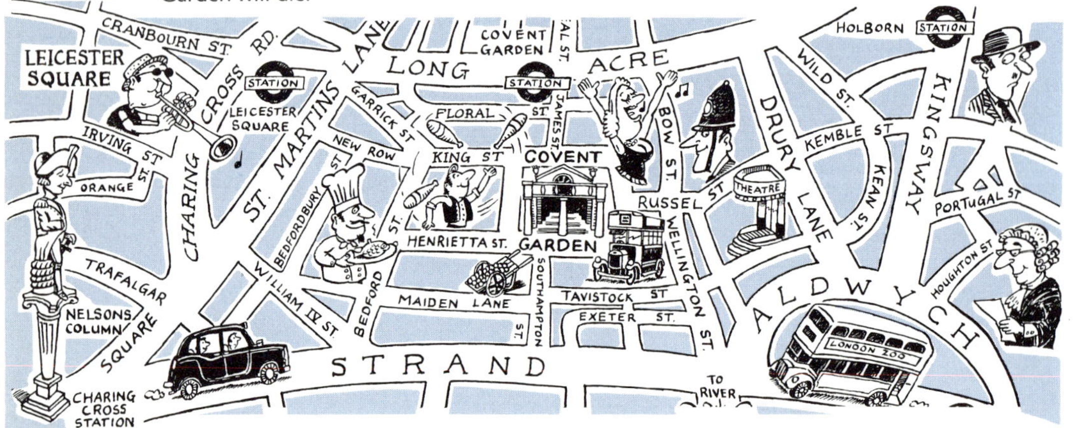

After a long fight, they persuaded the Greater London Council to keep the old market buildings and find a new use for them. And so, in 1980, the new Covent Garden opened. It soon became one of the most popular places in London. The old halls are now full of small, attractive shops, and pubs and cafés where visitors can sit outside and relax. Instead of fruit and vegetables, all kinds of interesting hand-made or home-made articles are sold in the shops and stalls. And the sounds that are heard aren't the noise of the market – instead, there's the music of the street musicians, or 'buskers'. Or you can listen to the street entertainers and hear foreign tourists speaking German, French, Italian, Japanese, Arabic and any other language you can think of.

Covent Garden has become a place where people can enjoy themselves – and that is just what they come and do: millions of them, every year. You don't need to buy anything. You can watch the entertainers or listen to the buskers. The performance is always good. Why? Well, because you may only busk in Covent Garden if you persuade the manager that you're good enough. And that's not easy.

Yet there's more to Covent Garden than just the market. In all the streets around it there are old shops and new ones where you can buy anything: from crazy posters and postcards to antiques, from tropical fruit to health foods. And because cars are not allowed in many of the streets, you can just wander – like thousands of others.

And what about the local people? Do they think the new Covent Garden is a good thing? Well, some do. They've made a lot of money out of the tourists. Others aren't so sure. As one of them said: 'They've destroyed the old atmosphere. Everything is made more expensive by all the tourists. People can't afford to live here any more. The old Covent Garden is dying.'

Well, perhaps it is. But there's plenty of life in the new one. You'll see that when you visit it.

Did you follow? 1

1 Look for information in the text and say if these statements are right or wrong. Correct the wrong ones.

1 Covent Garden was a fruit and vegetable market for more than 100 years.
2 The Greater London Council had to pull down the old market before it could build the new Covent Garden.
3 The new Covent Garden is full of shops and pubs.
4 Anybody can come to Covent Garden and play music.
5 The street entertainers all speak different foreign languages.
6 Everybody is happy about the new Covent Garden.

2 Answer these questions about Covent Garden:

1 When did the old fruit and vegetable market close?
2 What did the owners of the land at Covent Garden want to do with it?
3 Why weren't the local people happy about the owners' ideas?
4 What can you buy in the new Covent Garden market?
5 What else can you do at Covent Garden if you don't want to buy anything? Name one thing you can do.
6 Why is the music at Covent Garden always good?

3 When the old fruit and vegetable market closed, the owners of Covent Garden had good reasons for their plans. Find two.

4 Covent Garden has become one of the most popular places in London. Find three more things that the visitors can do there and in the streets around the market.

5 Which definition fits which word?
afford – atmosphere – busker – persuade – improve – plenty – wander

1 more than enough of something
2 make something better
3 walk slowly around without wanting to go anywhere
4 the feeling people have about a place
5 have enough money to buy something
6 make a person believe or do something
7 a person who plays music in the street

6 Local people don't all feel the same about the new Covent Garden. Find two different opinions from the text.

7 What do you think? Were the early plans of the owners good for Covent Garden and the local people, or is the new Covent Garden better? Give *your* reasons.

8 Find the words or phrases in the text which mean the same as the following:
destroy – very expensive – make somebody change their mind – people who play music in the street – make better – the people who live in an area

Watch your grammar 1

The passive 1 (Das Passiv 1)

Present passive (Passiv der Gegenwart)

All kinds of interesting hand-made or home-made articles **are sold** in the shops and stalls. And the sounds that **are heard** aren't the noise of the market.

Am häufigsten benutzt man das Passiv in Berichten über Ereignisse oder Handlungen, bei denen man die Ursache/den Verursacher bzw. den Auslöser nicht kennt oder nicht nennen will. Ferner ist zu beachten, daß im Passivsatz das Subjekt die Person oder der Gegenstand ist, mit dem „etwas geschieht".

Bildung: *to be* + **past participle**

REGELMÄSSIGE VERBEN	UNREGELMÄSSIGE VERBEN
to be + -ed He **is** visited at home.	*to be* + die 3. Form (s. S. 225) English **is taught** everywhere. The book **was taken** from my desk.

I	**am** (not)	**visited** often. **expected** at eight o'clock.
You/We/They	**are** (not) **aren't**	
He/She/It	**is** (not) **isn't**	

Gelegentlich kann es nötig oder wichtig sein, in einem Passivsatz die Ursache oder den Verursacher doch zu nennen. Man schließt die Ursache bzw. den Verursacher der Handlung durch *by (by-agent)* an (Subjekt eines entsprechenden Aktivsatzes).

	SUBJECT	VERB	OBJECT	BY-AGENT
AKTIVSATZ	The buskers	entertain	the tourists.	–
PASSIVSATZ	The tourists	are entertained	–	by the buskers.

Für das unpersönliche Aktiv mit **man** im Deutschen steht im Englischen das Passiv.

Covent Garden **isn't needed** any more. **Man braucht** Covent Garden nicht mehr.

Permission (Erlaubnis)

Anyone **can** walk around Covent Garden free.
You **may** only busk in Covent Garden if you persuade the manager that you're good enough.
If people **are allowed** to build offices here, it will destroy the whole area.

	NORMALER UMGANGSTON	BESONDERS HÖFLICHER UMGANGSTON
Erlaubnis gewähren oder verweigern	can, can't, cannot	may, may not
bestehende(s) Erlaubnis bzw. Verbot	be (not) allowed to	–
Um Erlaubnis bitten	can	could, may, might *(selten)*

Get it right 1

1 Present passive statements

Put the verbs into the present passive.

1 Mike and Jean *(take)* to school by car every day.
2 This kind of cake *(eat)* only at Christmas.
3 Customers who are angry about something *(send)* to see the manager.
4 The atmosphere *(improve)* by the street entertainers.
5 This newspaper *(read)* by more than a million people.
6 Covent Garden *(visit)* by many foreign tourists.
7 Hundreds of these toys *(sell)* every year.

2 Present passive negative statements

Make passive negative answers to these questions.

Example Why isn't Charlie here? *(children – take – to see horror films)*
Because children aren't taken to see horror films.

1 Why don't you take your letter to the post? *(letters – collect – on Saturday afternoons)*
2 Why don't you want to do the work? *(I – pay – very much for it)*
3 Why's the company selling that computer? *(it – need – any more)*
4 Why don't many English people speak Spanish? *(it – teach – in many English schools)*
5 Why did you buy that book in Germany? *(it – sell – in England)*
6 Why can't they go running in the park? *(the gates – open – before 9.30)*
7 Why haven't you gone home yet? *(I – expect – until ten o'clock)*

3 Passive statements with by

Make passive statements and use *by* to say who or what does the action.

Example letters – take – post – secretary
The letters are taken to the post by the secretary.

1 noise – make – wind
2 animals – feed – two o'clock – Mr Morris
3 Anne – teach – French – Frenchman
4 Covent Garden – enjoy – most of the visitors
5 fruit and vegetables – carry – market workers
6 this language – not speak – many people
7 radio programme – hear – millions
8 kind of music – not like – everybody

4 Translate these sentences into German

1 Two old people live next door to me.
2 The old man is ill and is often visited by his doctor.
3 The housework is done by the local council.
4 A younger woman is sent to them once a month.
5 The shopping and the cleaning are done by her.
6 The old people are visited by their children regularly.
7 The old man never goes out. His meals are brought to him in bed.

5 Asking and giving/refusing permission

Ask permission, then give it or refuse it. Use the normal form first, then make your questions/answers more polite.

Example look at – newspaper
Can (Could/May/Might) I look at your newspaper, please?
Yes, you **can (may)** – or
No, you **can't (may not)**.

1 sleep – house
2 have – one – sweet
3 Terry – come – us
4 open – window
5 Mike – listen – new record
6 speak – you – for a moment
7 ask – dance
8 eat – breakfast
9 pull – hair
10 throw away – English book

THE TRAIN IN THE DRAIN

There are some things that are so important that life in London would not be possible without them. One of them has its 125th birthday in 1988 – the Tube. That's the name that Londoners have given to their underground railway, because of the shape of its tunnels. In the early days, people used to compare the tunnels to the drains which carry away the city's waste water!

The Underground is the best way to beat the traffic in the centre of London. But the traffic is not just a modern problem. It was the same back in the nineteenth century, when it was all horse-drawn. That's why the Metropolitan Railway, the first underground railway in London, was built.

Work began in 1860 and took three years. Many workers were killed in accidents and flooding. 12,000 poor people were forced to leave their homes because the railway needed the land. But when the line was opened in 1863 it was a great success, and other lines soon followed.

Life wasn't very pleasant for the early Tube passengers. The trains were pulled by steam engines and it wasn't easy to get enough air into the tunnels. Breathing was sometimes quite a problem, especially in the rush hour.

You can see one strange result of this problem in Leinster Gardens, in Paddington. Numbers 23 and 24 look just like all the other houses in the road. If you go round the back, however, you'll see that there's just the front wall and nothing else! The special steam engines of the Metropolitan Railway used to save their steam while they were in the tunnel and let it all out when they came into the open at Leinster Gardens. The dummy houses were built to keep the smoke and steam away from the road. They're still there today.

Older Londoners remember spending the nights in the Tube during the war. They sheltered there from the bombs. Special trains came round to sell food and drink. Nowadays, people talk about the friends they made in those days, and the singing and the entertainments. Really, the Tube was dirty and full of rats. It smelled and it wasn't completely safe – even in the Unterground people were killed by bombs. But the bad side of things has been forgotten.

The Tube is the biggest underground railway system in the world, although others carry more passengers. The lines are about 1,240 kilometres long, including the world's longest railway tunnel, more than 27 kilometres long on the Northern Line. Nearly 24,000 people work on the Tube, and 541 million passengers use it every year – that's one and three quarter million every day. And it's still growing. Two new Tube lines, the Victoria and the Jubilee, have been opened since the beginning of 1969. Not bad for a railway they used to call the train in the drain!

Did you follow? 2

1 Answer these questions about the London Tube.
1 How old is the underground railway in London?
2 Why is London's Underground called the Tube?
3 What was the name of the first London Tube line?
4 How long did it take to build the first Tube?
5 Why were Tube journeys very uncomfortable at first?
6 What is unusual about the house at 24 Leinster Gardens?
7 How were Tube stations used during the war?
8 How many people use the Tube in a year?
9 What are the Jubilee and the Victoria?

2 Somebody wants to know more about the Tube. Can you give them more information?
1 Were there any problems building the first Tube?
2 The Tube has always been electric, hasn't it?
3 I'm sure people got hungry and thirsty when they were sheltering in the Tube during the war.
4 I expect at least a million people use the Tube every day, don't they?

3 Look for information in the text and say if these statements are right or wrong. Correct the wrong ones.
1 In the centre of London, it's quicker to go by car than by Tube.
2 There were no traffic problems in London when people used horses.
3 The steam engines didn't let all of their steam and smoke out into the tunnels.
4 The London Tube is used by more people than any other underground railway.
5 The world's longest railway tunnel is part of the Jubilee Line.

4 Which definition fits which word?
breathing – century – dummy – engines – force – passenger – rush hour – shelter – steam
1 make a person do something he or she doesn't want to do
2 in a city, this is what they call the time when most people are going to work or going back home
3 a person who is travelling in a bus or train
4 something which looks real, but isn't
5 go under something to get away from rain – or from anything which falls from the sky
6 if you stop doing this you will die
7 water turns into this at 100 °C
8 one hundred years
9 machines that pull trains or turn energy into movement

5 The London Tube has changed and grown a lot since the first line was built. Find at least five facts about the modern Tube which make it important for London or different from other underground railways.

6 There are two different ideas in the text about life in the Tubes during the war. Describe these ideas, then say which one *you* think is probably truer. Give reasons.

Watch your grammar 2

The passive 2 (Das Passiv 2)

1 Past passive Passiv der Vergangenheit

Many workers **were killed** in accidents and flooding.
When the line **was opened** in 1863, it was a great success.

Das **past passive** wird mit der Vergangenheitsform von *to be* und dem **past participle** des Verbs gebildet. Wie für das **present passive** (siehe S. 92) gilt auch hier, daß die Ursache oder der Verursacher einer Handlung oder eines Ereignisses nicht im Vordergrund steht, d.h. man kennt ihn nicht oder will ihn nicht nennen.

SUBJECT	FORM OF *TO BE*	PAST PARTICIPLE	
I/He/She/It	was (not) wasn't	sent	to America.
You/We/They	were (not) weren't		

2 Present perfect passive (Passiv des Perfekts)

The bad side of things **has been forgotten**.
Two new Tube lines **have been opened** since the beginning of 1969.

Das **present perfect passive** bildet man mit den Perfektformen von *to be* und dem **past participle** des Verbs.

SUBJECT	FORM OF *TO BE*	PAST PARTICIPLE
I/You/We/They	have been haven't been	taught well.
He/She/It	has been hasn't been	

Hyde Park in 1838

Get it right 2

1 Past passive statements

Put the verbs into the past passive.

1 The first London underground line *(open)* in 1863.
2 We *(not teach)* foreign languages when we went to school.
3 Many people's homes *(destroy)* when the line *(build)*.
4 The office *(not clean)* yesterday.
5 The first trains *(pull)* by steam engines.
6 I didn't tell him because I *(not ask)*.
7 Fans *(put)* in the Tube tunnels between 1920 and 1930.
8 In the war the Tube *(use)* by people to shelter from the bombs.
9 I'm sure that this dress *(not buy)* in England.

2 Present perfect passive statements

Put the verbs into the present perfect passive.

1 Many events of the past *(forget)*.
2 I'm afraid your suitcase *(leave)* in Valparaiso.
3 Our neighbour *(not see)* since last week.
4 Fred's hair *(not wash)* for a month.
5 We can drive there because the car *(repair)*.
6 All of our questions *(answer)*.
7 The letter *(not write)* yet.
8 This picture *(take)* from the local museum.

3 Past passive questions

Make past passive questions from these notes.

Example car – drive – by – woman?
Was the car driven by a woman?

1 when – first – London underground – build?
2 book – write – by – American?
3 how – they – bring – here?
4 glasses – make – Italy?
5 where – strange car – see?
6 first Tubes – pull – steam engines?
7 when – letter – send?

4 Present perfect passive questions

Make present perfect passive questions from these notes.

Example ticket – leave – here – for me
Has a ticket been left here for me?
how many – boxes – take?
How many boxes have been taken?

1 children's hair – wash – this week?
2 car – repair – yet?
3 how much – money – spend – already?
4 dog – feed – today?
5 all the coffee – drink – already?
6 how far – car – drive – today?

5 Past passive or present perfect passive?

Put in the right verb in the right form, past passive or present perfect passive.

bring – drive – find – leave – send – show – take – wake

On the day of his journey, Mr Corrigan ☐[1] by his wife at 6 o'clock. After a quick breakfast, he ☐[2] to the airport by his secretary. When he arrived, he walked over to the Flopair desk and spoke to the stewardess. 'My name's Corrigan,' he said. 'I believe a ticket ☐[3] here for me.'
'That's right,' she said. 'It ☐[4] down yesterday by Mr Branson.' Then Mr Corrigan ☐[5] the way to the plane by a friendly stewardess. When he arrived in New York, he couldn't find his suitcase. He ☐[6] to a comfortable office by another stewardess. There he waited for half an hour until she came back. 'Your suitcase ☐[7],' she said. 'Great,' said Mr Corrigan. 'Yes,' she said, 'it ☐[8] to Hong Kong.'

6 Some, any and their compounds (revision)

Translate these sentences into English. Use some or any or a compound in each sentence.

1 Brauchen Sie Geld?
2 War jemand hier, als du reinkamst?
3 Ich habe noch Äpfel, aber Kartoffeln brauche ich.
4 Da ist jemand im Schlafzimmer.
5 Paul und Anna sind irgendwo in Italien.
6 Ich habe etwas im Auge.
7 Ist irgendwo in der Nähe eine Telefonzelle?
8 Müssen wir etwas mitnehmen?
9 Es ist keiner da.
10 Wir haben kein Brot mehr. Fährt jemand heute in die Stadt?

OVER TO YOU

Listening

1 Listen to the tape. Find out who is speaking and what they are doing at Covent Garden.

2 Listen to the tape again. What do the people who are interviewed think is good about Covent Garden, and what do they think is bad about it?

3 Why do you think the last person talked to the interviewer like that? Do you think he was right?

Mindfield

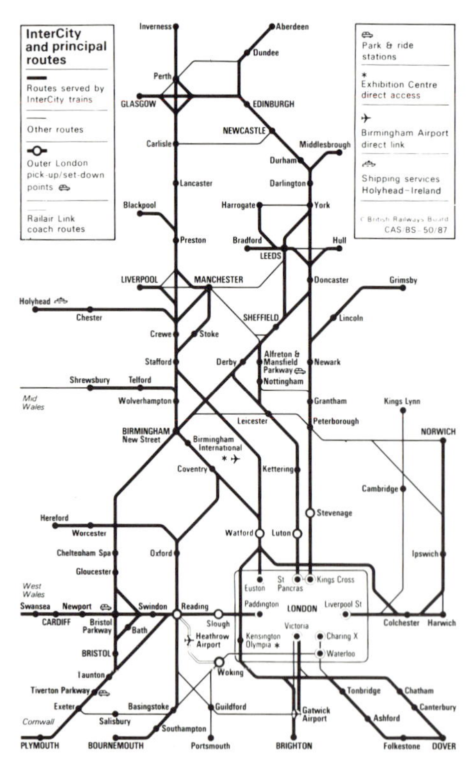

The InterCity Overground

Use these two maps to solve the following problems:

Example You're at Holborn Station and want to go to York.
I take the Piccadilly Line to King's Cross and change to British Rail for the InterCity to York.

1 You're in Birmingham and want to get to Oxford Circus.
2 You're at Green Park and want to go to Cardiff.
3 You're in Manchester and want to go to Brighton.
4 You're in Norwich and want to go to Portsmouth.

If you enjoy working with maps, set each other more problems like this.

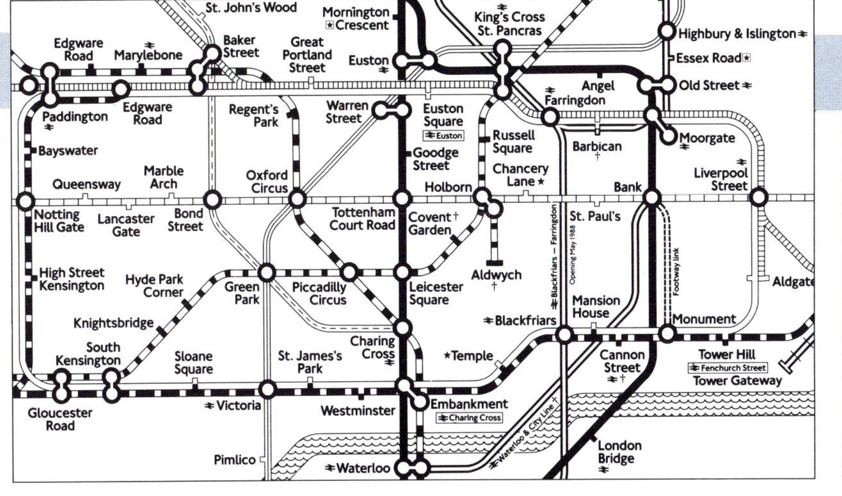

Part of the London Underground

(LRT Reg. User No. 88/E/413)

Key to lines

- Bakerloo
- Central
- Circle
- District
- Jubilee
- Metropolitan
- Northern
- Piccadilly
- Victoria
- British Rail

Interchange stations
Connections with British Rail
Connections within walking distance

Writing

Use these notes to write about the New York underground, which is called the subway. Begin like this: *The idea for a subway was first suggested in the 1860s. The first 300 feet ...*

1 300 feet of track – open – February, 1870
2 drive – by air – called – Beach Pneumatic Subway
3 first long subway – New York – build – between 1900 – 1904
4 cost – $35,000,000 – many men – kill – during construction
5 more lines – open – 1913
6 another line – build – 1930s
7 By 1960 – New York subway lines – 726 miles long

Working with words

Put in the right words.

1 Electric motors, steam engines and horse power are all forms of ☐.
2 Subways, undergrounds and the Tube are all types of ☐.
3 If something belongs to you, you are its ☐.
4 If you want a drink, you're ☐.
5 Buskers and people who play in the streets provide ☐ for passers-by.

Key words and phrases

It's a good way to travel.
There's more to London than the tourist sights.
Which is the best way to travel?/to the Tower?
Meet all kinds of people. What kind of people?
You might meet anyone.

entertain – entertainer – entertainment
subway – the Tube – underground

adjectives	nouns		verbs		quantifiers
	energy	railway	fight	persuade	plenty of
strange	market	result	force	smell	
thirsty	owner		grow	shelter	
			improve		

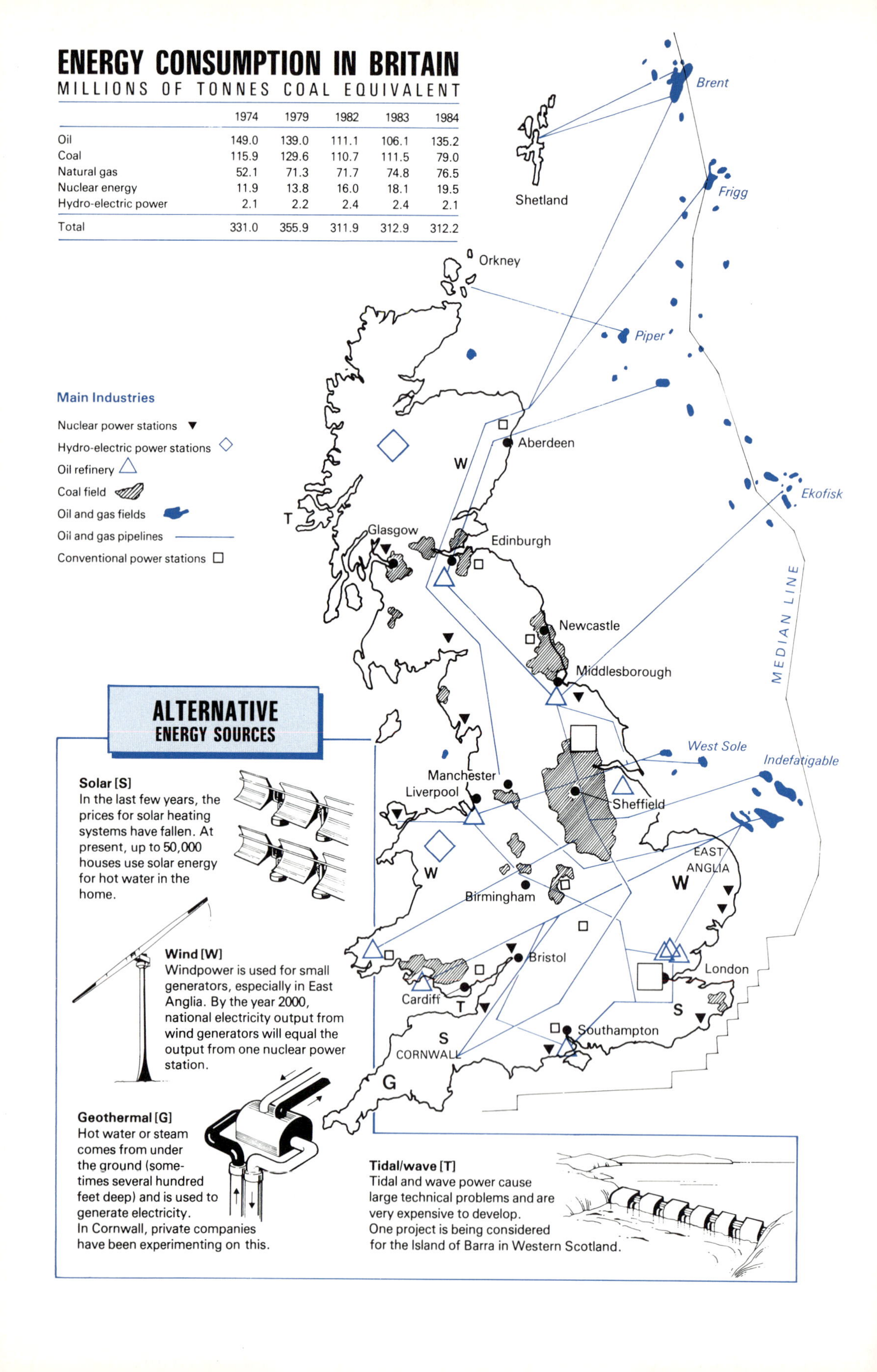

ENERGY CONSUMPTION IN BRITAIN

MILLIONS OF TONNES COAL EQUIVALENT

	1974	1979	1982	1983	1984
Oil	149.0	139.0	111.1	106.1	135.2
Coal	115.9	129.6	110.7	111.5	79.0
Natural gas	52.1	71.3	71.7	74.8	76.5
Nuclear energy	11.9	13.8	16.0	18.1	19.5
Hydro-electric power	2.1	2.2	2.4	2.4	2.1
Total	331.0	355.9	311.9	312.9	312.2

Main Industries

Nuclear power stations ▼
Hydro-electric power stations ◇
Oil refinery △
Coal field
Oil and gas fields
Oil and gas pipelines
Conventional power stations □

ALTERNATIVE ENERGY SOURCES

Solar [S]
In the last few years, the prices for solar heating systems have fallen. At present, up to 50,000 houses use solar energy for hot water in the home.

Wind [W]
Windpower is used for small generators, especially in East Anglia. By the year 2000, national electricity output from wind generators will equal the output from one nuclear power station.

Geothermal [G]
Hot water or steam comes from under the ground (sometimes several hundred feet deep) and is used to generate electricity.
In Cornwall, private companies have been experimenting on this.

Tidal/wave [T]
Tidal and wave power cause large technical problems and are very expensive to develop.
One project is being considered for the Island of Barra in Western Scotland.

CUMBRIA: INDUSTRY AND LOCAL GOVERNMENT

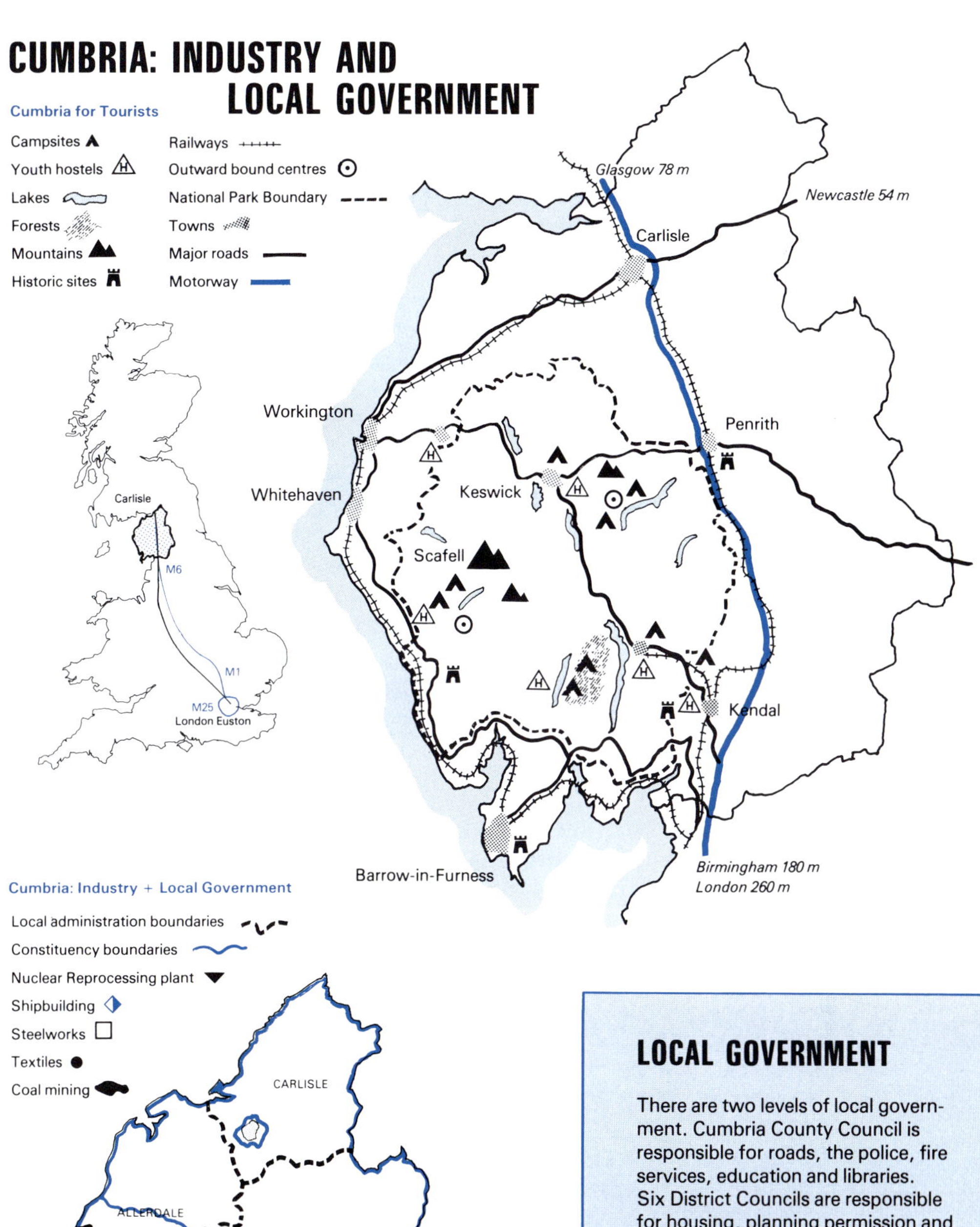

LOCAL GOVERNMENT

There are two levels of local government. Cumbria County Council is responsible for roads, the police, fire services, education and libraries. Six District Councils are responsible for housing, planning permission and refuse collection.

Cumbria is divided into 6 constituencies:
The electors of each constituency elect 1 MP to sit in the House of Commons in London.

The main industries in Cumbria are: Tourism, Chemicals (including BNFL), Shipbuilding (Submarines), Distribution & Road Haulage, Food Processing, Agriculture, Forestry & Mining.

10 Work and play

JOBS WITH A DIFFERENCE

Tony Green has a good view from his job. He is a thatcher who spends most of his days on the roof. But before you can enjoy the views you have to have a head for heights: 'From the top of a roof, it can look a long way down. You also need to be fit and good at climbing up and down ladders. Then you need a good eye to lay the reeds in a straight line.' 5

Tony, who is 19, started thatching straight after school. He did his training, four years of it, with a local company and now works for them as a full-time qualified thatcher. He loves working with natural materials. 'Working with concrete must be terrible. You can feel the life in the reeds we use. Even after they have been cut. And you're closer to the weather and the natural world, too. I'd hate to work in an office.' 10

Nothing much has been changed about the job for centuries. For example, reed is still cut during the summer and left to dry until it is needed. And even today the reeds are kept together on the roof with 30 cm-long sticks. They are split into four and tied around the reeds. 15

A thatched roof is built to last: at least 25 years and up to 40. And if you think thatching is dying out, forget it. 'There are hundreds of thatched roofs in our area alone. Some people are even putting them on new houses.' 20

Sharon Niblock thinks that people expect too much of nurses. 'We're not angels. People don't understand that we're human and get tired and angry like everyone else. But I love it. Nursing's like a drug. Once you've started it, it's hard to give up nursing.' 25

It's not an easy job, however. Nurses must be confident, as patients depend on them, and fit and full of energy, as they have to do a lot of walking and lifting. They must also be patient and like helping people.

Sharon also talked of the pressure. On her ward there are six qualified nurses and five trainees for day and evening work, seven days a week. This often means that the ward is looked after by one trained nurse and two trainees. 'You ask yourself – would you like your mother to be in here with so few nurses to look after her?' 30

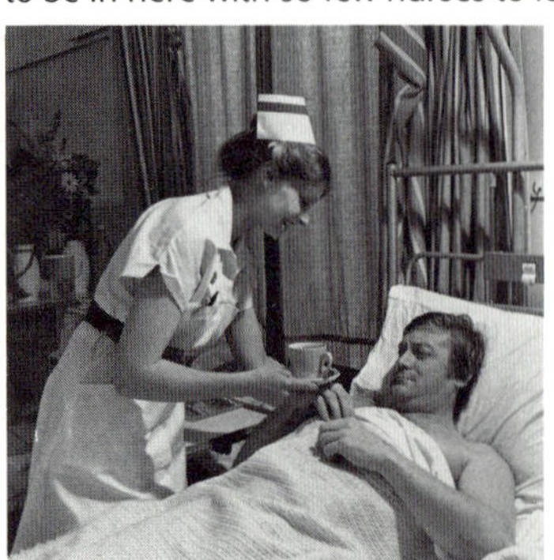

Hospital managers sometimes cause problems. They just want to get patients into and out of hospital beds as quickly as possible. 35

When people die the main trouble is that the nurses cannot give any help to the relatives. 'We often have to send people away alone after the death of a relative. It's terrible. There ought to be someone to help them, but we haven't got the time.' They have a cup of coffee, a cigarette and a good cry themselves. 40

'But it's not all depressing,' she says. It's wonderful that the nurses are able to give their ward such a warm atmosphere – in spite of all the problems. 45

Did you follow? 1

1 Answer these questions about a thatcher's job.
1 What are the roofs made of?
2 What happens to the reeds before they are used for thatching?
3 How are the reeds kept on a thatched roof?
4 How long does a thatched roof last?
5 What are the chances like for thatchers in the future?

2 Describe how Tony Green became a thatcher.

3 What are the things he prefers about his job to other jobs?

4 Answer these questions about the nurses' job described in the article.
1 Why are nurses not angels?
2 Why does Sharon Niblock compare nursing to a drug?
3 Why are there often only three nurses to look after Sharon's ward?
4 Why do hospital managers cause problems for the nurses?
5 What can the nurses do for the relatives of someone who has died?
6 What do the nurses do themselves when someone dies?
7 What sort of place is the ward in spite of all the problems?

5 Find four things you must have or be able to do if you are a thatcher. What reasons are given for these things?

6 Find four or five qualities a nurse must have. For which ones are reasons given in the text?

7 Find words from the text to fit these definitions.
1 the job of making roofs out of reeds
2 something that you use for climbing up and down
3 a thin piece of wood
4 something hard used in building
5 what you use to make something
6 the job of looking after people in hospital
7 something you need a lot of to work hard
8 that makes you feel bad
9 the place in a hospital where a nurse works
10 with the right training for a job

8 The word *patient* is used with two different meanings in the text. What sort of words (noun, verb, etc.) are they? How would you say them in German?

9 Say which of these jobs you would prefer. Give reasons for your choice.
builder – cleaner – cook – driver – gardener – mechanic – nurse – policeman – thatcher

I would prefer to be a … Being a … would be a better job for me I find being a … is a better job …	because	I would like to … I'm (not) … I can/can't … I love/hate … …

Watch your grammar 1

-ing form 1

1 Gerund (Gerundium)

Nursing is like a drug.
He did his **training** with a local company.

Die *-ing* Form eines Verbs kann wie ein Substantiv verwendet werden und zwar sowohl als Subjekt wie Objekt.

2 Nach bestimmten Verben

Nurses must **like helping** people.
It's hard to **give up nursing**.

Nach bestimmten Verben muß die *-ing* Form verwendet werden: nach Verben, die Gefallen oder Mißfallen ausdrücken (siehe S. 42), wie *like, hate, enjoy, mind* usw. Außerdem nach Verben, die Beginnen, Weitermachen oder Beenden ausdrücken wie *finish, stop, go on, can't help, give up.*

Noun endings (Substantivendungen)

ENDUNG	-age	-ance	-ment	-sion	-tion	-ure
VERB	pass	perform	govern	comprehend	direct	press
SUBSTANTIV	passage	performance	government	comprehension	direction	pressure

Get it right 1

1 Gerunds

Look at the two lists of verbs and adjectives and make statements about these activities. Use the -ing form of the verbs and words like *(not) very, too, quite, a bit, just, so,* etc.

Example **I think drinking is too popular.**

climb – beautiful
dance – dangerous
drink – difficult
drive – easy
fly – expensive
read – great
run – healthy
sleep – important
swim – old-fashioned
translate – popular
travel – safe

2 Verbs + -ing form

Look at this table which shows what some nurses think of their job. Make at least six statements about their feelings.

Example Most of them don't mind taking blood but one of them hates doing it.

\+ = like +? = quite enjoy
?– = don't mind – = hate

	+	+ ?	?–	–
Do night shift	2	3	2	6
Take blood	0	2	10	1
Wash patients	4	4	5	0
Talk to visitors	3	1	4	5
Give injections	1	5	5	2

3 Passive

Look through 'Jobs with a difference' again and find all the examples of verbs in the passive. Make a list and say what tense the verbs are in.

4 Passive of simple present

Look at the pictures and use the simple present passive to complete the description of how a thatched roof is made.
Use these verbs.
carry – collect – cut – lay – left – split – take – tie

Reeds **1** in the summer. The reeds **2** to barns and **3** there to dry. When dry, the reeds **4** by the thatchers. They **5** up on to the roof. Then they **6** in straight lines on the roof and **7** together with sticks which **8** into four.

5 Verbs + -ing form

Use these notes to make statements.

Example Tony/really/like/thatch
Tony really likes thatching.

1. Tony/give up/train/as mechanic/to become a thatcher
2. the other day/start/work/at 8 a.m.
3. go on/climb ladders/and lay reeds/all day long
4. enjoy/work/in the warm sun
5. only hate/thatch/when the wind/be/strong
6. that day/there was no wind/so/not mind/climb/up and down the ladder
7. feel/so good/can't help/smile
8. finish/work/at 6 p.m./and go home

6 Passive present perfect

Change these headlines into complete sentences by using the present perfect passive.

Example BOY KILLED IN ACCIDENT
A boy has been killed in an accident.

1. 100 NEW NURSES EMPLOYED
2. AMERICAN COMPANY BUYS BRITISH COMPUTER SYSTEM
3. FARMWORKERS GIVEN PAY RISE
4. GOVERNMENT DECISION SAVES 2,500 JOBS
5. COMPANY SELLS 100 HOUSES WITH THATCHED ROOFS
6. MORE SPENT ON TRAVEL THIS YEAR

7 Passive simple present and present perfect

Put the verbs in brackets into the correct passive form.

Example The number of hours nurses work *(cut)*.
The number of hours nurses work has been cut.

1. Roofs *(thatch)* the same way for centuries.
2. Every year more new cars *(buy)*.
3. This year fewer goods *(send)* from Great Britain to other countries.
4. Problems in Britain *(make)* worse by what happens in the rest of the world.
5. Thatchers *(not worry)* by these general problems.
6. More new houses with thatched roofs *(build)* this year than since last century.

8 Noun endings

1. Find nouns that are formed from these verbs.
   act – enjoy – entertain – marry – mix – organize – pay – state
2. Find verbs from which these nouns are formed.
   agreement – concentration – decision – definition – description – invention – performance – pleasure
   Check your answers in a dictionary.

PLAY, PLAY, THE U.S. WAY

This week *Crystal* looks at some American activities played by young Britons and Americans. Our reporter spoke to some of the people who enjoy American sports.

During the week, **John Walters** works as a trainee supermarket manager. On Friday evenings, John puts on a helmet and 14 pounds of protective padding and trains for his next game of American football. But it won't be in the USA. John's team comes from Birmingham, England. Their opponents are a team from London. John says, 'I've never been to the States but I love their style of football. The sport has been going since 1982 in Britain. 150 British clubs have been formed with 14,000 players. Some matches get more supporters than regular soccer matches. People think American football is very violent and physical and they're right! But it's like chess with violence. You need mental concentration, too. Every move is carefully planned. After the game we watch ourselves playing on video. For me it's a good way of keeping fit.' The league is supported by an American beer company. Its national team is trained by four American coaches. The players come from different backgrounds: there is a miner, a salesman, a policeman and a car worker in the team. But under their helmets, they all look the same.

Liz Greenwood is one of the cheerleaders at her local American football club, the Redskins. Monday to Friday, she is a hairdresser: in her spare time, she meets the seven other Redskins' cheerleaders. They practise their routines to disco music. They dance, do high kicks, sing and chant. Practice usually lasts an hour a week. Their latest chant is, 'We got power, we got style, See us come and run a mile! Redskins, Redskins, Ra-ra-ra!' Liz told *Crystal*, 'Cheerleaders and players have a great social life together after the games. At games, we wear red tights, red pullovers and red coaches' caps. Some people say there's no point in having cheerleaders. But it's worth spending time on it. The supporters look forward to seeing us, you see. And our team has a feeling of confidence when we're there'.

Californian **Richie Caudwell** is the fastest teenager on wheels in his street. Instead of watching TV or joining his friends at the drugstore, he goes skateboarding after college. He became interested in skateboarding after seeing the National Championships on TV when he was eight years old. Six-foot Richie has taken part in the Skateboard Association championship. In spite of training regularly, he is still not happy with his performance. 'It's always worth doing what you enjoy. But by training hard you can enjoy it more. But I don't seriously want to be U.S. Champion,' he told *Crystal*. 'I go skateboarding because it helps me relax after college.'

In fact, all three youngsters saw more in their sports than just the sport itself. *Crystal* would like to hear from any other young people in Britain who play typical American sports. Write to us at …

Did you follow? 2

1 Answer the questions on the text about John Walters. If the information is not in the text, say so.

1 What is John's job?
2 How old is he?
3 When does he usually practise for games?
4 Is John an American?
5 How does he describe American football? Name two things.
6 What is his team called?
7 He says he likes American football. Does he say why?
8 Find as many facts (not opinions) as possible about the sport from the text.

2 Answer the questions on the text about Liz Greenwood. If the information is not in the text, say so.

1 Where does Liz live?
2 What does she like about cheerleading?
3 How many others are in her group?
4 Where do they practise?
5 What colour uniforms do they wear?
6 How long and how often do they practise?
7 How long has Liz been in the group?
8 Why does she say, 'It's worth spending time on it'?

3 Answer the questions on the text about Richie Caudwell. If the information is not in the text, say so.

1 Describe Richie Caudwell. Name two things.
2 How did Richie start skateboarding?
3 Where does he practise?
4 What do his friends often do while he is skateboarding?
5 What is his opinion about training?
6 When does Richie practise?
7 Which other sports does he play?
8 What is his opinion about becoming skateboard champion?

4 Find words from the text for these definitions.

1 the fans of a team
2 the players who play for their country
3 thinking very hard about something
4 to train for a sport
5 the person/people you play a game or sport against
6 the opposite of physical
7 someone who trains a team for a sport

5 Which of the three sports or activities have you tried/would you like to try? Give your opinions about the three sports or activities described in the text.

Playing American football Cheerleading Skateboarding...	is sounds ...	...

Watch your grammar 2

-ing form 2

Die *-ing* Form wird verwendet, wenn ein Verb in folgenden Konstruktionen gebraucht wird:

1 After prepositions (Nach Präpositionen)

For me it's a good way **of keeping** fit.
By training hard you can enjoy it more.

Typische Präpositionen: *by, for, in, like, of, on, to.*

2 After prepositional phrases (Nach präpositionalen Wendungen)

Instead of watching TV or **joining** his friends at the drugstore, he goes skateboarding after college.
In spite of training regularly, he is still not happy with his performance.

Typische Wendungen: *according to, apart from, as a result of, because of, due to, except for, in spite of, owing to.*

3 After adjective + preposition (Nach Adjektiv + Präposition)

He is **good at playing** physical sports.
I'm more **interested in watching** them on TV.

Typische Beispiele: *afraid of, glad about, good at, interested in, keen on, mad about, tired of, used to, worried about.*

4 After set phrases (Nach feststehenden Redewendungen)

Some people say **there's no point (in) having** cheerleaders.
But **it's worth spending** time on it.

Typische feststehende Redewendungen: *it's no good, it's no use, it's (not) worth, there's no point (in).*

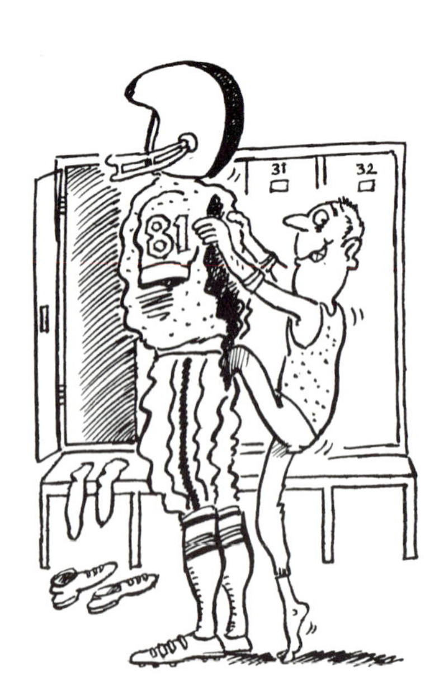

Get it right 2

1 -ing forms

Put in the right verbs in the -ing form.
do – lose – practise – see – spend – talk – train (2x) – *write*

1 The reporter went to watch them □ their sports after work.
2 He was glad of the chance of □ them as he was thinking of □ about them.
3 □ hard was very important for them all.
4 All of them enjoyed □ their □ in spite of □ two or three evenings a week.
5 We heard him □ to Liz about cheer-leading.
6 She told him that it was worth □ time on it because the supporters like it.

2 -ing form

Translate the following sentences into German.

1 It is worth spending time on a sport or hobby.
2 It is a good way of relaxing after college.
3 People look forward to playing sport at the weekends.
4 There's no point in worrying about championships.
5 Many people never win championships in spite of practising regularly.
6 By practising often you can enjoy a sport more.
7 Many people watch sport instead of playing it.

3 -ing form after prepositions

Put in the missing prepositions and -ing forms of the verbs from the lists. The first one is done for you.
□ *about – at* (2x) *– by – in – in spite of – of – to*
■ *become – choose – concentrate – give up – go – play – train – try*

Example Jim Jones can break a piece of wood with his hand □ ■[1] hard on it.
Jim Jones can break a piece of wood with his hand **by concentrating** hard on it.

He has always been good □ ■[2] both mental and physical games and became interested □ ■[3] karate. Five years later, □ ■[4] every week, he was still only a beginner. He has not had any success □ ■[5] an expert yet, but he still looks forward □ ■[6] to the karate club twice a week. 'I'm happy □ ■[7] karate. I have no thoughts □ ■[8] the sport. I feel much fitter now.'

4 -ing forms

Look through 'Play, play, the U.S. way' and find all the -ing forms of verbs. Say why these forms are used in the text.

5 Passive past simple

Use these notes to write a short report on the world snooker championships. Use past simple passives of the underlined verbs to describe what happened. Begin like this:
At 2 p.m. on the 24th April the championships **were opened**. *The first …*

1 opening of championships – 24th Apr., 2 p.m.
2 first match – start – 3 p.m.
3 750 people watched
4 also showing on TV
5 first day – playing only four matches
6 2nd round – young star beats world champion
7 After match – champion and new star – interviews – TV reporters
8 next round – new star – also beaten
9 in the end – world No. 2 wins championship

6 Passive

Put the verbs in brackets into the right form of the passive.

Example The world snooker championship never *(win)* by a German.
The world snooker championship **has** never **been won** by a German.

1 Skateboarders often *(injure)* during practice.
2 The karate club *(build)* nine years ago.
3 A reporter *(send)* to the club last week.
4 He *(surprise)* by what he saw.
5 He also *(take)* to watch an American football game.
6 American football *(make)* popular in the last few years by TV.
7 The game you see on TV *(play)* by huge men in helmets and padding.
8 Nowadays a lot of money *(earn)* by the best players in the USA.

7 Nouns made of two words

Make ten proper English words from this list of twenty. Use each word once.
bike – burger – business – card – centre – cheese – head – job – line – man – motor – news – paper – post – pot – shop – table – tea – time – work

OVER TO YOU

Listening

1 Listen to this extract from a radio programme.

1 Give the following information about the young people you hear: – name, age, what they do (job etc.).
2 Who are the other people you hear?
3 What do the young people talk about?

2 Listen to the tape again and find out the following things about the three young people:
– whether they are happy with their situation or not.
– what reasons they give for this.
– what spare time activities they do/do not do.
– what things they would like to change so that they could enjoy life better.

3 Compare what these average young people from Britain do in their spare time to your own spare time activities.
What different things do you do? What do you do more/less of? Do you have the same/different problems? Do you think you have a better/worse time than the ones on the tape?

Writing

1

GALVANISER with chrome plating experience. Salary plus tax free allowance and bonus scheme. Please apply Field Aircraft Services (Heathrow) Ltd. Tel: 01-759 1392 Agy 398.

MACHINE TOOL Cutter Grinders Salary plus tax-free allowance and bonus scheme. Please apply Field Aircraft Services (Heathrow) Ltd. Telephone 01-759 1392. Agy: 399.

MACHINE TOOL Cutter Grinders. Salary plus tax-free allowance and bonus scheme. Please apply Field Aircraft Services (Heathrow) Ltd. Tel: 01-759 1392 Agy 399.

We are looking for a **FARM-WORKER**

PIPE FITTERS. Hydraulic / Pneumatic With Machine Tool Experience. (Pipe 6mm to 40mm

We would like to employ a **SECRETARY**

TOOLMAKERS, Herts contract. Staffhire 0920 5921.

TURNERS and millers Surrey conts. Rapid agy 0438 815333.

VENDING MACHINE Serv/Engs Must have basic Electrical/Mechanical knowledge, clean driving license. Required for Overseas Contract. Salary plus tax-free Overseas allowance. Please Apply Field Aircraft Services (Heathrow) Ltd. Telephone 01-759 1392. AGY 397.

VENDING MACHINE Service Engs. Must have basic electrical/ mechanical knowledge. Clean Driving Licence. Required for overseas contract. Salary plus tax free overseas allowance. Please apply Field Aircraft Services (Heathrow) Ltd. TEl: 01-759 1392 Agy. 397.

FREE BROCHURE AND NEAREST COURSE ON (0602) 609941 or 621206

£15.000 P.A. Qualify as a Driving Instructor in 1988. 0932 221434.

SALESMAN or **SALESWOMAN** wanted

AIRCRAFT FINAL ASSEMBLY FITTERS With F28 and F100 experience required for immediate contracts. Salary plus tax-free allowance and bonus. Please apply Field Aircraft Services (Heathrow) Ltd. Tel: 01-759 1392 Agy B394.

AIRFRAME ENGINE FITTERS. 737 exp pref. Various conts. Staffhire 0920 3044.

The texts of these three job adverts have been mixed up. Decide which sentences are from which advert and write the adverts out in full. Compare your answers with other people's in the class. Decide what the best adverts are.

– S/He must have a driving licence
– and be polite.
– and be practical.
– S/He should be confident
– and sensible.
– S/He must have a good telephone voice
– and like contact with customers.
– and like working outside.
– and be good at typing.
– S/He must have lots of energy
– S/He should be strong
– S/He should be friendly

2 Now write an advert like this for one of these jobs:
cleaner – clerk – mechanic – nurse – hairdresser
These words and phrases might help you:

S/He	should ought to must	be	careful – clever – confident – exact – friendly – intelligent – modern – patient – polite – practical – quiet – sensible – serious – strong – thoughtful – …
		have	lots of energy – at least two years experience – a driving licence – …
		like	working with computers – working in an office – taking responsibility – …
		be able to	make decisions – answer enquiries – …
		be good at	spelling – typing – …

Working with words

1 In the following sentences one of the words is wrong. Find it and replace it with the right word from the same word family.

1 The dead of a young patient is always very depressing.
2 Sports like American football might look very violence but they are not really dangerous at all.
3 If you want success at any sport you have to do a lot of practise.
4 Success is a great feel.
5 You just have to concentration on getting better.

2 Put in the missing words or phrases.

1 After four years of training he became a ▭ mechanic.
2 There's ▭ in doing the training unless you like the job.
3 You really have to have the right ▭ if you want to have any success.
4 Of course, ▭ working so much, he also has a great ▭ in the evenings.
5 He really enjoys his ▭.

Key words and phrases

concentrate *(v)* – concentration *(n)*
die *(v)* – dead *(adj)* – death *(n)*
dry *(v)* – dry *(n)*
feel *(v)* – feeling *(n)*
form *(v)* – form *(n)*
practise *(v)* – practice *(n)*
press *(v)* – pressure *(n)*
surprise *(v)* – surprising *(adj)* – surprise *(n)*
violent *(adj)* – violence *(n)*

mental ▶◀ physical

in spite of …ing
be good at …ing/something
do a lot of …ing
it's worth …ing

– be a qualified …
– They're all … to me.
– there's no point (in) …ing

attitude
energy
relative
size
social life
spare time

lay
miss

11 Legend

Leg·end ['ledʒənd] *n* ... a person famous for a particular activity esp. after death

GIVE PEACE A CHANCE

'I can go out this door right now and go into a restaurant. You want to know how great that is? People will come up and ask you for autographs, but they don't bug you. When I left England, I couldn't even go to a restaurant. I've been walking the streets here for the last seven years.' John Lennon talking about life in New York in a BBC Radio 1 interview with Andy Peebles a few hours before he was shot.

'Do you know what you just did?'

John Lennon was murdered by a smiling gunman at 11 p.m. on Tuesday, 9th December 1980 outside his New York home. Lennon, who was just 40, was shot five times by a .38 revolver. He tried to walk but fell after only five steps. 'Do you know what you just did?' the shocked doorman shouted at the gunman. 'I just shot John Lennon,' the gunman answered and threw down the gun. Lennon was taken to hospital in a police car but was dead when he arrived.

'Gunman a Screwball'

A 25-year-old man, Mark David Chapman of Honolulu, Hawaii, was arrested for Lennon's murder. Chapman had succeeded in getting Lennon's autograph earlier in the evening as John and Yoko Ono left their 25-room home near Central Park. A number of people saw him waiting around the building for several hours. Chapman, who New York police described as a *screwball*, was a printworker in a Honolulu hospital.

A huge crowd of fans, holding lit candles, sang Lennon's 'Give Peace a Chance', which became the favourite song of the peace movement all over the world.

Pop changed forever

John Lennon of the Beatles was, with Elvis Presley and Bob Dylan, one of the three most important pop musicians since the war. The Beatles were formed in 1960. Two years later, their first record, 'Love Me Do' reached number 17 in the Top 20 and their second record, 'Please, Please Me' reached Number 1. The Beatles legend began. Since then, two hundred million Beatles records have been sold. By 1969, the music of the Beatles was world-famous and the four Beatles had become millionaires. John alone was receiving more than £5,000,000 a year from sales of records and songs. In that year, the

group broke up but pop music had been changed forever. John Lennon married Yoko Ono, a
10 Japanese artist. In 1969 John and Yoko moved to New York. John tried making records there without the Beatles. After five years of 'baby-sitting' for his son, Sean, born in 1975, either in their home in the Dakota building or on their farm in the Catskill mountains, John decided to return to the music business. He was coming home from a recording studio when he was shot.

A legend that the whole world will miss

15 Paul McCartney, when told of the death of his friend, said, 'I'm shocked. I really loved that guy and the whole world will miss him.' George Harrison said, 'It's such a waste of life.'

Carol Bellamy, leader of the New York City Council, called for better gun-control. She said 'Killers can buy guns as easily as lollipops.'

Did you follow? 1

1 Say if these statements about the first part of 'Give peace a chance' are what Lennon said (right or wrong).

1 John Lennon was giving a radio interview.
2 He liked New York.
3 He preferred New York restaurants.
4 It was difficult for him to go to a restaurant in London.
5 He could not go to restaurants in New York.
6 People were unfriendly in both London and New York.
7 He was able to walk around New York safely for years.

2 Answer the questions about 'Do you know what you just did?'.

1 Who killed John Lennon?
2 At what time was he killed?
3 Where was he shot?
4 What was the date of his murder?
5 How was he killed?
6 What did the murderer do after the murder?
7 Where did Lennon die?

3 How much information about the killer can you find in 'Gunman a Screwball'? Think of: *name – age – home town – job.*

4 Find out from the text 'Gunman a Screwball'.

1 Where did John Lennon and Yoko Ono live?
2 What did the police think of the murderer?
3 How did many young people react to the news of Lennon's death?

5 Answer the questions about 'Pop changed forever'.

1 Who are described as the most important figures in pop music since 1945? Do you agree?
2 When did the Beatles have their first number 1 hit record?
3 When did the Beatles become rich?
4 Where did Lennon get his money from?
5 When did the Beatles start and when did they finish?
6 What did Lennon do in the year that the Beatles broke up?
7 Did Lennon give up music after the Beatles broke up?
8 What did he do between 1975 and 1980?
9 What did Lennon plan to do in 1980?

Watch your grammar 1

-ing form 3

1 After verbs of perception (Nach Verben der Sinneswahrnehmung)

A number of people **saw** him **waiting** around the building for several hours.

Hier stehen die *participles* nach Verben der Sinneswahrnehmung
feel, hear, listen to, look at, notice, see, watch
mit der Konstruktion Objekt + *-ing* Form, weil der **Ablauf** der Handlung betont wird.

2 Expressions with prepositions + -ing form.

Chapman had succeeded **in getting** Lennon's autograph.

Nach Verben oder Adjektiven, die mit einer Präposition gebildet werden, muß das Verb stets in der *-ing* Form sein.

3 Verbs which take the -ing form or the infinitive

John **tried making** records there without the Beatles.
He **tried to walk** but fell after only five steps.

Wie einige andere Verben auch kann *try* entweder mit der *-ing* Form oder mit dem Infinitiv gebildet werden:

-ING FORM	INFINITIVKONSTRUKTION
Es war möglich, die Handlung als Versuch durchzuführen.	Es war nicht möglich, die Handlung als Versuch durchzuführen.

Andere Verben, denen beide Formen folgen können, die aber dadurch unterschiedliche Bedeutungen haben: *dislike, forget, go on, like, prefer, remember, start, stop.*

Definite and indefinite article
(Bestimmter und unbestimmter Artikel)

Chapman was **a** printworker in a Honolulu hospital.
The cars built in the sixties ...

Im Gegensatz zum Deutschen braucht man bei **Berufsbezeichnungen** im Englischen den unbestimmten Artikel *a* bzw. *an.*
Spricht man über bestimmte Menschengruppen, benötigt man ebenfalls einen Artikel: **the** people in London, **the** farmers in the USA usw.
Spricht man hingegen über Menschen, Landwirte, Autos usw. als Gesamtheit, fällt der Artikel weg: people, farmers, cars usw.

Life in New York ...
Pop music had been changed forever.
Unemployment was rising.

Bei abstrakten Begriffen wie Leben, Tod, Ehrlichkeit, Musik usw. benötigt man einen Artikel nur, wenn man den Begriff näher beschreibt:
The music **of** the Beatles
The death **of** his friend

Get it right 1

1 Verbs of perception

Join the two sentences using the -ing-form.

Example The boy played football.
I saw him.
I saw the boy play**ing** football.

1. Mrs Wilkins talked to her neighbour. I heard her.
2. You were smoking in school. The teacher saw you.
3. My grandparents talked about their school days. My brother and I listened to them for half an hour.
4. Two ships arrived in Dover. I could see them.
5. The water got higher and higher. I felt it.
6. The music was being played in the bedroom. I heard it.
7. The wind was getting colder. I could feel it.
8. A dark figure waited under the trees. A neighbour noticed it.

2 Definite and indefinite article

Which sentences need *a/an, the*?
Which sentences do not need an article?

1. My neighbour is ▭ musician.
2. ▭ farmers always work long hours.
3. Do you believe in ▭ life after ▭ death?
4. I'd like to be ▭ expert on Chuck Berry's music.
5. ▭ life is short.
6. ▭ life of ▭ salesman can be very difficult.
7. Some people find ▭ history interesting.
8. ▭ history of pop music was changed forever.

3 Possessives

Put in the correct possessive.
its – their – his – her – our – your – my

▭[1] sister Linda and I loved listening to stories from ▭[2] grandparents when we were very young. My grandmother always asked, 'What is ▭[3] favourite story? I said, '▭[4] favourite story is about grandfather and ▭[5] first car.' ▭[6] sister said ▭[7] favourite story was about grandmother and ▭[8] visit to Chicago and ▭[9] dangers when she was twenty. My grandfather didn't like telling ▭[10] stories, so ▭[11] wife always told ▭[12] stories for both of them.

4 Expressions + preposition + ing form

Complete the sentences.

Example Do you ever think about ▭? *(buy your own car)*
Do you ever think about **buying** your own car?

1. I often worry about ▭. *(get a good job after college)*
2. My friends agree with ▭. *(work hard on weekdays and have a good time at the weekends)*
3. My parents believe in ▭. *(earn a lot of money while they are still young)*
4. I dream about ▭. *(be rich)*
5. Who knows about ▭? *(programme computers)*
6. I've always wanted to succeed in ▭. *(make friends)*
7. When I see my friends we often talk about ▭. *(go on holiday together)*
8. Why do people look at ▭? *(other people play sport)*

5 Pronouns

Put in the correct pronoun.

Many industries already use a large number of computers. Workers who work with ▭[1] are often pleased that their work has become easier; but what about the factory worker who loses his job, because a computer has replaced ▭[2]? Or the secretary who finds that a computer has replaced ▭[3] and three other secretaries in the office? A modern computer can help ▭[4] in my work and ▭[5] in your work, in other words, ▭[6] can help all of ▭[7]. All, except those workers who have been made unemployed by these wonderful machines. ▭[8] probably have a very different opinion of ▭[9].

6 Tenses

Put in the correct forms of the verbs.

Example Harriet *(be)* an ordinary sort of girl.
Harriet **was** an ordinary sort of girl.

She *(work)*[1] in an office in town. One evening, she *(have to)*[2] work late. She *(be)*[3] alone in the office and the building *(be)*[4] empty. While she *(type)*[5], she suddenly *(feel)*[6] a hand on her arm. Too afraid to look, she *(say)*[7], 'Who *(be)*[8] there?'. After she *(say)*[9] it, the hand *(go away)*[10] and she *(look)*[11] round and *(see)*[12] nobody. She *(not work)*[13] alone in the office since then and she *(say)*[14] she *(never work)*[15] alone again in future.

THE MAN WHO NEVER DIED

I dream'd I saw Joe Hill last night
Alive as you or me.
I says, 'But Joe, you're ten years' dead.'
'I never died,' says he.
'I never died,' says he.

'Joe Hill ain't dead,' he says to me,
'Joe Hill ain't never died.
Where working men are out on strike
Joe Hill is at their side.
Joe Hill is at their side.'

Hard times

Joe Hill was a singer, songwriter and union organizer before the First World War in the U.S.A. His real name was Joel Hägglund and he was born in Sweden in 1879. After he had emigrated to the U.S.A. in 1902, he worked in factories, farms and mines. In 1905, unemployment was rising and wages were falling. Only skilled white workers belonged to the conservative trade unions. 5 The majority of unions were closed to unskilled workers or minorities, such as European immigrants and blacks. These minorities earned, on average, the lowest wages. For that reason, the organizations formed a new industrial union to fight for higher wages for these groups. The IWW – the Industrial Workers of the World – wanted the unionization 10 of all workers – skilled and unskilled – into 'One Big Union'. Some employers used violence to stop their employees joining the IWW and fighting for higher wages. Union meetings were broken up by gangsters paid by the bosses, so being an IWW organizer was dangerous. Many lost their lives. 15

Songs for the workers

In 1910 Joe Hill joined the IWW. He moved from town to town, organizing IWW meetings. Tens of thousands of workers joined. While he was working for the union, Joe Hill wrote many songs. These songs were popular amongst the workers, particularly amongst black and immigrant workers. His music was sung at meetings 20 and at strikes. Joe Hill used well-known tunes with bitter new texts in simple English. They opposed the employers and those workers who supported their bosses.

'Don't mourn, organize!'

In January 1914, after a long strike in the Utah copper mines, he was arrested for murder. Joe Hill denied it. He was sentenced to death in 1915, although there had been no real evidence 25 against him. The sentence caused a huge protest in the U.S.A. and Europe. Even U.S. President Woodrow Wilson called for his release. Joe Hill 30 was shot in November 1915 in Utah. Before he was shot, he said this, 'Don't mourn, organize!' After his death he became a legend in the labour 35 movement; the song about him is still often sung in the English-speaking labour movements, together with many of those songs written 40 for the workers by Joe Hill himself.

Did you follow? 2

1 Answer the questions on 'Hard times'.
1 Where and when was Joe Hill born?
2 What was his name in Sweden?
3 When did he go to the U.S.A.?
4 Where did he work?
5 How does the text describe the U.S.A. in 1905? Say two things.
6 Who belonged to the trade unions?
7 What did the IWW want to do?
8 How did employers react to the IWW?

2 Answer the questions on 'Songs for the workers'.
1 When did Joe Hill become a member of the IWW?
2 Where were union meetings organized?
3 How did Joe Hill help the union?
4 What did the workers think of his music?
5 What sort of music did Joe Hill use for his songs? Why do you think he used that sort of music?
6 He wrote songs with simple texts. Why do you think he used simple English?
7 Were his songs only against the employers?

3 Answer the questions on 'Don't mourn, organize!'
1 Why did Joe Hill's union work stop in 1914?
2 What did the police say he had done?
3 How did people feel about the death sentence?
4 How did Joe Hill die?
5 Did people forget Joe Hill after his death?

4 Prepositions
amongst – for – in – of – on – to (2x)
1 Joe Hill emigrated ▭ the U.S.A. ▭ 1902.
2 Only skilled white workers belonged ▭ the conservative trade unions.
3 Immigrants and blacks earned, ▭ average, lower wages than white Americans.
4 Many organizations formed a new industrial union ▭ all workers.
5 Joe Hill's music was popular ▭ the workers.
6 His songs made fun ▭ those workers who supported their bosses.

5 What do you think 'Don't mourn, organize!' means?

6 Make notes from the text. Write a short lifestory (born, worked, died) of Joe Hill, giving dates and facts about his life.
Why do you think the story of Joe Hill is a legend?

FACT	DATE
born in Sweden ...	1879 ...

Watch your grammar 2

Infinitive construction to show intentions (Infinitivform, um eine Absicht auszudrücken)

Some employers used violence **to stop** their employees joining.

Participle construction to shorten sentences 1 (Satzverkürzung durch Partizipformen 1)

'Joe Hill went from town to town, **organizing** IWW meetings'
oder '**Going** from town to town, Joe Hill organized IWW meetings.'
= 'Joe Hill went from town to town. Joe Hill organized IWW meetings.'

Man kann *participles* in der *-ing* Form benutzen, um zwei Sätze oder Satzteile zusammenzufügen, in denen
1 die handelnde Person gleich ist, und
2 die Handlungen gleichzeitig durchgeführt werden.

Der Satzteil mit der *-ing* Form kann entweder als erster oder als zweiter Satzteil stehen, je nachdem, was man betonen möchte.

Past tenses so far (Bisher behandelte Vergangenheitsformen)

In 1910 Joe Hill **joined** the IWW.

Das **simple past** benutzt man, um einmalige, abgeschlossene Handlungen und Ereignisse zu beschreiben.

While he **was working** for the union, Joe Hill wrote many songs.

Das **past continuous** drückt aus, daß eine Handlung in der Vergangenheit zu einem bestimmten Zeitpunkt **noch im Verlauf war**. Das Ereignis, das diese Handlung unterbrochen hat, wird im **simple past** beschrieben.

After he had emigrated to the USA in 1902, he worked in factories, farms and mines.

Sollen zwei Handlungen beschrieben werden, die in der Vergangenheit aufeinanderfolgten, benutzt man das **past perfect** für die zeitlich vorausgehende, d.h. erste Handlung. Für die zweite, zeitlich spätere Handlung wird das **simple past** verwendet.

This, these, that, those

Before he was shot, he said **this**, 'Don't mourn, organize!'
These songs were popular amongst the workers.
For **that** reason, the organizations formed a new union for all workers.
They opposed **those** workers who supported their bosses.

THIS – THESE (PLURAL)
Verweis auf 1 (einen) nahegelegene/n Gegenstand/Gegenstände; 2 etwas, was erwähnt werden wird.

THAT – THOSE (PLURAL)
Verweis auf 1 (einen) entfernte/n Gegenstand/Gegenstände; 2 etwas, was gerade erwähnt worden ist.

Get it right 2

1 Passive – past, present, present perfect

Put these sentences into the passive. Make the words in **bold** into the subject of the new sentence. If the agent is important, use *by + agent*. If it is not important, leave it out.

Example Gangsters broke up **union meetings**.
Union meetings were broken up by gangsters.

1 Many organizations formed **the IWW** to fight for all workers.
2 Joe Hill wrote **many songs** for the IWW.
3 People sang **his songs** at meetings.
4 The police arrested **Joe Hill** in 1914.
5 The state of Utah killed **Joe Hill** in 1915.
6 People often sing **Joe Hill's songs** today.
7 People have sung **his songs** for seventy years.

2 This, these, that, those

Put in the correct words.

1 I need a video cassette. Have you got one like □ one here?
2 Can I have one of □ cheeseburgers, please?
3 □ is how you switch on the lights.
4 □ are very popular.
5 □ was a difficult test!
6 What's □?

3 Infinitive constructions

Use infinitive constructions to join the two sentences.

Example I am going into town this evening. I want to meet my friends.
I am going into town this evening **to meet** my friends.

1 The farmer drove out to the fields. He wanted to check the sheep.
2 The young man worked hard. He wanted to be a doctor.
3 Susie got a weekend job. She wanted more money.
4 Dan often visited his old aunt. He liked talking about the past.
5 Jim rode his motorbike fast along the mountain road. He was trying to get away from the police.
6 In the sixties, the USA spent a lot of money on NASA. They wanted to put a man on the moon before the Russians.
7 The union was formed before the first world war. It wanted to fight for the lower-paid workers.
8 A friend of mine went to South America for a year. He was interested in looking at the animals there.

4 Participle constructions

Use participle constructions to link the two sentences which have the same subject.

Example I walked along the road. I sang to myself.
I walked along the road, **singing** to myself.

1 Gerry cooked the dinner. He drank sherry all the time.
2 Caitlin did her homework in the living room. She listened to music.
3 Dave lay on his bed. He thought about Saturday evening.
4 Mrs Jenkins told us about the accident. She ate toast and smoked at the same time.
5 Ray walked along the road. He tried to remember the telephone number as he went.
6 Arthur went out the front door. He put his hat on his head as he did so.
7 The doctor listened to the woman. He smiled and looked at her.
8 An old man got on to the plane. He carried a large suitcase.

5 Simple past questions

Find questions to which these sentences are the answers. Ask about the words underlined.

how long – how much – what – when – where – who – why

Example Joe Hill joined the IWW in 1910.
When did Joe Hill join the IWW?

1 Joe Hill emigrated to the USA in 1902.
2 He worked in factories, farms and mines.
3 European immigrants and blacks, earned, on average, the lowest wages.
4 Joe Hill spent several years organizing IWW meetings.
5 Joe Hill wrote many songs for the union.
6 The death sentence caused a huge protest because there had been no real evidence against Joe Hill.
7 President Woodrow Wilson called for his release.

OVER TO YOU

Listening

The Legend of JOE HILL

1

I dream'd I saw Joe Hill last night
Alive as you or me.
I says, 'But Joe, you're ten years' dead.'
'I never died,' says he.
'I never died,' says he.

2

'In Salt Lake, Joe, by God,' says I,
Him standing by my bed,
'They framed you on a murder charge.'*
Says Joe, 'But I ain't* dead.'
Says Joe, 'But I ain't dead.'

3

'The copper bosses* killed you, Joe,
They shot you, Joe,' says I.
'Takes more than guns to kill a man,'
Says Joe, 'I didn't die.'
Says Joe, 'I didn't die.'

4

And standing there as big as life,
And smiling with his eyes,
Joe says, 'What they forgot to kill
Went on to organize.
Went on to organize.'

5

'Joe Hill ain't dead,' he says to me,
'Joe Hill ain't never died.
Where working men are out on strike
Joe Hill is at their side.
Joe Hill is at their side.'

6

'From San Diego up to Maine
In every mine and mill,
Where workers strike and organize,'
Says he, 'You find Joe Hill.'
Says he, 'You find Joe Hill.'

Words by Alfred Hayes

Music by Earl Robinson

* framed you on a murder charge – made you appear a murderer *(jmdn. mit einer fingierten Mordanklage reinlegen)*
* copper bosses – owners of a copper mine *(Kupfermine)*
* ain't – am/are/is/have/has not

1 Listen to and read the song text carefully. Look up any new words in the wordlists at the back of the book.

2 Complete these sentences about Joe Hill:
America – enough – dead – organizing – shot – workers
Joe Hill had been ☐[1] for ten years, but the dreamer saw him in a dream. The dreamer said Joe Hill had been ☐[2], but Joe said he had not died. He said that guns were not ☐[3] to kill him. He said part of him had died, but the other part was still ☐[4]. Joe Hill said he was always where ☐[5] were on strike. He was in all parts of ☐[6], helping the workers.

3 What do think of this song?
– very/really interesting/sad/bad/boring/...
– doesn't mean anything to me/can't understand it/makes me think ...

Writing

What do you know about these legendary figures? Robin Hood, Marilyn Monroe, Florence Nightingale, Elvis Presley, Schinderhannes, Che Guevara?
Either write the main facts about a famous person or a short lifestory of a person who has become a legend.
Or write the story of a group or musician that you like. Say when s/he started, when the first/best record was made, how successful it was, what happened since then, etc. Find *facts* and *dates* as you did with Joe Hill.

Mindfield

Write the missing part of one of these stories.

A young German arrived in the USA at the end of 1913. He could not find a job in New York, so he travelled across the country to Utah and found a job at a copper mine near Salt Lake City. Wages were low and the workers were unhappy. One day, a stranger arrived at the mine. He stood on a box and started to sing. …
… And that was how he met a legend.

Nancy Jones was a good nurse. She was not only qualified but also experienced. She had worked at Saint Andrew's Hospital for five years. Suddenly, she decided to leave the hospital. She wanted something new. She put an advert in the local newspaper – 'Nurse wants interesting new job. Able to travel. Box 3393.'
A few days later, she got an answer. …
… And so Nancy Jones went back to work at Saint Andrew's.

Working with words *Obituary*

John Winston Lennon was born in Liverpool on 9th October 1940. He went to Quarry Bank High School. In 1955 he formed a pop group at school called 'The Quarrymen'. In 1956, Paul McCartney joined the group, whose name was changed to 'The Beatles' in 1960. In 1962 Lennon married his first wife, Cynthia, an art student. The marriage ended in divorce in 1968. They had one son, Julian. In 1969 John was married to Yoko Ono. They had one son, Sean. Lennon leaves £100,000,000.

Finden Sie aus dieser Todesanzeige und aus dem gesamten Text folgende Informationen über John Lennon heraus:
Geburtsort / vollen Namen / Geburtsdatum / Namen der Schule / Datum der Gründung seiner Musikgruppe / Namen der Gruppe / Datum der Namensgebung der 'Beatles' / Beitritt Paul McCartneys in die Gruppe / Daten der ersten/zweiten Ehe / Namen der ersten/zweiten Ehefrau / Anzahl, Namen und Geschlecht der Kinder / Todesdatum und -ort / Vermögen / letzten Wohnort.

Key words and phrases

The difference between this and that

be popular amongst the workers
be arrested, deny
In the nineteenth/twentieth century

form an organization
join an organization

adjectives	nouns	verbs
	emigrant	emigrate
	emigration	
	immigrant	immigrate
	immigration	
alive ▶◀ dead	life ▶◀ death	live ▶◀ die
skilled ▶◀ unskilled	trade union	
conservative	unemployment	

12 Head in the clouds

SPACE FLYING

'British Airways flight 123 is about to leave London for Sydney, Australia. Our flying time will be just sixty-seven minutes. During our flight we shall leave the earth's atmosphere. Fasten your seat belts for take-off.'

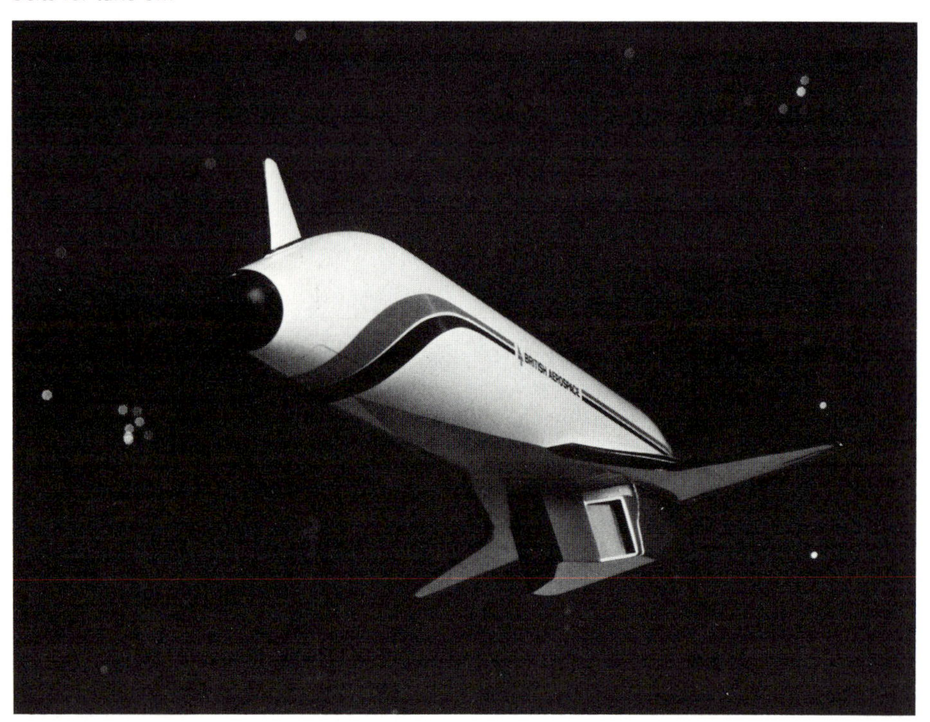

While the captain is talking, the space plane, HOTOL, takes off from the runway at a speed of 335 mph. Two minutes later it is supersonic. After four and a half minutes it is above commercial flight lanes at twelve kilometres. Five minutes later the captain speaks again: 'We are flying at a height of 79,000 feet or twenty-four kilometres. Our speed is 3,250 mph – that's 5,200 kph. You may now smoke.'

HOTOL's engines, which use liquid hydrogen and oxygen fuel, take it to a height of 90 kilometres before it returns to the atmosphere. It glides towards Australia. Just one hour after leaving London, the 70 passengers on flight BA 123 land safely in Sydney.

This may sound like a science fiction story – but it might be reality by the next century. For the Government has asked British Aerospace and the jet-engine manufacturer Rolls-Royce to show that their idea for a space plane called HOTOL is realistic. Their experiments will last two years.

HOTOL stands for **Ho**rizontal **T**ake-**O**ff and **L**anding, which tells us why this space plane could be used commercially. If it were ever built, it would be able to take off and land on the runways at ordinary airports.

However, before you rush to book your ticket, there is a long way to go before commercial travel by HOTOL becomes reality. Technically, there's little doubt it's possible, but the development costs could be as high as £4 billion. Even if enough money were found, HOTOL would have to be tested in space before it carried passengers. But if it passed all these stages successfully, it would certainly be realistic. So one day spending the weekend in Australia might be more than just a daydream.

Did you follow? 1

1 Answer these questions on the text.

1 Which British companies are working on the HOTOL project?
2 What are these companies trying to show in their experiments?
3 How long will these experiments take?
4 When will HOTOL be used commercially?
5 Why could HOTOL be used commercially?
6 What advantage will HOTOL have over other planes?
7 Why will it take such a long time before HOTOL becomes reality?

2 The text gives us lots of technical information about HOTOL. Use the text to make sentences about the following.

Example Number of passengers: **HOTOL can carry 70 passengers.**

1 flight time from London to Sydney
2 speed at take-off
3 height four and a half minutes after take-off
4 speed ten minutes after take-off
5 fuel
6 greatest height during flight

3 Which definition fits which word or phrase?

airport – atmosphere – development – experiment – fuel – glide – runway – seat belt – realistic

1 the planning and making of something new
2 a place where passengers get on and off planes
3 something that is possible and practical
4 a test which gives new information about something
5 fly very smoothly – fly without engines
6 something that keeps you safe in a car or plane
7 the air around the earth
8 what cars, planes etc. need to run
9 what a plane lands on and takes off from

4 Do you think it is a good idea to develop planes like HOTOL? Give reasons for or against it.

5 Would *you* like to go on a trip in HOTOL? Why/Why not?

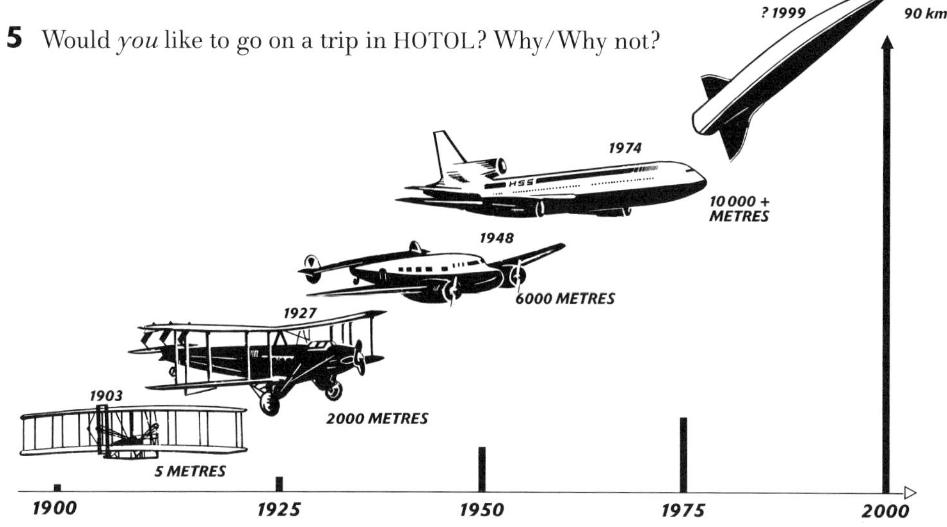

Watch your grammar 1

Conditional 2 if + simple past + would (Bedingungssätze 2)

If we **saved** £500, we **would** buy a car next year.
If I **won** a million pounds, I'**d** stop working.
If I **were** you, I'**d** stay at college.

Mit *if* werden Bedingungssätze gebildet (vgl. S. 76).

If-Sätze vom Typ 2 können zwei Bedeutungen haben: der Bedingungssatz bezieht sich auf die

ZUKUNFT	GEGENWART
Die Handlung ist möglich, aber unwahrscheinlich.	Die beschriebene Situation ist unrealistisch, wenn auch theoretisch möglich.

Das Verb *to be* kann in diesen Konditionalsätzen ausnahmsweise eine besondere (Konjunktiv-)Form – *were* (unveränderlich bei allen Personen) haben.

Im *if*-Satz Typ 2 werden folgende Zeiten verwendet:

HAUPTSATZ	*IF*-NEBENSATZ
would (could, might) + Grundform des Verbs	simple past

May and might

My friend hasn't come; he **might** be/**may** be at the club.
Air fares on HOTOL **may** cost/**might** cost a lot of money.

Wir verwenden **may** und **might**

FÜR ZUKUNFTSBEZOGENE SÄTZE,	FÜR DIE GEGENWART,
wenn etwas geschehen bzw. die darin beschriebene Sachlage sich bewahrheiten könnte.	wenn es sich um denkbare *(may)* oder entfernt mögliche *(might)* augenblickliche Handlungen bzw. Ereignisse handelt.

During/while

During your flight to Australia you will see a good film.
While you are in Australia, you can go sightseeing.

During (Präposition)

Man verwendet *during* in Zusammenhang mit einem Zeitraum: *during your flight, during the experiments.*
During kann man aber nicht als Einleitungswort in einem Nebensatz verwenden.

While (Konjunktion)

Mit *while* leitet man einen Nebensatz mit eigenem Verb ein. In diesem Nebensatz wird die zeitliche Begrenzung einer Handlung festgelegt.

Get it right 1

1 Complete the following sentences.

Example If I were ill …
If I were ill, I would go to the doctor's.

1 If my English were perfect, …
2 If I didn't have to come to school, …
3 If I had a million marks, …
4 If there were space flights to Australia, …
5 If I had my own flat, …
6 If my father were English, …
7 If …, I would stay at home all week.
8 It would make life easier if …
9 We could all go on holiday to the moon if …
10 I would live in the country if …

2 Answer these questions on the HOTOL project.
Sometimes, you won't know the exact answer and will have to give your own ideas. Use *may* and *might* as in the example.

Example **Question** When will space flights to Australia be possible?
Answer They may (might) be possible by the next century.

1 How long will the project development take?
2 How much will it cost?
3 How long will the flight time to Australia be?
4 Will tickets be very expensive?
5 Will there also be flights to other countries?
6 Will HOTOL be in operation before the Americans build a plane like it?
7 Will HOTOL be able to fly to the moon?
8 Do you think HOTOL will be more popular than normal planes?

3 This short text is an advert from a holiday brochure, describing what travellers will do on a holiday in Australia. Fill in the gaps in the text with *during* or *while*.

Example You will see a lot of kangaroos **during** your holiday in Australia.
While you are on holiday, you will do some sightseeing.

> Your holiday begins on the plane. ▭[1] your flight, you can try some of our wonderful food, and ▭[2] you are eating, you can watch one of our films. When you arrive, you are taken to our luxury holiday centre just outside Sydney. There will be plenty to do and see ▭[3] your stay in Australia, so first, we explain our programme ▭[4] you're relaxing with a welcoming drink in the hotel. ▭[5] the first few days of your holiday there will be a sightseeing tour of the city, and lots to do at night. ▭[6] you're busy enjoying the sun and the city, we'll look after everything else. Sounds good? Yes, and we even take care of your children ▭[7] you are out ▭[8] the evenings!

METRIC MIX-UP DOWNS JUMBO JET

A Canadian jumbo jet ran out of fuel at 39,000 feet last week because someone had mixed up imperial and metric measures. Air Canada's 8 p.m. flight 143 from Montreal to Edmonton had already stopped at Ottawa on the first stage of its journey, and had taken off again for the 2,000 mile trip to Edmonton. Passengers were watching a film as they flew over Winnipeg, when suddenly the engines went silent. Then, from the cockpit, the captain told them to fasten their seatbelts. He explained the emergency procedures for a crash landing.

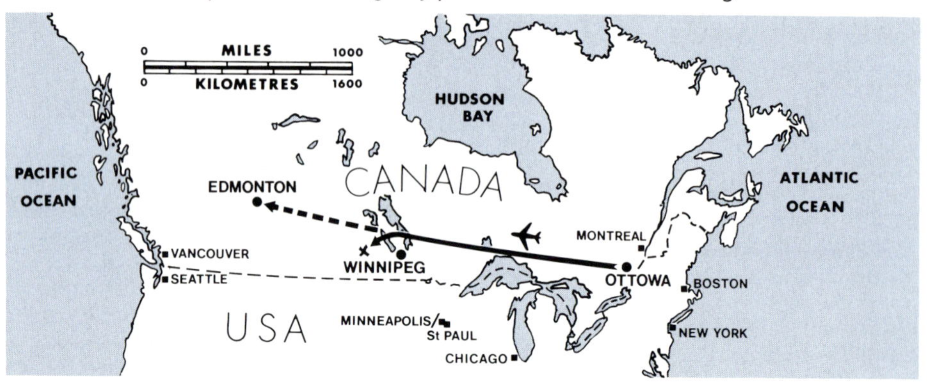

During their 100-mile glide to earth, the cabin crew calmed the passengers, but as the crash landing came nearer, there was a lot of panic. The jumbo came down hard. The captain managed to put the plane down on an old airforce airfield. A wheel came off as he braked hard. The jet stopped only 150 yards from a group of tents where some families were camping.

As passengers quickly left the plane by the emergency chute, car drivers raced to the plane and used their fire extinguishers on its smoking tyres. Luckily, there were only a few minor injuries. The co-pilot had flown to the airfield many times as an airforce pilot. He knew its exact position. And if he had not been a glider pilot, the accident would have been much more serious.

The amount of fuel on board is normally checked by the pilots from an electronic system. Before this flight, however, the system failed. Ground staff told the crew how many fuel units they had put in. The plane should have had 22,300 kilogrammes of fuel (or 49,060 lb) at Montreal. Instead it only had 22,300 lb on board when it left.

The 767 is Air Canada's first plane to use the metric system for fuel. Up to now, the airline has used the imperial system for all its planes. The airline admitted a mistake in changing figures from the imperial to the metric system. It said that in future its planes would only be allowed to fly if all fuel measuring systems were working.

Did you follow? 2

1 Answer these questions on the text.

1. Where was the plane when it ran out of fuel?
2. How far did the plane have to travel without fuel?
3. Where did the plane finally land?
4. What experience did the co-pilot have which helped in the crash landing?
5. What exactly caused the plane to run out of fuel?
6. How was the plane damaged?
7. Why didn't the pilots know how much fuel they had?
8. How does the airline want to stop such mix-ups in the future?

2 Are the following statements right or wrong? Correct the wrong ones.

1. The plane had 22,300 kg of fuel on board.
2. The passengers started shouting when the engines went silent.
3. The pilot managed to land the plane smoothly.
4. Nobody was seriously injured.
5. The plane caught fire and car drivers had to put the fire out.
6. The pilots were told before take-off how much fuel they had on board.
7. The pilots broke the rules because they took off although the fuel measuring system was not working.
8. The airline uses the imperial system to measure fuel on the majority of its planes.

3 Find how these ideas were written in the text.

1. Somebody had used the wrong system of measurements.
2. While the plane was coming slowly down.
3. The pilot was able to land the plane.

4 Complete these sentences with words or phrases from the text.

1. The ▭ helped the captain to land the plane safely.
2. When the fuel ran out the engines became ▭.
3. Because of their training and experience the pilots ▭ to get the plane down in one piece.
4. Later Air Canada ▭ that there had been a mistake about the ▭ of fuel on board.
5. Air Canada said that in ▭ its planes would not be allowed to fly if their fuel measuring systems ▭.

5 Countries like Britain, the USA and Canada still use the imperial system in many areas of life. What do *you* think? Should they go 'completely metric'? Or is it good to be different? What problems or advantages could there be with this system for – industry? – foreign tourists?

Watch your grammar 2

Conditional 3 if + past perfect + would have (Bedingungssätze 3)

If the plane **had had** enough fuel, it **would have reached** Edmonton.
The accident **might have been** much worse if the co-pilot **had not known** about the old airfield.
If I'**d not been** ill, I **could have gone** yesterday.

Mit *if* werden Bedingungssätze gebildet (vergl. S. 77 und S. 123).
If-Sätze vom Typ 3 werden verwendet, wenn wir von einer Handlung in der Vergangenheit reden, die zwar nicht passiert ist, die aber hätte geschehen können.

Im *if*-Satz Typ 3 werden folgende Zeiten verwendet:

IF-NEBENSATZ	HAUPTSATZ
past perfect	would have, could have, might have + Verb

'd ist die Kurzform für sowohl *had* als auch *would*.

Für alle Bedingungssätze (Typ 1-3): der *if*- Nebensatz kann **vor** oder **nach** den Hauptsatz gestellt werden. Wird der *if*-Nebensatz vor den Hauptsatz gestellt, setzt man normalerweise ein Komma zwischen Haupt- und Nebensatz.

Indefinite quantifiers – much, many, a few, a little (Unbestimmte Mengenangaben)

We didn't have **much** difficulty doing these exercises.
Many people are not very keen on flying.
I have **a few** questions to ask.
There's only **a little** time left.

MANY	A FEW	MUCH	A LITTLE
Das Substantiv, auf das sich *many* bezieht, ist **zählbar** *(people, questions, books*, etc.) eine große Anzahl	eine kleine Anzahl	Das Substantiv, auf das sich *much* bezieht, ist **nicht zählbar** (*time, money*, etc.) eine große Menge	eine kleine Menge

Get it right 2

1 Rewrite the following sentences using *if*.

Example The airline made a mistake with their metric measures, so the plane did not have enough fuel.
If the airline **had not made** a mistake with their metric measures, the plane **would have had** enough fuel.

1 The co-pilot had had experience as a glider pilot, so he was able to bring the plane down.
2 The plane did not catch fire, so there weren't any serious injuries.
3 The fuel measuring system was out of order, so the pilots didn't know about the mistake.
4 The co-pilot had been an airforce pilot, so he knew about the old airfield.
5 Passengers kept calm during the crash landing, so they were able to leave the plane very quickly.
6 The plane did not have enough fuel, so it was not able to reach Edmonton.

2 There are lots of ways of travelling – and everyone has their favourite. Compare these means of transport using the adjectives in the list.
Adjectives: *comfortable, dangerous, cheap, popular, expensive, fast, relaxing, safe, big, convenient, good.*

Example *car – train*
I prefer travelling by car, because cars are cheaper than trains/not as expensive as trains.

1 train – plane
2 car – bus
3 coach – train
4 plane – space vehicle
5 ship – plane
6 moped – car
7 bicycle – car
8 motorcycle – car
9 Underground – bus
10 bus – moped

3 Fill in the gaps in the questions and answers with *a few, a little, much* or *many*. After the plane crash, a journalist interviewed one of the pilots.

Example **Journalist** How **many** passengers were on board?
Pilot Only **a few** – 69, I think.

Journalist You ran out of fuel, didn't you? How ☐[1] fuel did you have?
Pilot Well, after we'd left Ottowa we only had ☐[2] fuel left. And then we ran out over Winnipeg.
Journalist And you flew the plane like a glider. Have you had ☐[3] experience as a glider pilot?
Pilot Only ☐[4] , I'm afraid. But my co-pilot was a glider pilot for ☐[5] years, so he didn't have ☐[6] difficulty controlling the plane.
Journalist How did you find the airfield?
Pilot Again, it was my co-pilot. He was in the airforce for ☐[7] years, from 1976 to 1979, so he knew about the airfield. But still, flying a hundred miles without fuel wasn't ☐[8] fun!
Journalist How ☐[9] years have you been a pilot?
Pilot I started with this airline 10 years ago, and I've flown this route ☐[10] times before without any trouble. But this time somebody made a big mistake!

4 Translate into German.

1 My brother has been in hospital since April.
2 He had an accident on his motorbike on his way home. He hit a car.
3 If he had not been late, he would not have ridden so fast.
4 If the road had not been wet, he would have been able to stop in time.
5 His injuries would not have been so bad if he had been wearing a helmet.
6 He will be able to leave hospital in a few weeks if all goes well.

OVER TO YOU

Writing

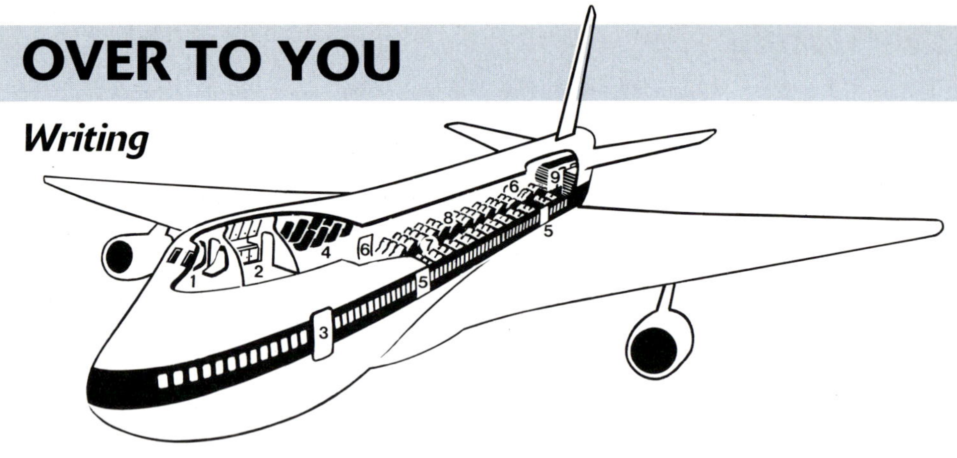

Which words below match which numbers on the picture of the plane?
Do not write in the book! Use a piece of paper!
aisle – cockpit – emergency exits – first class – galley – tourist class – main door – seats-toilet

Listening Welcome aboard

Listen to the tape. You will hear an announcement. Work alone or in groups.

1 Who is speaking? Who is she speaking to? Where is she? What is she doing?

2 What do you think the following items could be?
armrest – audio channel – cabin staff – cruising altitude – fresh air control – reading light – refreshments – oxygen masks

3 Give each part of the tape the best heading.

1 general flight information
2 food and drink
3 emergency instructions general
4 emergency instructions for water
5 smoking
6 seat controls

4 Which parts of the tape couldn't you understand? Do you think you missed any important information? Use your English to ask other pupils or your teacher *generally* or *exactly* what those words or sentences mean which you could not understand.

I don't understand ...
What does ... mean?
What does she mean by ...?
I know what ... means, but what does ... mean?

5 A lot of people are not keen on flying because of the danger – real or imagined. Do you agree that planes are safe enough?
accidents – boats – cars – planes – safety – trains – no smoking rules – trained cabin crew – regular safety checks

When	a car crashes a train crashes a ship sinks a plane crashes	a lot of most many some a few	passengers people	are	injured. killed.

Mindfield

There are some nonsense words in the following text. Can you guess what they should be? Read the whole text before you answer.
'Ladies and togglebigs, welcome aboard this googledrop to Oslo. We shall be striffling at 25,000 feet and our arrival time in Oslo will be 12.15 p.m. During flipjerking, please do not smoke. Smoking is not allowed in the aisles or in the thunderhuts. After flipjerking, our hagglermen will be serving refreshments. The awlrapping in Oslo is fine and the temperature there is 18 degrees. We wish you a pleasant googledrop.'

Working with words

Some of the words in these sentences do not fit or are not in the correct form. Find them and correct them.

1 'The next fly to Rome will taking off at 9 o'clock. Will all passenger for Rome who has not check-in, please go to the check-in now?'
2 London Heathrow is one of the busiest airlines in the world. A plane takes off or crashes every minute.
3 A space plane is technical possible, but it may not be commercial realistic.
4 'Please brake your seatbelts now. Smoke is not allowed during take-off or land.'
5 'The captain will bring you tea or coffee while the flight.'
6 'Our cabin crew will now explain emergency procedures. If there is an emergency, please panic.'

Key words and phrases

The passengers arrive at the airport.
The airline employs a lot of staff.
The ground staff check the plane before the flight.
The amount of fuel on board is checked by an electronic system.
The cabin crew look after the passengers in the air.
The captain flies the plane.

pilot – captain – cockpit
technical – commercial – development – realistic

miles/kilometres per hour – mph/kph
kilogramme/pound – kg/lb

seatbelt – emergency procedures – crash landing – chute

take-off ▶◀ landing
stay calm ▶◀ panic

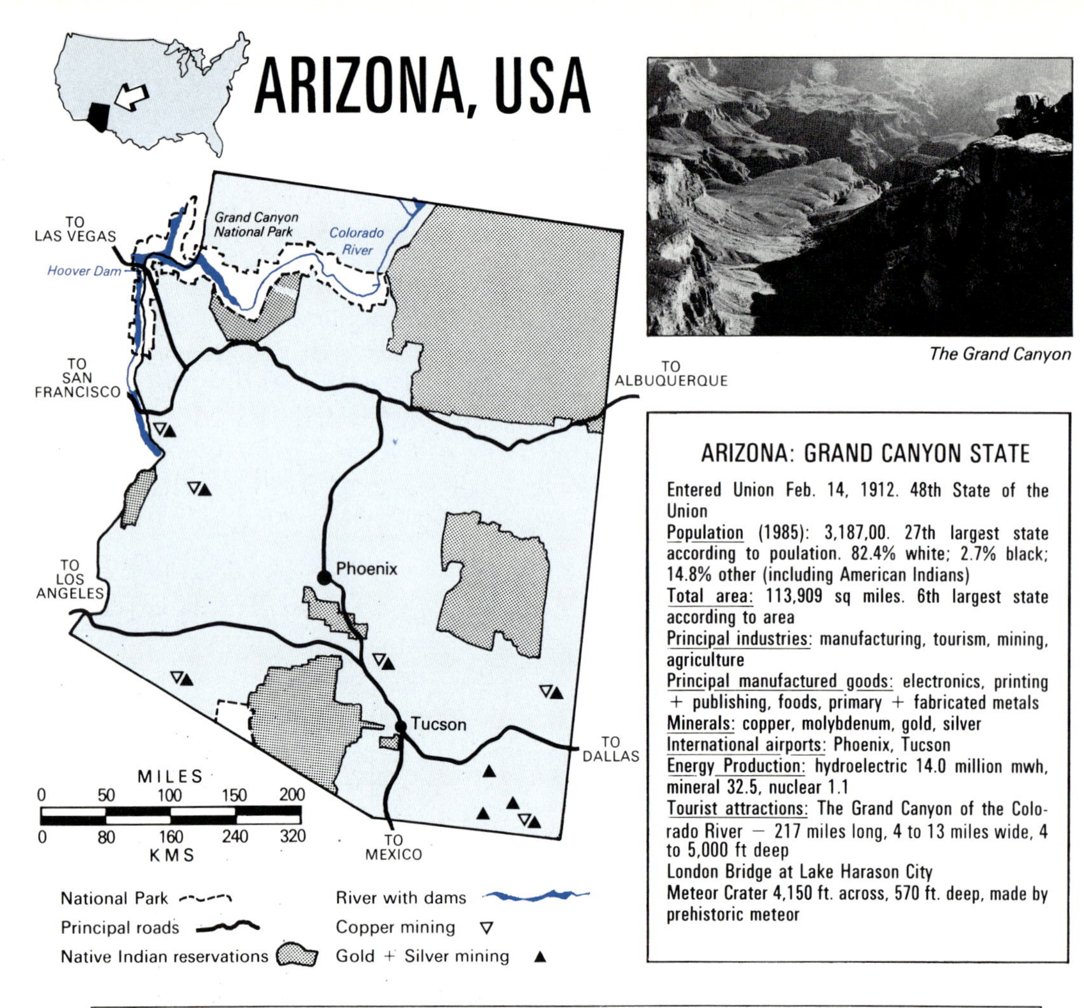

The Grand Canyon

ARIZONA: GRAND CANYON STATE

Entered Union Feb. 14, 1912. 48th State of the Union
Population (1985): 3,187,00. 27th largest state according to poulation. 82.4% white; 2.7% black; 14.8% other (including American Indians)
Total area: 113,909 sq miles. 6th largest state according to area
Principal industries: manufacturing, tourism, mining, agriculture
Principal manufactured goods: electronics, printing + publishing, foods, primary + fabricated metals
Minerals: copper, molybdenum, gold, silver
International airports: Phoenix, Tucson
Energy Production: hydroelectric 14.0 million mwh, mineral 32.5, nuclear 1.1
Tourist attractions: The Grand Canyon of the Colorado River — 217 miles long, 4 to 13 miles wide, 4 to 5,000 ft deep
London Bridge at Lake Harason City
Meteor Crater 4,150 ft. across, 570 ft. deep, made by prehistoric meteor

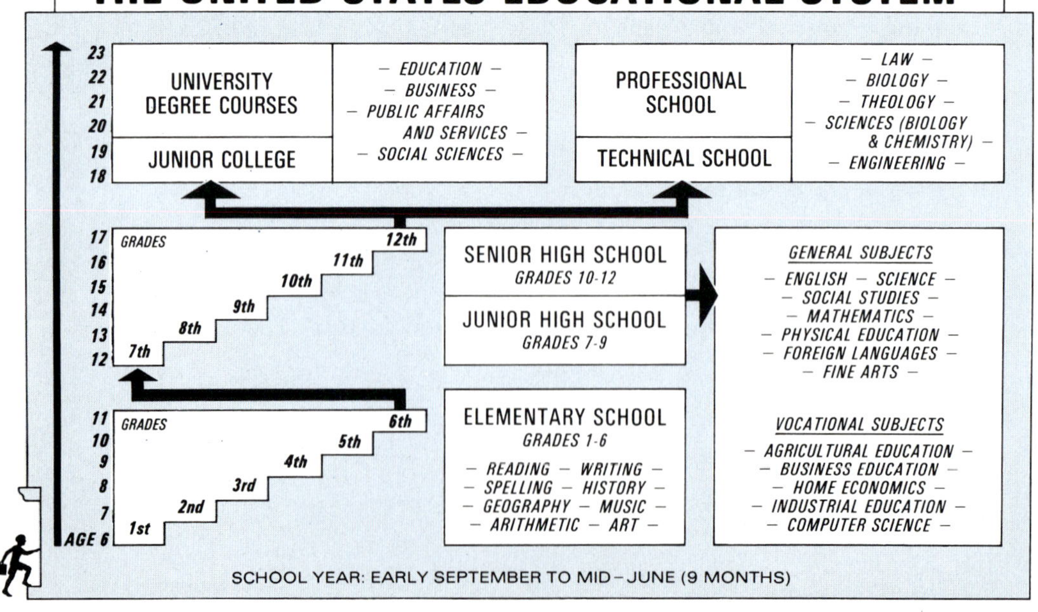

THE CONSTITUTION OF THE UNITED STATES: A SYSTEM OF CHECKS AND BALANCES

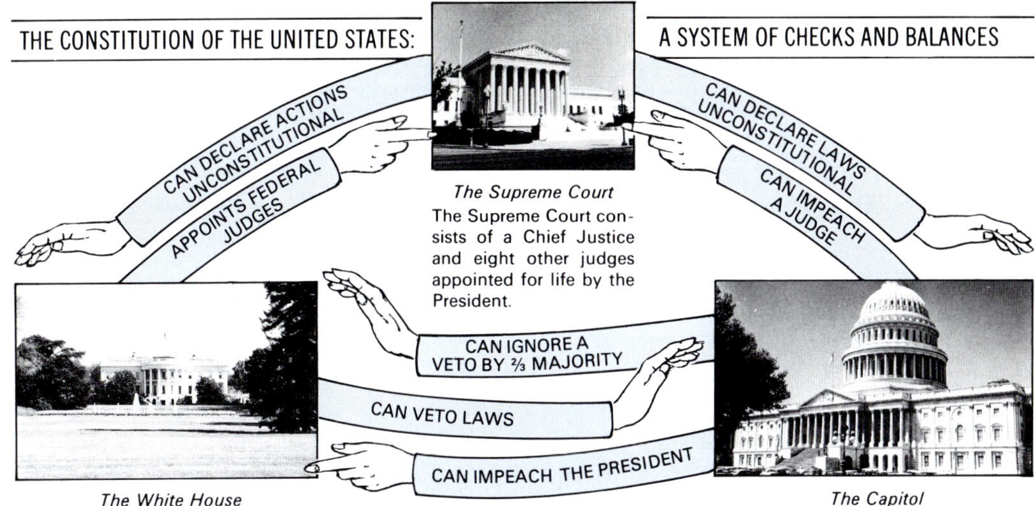

The Supreme Court

The Supreme Court consists of a Chief Justice and eight other judges appointed for life by the President.

The White House

The President is elected for four years by the people.

Each state elects 2 Senators and a number of Representatives according to size. California has 45 Representatives, Florida 19 and Delaware 1.

The Capitol

Congress has two chambers: the House of Representatives elected for 2 years by the people; the Senate elected for 6 years by the people.

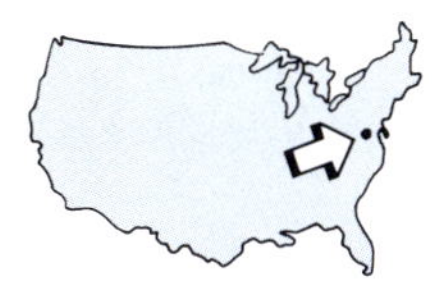

WASHINGTON, D.C.

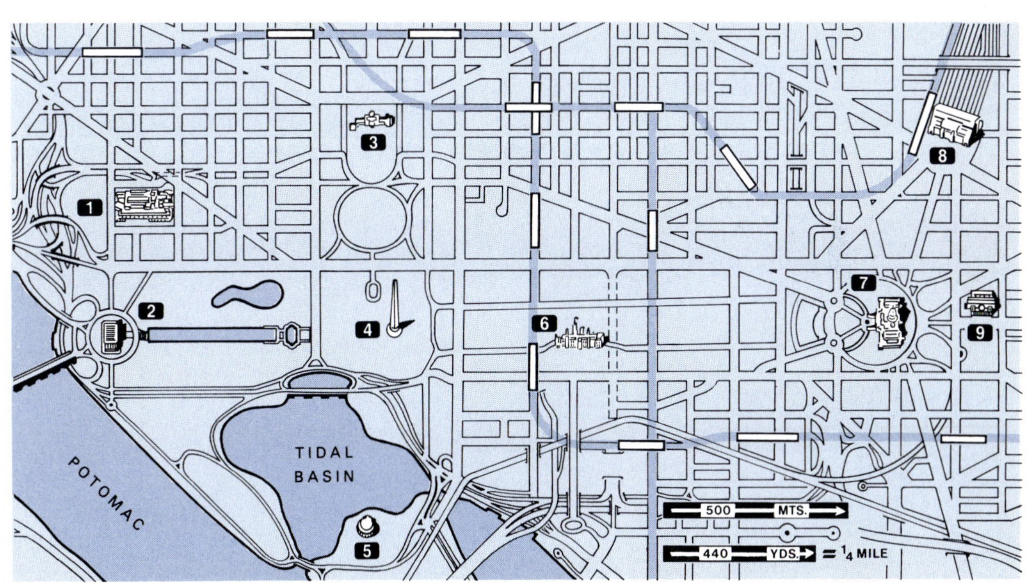

(1) State Department (2) Lincoln Memorial (3) White House (4) Washington Monument (5) Jefferson Memorial (6) Smithsonian Institute (7) The Capitol (8) Union Station (9) Supreme Court

The site for the capital of America was chosen in 1790 by President Washington. On June 10, 1800 the capital was moved from its temporary home in Philadelphia.

Today, Washington has a population of 625,000, 2 airports, a metro system, railway station and local and long distance bus services. There are 8 TV stations and 40 radio stations, 43 hospitals and 6 universities and colleges.

Washington is the home of the Federal Government of the United States. The Federal Government is responsible for:

Armed Forces	Federal Taxation
Foreign Policy	FBI and CIA

Each State, such as Arizona, is responsible for:

Public Health	Education
Police/Highway Patrol	Welfare

13 Downtown and uptown

CENTRAL CITY U.S.A.

Almost 80% of Americans live in the cities and suburbs of the U.S.A. So what happens there is what happens in the country as a whole. Here are two views of the situation in central city areas.

Black days for America's cities

American cities have always had problems like overcrowding, poverty, social conflict and criminal violence. These grew worse after the war, however. One expert, Marshall Kaplan, says that the 5 problems people were concerned about in the '60s and '70s have not gone away. 'The people who were concerned about them have gone away, but the problems have not.' In the U.S., city centers are now seen as the worst places to live. So people move out to the suburbs as soon as they can afford it. They want cleaner air and more privacy, less noise and less automobile traffic.

Businesses have followed people to the suburbs. 10 Fewer people and fewer businesses mean less tax income for the central city areas. They are now often unable to keep up social services because their incomes have decreased while social problems have increased. 15

Not everyone can afford to move out of the central city areas. Another expert states in an article that the people who live in city centers have the most trouble with city life. They have little education, few skills and are the poorest citizens. They are also often the new- 20 comers to a city – since 1945 more and more blacks, Hispanics and Asian immigrants.

Can the problems be solved? Some experts say that this is as difficult as ever. Since 1970 the population of the suburbs of US cities has risen 25 by 20 million, which means less political power for the central cities. That is perhaps one reason why the government in Washington does not seem very interested in helping.

A bright future 30

Neal Peirce, a city expert, says that people from all income groups are returning to the central areas of a large number of American cities. He is optimistic about the future of these areas for six main reasons:

1 The number of people looking for housing has increased and they cannot all go to the suburbs.
2 There are more single people now, who may not prefer life in the suburbs. 35
3 The smaller size of families means that living in apartments is easier.
4 The lifestyles of young people especially have changed. They want good restaurants, theaters, museums, housing with character, etc. – all things not found as often in the suburbs.
5 The rise in gasoline costs, which means that people want to live nearer to work.
6 It is cheaper on average to renovate a building than to put up a new one. 40

Peirce argues that all these and a few other things are signs of new hope for the central cities.

Renovation of housing is taking place in 70 per cent of US city centers. Renovated apartments are usually mixed with new stores and restaurants. So far the renovation of these areas is still
45 a minority trend. If the optimism lasts, however, America's city centers will have a bright future.

Did you follow? 1

1 Answer these questions on the first part of the text.
1 Are the problems in American cities new? Which parts of the text tell you this?
2 What has changed since the 1960s and 1970s?
3 Which parts of American cities do people now prefer to live in?
4 What do they hope to find there?
5 Why do cities now have less money for their social services?
6 What sort of people remain in the central city areas?
7 What newcomers have moved into cities since the war?
8 Is the situation going to change soon according to this part of the text?
9 Why doesn't the government help?

2 Answer these questions about the second part of the text.
1 What sort of people are returning to American cities?
2 What are Neal Peirce's feelings about the situation?
3 What is happening to housing in 70% of American cities?
4 What else happens when housing is renovated?
5 What does the future of American cities depend on?

3 Neal Peirce gives six reasons for his optimism about the future of American cities. Match these statements to the numbers in the text.
1 People without big families do not need a house.
2 New houses cost more to build than renovating old ones.
3 People are looking for things in life that cannot be as easily found out in the suburbs.
4 The suburbs are often too lonely for people who live alone.
5 Travelling in to work from the suburbs, especially by car, is becoming too expensive.
6 With more people looking for somewhere to live, more will choose the city centres.

4 Say what these words and phrases from the text mean in your own words.

1 income	3 newcomer	5 poverty	7 suburb
2 concerned	4 overcrowding	6 social services	

5 Put in the correct word or phrase from the text.
1 Murder is the worst form of ▭.
2 When people have to live together in bad conditions it always leads to ▭.
3 The city council has changed its attitude. Instead of pulling down old houses now, it always tries to ▭ them if possible.
4 I think American cities have a wonderful future. I'm very ▭ about what is happening in them.
5 The movement back into the central areas is one ▭ that gives us all hope.

Watch your grammar 1

Reported speech 1 (Indirekte Rede 1)

1 Statements (Aussagesätze)

'The problems have not gone away.'
Marshall Kaplan **says (that)** the problems have not gone away.
'I'm very optimistic about the future of our cities.'
Neal Peirce **tells everyone (that)** he's optimistic about the future of their cities.

„Die Probleme sind nicht gelöst."
Marshall Kaplan sagt, daß die Probleme nicht gelöst seien.
„Ich sehe die Zukunft unserer Städte als sehr optimistisch an."
Neal Peirce erzählt jedem, daß er die Zukunft ihrer Städte als optimistisch ansehe.

Die indirekte Rede verwendet man, um zu berichten, was jemand gesagt oder geschrieben hat. Wie im Deutschen müssen im Englischen bei der Wiedergabe eines Satzes der direkten Rede in der indirekten Rede eine Reihe von Veränderungen beachtet werden:

1 Man verwendet sehr oft die Verben *say* und *tell*, wobei *tell* immer ein Objekt benötigt, z. B. *tell someone.*
Nach *say* kann *that* eingesetzt werden.
Weitere Verben: *agree, answer, argue, be sure, know, remark, think.*
2 Abweichend vom Deutschen steht **kein** Komma vor der indirekten Rede, z. B. *Neal Peirce tells everyone he's ...*
3 Abweichend vom Englischen wird für die Übersetzung ins Deutsche der Konjunktiv benötigt, z. B. **habe, sei.**
4 Ähnlich wie im Deutschen müssen Personal- und Possessivpronomen der 1. und 2. Person häufig verändert werden, aber nur, wenn es der Sinn des Satzes verlangt.

PERSONALPRONOMEN		POSSESSIVPRONOMEN	
DIREKTE REDE	INDIREKTE REDE	DIREKTE REDE	INDIREKTE REDE
I, you *(sing.)* we, you *(plur.)*	→ he, she → they	my, your *(sing.)* our, your *(plur.)*	→ his, her → their

Steht das einleitende Verb im **simple present, present perfect, will-future**, wird das Tempus der direkten Rede in der indirekten Rede **nicht** verändert.
Das Tempus der direkten Rede kann auch erhalten werden, wenn die Aussage allgemein gültig ist oder noch zutrifft.

2 Modals in reported speech (Modale Hilfsverben in der indirekten Rede)

'We should move to the centre of New York.'
He **says (that) they should** move to the centre of New York.

Die modalen Hilfsverben *would, could, should, might, ought to* werden in der indirekten Rede nicht verändert.

American English (Amerikanisches Englisch)

Amerikanisches Englisch unterscheidet sich vom britischen Englisch vor allem in Aussprache und Wortschatz, daneben in der Rechtschreibung, selten in der Grammatik. Hier einige Beispiele:

BRITISH ENGLISH (BE)			AMERICAN ENGLISH (AE)
	RECHTSCHREIBUNG		
colour, neighbour	*-our*	*-or*	color, neighbor
theatre, centre	*-re*	*-er*	theater, center
telegramme, programme (computer program *auch im BE*)	*-amme*	*-am*	telegram, program
practice, defence	*-ce*	*-se*	practise, defense
(In Einzelfällen weisen Wörterbücher auf die Unterschiede hin.)			
	WORTSCHATZ		
car			auto(mobile)
flat			apartment
petrol			gas(oline)
town/city centre			downtown

Get it right 1

1 Reporting statements

Look at Neal Peirce's six arguments in the second part of 'Central City U.S.A.'. Report what he says. Use verbs like *say*, *think*, *argue* in the simple present.

2 Reported speech

Look at these extracts from the text. What do you think were the words the people used?

1 One expert, Marshall Kaplan, says that the problems people were concerned about in the '60s and '70s have not gone away.
2 Another expert states in an article that the people who live in city centres have the most trouble with city life. They have little education, few skills and are the poorest citizens.
3 Peirce argues that all these and a few other things are signs of new hope for the central cities.

3 Reporting statements

Read these sentences from newspaper articles. How would you report them to someone else?

Example 'Detroit is the most dangerous city in U.S.'
It says here that Detroit is the most dangerous city in the U.S.

1 '83% of city workers go to work by car.'
2 'Los Angeles will be larger than New York by the year 2000.'
3 'Chicago has the best public transport system of any U.S. city.'
4 'The cities in the south and west of the country are growing fastest.'
5 '8.5% of city residents are unemployed. In the suburbs it's only 5.6%.'
6 'There is 16.5% unemployment amongst blacks in city centres.'
7 'Cities are better off than they were before.'
8 'Cities like New York, Boston, Baltimore and Washington D.C. have renovated large parts of their central districts.'

4 If-clauses I

Connect the right sentences together. Use if-clauses.

Example **If the cities receive less income from businesses and residents, they will find it harder to continue their social services.**

1

1 *The cities receive less income from businesses and residents.*
2 More people leave the city centres.
3 Social services in the central city areas get worse and worse.
4 The move to the suburbs goes on.

a Businesses will follow them.
b The cities will get poorer and poorer.
c Nobody will want to return to them.
d *They will find it harder to continue their social services.*

2

1 High-income residents return to the city.
2 The city centre is a better place to live.
3 You want a little colour in your life.
4 The renovation programme continues.

a You'll have to find an apartment downtown.
b The city centre will be a lot more attractive.
c People will move back from the suburbs.
d Services will also improve.

TWIN CITY NEWS

A new study says that the *Twin Cities* of Minneapolis and Saint Paul have eight different types of residential areas or zones. We talked to residents of some of these zones.

Zone One. 'I could live in a better area. I have enough money.' David Ngo Diem opens the door to the yard. The street in the Summit-University district of Saint Paul is a mixture of small single and two-family homes. A block away is an old people's highrise. Some of the houses seem extremely well maintained but others are badly decayed.

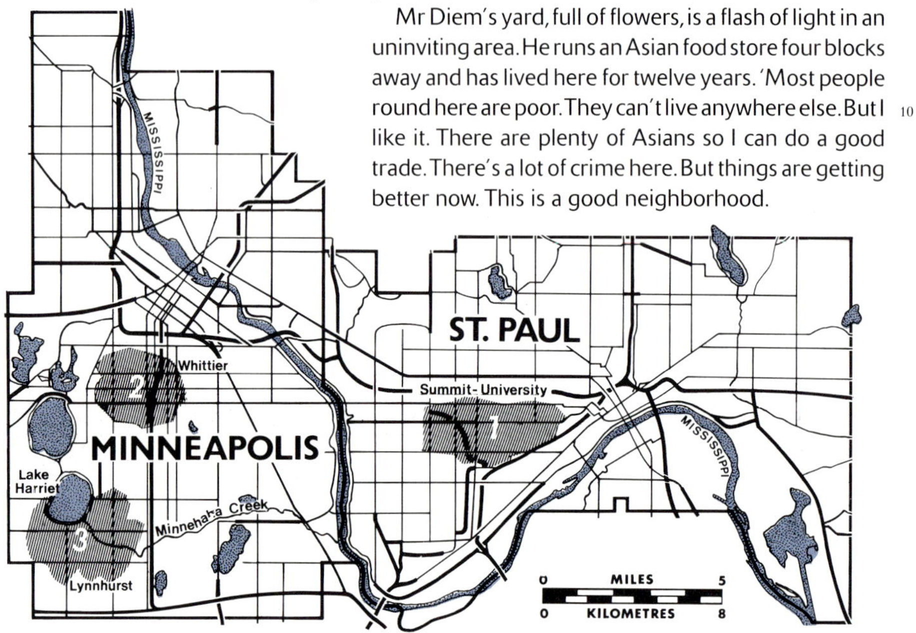

Mr Diem's yard, full of flowers, is a flash of light in an uninviting area. He runs an Asian food store four blocks away and has lived here for twelve years. 'Most people round here are poor. They can't live anywhere else. But I like it. There are plenty of Asians so I can do a good trade. There's a lot of crime here. But things are getting better now. This is a good neighborhood. We have a neighborhood housing group and we're improving things. It's only the multi-family units that are decaying. The owners don't live in them so nobody looks after them. That's a shame. But those people have got no money and nowhere else to go.'

Zone Two. This zone has seen more changes than any other. What used to be a high income area in the 19th century turned into a slum over the years. Now it's turning back again. Molly Vance, who is over 78 now, has lived in Whittier, Minneapolis since 1928. Her small house is in an area that also has some grand old houses from the turn of the century and a few highrise condominiums. Sitting in front of her house, she tells us about the neighborhood.

'I blame the middle classes,' she says. 'They all left in the '50s and '60s. Just went and left the problems behind. Went out to the suburbs. No problems out there. This place was almost a slum. Now they're coming back. You know, they're renovating old houses, buying units in these new condominiums. They want to be closer to downtown. House prices are rising. The old residents can't afford to live here any more. That's a shame. But I guess it's better than a slum. You know, there are restaurants and bars and fancy stores. A lot more life to the place nowadays. I really don't know if it's a good or a bad thing, I really don't.'

Zone Three. The view from the Bergstroms' front room could hardly be better. Lake Harriet shines in the sun. They have lived in the Lynnhurst district of Minneapolis for almost 10 years. Their two children go to school there. Anna's parents also live in the area. 'Their house is on Minnehaha Creek,' she tells us. 'I grew up with water out front. That's why I like it here on the lake.'

The people who live in this zone have no money problems. Almost all own their expensive houses which are close to amenities such as lakes, the Mississippi, parks or hills. There is very little crime in the area and lots of open space. Residents here do not suffer from noise or other environmental problems. In fact, the only problem they do have there is that the area has lost some public elementary schools. 'We're lucky to live here and we definitely wouldn't want it to change.'

Did you follow? 2

1 Answer these questions about zone one.
1 What sort of housing can you find in this district?
2 How can you describe the people who live there?
3 What are the biggest problems the area has?
4 Describe Mr Diem's house.
5 What does he do for a living and how long has he lived in the area?
6 Why does he like living there?
7 What information does he give about housing in the area?

2 Answer these questions about zone two.
1 What has happened to zone two over the years?
2 What is Molly Vance's home like?
3 What information is there about other housing in the area?
4 According to Molly Vance, why did the area start becoming a slum in the '50s and '60s?
5 What does she think about this?
6 Who is now returning to the area and what are they doing there?
7 What results is this return having for the old residents?
8 How else is it changing the area?

3 Answer these questions about zone three.
1 Where do the Bergstroms live?
2 What can they see from their house?
3 What information is given about their children and Anna's parents?
4 What do you know about the housing in the zone and the people who live there?
5 What things give the zone a high quality of life?
6 What is the only problem people have there?

4 In what zones would these people live? Explain why.
1 'The children wanted to live closer to the city. But we preferred this house because of the river. Although it was quite expensive. It's a wonderful view.'
2 'The only good thing about our apartment is that it's close to downtown. It's just falling down. Bit by bit. I work downtown, but the job's terrible. But I can't find another one. No chance at the moment.'
3 'We lived in the suburbs for years. But I hated driving in on the freeway. I work in downtown St. Paul, so we bought this condominium close to the city. I walk to the office in fifteen minutes now.'

5 Why are Minneapolis and Saint Paul called the *Twin Cities*?

6 Find words or phrases from the text which mean:
1 in good condition
2 a house for two families
3 a very high building
4 one part of a street in American cities between two side streets
5 a place or a service useful for people living in a city
6 the people who live in an area
7 an apartment that belongs to the people living in it
8 an area of very bad housing in a city

Watch your grammar 2

Adverbs 3 (Adverbien 3)

1 Adverbs of time and place (Adverbien der Zeit und des Ortes)

They all left **in the '50s and '60s**.
There's a lot of crime **here**.
He has lived **here for twelve years**.

Adverbien der Zeit und des Ortes stehen meistens am Satzende. Im allgemeinen steht **Ort** vor **Zeit**.

In the Twin Cities there are eight residential zones.

Will man die Adverbien besonders betonen, können sie auch am Satzanfang stehen.

She bought her house **in June 1987**.
Before that she lived **in a small apartment in downtown Saint Paul**.

Wenn zwei Adverbien des gleichen Typs zusammentreffen, steht der genauere Ausdruck vor dem weniger genauen.

ADVERBIEN DES ORTES	ADVERBIEN DER ZEIT
anywhere, below, everywhere, far, here, inside, nowhere, outside, somewhere, there	afterwards, already, at once, early, immediately, just, lately, next, now, soon, then, today, tomorrow, tonight, yesterday

2 Adverbs of degree (Adverbien des Grades)

Some of the houses seem **extremely** well maintained but others are **badly** decayed.
We **definitely** wouldn't want it to change.

Gradadverbien verwendet man, um eine Aussage zu verstärken oder abzuschwächen. Sie stehen meist unmittelbar **vor** dem Ausdruck, den sie näher bestimmen.

GRADADVERBIEN
almost, certainly, completely, definitely, even, extremely, fairly, hardly, just, nearly, only, quite, rather, really, so, too, very

American English (Amerikanisches Englisch)

BRITISH ENGLISH *(BE)*	AMERICAN ENGLISH *(AE)*
block *(ein Häuserblock, umgeben von vier Straßen)*	block *(die Häuser entlang einer Straße zwischen zwei Querstraßen)*
detached house semi-detached house *(Doppelhaushälfte)* owner-occupied flat *(Eigentumswohnung)* shop	single-family home/house two-family home/house/duplex *(Zweifamilienhaus)* condominium store

Get it right 2

1 Adverbs of time and place

Put the adverbs and adverbial phrases in brackets into the sentences in the right place.

1. We are going to start renovating the houses. *(in Ruth St. – soon)*
2. Zone one will be smaller. *(in Minneapolis – in ten years' time)*
3. Zone four will be bigger. *(then)*
4. More and more people have moved. *(out of the city – since the 1960s)*
5. The freeways made travelling easier. *(after the war – downtown)*
6. But parking has been a lot harder. *(since then – there)*
7. A lot of people go to their local shopping centres. *(in the suburbs – nowadays)*
8. You can get anything you want. *(all day long – there)*

2 Adverbs of time and place

Use these notes to talk about things happening in Minneapolis.

Example Minnesota Orchestra concert – Orchestra Hall – Saturday evening
There will be a Minnesota Orchestra concert at the Orchestra Hall on Saturday evening.

1. Mississippi River – 9 a.m. Sunday – special boat trip
2. Como Park, St. Paul – flower show – Japanese Garden – weekend
3. Children's Museum, First St. – group tour – Tuesday afternoon
4. Minnesota North Stars game – Met Center – Bloomington – Saturday
5. Opening of the Republic Museum – Airline Drive, Minneapolis – next week
6. Rare books – on show – Meredith Wilson Library – University of Minnesota, Minneapolis – in June.

3 Adverbs of degree

Put in the missing words. Use each adverb only once.

almost – certainly – completely – extremely – just – quite – really – too

Twin Citians ☐[1] talk about the weather a lot. But that's not ☐[2] surprising because it gets ☐[3] cold in winter and, some people say ☐[4] hot in summer. Others say that summer temperatures in the *Twin Cities* are ☐[5] perfect. In the summer there are ☐[6] often tornados in the area but they ☐[7] never hit the downtowns. Although *Twin Citians* love talking about their weather, they never ☐[8] agree about it.

4 If-clauses II

Finish these statements from what you know about Minneapolis and Saint Paul.

Example If my house was/were on a lake, **… it would be in zone three.**

1. If you were poor, …
2. If I lived in zone three, …
3. If more middle class people moved to zone one, …
4. If more houses in Whittier were renovated, …
5. If I had a job in downtown Minneapolis, …
6. If the houses in Lynnhurst were too expensive, …

5 If-clauses III

Use the notes to make statements about the Twin Cities.

Example so many Swedes – not come to Minnesota – Twin Cities – have different character.
If so many Swedes had not come to Minnesota, the Twin Cities would have had a different character.

1. there not be – waterfall – on Mississippi River – Minneapolis – not be built there
2. no water power there – Minneapolis – not become – commercial centre
3. so many Yankees – come to St. Paul – not be called – 'Boston of the West'
4. railway come to Minnesota earlier – the river not be as important for Twin Cities
5. wheat – not be main farm product – Minnesota – Minneapolis – not become – world's largest wheat market
6. not be 16 lakes in area – not be given name Minneapolis

6 Comparison

Use the information from the year 1983 in the table below to compare the twin cities of Minneapolis and Saint Paul.

	M	SP
Population	364,000	269,000
Land area km^2	147	135
Water area km^2	5	8
Drinking water	Mississippi	lakes
Elementary schools	78	73
High schools	35	20
Average family income per year	\$23,178	\$24,058

OVER TO YOU

Listening

ALLENTOWN – Billy Joel

And we're living here in Allentown
And they're closing all the factories down
Out in Bethlehem* they're killing time
Filling out forms
5 Standing in line
Well our fathers fought the Second World War
Spent their weekends on the Jersey Shore
Met our mothers at the USO*
Asked them to dance
10 Danced with them slow
And we're living here in Allentown
But the restlessness was handed down
And it's getting very hard to stay
Well we're waiting here in Allentown
15 For the Pennsylvania we never found
For the promises our teachers gave
If we worked hard
If we behaved
So the graduations hang on the wall
But they never really helped us at all 20
No they never taught us what was real
Iron and coke
Chromium steel
And we're waiting here in Allentown
But they've taken all the coal from the ground 25
And the union people crawled away
Every child had a pretty good shot
To get at least as far as their old man got
But something happened on the way to that place
They threw an American flag in our face 30
Well I'm living here in Allentown
And it's hard to keep a good man down
But I won't be getting up today
And it's getting very hard to stay
And we're living here in Allentown 35

* Bethlehem – town in Pennsylvania, home of Bethlehem Steel Corporation
* USO – United Service Organizations, sort of social club for soldiers and ex-soldiers

1 Listen to the song and read the words at the same time.
Now describe in your own words what the song is about for someone who does not know it. These points may help you:
- who is the song about?
- where is Allentown, what sort of town is it, what is happening to it?
- what does this mean for the people who live there?
- what does the song say about the past?
- what has been the result of the education people received? Why?
- what sort of music is it?
- what else gives the song the atmosphere of Allentown?

2 Look at the following lines in the song and say what you think they mean.
1 lines 27-30 2 lines 32-33 3 line 34

3 What's your opinion of the song? Say what you think about:
- the words
- the music
- the singing

Writing

1 What information would you give to someone coming to live in your area for the first time?
Write down what you think is important to know about the following things. Be careful to make it clear. Remember – it is for someone who knows nothing about the area.
- public transport: inside town/area – to other places
- types of housing
- residential areas
- the weather
- important public facilities

- schools
- entertainment
- sightseeing
- government offices
- shopping
- ...

You could make what you write into a small brochure by using photos, tables, maps, etc.

2 Write a report of about fifty words on what you know about the Twin Cities of Minneapolis/Saint Paul. Here are some words to help you:
business – city centres in the U.S.A. – crime – downtown – entertainment – financial problems – population – residential areas – shopping – suburbs – types of housing – ...

Working with words

1 Put in the missing words:
after – before – for – immediately – lately – now – since – then – when

1. He grew up in the city centre. ▭ he moved out to the suburbs. ▭ he had married he moved back into the city.
2. ▭ she got a job in Boston she had lived all her life in the country.
3. She has been there ▭ ▭ six years.
4. ▭ her arrival she has grown to love big city life.
5. ▭ she arrived she ▭ started looking for an apartment.
6. She has moved to a new apartment ▭.

2 Write clues for this crossword puzzle. Use a piece of paper. (Across 2, 3, 5, 8/ Down 1, 4, 6, 7)

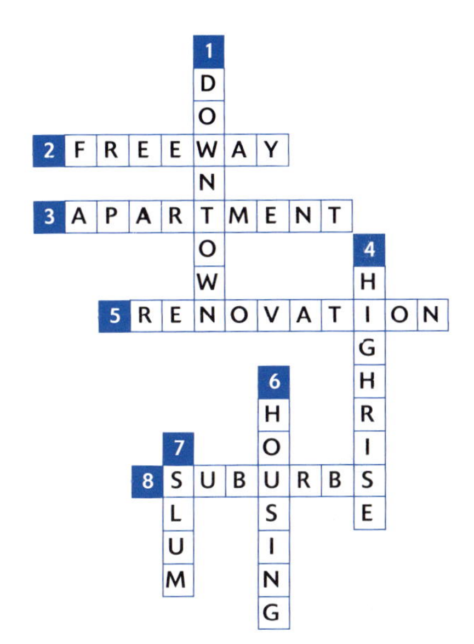

Key words and phrases

crime – criminal
central city area – city centre
downtown *(AE)*
freeway *(AE)*
highrise *(AE)*
overcrowding
renovate – renovation
resident – residential
slum
suburb
zone

That's a shame.
I guess ... *(AE)*
... runs a (food store).

afterwards
so far

extremely
immediately
lately

useful

14 Can you believe it?

IN MY BEAUTIFUL BALLOON

BRANSON'S FAREWELL MESSAGE

DAREDEVIL Richard Branson wrote a last love letter as he faced death in his hot air balloon.

5 He said he grabbed a pen and wrote a love note to his girlfriend Joan.

'In it, I said I loved her and our two children.'

10 The 36-year-old millionaire, whose record-breaking flight across the Atlantic almost ended in disaster, explained: 'I

'I LOVE YOU,' HE WROTE AS BALLOON FELL

left the note in the capsule so that it would be found if I was killed.'

Clothes

But Richard was full of life after four hours of sleep in an Ayrshire hotel.

And before breakfast he was back in the water – in the hotel swimming pool with his children, Holly, five, and Sam, 18 months. 25

Richard had to borrow clothes from hotel guests and staff. Wearing a pair of yellow socks he said: 'It's wonderful to be alive today. I've told Joan that I have given up this sort of adventure. In future my adventures will be carried out at my desk.' 30

Private

Joan said: 'I was watching TV when a message came on. It said the balloon had a major problem. I almost had a heart attack.' 35

But Richard would not answer questions that he might now marry Joan. 40

'I never talk about my private life,' he said.

Yesterday the Guinness Book of Records said Richard would go into the next edition for his balloon flight across the Atlantic. 45

Branson's own hot air to blame

MILLIONAIRE Richard Branson's transatlantic crossing almost ended in disaster yesterday when his hot air balloon fell into the Irish Sea off the coast of Scotland.

5 Mr Branson's own thirst for publicity may have been responsible. There were so many live interviews with radio and television stations that electric power needed to separate the capsule from the balloon may have been too low. Mr Chris Witty, 10 manager of Branson's special projects, said that they knew that power was low but added: 'You can't stop Richard talking to the media.'

Branson will go down in history as pilot of the first transatlantic balloon crossing. He also broke three other records: his balloon was the largest and the 15 fastest and the flight was the longest – 3,000 miles, with the record standing at 913 miles before.

Branson threw himself into the sea when the balloon hit the waves and was picked up by HMS Argonaut. His co-pilot, Per Lindstrand, was found 20 an hour later. Neither was injured.

Mr Branson said that this episode marked the end of his daredevil days. He will now devote his time to business and charity work.

Did you follow? 1

1 Look for the following information about Richard Branson's balloon flight in the two articles. State which article you found the information in. If the information is in neither article, say so.

1 Where the flight started.
2 Where it ended.
3 What it crossed.
4 When it took place.
5 How long the journey was, in distance and in time.
6 Why there was trouble at the end.
7 What Branson did at this point.
8 What happened when the balloon crashed.
9 How Branson was rescued.
10 Who else was in the balloon.

2 What do we learn from these articles about Branson's personal life? Make a list of facts and say which article they come from.
What do the articles call Branson?
Which article is more interested in him as a person?

3 What are Branson's plans for the future?

4 Look at the two headlines. What do they mean? What do they say about the attitude of the articles?

5 Which article is more positive about what Branson did? Give reasons.

6 Which article is more difficult to read? Look at the length of the sentences and the paragraphs. What differences do you notice?

7 What other differences are there between the two articles?

8 If one article comes from a popular newspaper and one from a serious paper, which article comes from which type?

9 What information in the two articles do you find uninteresting or silly?
Say which article gives a better report of what happened. Give reasons.

10 Do you read popular or serious newspapers? Give examples.

11 In your own words, explain what these words and phrases from the text mean.

1 farewell message (text 1, headline)
2 hot air (text 2, headline)
3 record-breaking (text 1, line 11)
4 capsule (text 1, line 14)
5 heart attack (text 1, line 37)
6 transatlantic (text 2, line 1)
7 thirst for publicity (text 2, line 5)
8 media (text 2, line 12)
9 daredevil (text 2, line 23)

Watch your grammar 1

Reported speech 2 (Indirekte Rede 2)

1 With back-shift of tenses (Mit Zeitenverschiebung)

'I **love** you and our two children.'	He **said** he **loved** her and their two children.
„Ich liebe Dich und unsere zwei Kinder.“	*Er sagte, er liebe sie und ihre zwei Kinder.*
'Richard **will** go into the next edition.'	The Guinness Book of Records **said** Richard **would** go into the next edition.
„Richard wird in der nächsten Ausgabe stehen.“	*Das Guinness Buch der Rekorde sagte, Richard werde in der nächsten Ausgabe stehen.*

Wie bereits unter **reported speech 1** (S. 132) aufgeführt, müssen bei der Wiedergabe eines Satzes der direkten Rede in der indirekten Rede Veränderungen beachtet werden.
Steht das einleitende Verb im **simple past**, z. B. *said, remarked, thought, told*, müssen in der indirekten Rede andere Zeiten verwendet werden *(back-shift)*.

DIREKTE REDE		INDIREKTE REDE	
simple present	aren't	weren't	*simple past*
present continuous	is beginning	was beginning	*past continuous*
present perfect	have seen	had seen	*past perfect*
simple past	went	had gone	*past perfect*
past continuous	was watching	had been watching	*past perfect continuous*
going to-future	is going to	was going to	*was/were going to*
will-future	will/'ll	would	*would + infinitive* (ohne *to*)

Folgende modale Hilfsverben verändern sich:

can → could
may → might
shall → should

Vor allem in der informellen Sprache kommt es auch vor, daß ein Verb im **simple past** oder **past continuous** in der indirekten Rede nicht geändert wird.

'I **grabbed** a pen and **wrote** a love note.'	He **said** he **grabbed** a pen and **wrote** a love note.
'The balloon **was falling** fast.'	He **told** us that the balloon **was falling** fast.

2 Adverbs in reported speech (Adverbien in der indirekten Rede)

'It's wonderful to be alive **today**.'	He said it was wonderful to be alive **that day**.
'I am very happy to be **here**.'	He said he was very happy to be **there**.

Ähnlich wie im Deutschen müssen Adverbien des Ortes und der Zeit häufig in der indirekten Rede verändert werden, aber nur, wenn die Sprechsituation es verlangt. Ausschlaggebend ist, **wann** und **wo** jemand über etwas berichtet.

Mögliche Änderungen:

here → there
today → that day
yesterday → the day before
... ago → ... before
last week → the week before/the previous week
tomorrow → the next/following day
next week → the following week/a week later

3 Imperatives in reported speech (Befehle in der indirekten Rede)

Die Befehlsform in der indirekten Rede wird durch einen Infinitiv mit **to/not to** wiedergegeben. Das gilt für alle Zeiten. Zur Einleitung können u.a. folgende Verben verwendet werden: ask, order, tell, die alle ein Objekt brauchen (z.B. order **us**, tell **the men** usw.).

DIREKTE REDE	INDIREKTE REDE
'Speak to the newspapers, Chris.' *'Rede mit den Zeitungen, Chris.'* 'Give me the yellow socks, please.' *'Geben Sie mir die gelben Strümpfe, bitte.'* 'Don't do anything like that again, Richard.' *'Mach so etwas nie wieder, Richard.'*	He ordered Chris to speak to the newspapers. *Er befahl Chris, mit den Zeitungen zu reden.* He asked the guest to give him the yellow socks. *Er bat den Gast, ihm die gelben Strümpfe zu geben.* She told Richard not to do anything like that again. *Sie sagte, Richard solle so etwas nie wieder machen.*

Get it right 1

1 Reported Speech

Find five examples of reported speech in the two articles.
What were the actual words the people used?

2 Reported Speech

Put these quotes from the articles into reported speech. The reporting verb should be in the past simple.

Example 'I left the note in the capsule.' – explain
He explained that he had left the note in the capsule.

1 'It's wonderful to be alive today.' – Richard Branson say
2 'I've given up this sort of adventure' – go on
3 'In future my adventures will be carried out at my desk.' – tell reporters
4 His girlfriend say – 'I was watching TV when a message came on.'
5 'I almost had a heart attack.' – add
6 Mr Branson tell reporters – 'I never talk about my private life.'
7 Chris Witty add – 'You can't stop Richard talking to the media.'

3 Reported speech

You are telling someone about a conversation you heard at school. Report the conversation. Use verbs like *reply*, *answer*, *tell*, etc.

Example **Rick** 'I've just had a maths test and I've probably not passed it. We have another test soon, and I'm really worried'
Jane 'Oh dear – I'll help you with the next one!'
Rick said he'd just had a maths test and he'd probably not passed it. He said he had another test soon and he was really worried. Jane told him that she would help him with the next one.

Rick 'That's very nice of you. I really need some help, because I've not passed any of the tests so far.'
Jane 'I'll bring my maths books round to your house on Saturday so we can look at them together.'
Rick 'But I'm going out on Friday night, so I can't get up early on Saturday morning!'
Jane 'It doesn't matter – we can meet in the afternoon.'
Rick 'I've arranged to go to a football match on Saturday afternoon, and I won't be back until quite late.'
Jane 'Well, there's still time on Sunday ...'
Rick 'I usually sleep late on Sundays, and on Sunday afternoon I'm playing tennis. But I'll have some time on Sunday evening.'
Jane 'I'm sorry, but I've made a date to go to the cinema on Sunday evening.'
Rick 'What! But I need help! You must come on Sunday! The test is on Monday morning!'
Jane 'Well, if you don't go out at the weekend, you'll have lots of time to learn some maths for the test!'

4 Reported speech (imperatives)

Put these sentences into reported speech.

Example 'Be careful,' the old man said to us.
The old man told us to be careful.

1 He said to us: 'Look for a hot air balloon.'
2 'Don't worry about the balloon,' he ordered.
3 'Find the two pilots quickly and rescue them,' he said.
4 'Ask about their injuries,' he told us.
5 'Then return to the airport as quickly as possible,' he said.
6 'Please don't forget to radio for an ambulance,' he said.

Newspaper News

DAILY CIRCULATION FIGURES FOR UK NATIONAL NEWSPAPERS.

1987

Newspaper	Circulation
Sun	3,993,031
Daily Mirror	3,122,773
Daily Mail	1,759,455
Daily Express	1,697,229
Daily Star	1,288,583
Daily Telegraph	1,146,917
Guardian	493,582
Times	442,375
Today	307,256
Independent	292,703
Financial Times	279,762

FAREWELL TO FLEET STREET

Many of the national daily and Sunday newspapers are leaving Fleet Street in the City of London and moving east to new works and offices in the Docklands. This is just one of a series of major changes that is giving a new face to the British newspaper industry.

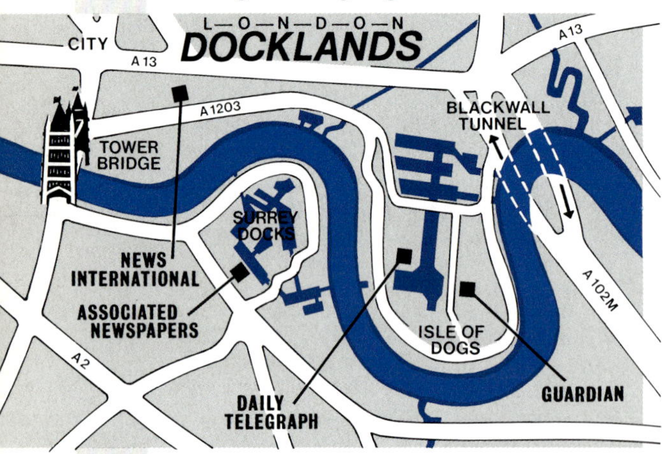

We asked spokesmen from the trade union and from the management side how they saw the future of the industry. One thing they agreed on was that new technology is already having a big effect.

The owners and management claimed that the only hope for the future could be found in one word: computers. Journalists can now type their articles directly into a computer system. In fact, the whole newspaper can now be put together electronically on computer screens. The printworkers who used to set and make up the pages are no longer necessary. If newspapers were to survive, the management spokesman told us, they had to be produced more cheaply. This was possible with the direct input of material into a computer system because one whole work process disappeared. That saved time and money. And that was the only way to save jobs. If new technology was not used, more newspapers would die and more printworkers lose their jobs.

We wanted to know whether the trade unions agreed with this view. Of course, they saw things differently. The direct input system would put many of their members out of a job. Associated Newspapers, for example, had cut jobs from 4,000 to 3,100. Others were doing the same. Management were only interested in it because it would increase profits tremendously. Why should printworkers believe the owners' promises about saving jobs in the industry? Most of the news in their papers was anti-union. New technology would only be acceptable, the trade union spokesman told us, if society controlled it properly. At the moment the benefits of this new technology went only to the owners. It was used for rationalization. Workers just lost their jobs. Until they also had their share of the benefits, new technology would be of no use to them.

Did you follow? 2

1 Use the table of circulation figures and the photograph to answer the following questions.
1 Which sort of papers sell better – serious or popular?
2 Which is the best-selling serious paper?
3 Do any serious papers sell more than any popular papers?
4 Which popular newspaper has the smallest circulation?

2 Answer these questions on *Farewell to Fleet Street.*
1 Does the article tell you why newspapers are moving away from Fleet Street?
2 Where are the newspapers going?
3 What do newspaper owners and trade unions have the same opinion about?

3 Look at these statements. Which spokesman – the one for the management or the one for the trade union – might make which statement?
1 'Computer systems are only being used to increase profits.'
2 'With new technology producing newspapers costs much less – and that is the only way to save jobs.'
3 'Only the use of computers will save the newspaper industry.'
4 'New technology will not save jobs but destroy them.'
5 'Without new technology a lot of newspapers would not be able to stay in business.'
6 'Society is not controlling the use of new technology properly – only the owners of it receive its benefits.'

4 What did journalists use to write their articles on before? How do they do it now?

5 What jobs that printworkers used to do can now be done using computers?

6 Find words in the text which fit these definitions.
1 a type of newspaper with a lot of pictures and large headlines
2 where the words appear when you type into a computer
3 something you put into a computer is called this
4 the general term for ways used to cut the cost of producing goods in industry
5 the people who run a business
6 someone who works making books, magazines or newspapers, but does not write or edit them
7 the good results of something
8 the money that a company earns
9 a general term for new systems or machines for doing things.
10 someone who belongs to an organization
11 someone who is responsible for giving the opinions of an organization

7 Whose opinion do you agree with? The owners or the trade unions? What other reasons can you think of *for* or *against* using new technology in industry?

Watch your grammar 2

Reported speech 3 (Indirekte Rede 3)

1 Indirect questions (Indirekte Fragen)

'How do you see the future of the industry?'	We **asked** them **how they saw** the future of the industry.
'Do the trade unions agree with this view?'	We **wanted to know whether** the trade unions **agreed** with this view.

1 Indirekte Fragen werden oft mit Verben wie *ask*, *want to know* oder *wonder* eingeleitet.
2 Die Verschiebung der Zeiten *(back-shift)* gilt auch für Fragen.
3 In indirekten Fragen bleibt die Wortstellung von Aussagesätzen erhalten (Subjekt – Prädikat – Objekt).
4 Bei Fragen ohne Fragewort *(yes/no questions)*, die man mit *Ja* oder *Nein* beantworten kann, bildet man die indirekte Frage mit *if* oder *whether* (ob).

DIREKTE REDE	INDIREKTE REDE
'Is your father in?'	He **asked** him **if** his father **was** in.

5 Bei Fragen mit den *question words who, when, what, how, how many, where, why* verwendet man auch in der indirekten Rede diese Fragewörter.
Dabei muß besonders auf die Wortstellung geachtet werden.

DIREKTE REDE	INDIREKTE REDE
'Why did the accident happen?' 'What do the police know about the accident?'	I asked **why** the accident **had happened**. I wanted to know **what** the police **knew** about the accident.

Get it right 2

1 Indirect questions – yes/no questions

Mr Swan, a friend of Andrew's father, phones him when he's out. When his father comes back, Andrew tells him about the call. Here are Mr Swan's questions. How did Andrew report them to his father later?

Example **Mr Swan** Is your father in?
Andrew Mr Swan asked **if/whether you were** in.

1 Has he gone to London?
2 Did he leave early?
3 Is he coming back tonight?
4 Did your mother go with him?
5 Is it a business visit?
6 Has he taken the car?
7 Does he usually come back late?
8 Can he ring me back tonight?
9 Will he have any time tomorrow morning?
10 Can he drive me to work tomorrow?

2 Indirect questions – with question words

A journalist interviewed some people about a road accident. When he arrived back at the newspaper office, his boss wanted to know what questions he had asked. Here are the questions the journalist asked. How did he report them to his boss?

Example What happened?
I asked **what had happened**.

1 How many people were in the accident?
2 When did the police arrive?
3 Where are the people who were in the accident?
4 How were they injured?
5 Where do they live?
6 What are their names?
7 How dangerous is the road?
8 How often do accidents happen here?
9 What have the police found out about the accident?
10 Why did the accident happen?

3 Passives – past simple and present perfect

This is the journalist's article. Put in the passive forms which are missing.

PART ONE – ***Past simple***

> Two people *(hurt)*[1] in a car accident which happened at 2 p.m. today on Musgate Road, Highborough. They are Linda Rogers and Jane Markham, of Park Road, Highborough. Two cars *(involve)*[2] in the accident. The driver of the second car, Mr John Ridgeway, *(take)*[3] to hospital, but *(sent)*[4] home after treatment.

PART TWO – ***Present perfect***

> The injured women *(not yet, interview)*[1] by police. Miss Rogers, who was driving the car, *(treat)*[2] for shock, and her friend, Miss Markham, is still unconscious. But the police *(already, tell)*[3] by people who saw the accident that Miss Rogers was driving too fast. The road *(now, clear)*[4] and the two cars *(take)*[5] away.

4 Passives – present simple

Use these notes to say how an article gets into a modern newspaper.

Example subject/article/research/journalist
The subject of the article is researched by a journalist.

1 then/type/into/computer system
2 text/article/show/screen
3 can/then/edit/screen
4 article/can/also/set/computer system
5 page/article/on/show/screen
6 article/insert/into/page

5 Present simple passive

Put the verbs in the following sentences into the passive:

Example English *(speak)* everywhere in the world.
English **is spoken** everywhere in the world.

1 When the weather's hot, we *(send)* home from school.
2 We *(always take)* to school by car.
3 A lot of old people *(look after)* by nurses.
4 Today many newspapers *(make)* by computers.
5 A lot of accidents *(cause)* by bad driving.

6 A questionnaire

A questionnaire asked people these questions about reading newspapers and getting information. How would you have answered? Do not write in the box!

> **1** Do you get your news mainly from
> **a)** newspapers **b)** TV
> **c)** radio **d)** magazines
> **e)** other?
> **2** How often do you read a newspaper?
> **3** What sort of newspaper do you read most often?
> **a)** national daily **b)** regional daily
> **c)** evening paper **d)** weekly paper
> **e)** free paper **f)** none
> **4** How often do you buy a newspaper? Which sort from above?
> **5** Do you subscribe to (abonnieren) a newspaper?
> **6** Do you know the names of any local newspapers?
> **7** Do you read popular or serious newspapers more often?
> **8** Do you prefer newspapers with a lot of photographs or with longer articles?
> **9** When you read a newspaper, which parts do you read?
> national news gossip
> international news women's page
> local news job ads
> sport small ads
> culture/arts cartoons
> TV/showbusiness etc. entertainment
> business news fashion
> **10** Which part of a newspaper do you read first?

Look at your answers. Do they say anything about you as a person? Talk to other people in the class about their answers. Do they use newspapers in the same way as you or are they very different?

OVER TO YOU

Listening

1 Listen to both parts of the tape. What have you heard?

2 Listen to both parts again and answer these questions about what happened.
1 What caught fire?
2 Where and when did it happen?
3 What was the result of the fire?
4 What caused the fire?
5 Why did the firemen get to the fire so late?
6 How many people were injured?

3 Which part of the tape had the information you needed to answer the questions? The first and second for all six questions or sometimes only one?

4 Which part (first or second) did not only give information about the fire but also opinions about what happened? How are the opinions expressed?

5 The two reports of the fire have very different styles. What things give them their style?

6 Which report did you prefer? For what reasons? What sort of radio station or programme do you think the reports came from?

Mindfield

Find the couples who are going out with each other.
Read the descriptions of these six people and decide who is going out with whom. Give reasons for your decision.

Vernon was born in Jamaica and came to England as a boy. Most of his friends are black, too, but he doesn't like the same music as they do. He prefers punk and met his girlfriend at a punk music festival. But his clothes don't go with the music because he loves to wear jackets and ties.

John works in a bank. He's 23 years old and a very good dancer. He spends many hours a week listening to his mother's old dance music. He can't stand modern music and loves cooking Chinese food.

Cindy goes to technical college. She's only seventeen and a bit old-fashioned. She likes her boyfriend to be that way, too. She doesn't like many boys at college because they never wear jackets and ties.

Philip's parents have a Chinese restaurant and he sometimes works there in the evenings. They want him to get married to a nice Chinese girl and stay in the restaurant business, but his girlfriend is English and goes to the same college as he does. He wants to work with computers and knows a lot about them.

Marion has blue and red hair, but not long ago it was black. She always paints her fingernails to go with her hair. She loves dancing. She usually wears black clothes and people always notice her in the street. Her parents come from Hong Kong.

Tania works hard at college because she wants to pass her exams. She's especially interested in maths. She also loves cooking and hates it when her friends just eat hamburgers and fish and chips. On Saturday mornings she goes to the Jamaican supermarket because she thinks Caribbean food is wonderful. She also has lots of black friends.

Working with words

1 Replace the underlined words or phrases with others that mean the same.

1 Newspapers, radio and television have the important job of providing people with information.
2 The part that newspaper reporters play is different to that of those in television.
3 If you work for a paper that comes out every day you often do not have much time to write your stories.
4 Popular papers sell a lot more copies than the serious ones.

2 Put in the missing words.

▭[1] is a big problem for a lot of workers. Their companies use ▭[2] ▭[3] to make their products cheaper. The new machines and systems can work more quickly; they do not need sleep or holidays. So ▭[4] uses them to replace workers. It is especially bad when whole ▭[5] ▭[6] disappear. People who do a special job find that that job no longer exists.

Key words and phrases

newspapers
daily, weekly
regional, national
popular, serious
circulation figures
journalist
print/printing/printworkers
media
publicity
article

management
spokesman
work process
new technology
rationalization
produce

computer system
direct input
display
electronically
screen

go down in history
break a record
add
arrange
survive
benefit
effect
message

clear
major

15 Cleaning up

FRIDAY, 13TH FEBRUARY 1987

AN OILY MESS

On 24th November 1986, the cargo ship 'Kowloon Bridge' ran on to rocks off Cork, Eire. She was carrying a cargo of iron ore, some highly toxic paint and 1,800 tonnes of fuel oil. A recovery firm tried to pull the 160,000 tonne ship off the rocks. They failed and left. Now she is on the seabed and has been there since she sank on 3rd December. Since then, one tonne of oil has been leaking into the sea a day. There is enough oil in the ship to pollute the sea for the next five years. Much of it is coming ashore on the Cork coastline, famous for its wildlife.

Danger to wildlife and people

For the eleven weeks since the accident, local people have not been waiting for others to do something. Patrols have been collecting and washing oiled seabirds; in all they have received reports from fishermen of between 2,000 and 3,000 birds, dead or alive. Patrols have found a number of dead seals on the beaches. The pollution will probably also stop many birds from breeding this year. Heavy metals in the iron ore and the toxic paint could get into the food chain; the Cork breeding ground for herring is internationally important. This accident off the Irish coast could affect food in large parts of Europe.

Why no action?

Since the accident, many people have been asking why the recovery firm didn't make the ship safe; while the ship was still on the rocks it was possible to pump the oil out. Instead, they tried to pull her off the rocks. The reason was, of course, money. If they had succeeded, they would have earned huge profits from the insurance company. But under international law only the ship's insurance company, not governments, can employ a firm to recover a wrecked ship. If the Irish government touches the ship, the insurance company can refuse to pay. For eleven weeks the ship has been waiting for a firm to pump her out.

While the government is waiting for private firms to clean up the mess, huge damage is being done. The sinking of the Kowloon Bridge may have been an accident but commercial interests have made the pollution much worse.

The sea as a rubbish dump

Commercial interests also cause much of the world's oil pollution. Because it costs money to clean a ship's tanks in port, some tanker captains empty oil left in their tanks at sea. Although this is illegal, it is very difficult to catch the ships doing it. We have been using the sea as a rubbish dump since the industrial age began. For years, very few people believed that this could do any serious damage. The world's oceans seemed too large. Nowadays, they are beginning to seem very small indeed.

Did you follow? 1

1 Answer the questions on the first part of the text.
1 When did the 'Kowloon Bridge' hit the rocks?
2 When did the ship sink?
3 What was her cargo?
4 What can you say about the paint on the ship?
5 What happened when they tried to recover the ship?
6 What has been happening since she sank?
7 How long can the problem last?
8 Where is the oil going?

2 Answer the questions on the second part of the text.
1 When was this article written?
2 What have people on the Cork coast been doing since the accident?
3 How many oiled birds have been seen?
4 Have only birds been affected?
5 Is the danger to birds over?
6 What problems are there for people?
7 Is this only an Irish problem?

3 Answer the questions on the third part of the text. Use these words.
private firm – want profits – did not pump out oil tanks – recover the ship – earn money – insurance company
1 When was it possible to stop the oil pollution?
2 What did the recovery firm do? Why?
3 Why hasn't the Irish government recovered the ship?
4 'Commercial interests have made the pollution much worse.' What does this mean?

4 Summarize each of the four sections of the newspaper article in German. Do not try to translate the article word for word. Look for the main facts or ideas in each section.

5 Translate into German.
The pollution will probably stop many birds from breeding this year. Heavy metals in the iron ore and the toxic paint could get into the food chain; the Cork breeding ground for herring is internationally important. This accident off the Irish coast could affect food in large parts of Europe.

6 Find the antonyms in the text for the following:
dangerous – dead – easy – legal – push – succeed

Watch your grammar 1

Present perfect continuous (Verlaufsform des Perfekts)

1 Statements and negatives

Since then, one tonne of oil **has been leaking** into the sea a day.
Patrols **have been collecting** and **washing** oiled seabirds.
Since the accident, local people **have not been waiting** passively.

2 Questions and short answers

Have you **been working** on this patrol long? – Yes, I **have**.
Hasn't John **been staying** at your house? – No, he **hasn't**.

Das **present perfect continuous** bildet man mit *have been/has been* (Perfekt von *to be*) und der *-ing* Form des Verbs.

SUBJEKT	PRÄDIKAT		ERGÄNZUNG
I/You/We/They	have been haven't been	waiting	for a long time.
He/She/It	has been hasn't been		

Mit dem **present perfect continuous** drückt man aus, daß eine Handlung oder ein Vorgang in der Vergangenheit angefangen und bis zu bzw. bis kurz vor dem Zeitpunkt der Äußerung angedauert hat. Oft wird es auch verwendet zum Ausdruck eines Gefühls z. B. Ärger, Freude usw. Dabei wird (im Gegensatz zum **simple present perfect**) auf **das Andauern** eher als auf das Ergebnis der Handlung Nachdruck gelegt.

Ferner drückt man mit dieser Form auch aus, daß – angefangen in der Vergangenheit – eine Einzelhandlung bis zu bzw. bis kurz vor dem Zeitpunkt der Äußerung wiederholt oder andauernd ausgeführt wurde.

Present perfect, simple present and present continuous – Revision (Perfekt und Gegenwart – Wiederholung)

Now she **is** on the seabed and **has been** there since she sank on 3rd December.
While the government **is waiting** for private firms to clean up the mess, huge damage is being done.
The ship **is** still **waiting** for a new recovery firm.

Im Gegensatz zum Deutschen wird nicht die Gegenwart, sondern das **present perfect** verwendet, um zu beschreiben, **wie lange schon** oder **seit wann** ein Zustand anhält.

Present perfect and simple past – Revision (Perfekt und einfache Vergangenheit/Präteritum – Wiederholung)

1 Present perfect

Commercial interests **have made** the pollution much worse.
In all the patrols **have received** reports of 2,000 to 3,000 birds.

Das **present perfect** benutzt man, um über Ereignisse bzw. Handlungen in der Vergangenheit zu reden, deren Wirkung **heute noch** spürbar ist.

2 Simple past

On 24th November 1986, the 'Kowloon Bridge' **ran** on to rocks.

Das **simple past** benutzt man, um über **abgeschlossene** Ereignisse bzw. Handlungen in der Vergangenheit zu sprechen. Deshalb wird es z. B. sehr häufig in Berichten oder Geschichten verwendet.

Wörter wie z. B. *ago, last week/month/year, yesterday, in 1986*, oder überhaupt die Angabe vom Zeitpunkt eines Ereignisses deuten an, daß es sich um abgeschlossene Zeiträume oder Ereignisse handelt. Eine Zeitangabe – außer *since* oder *for* – kann als Signal verstanden werden, daß das **simple past** benutzt werden soll. Folglich darf man mit solchen Ausdrücken das **present perfect** nicht verwenden.

Diese Regeln gelten für alle Formen des **simple past** bzw. des **present perfect**: Sowohl für die einfache wie auch für die Verlaufsform, für das Aktiv wie auch für das Passiv.

Get it right 1

1 Present perfect continuous statements

Put the verbs in brackets into the present perfect continuous tense.

'Are you interested in the old canal? You *(stand)*[1] here looking at it for quite a long time. People *(use)*[2] it as a rubbish dump since it was closed to boats ten years ago. They *(throw)*[3] everything in there: old cans, bottles, bikes, even an old car. And of course, all this time, the canal *(get)*[4] dirtier and dirtier and more and more dangerous. Children like to play on the banks, and they *(fall in)*[5] regularly. But things have started to move. A man *(walk)*[6] around. He *(measure)*[7] things and taking notes. People *(say)*[8] they're going to restore the canal in one of those community projects. I *(live)*[9] here for twenty years now. I can remember all the boats going up and down. We *(hope)*[10] they'd come back one day.'

2 Present perfect continuous and present continuous (revision)

Put the verbs in brackets into the right tense: present perfect continuous or present continuous.

1 Chris *(talk)* to Brian on the phone. They *(talk)* since ten o'clock.
2 What terrible weather. It *(snow)* for a week now.
3 We *(go)* for a picnic in the country today.
4 *(come)* Philip yet? We *(wait)* for ages.
5 The family *(live)* in that house since David was born.
6 Since you *(not do)* anything at the moment, you can come and help me.
7 Paul and Val *(work)* on an environmental project at the weekend. They *(help)* on the project for quite a few months now.
8 The driver of that car *(act)* very badly. He *(try)* to get past me for miles.

3 Simple past or present perfect

Put the verbs in brackets into the right tense.

The population of US city suburbs *(rise)*[1] by 20 million since 1970. The Mitchell family *(live)*[2] in the city center of Philadelphia until 1984. In that year they *(move)*[3] out to a suburb. 'Since 1984 we *(enjoy)*[4] life more,' says Billy Mitchell. 'When we *(live)*[5] in the city centre, we *(be)*[6] always worried about something. Since our move here we *(feel)*[7] more relaxed.' The Mitchells' friends, the Carter family are still in the city center. Mrs Carter says, 'A lot of our friends *(leave)*[8] in the eighties. But a lot of people from the suburbs *(come)*[9] back to the center now. It's more fun here.'

4 Translate these sentences into German.

1 How long have you been going to college?
2 The workers have been cleaning the walls of the college for four weeks.
3 Somebody has been damaging bicycles in the college car park for some time now.
4 Where have you been all morning? I have been looking for you for hours.
5 Have I been boring you?
6 Mandy and Joe haven't been speaking to each other for weeks.
7 Frank has been looking very ill since his accident.
8 He has been smoking too much since he came home.

STOPPING THE ROT

Everywhere you go nowadays, you see the signs of industrial decay or environmental pollution. Nobody can go anywhere in our large industrial cities without noticing this. There is always something to remind you of the problem. Some people think that there is nothing they can do about it. This isn't true. Anybody can help somewhere, and everyone should.

In Birmingham, as in many European cities, traditional heavy industries have been dying out for many years. The result? Well, many parts of Birmingham and other cities are a bit like rubbish dumps. All the cities are trying to clean up such areas. Unfortunately, cities which have lost their main industries can't afford to spend huge amounts of money on stopping the rot.

I visited an unusual project to tackle this problem in Bordesley Green, Birmingham: the Wheels Project. The project is not finished yet, but it has turned 28 acres of wasteland into an adventure park with tracks where young people can do anything on wheels: from roller-skating to racing BMX bikes, go-karts, or motorbikes.

Before the project started, the land was full of toxic waste, dead animals and other rubbish. The rubbish used to catch fire in summer and burned for weeks on end. Now the whole area has been covered in fresh soil and landscaped. The tracks have been laid out and grass, bushes and trees have been planted. They have even made good use of old materials. Some of the banks are built of thousands of old tyres, which have rock plants growing in them. A thousand or more young people use the park every day and BMX clubs and others will be holding international championships there.

This project is just one part of the Community Programme, organized by the people who run YTS. Untrained unemployed young people work with skilled older people on projects to improve the environment. Old or young, skilled or unskilled, they all have one thing in common: they want to do useful work and earn money at the same time. A new UK2000 programme will raise the number of projects so that more cities will be able to start cleaning up.

Carol Innes, 18, who has been working on the Wheels Project for three months, told *Crystal*, 'It's a great idea. It's a way of giving people work and making things more pleasant for everybody. People on projects like this have been making parks, wildlife reserves or even city farms out of waste industrial land. Some of them have been restoring old factory buildings and railways as museums. Then there are the old canals which are unused. There are hardly **any** fish in them nowadays. This Wheels Project is super. This place was just a rubbish dump, but now it's a real playground for

everybody – not just for kids. I have been learning a lot, working with skilled people like gardeners and engineers. The disadvantages? We aren't paid very much – about £67 a week. And I won't be working here next year. We're only allowed to work for one year – then we have to go. After that I'll be looking for another job. I think most of us will go back on the dole. It's a waste! There's still so much to do!' 40

Did you follow? 2

1 Answer the questions on the first part of the text.

1. What did the *Crystal* reporter visit?
2. What effect on the environment has industry had?
3. What kind of land was the Wheels Project built on?
4. Why do you think it is called the 'Wheels Project'?
5. How long can people work on projects like this?
6. What kind of waste materials have been useful at Bordesley Green?
7. What does Carol Innes like about the Wheels Project and what doesn't she like?

2 Community Programme and Voluntary Projects Programme workers clean up the environment in many different ways.

- Which ones are mentioned in the text? Find as many as you can.
- Are people working on projects like these in your area? Say what kind of projects there are already, and what other projects could be started.

3 Look for information in the text and say whether these statements are right or wrong. Correct the wrong ones.

1. The cities do not want to clean up industrial wasteland.
2. Before the Wheels Project was started, people used to go roller-skating on the land.
3. Everybody who joins the Community Programme has been unemployed.
4. All the workers are unskilled.
5. Some old industrial buildings have become museums.
6. There are no fish in the canals nowadays.
7. Bordesley Green is now a popular place.
8. Carol Innes would like to stay with the project longer.

4 What does the government hope to do with programmes like the Community and Voluntary Projects Programmes and UK2000? You can use these words and phrases:
hope to – want to – try to – improve wasteland – employ – unemployed – clean up – factory – canal – rubbish dump – park – playground – museum

Watch your grammar 2

Future continuous (Verlaufsform der Zukunft)

1 Statements and negatives

BMX clubs **will be holding** international championships there. I **won't be working** here next year.

2 Questions and short answers

Will you **be swimming** in the sea next holiday? Yes, I **will**/No, I **won't**.
What time **will** you **be leaving** tomorrow?

Die Verlaufsform der Zukunft bildet man mit *will be (will-***future** von *to be)* und der *-ing* Form des Verbs.

SUBJEKT	PRÄDIKAT		
I/You/We/They He/She/It	will be won't be (will not be)	staying	for a month.

Das **future continuous** benutzt man:
1 um über Pläne und Absichten zu sprechen, die mit ziemlicher Sicherheit in Erfüllung gehen werden;
2 um das Andauern einer zukünftigen Handlung oder eines Vorgangs zu betonen;
3 um auszudrücken, daß etwas als völlig selbstverständlich im natürlichen Laufe der Dinge geschehen bzw. beabsichtigt wird, oder um danach zu fragen;
4 um Absichten und Fragen nach Absichten taktvoller auszudrücken.

Simple present and present continuous – Revision

Simple present

Many parts of Birmingham and other cities **are** a bit like rubbish dumps.
A thousand or more young people **use** the park every day.

Mit dem **simple present** drückt man aus,
- daß etwas allgemein wahr ist.
- oder daß es häufig oder regelmäßig geschieht.

Wörter wie z. B. *want, like, love, hate, think, see, hear* u. a., mit denen man Meinungen, Gefühle und Sinneswahrnehmungen ausdrückt, werden in der Regel nur in der einfachen Form gebraucht.

Present continuous

All the cities **are trying** to clean up such areas.
My sister **is working** for a project to clean up the environment.

Mit dem **present continuous** drückt man aus,
- daß eine Tätigkeit zum Zeitpunkt der Äußerung geschieht.
- daß eine Tätigkeit zwar nicht unbedingt im Moment, aber doch während einer längeren Zeitspanne stattfindet, die die Gegenwart einschließt.

Get it right 2

1 Future continuous statements and negatives

Put the verbs in brackets into the future continuous.

1 Gary and Mike *(work)* on a community project for a year.
2 We *(not visit)* the seaside this year because of the pollution.
3 The countries around the North Sea *(dump)* millions of tons of rubbish there this year.
4 Britain *(clean up)* its old industrial land for many years to come.
5 Don't ring at nine. I *(watch)* my favourite TV programme then.
6 I'm afraid Janet *(not stay)* long this evening. She *(leave)* for Scotland at nine.
7 Come round any time tomorrow. We *(not do)* anything special.
8 Lucky you! At this time tomorrow, you *(lie)* on a beach in sunny Italy.

2 Future continuous questions and statements

An English-speaker might find these questions and statements a little impolite. Use the future continuous to make them more polite.

Examples When *will you pay* me for this work?
When **will you be paying** me for this work?
I *want* that book back tomorrow.
I'll be wanting that book back tomorrow.

1 I'*ll need* the car this evening.
2 When *will you do* that job for me?
3 Gerry *will sleep* in that bed.
4 I'*m taking* that book you're reading with me.
5 When *are you leaving*?
6 You'*ll carry* the rucksack on Saturday.
7 When *will you give* me my money back?
8 *Do you need* the computer this after-noon? I *want* to use it.
9 Pete and Kirstie are coming to dinner tonight. When *will you cook* the food?
10 I'm painting the house at the weekend. You'*ll help* me, won't you?

3 Future continuous and simple present

Put in the right verbs from the list in the right tense.

Example They ☐ dinner when we ☐.
(have – arrive)
They will be having dinner when we arrive.

arrive – cook – cry – do – end – get – land – leave – look – ring – speak – start – use – wait – watch – work

1 What (you) ☐ when the match ☐ ?
2 They ☐ for us when our plane ☐.
3 The audience ☐ when the film ☐.
4 Don't disturb mother. She ☐ dinner if we ☐ now.
5 He's too late. The train ☐ when he ☐ to the station.
6 Who ☐ the computer when the visitors ☐ round?
7 Where (the men) ☐ when the new workers ☐ ?
8 Everybody ☐ TV when the President ☐.

4 Present continuous and simple present (revision)

Use the notes to make answers to these questions and comments. Use the right tense of the verbs: present simple or present continuous.

Example Why are you standing around here?
wait – Mark. always – arrive – late
I'm waiting for Mark. He always arrives late.

1 What's wrong with the North Sea?
many people – believe – slowly – die
2 What's the cause of that?
Britain – European countries – dump – millions of tons – waste – year
3 Where are Andrew and Sarah?
work – old canal
4 The old canal? I didn't think anybody worked there!
Oh, yes. *They – clean up – restore – community project.*
5 What's wrong?
think – I – have – cold
6 Oh you poor thing.
It's okay. often – get – but – never last – long
7 Is it fine outside?
No, it – rain. always – rain – when – want – go – picnic.
8 Why don't you go and sit outside in the sun?
read – book. not like – sit – outside – when – read.

OVER TO YOU

Listening *Years ago . . .*

1 Listen to the tape. While you are listening, try to decide what the right answers to these questions are.

1 What kind of person is talking?
2 What was his job?
3 What is he talking about?
4 How does he feel about it?

2 Listen to the tape again, and write down any differences in the canals past and present.

3 Explain why the speaker feels like he does. Say whether or not you feel the same about a place near you and explain why.

Mindfield

Picture story composition

Tell the story in the pictures. Use past tenses. Do not use direct speech.
Use adjectives and adverbs of place, manner and time to make the story more interesting. Start like this:
Goofy and Snap (or you can use different names) went to the beach for the day.

Working with words

Translate into German.

In our town, we used to be proud of our community. We had a lot of factories and mines. Everybody had a job. But then most of the factories closed and they became wasteland. People used the land as a rubbish dump. Then the council started a new project to clean up the mess. I was unemployed so I applied for a job with the project. Our job was to turn the wasteland into a playground for children and a sports centre for adults; another team's job was to turn one part of the land into a wildlife reserve. Most of us knew nothing about gardening but we had help from skilled landscape gardeners. We will be finishing the project in a few months. We are all very proud of the new playground and the sports centre. The wildlife project finished a few months ago; there are already many kinds of birds breeding there. It all looks great.

Key words and phrases

A lot of people are taking part in a project to restore wasteland.
They are trying to clean up the mess.
They have a lot in common.
They want to be proud of their community.
sea – beach – coastline – wildlife reserve
pollute ▶◀ protect the environment
the advantage ▶◀ disadvantage of doing something

16 Prejudice

BELLEFONTAINE PARK

Linda Archer put the book into her bag. She was too tired to read on the bus. She had had to work on the accounts until ten o'clock this evening and then had to run through the rain, just catching the last bus home. The bus was almost empty. Just one old lady and a young black man, wearing a black jacket and jeans. She had never seen him before. He sat, eyes closed, listening to a cassette on his walkman, concentrating on the music. The bus stopped and the old lady got off. It moved off again 5 noisily. One more stop before Linda had to get off. Outside, the sky was nearly dark. Her house was half a mile from the bus stop. There were two ways of getting home from there. She could either walk through Bellefontaine Park or take the much longer way round the park. On summer evenings, she generally went through the park after work. In the winter she usually went the long way round. She did not mind walking the extra distance round the park. In fact, she enjoyed the 10 exercise.

She had lived alone in her parents' house in Moline Acres ever since her parents died. The neighborhood of St. Louis where she lived was very depressing. Not exactly slums, but there were a lot of problems. There was a lot of violence and vandalism and there seemed to be a mugging almost every day. Earlier this year, there had even been a brutal murder in the park. It was not surprising 15 that people moved in and out of the area all the time. She had lived in the house for ten years and in that time there had been four different families in the house next door. Yesterday, a new family had moved in. She had not seen them yet, but she had heard them playing soul music noisily until the middle of the night. Linda felt so tired that she decided she would cross the park this evening. It was dark already, but she wanted to get home quickly and go to bed early. The bus stopped and she got 20 off. She went through the park gates without looking round. The black teenager got off at the same stop, following her into the park.

The street lights in the park gave a poor yellow light. Linda Archer thought of the murder which had happened in the park in the summer. Someone tried to steal an old woman's purse, beating her savagely and leaving her to die. Nobody saw it happen. The old lady was found dead near the lake 25 next morning. Linda walked quickly with her hands pushed into the pockets of her raincoat and her head held low. It was raining harder now. Suddenly, she turned and looked behind her. Under a street light she saw the dark figure of the young man who had been on the bus. She walked on quickly. 'I must be crazy,' she thought nervously. 'Why did I come this way in the dark? It's unsafe.' The teenager in the black jacket and jeans was nearer now, only twenty yards behind her. Linda 30 increased her speed. She was right in the middle of the park, near the lake. Everything was quiet. 'Only a few more minutes. Faster, and you'll be safe,' she told herself. She was running now.

Finally, she saw the park gates in the distance. She was almost there! Suddenly, her bag fell from her nervous fingers and lay under the street light on the wet road. She went back and as she picked the bag up, she saw the black face of the young man. He was only a few yards away, moving into the 35 light. A voice called to her, 'Hey, wait a minute, miss.' Linda, almost crying with fear, turned and ran towards the gates. Her house was only ten yards away. Another minute and she would be safe. 'Miss!' Her house was dark. She should have left a light on. He would know there was no one home. She reached her garden gate and pushed it open. The teenager stopped at her gate, smiling. 'Sorry, you're Miss Archer, aren't you? I saw you going to work this morning. We've just moved in next 40 door. My mum said I should say hi when I saw you. Hope I didn't scare you.'

Did you follow? 1

1 Answer the questions about the first part of the text (lines 1-11).
1 Where was Linda Archer?
2 What did she try to do there?
3 Why did she stay at the office so late?
4 How did she travel home from work?
5 How many passengers were on the bus?
6 Describe the young man's clothes.
7 What did Linda know about him?
8 What was the advantage of going home through the park?

2 Answer the questions about the second part of the text (lines 12-22).
1 Why did Linda live alone now?
2 What sort of problems and crimes were there in the area?
3 Where did the worst crime that year happen?
4 Did people stay in her area long?
5 How long had she been in her house?
6 How long had her neighbours been in their house?
7 What experience had she had of them?
8 Did she decide to take the long or the short way home?
9 Why do you think she chose that way?
10 Did she go into the park alone?

3 Answer the questions on the third part of the text (lines 23-32).
1 What happened to the old woman in the park?
2 Why didn't anybody help her?
3 What happened to her murderer?
4 Why do you think Linda had her hands in her pockets and her head held low?
5 Who could she see when she looked behind her?
6 How did she feel when she saw the figure?
7 Why did Linda increase her speed?
8 Who was she talking to when she said, 'Faster, and you'll be safe'?

4 Answer the questions on the fourth part of the text (lines 33-41).
1 How did she know that she had nearly crossed the park?
2 Why did she stop and go back?
3 What else did she see in the light?
4 What did the voice ask her to do?
5 What did her house look like when she reached it?
6 Linda was sorry that she had not done something. What hadn't she done?
7 Why was she sorry about that?
8 Where was Linda when the teenager stopped at her gate?
9 Who was the young man?

5 Find synonyms for these words from the text.
Example brutally – **savagely**
1 generally 2 edge 3 quickly 4 call loudly 5 middle 6 unsafe 7 nearly

Find the opposites of the words from the text:
1 edge 2 quickly 3 middle 4 unsafe 5 completely

Watch your grammar 1

Participle construction to shorten sentences 2 (Satzverkürzungen durch Partizipformen 2)

1 Present participle showing simultaneous action (Partizip Präsens zum Ausdruck von Gleichzeitigkeit)

He sat, eyes closed, **listening** to a cassette on his walkman, **concentrating** on the music.	He sat. His eyes were closed. As he sat, he was listening to a cassette on his walkman. As he listened to the cassette, he was concentrating on the music.

In komplexeren Sätzen mit Nebensätzen, in denen das Subjekt gleich ist, können ein oder mehrere Nebensätze mit der *-ing* Form zeigen, daß verschiedene Handlungen gleichzeitig passieren.

2 Present participle showing preceding actions (Partizip Präsens zum Ausdruck von Vorherigkeit)

Someone tried to steal an old woman's purse, **beating** her savagely and **leaving** her to die.	Someone tried to steal an old woman's purse. He beat her savagely and then left her to die.
She stayed until they were finished and then had to run through the rain, just **catching** the last bus home.	She stayed until they were finished. Then she had to run through the rain. Then she just caught the last bus home.

In komplexeren Sätzen mit Nebensätzen, in denen das Subjekt gleich ist, kann ein Nebensatz mit der *-ing* Form das Subjekt ersetzen. Es bedeutet, daß zwei Handlungen nacheinander passiert sind.

3 Past participle to shorten sentences in the passive (Partizip der Vergangenheit zur Verkürzung von Passivsätzen)

He sat, eyes **closed**.	He sat. His eyes were closed.
Linda walked slowly with her hands **pushed** into the pockets of her raincoat and her head held low.	Linda walked slowly. Her hands were pushed into her raincoat. Her head was held low.

Das present participle (*-ing* Form) dient zur Verkürzung von Aktivsätzen, das past participle (*-ed* Form) zur Verkürzung von Passivsätzen.

Get it right 1

1 Full forms instead of participle constructions

Write out these sentences again but do not use the ing-form. Use the correct full tenses and structures.

1. The road running through the middle of the park was wide and straight.
2. He was only a few yards away, moving into the light.
3. Linda, almost crying with fear, turned and ran towards the gates.
4. The teenager stopped at her gate, smiling.

2 Participle constructions

Join the sentences using the ing-form to make them shorter.

1. I saw some children in the park. They were playing football.
2. The teenager sat in the bus. He looked out of the window.
3. The road ran through the trees. It went under a railway bridge.
4. The office work was hard. It tired her and made her unhappy.
5. She could hear the manager and his secretary in the office. They were arguing noisily.
6. Simon ran along the road. He just caught the bus.
7. The old man sat up in bed. He drank his tea.
8. Pat and Jill crossed Europe by car. They stopped in all the capital cities.

3 Adverbs of manner, time and place

Look at 'Bellefontaine Park' again. Make a list of the adverbs or adverbial phrases of

1. place – example: **in the park, home**
2. manner – example: **quickly, alone**
3. time – example: **one evening, at that time**

Find out in which order they appear when they appear in the same part of the sentence. Which sort of adverbs come first, second and third?

4 Paraphrasing

Express the following in your own words. Do not use more than one word from the original sentence. You can make more than one sentence.

1. The bus was almost empty.
2. The bus moved off again noisily.
3. Linda increased her speed.
4. Linda, almost crying with fear, turned and ran towards the gates.
5. We've just moved in next door.

5 Adverbs of manner

Find adverbs of manner for the verbs in these sentences.

1. The college basketball team practises ☐.
2. I thought the book was ☐ criticized in the newspaper.
3. All of my family support the trade unions ☐.
4. Two dogs fought ☐ in the road.
5. Colin always drives home ☐ after a party.
6. People in Germany live more ☐ than ten years ago.
7. I always try to arrive ☐ for interviews.
8. Last Friday, three young men were found guilty of riding their motorcycles ☐.

6 Tenses

Put the verbs in the right tenses.
Say which tenses you used.
'When I *(grow up)*, I *(be)* a fireman,' *(say)* the little boy in the school playground. 'My dad *(be)* a fireman for years and years and he *(think)* it *(be)* a good job for me, if I *(not mind)* getting dirty. I *(see)* my dad working. He *(fight)* a fire in the city centre when I *(see)* him. It *(be)* very exciting!' 'I *(want)* to be a train driver when I *(be)* your age,' I *(say)*. 'But I *(become)* a school teacher instead. I often *(travel)* by train, but I *(be)* a passenger instead.'

7 Tenses

Put in the right tenses. Say which tense you used.
John MacIntosh moved in next door last month. Without his uniform you *(never know)*[1] that John *(be)*[2] a policeman. I *(meet)*[3] him and his wife two days after they *(move in)*[4]. We *(talk)*[5] in their kitchen, when suddenly the telephone *(ring)*[6] and John *(run)*[7] into his bedroom. When he *(come out)*[8], he *(wear)*[9] his uniform. He *(say)*[10] he *(have to)*[11] go to the police station. I *(not be able)*[12] believe my eyes. I *(visit)*[13] them often since then, and I think we *(be)*[14] good friends in future. It *(be)*[15] nice if you *(have)*[16] friendly neighbours.

8 Translation

Translate into German.
Keith knows the coast well. He has lived there since he was thirteen years old. He normally goes out on his boat with friends but for some reason he wanted to go alone this time. He has always enjoyed sailing and does not mind working hard when the wind is strong. I often see him sitting in his boat, eyes closed, enjoying the wind on his face.

'GIRL IN A MILLION'

Gina Underwood is undeniably a girl in a million. At eighteen, she has the improbable job of being Britain's only female cowherd, responsible for a herd of forty dairy cattle. As far as Gina is concerned, it's a fine job for women as well as men.

Q Gina, how did you get the job?

A I've always wanted a job looking after animals although I grew up in a town. I saw an ad for a cowherd in a farming journal and I just applied. Naturally, the farmer was very unsure about me. Apparently, no girl has ever applied for this sort of job before. Anyway, I went for an interview.

Q Were you the only girl?

A There were over thirty applications. I went in for the interview, with lots of other applicants sitting there and looking at me. They were all boys. The interview was very nice and informal. I think the owner thought it was quite amusing. He said he would give me a chance but on a temporary basis. If I was irresponsible or couldn't cope with the work, he said, I'd have to go.

Q Did you experience any prejudice in the interview?

A Well, I was asked if I could cope with the heavy work. I was asked if I could lift the 50 kilo bags of feed. I said I was sure I could. In fact, I'd never tried. Well, when I started work, I had to lift a bag on the first day. It was completely unliftable. Fifty kilos are unbelievably heavy.

Q What did you do?

A I cut the bag open and shovelled half the feed into a wheelbarrow. After I had lightened it, I could lift it. Anyway, the owner laughed when he saw it. I said it was illogical to have such heavy bags. He said he was pleased to see I wasn't helpless. And he said muscles were irrelevant if you had brains. I can do all the other jobs all right.

Q Many farmworkers are overworked and underpaid. What about your pay?

A Financially, the job isn't very good yet. But I'm still a trainee. I go to college twice a week. And I enjoy hard work.

Q What are your plans now?

A I want to manage a dairy when I'm older and have finished my training. I'm taking my college exams this summer.

Q Is what you learn at college helpful in your work?

A Oh, yes, very. I have to know about diseases and hygiene and about special diets to fatten the animals. And learn about keeping the books. That's the disadvantage in being a manageress. Anyway, after I've passed the exams, I think I'll be ready for my own herd.

Gina is pleased that she was given a chance. Other girls who leave school this summer should take a tip from her – if you're asked by an employer if you think you can do a job, be positive! You may be like Gina and become the first girl to do a job which has traditionally always been done by men.

Did you follow? 2

1 Answer the questions on the first part of the text.
1 What does Gina have to do in her job as a cowherd?
2 How many girls have the same job as Gina?
3 How did she find out about the job?
4 Did she have much experience of working on a farm?
5 How many other girls applied for the job which Gina got?
6 Who else was in the building where the interviews took place?
7 What can you say about the other applicants?
8 Under what conditions did the owner give Gina the job?

2 Answer the questions on the second part of the text.
1 What was the owner particularly interested in at the interview?
2 How did Gina cope with the question about the feed bags?
3 What problem did she have on her first day at work?
4 What did Gina do about the problem?
5 What was the owner's reaction to what she did?
6 How does Gina cope generally on the farm?
7 Does Gina agree that she is 'overworked and underpaid'?
8 What does college offer her at the moment? Is that useful to her?

3 What do the following sentences mean? Explain them in your own words.
1 Gina Underwood is undeniably a girl in a million. At eighteen, she has the improbable job of being Britain's only female cowherd.
2 Naturally, the farmer was very unsure about me.
3 If I was irresponsible or couldn't cope with the work, he said I'd have to go.
4 I was asked if I could cope with the heavy work.
5 The bag was completely unliftable.
6 Financially, the job isn't very good yet.
7 I want to manage a dairy when I'm older.

4 Find questions for the underlined words.
Example I grew up <u>in a town</u>.
<u>Where</u> did you grow up?
1 I saw <u>an ad for a cowherd</u> in a farming journal.
2 There were <u>over thirty</u> applications.
3 The interview was <u>very nice and informal</u>.
4 I had to lift <u>a bag</u> on the first day.
5 I go to college <u>twice a week</u>.
6 I'm taking my college exams <u>this summer</u>.

5 Find the words in the text which mean the same as the following sentences/phrases.
1 a person who looks after cows
2 a talk with a possible future boss about a job
3 what cows are sometimes given to eat
4 a magazine for people who work on farms
5 not getting high enough wages
6 an unfair opinion without good reasons

Watch your grammar 2

Prefixes and suffixes (Vor- und Nachsilben)

PREFIXES TO NEGATE	ADJECTIVES	NOUNS	VERBS
dis-	**dis**united	**dis**advantage	**dis**like
un-	**un**liftable **un**clear **un**helpful	**un**rest	**un**dress **un**do
in-	**in**formal	**in**action	–
il-	**il**logical	–	–
im-	**im**probable **im**possible	**im**patience **im**politeness	–
ir-	**ir**responsible **ir**relevant	**ir**regularity **ir**relevance	–

Die häufigste Verneinungsform für Adjektive und Verben ist *un-*.
Bei vielen Wörtern wird die Negativform mit *in-* gebildet.
Der Anfangsbuchstabe des verneinten Wortes beeinflußt die Endung:
il- vor manchen Wörtern, die mit **l-** anfangen;
im- vor manchen Wörtern, die mit **p-**, **b-**, **m-** anfangen;
ir- vor manchen Wörtern, die mit **r-** anfangen.
Ausnahmen: z. B. **un**reliable, **un**reasonable, ...

PREFIX *OVER-*	ADJEKTIVE
... worked ... heated	**over**worked **over**heated

PREFIX *UNDER-*	ADJEKTIVE
... paid ... used	**under**paid **under**used

Die prefixes *over-* und *under-* zeigen an, daß etwas nach Meinung des Sprechers zu sehr oder zu wenig geschieht.

SUFFIX *-ABLE, -ABLY*	ADJECTIVES	ADVERBS
lift ... like ... rely ...	lift**able** like**able** reli**able**	– – reli**ably**

-able zeigt an, daß es möglich ist, dieses zu tun.
-ably ist die adverbiale Form von *-able*

Bei Wörtern mit auslautendem -y wird -y zu -i (*deny* – *den***iable**).

SUFFIX *-EE*	NOUNS
train ... employ ...	trainee employee

Die Person, mit der etwas passiert (ist).

SUFFIX *-ER, -OR*	NOUNS
train ... employ ... act ...	trainer employer actor

Die Person, die eine Handlung durchführt.

SUFFIX *-ESS*	NOUNS
manager actor waiter	manageress actress waitress

Die weibliche Form von Substantiven auf *-er*, *-or* läßt sich nicht mit beliebigen Substantiven kombinieren. Sie beschränkt sich auf einige wenige Berufsbezeichnungen (siehe links). Sie wird zunehmend durch die Form *-person* (z. B. *spokesperson*, *chairperson*) ersetzt, die für die männliche **und** weibliche Form steht.

SUFFIX *-EN*	VERBS
light ... short ... wide ... length ... fat ...	lighten shorten widen lengthen fatten

So werden oder etwas so machen, z. B. *to lighten = to make lighter.*

SUFFIX *-LESS*	ADJECTIVES
help ... weight ... sense ... cash ...	helpless weightless senseless cashless shopping

Ohne die betreffende Eigenschaft.

PREFIX *UN-*	ADJECTIVE OR VERB	SUFFIX *-ABLY, -ABLE*
... deny ... ... lift ...	undeni ... unlift ...	undeniably unliftable

Prefixes und suffixes können kombiniert werden, z. B.
un- ... -able zeigt an, daß es unmöglich ist, dieses zu tun.

Get it right 2

1 Opposites

Find the opposites of the words in brackets.

1 The cows are *(underfed)* and the milk is *(overpriced)*.
2 When I was *(older)* I earned *(more)* money.
3 I'm looking for a *(permanent)* job which isn't too *(interesting)*.
4 My firm *(sends)* *(a lot of)* letters.
5 We *(buy)* *(few)* products *(in this country)*.
6 I *(finish)* my training soon.

2 Negatives

Find the negative forms of the words in brackets.

1 The job they gave me was *(possible)*.
2 Their ideas are completely *(logical)*.
3 The boss is always very *(formal)*.
4 But when you have a problem, the secretaries are really *(helpful)*.
5 I think it is *(relevant)* if you are a boy or girl.
6 Our products are *(saleable)* because they are so *(reliable)*.

3 Synonyms

Find words in the text which have the same meaning as the words in brackets.

1 Sometimes it isn't a *(bad thing)* being a girl.
2 I'm still *(being trained)*.
3 I haven't *(qualified)* yet.
4 I decided to *(make the bag lighter)*.
5 The boss thought the idea was *(funny)*.
6 The farm is quite *(a relaxed)* place.

4 Prefixes and suffixes

Replace the words in brackets with one word using suffixes or prefixes.

1 The box was so heavy it was *(impossible to lift)*.
2 The story he told was *(impossible to be denied)*.
3 One of the manager's jobs is *(to make)* the cows *(fatter)*.
4 I told her she was *(not helping much at all)*.
5 Very often *(people who are being trained)* are completely *(not able to help themselves)*.
6 As far as time is concerned we are *(not able to be beaten)*.

OVER TO YOU

Use your head

Look carefully at the four pictures. Choose the two pictures that you like best. Use your imagination and talk (or write) about these pictures. Who are the people? Where are they? What has just happened? Why? What is going to happen next?
Compare your results. Who has got the most original answer?

Speaking or writing

Tell the story of Linda Archer for somebody who does not know it. Include some information about the following:
who she was – where she lived – how she lived – where she was going – what happened in the park – what she thought was going to happen – what really happened
Say if you liked or disliked the story. Say why. Say if you think other people should read it or should not read it.

Mindfield

Either

Write your own ending for the story about Linda Archer. Start from 'He was only a few yards away, moving into the light.' (line 36)
Write a minimum of 5 sentences.
Compare your results. Who has written the best ending?

Or

Both texts 'Bellefontaine Park' and 'A girl in a million' are about prejudice. Explain what kind of prejudice Linda Archer shows and Gina Underwood experienced. Do you think Linda Archer could learn anything from her experience in the park? Do you think employers could learn anything from Gina's way of coping with the heavy feed bags? Write what you think.

Key words and phrases

She applied for a job; a job application; an applicant for a job.
She's working here on a temporary/permanent basis.
She has to do the accounts.
She can cope with the work/with the problems.
Most people say they are overworked and underpaid.
Is your boss prejudiced against women?
As far as I'm concerned, she's OK.
I'm on a diet; a healthy diet.

amusing, exciting, interesting, boring
brains and muscles
muggings, vandalism and other crimes

logical ▶◀ illogical
helpful ▶◀ unhelpful/helpless
responsible ▶◀ irresponsible

READING TEXTS

1 AN ENGLISH-SPEAKING WORLD

An old dream is becoming a reality. There is now one language which is used at least once a day by a thousand million people. It is used in half of all telephone conversations in the world and three-quarters of all telexes, telegrammes and letters are written in it. Pilots who take off or land in over 150 countries use it and half of the world's 10,000 newspapers are written in it.

The language itself is a mixture of old German, old French, Latin, Greek and old Norse, the language of the Vikings. Its grammar is simple, its vocabulary is much larger than that of French or German and its spelling is often strange. It is the language of computers, space travel, pop music and the cinema; it links people across borders and continents. Its name, of course, is English.

Outside Britain and the North American continent with over 300 million native speakers, English is spoken in every continent. In countries which have many local languages, English is a neutral language. For example, it is an important link language for India and many African and Asian countries. English is taught in schools in sixteen African countries; at least 200 million Africans speak a form of English. Today there are over 750 million people in India; of these, about 70 million can read, write and speak English well.

In the Philippines and the Caribbean, in Indonesia and Egypt you will find millions of people using English. There are English-language newspapers in Iran, Japan, Greece, Egypt, Israel, Argentina and France.

All over the world, English is mixed with hundreds of different local languages. So what do people mean by 'English'? Normally, people speak of 'BBC English' or the 'Queen's English'. Actually, only about 10 % of Britain's population speak the 'Queen's English'. The others speak English with regional accents but they will all *understand* the 'Queen's English' whether they speak it themselves or not. In fact, this kind of English, or 'General American', are the types of English which people all over the world understand best when they are speaking English. Speaking and reading English does not mean losing your own language and your own culture; it is a way of talking to the world and getting the best out of it.

Exercises

1 Answer these questions about the text.

1 How many people speak English every day?
2 In which four written forms of communication is English often used?
3 Of how many languages is English a mixture?
4 Are there more words in German or English?
5 In which hi-tech areas is English used?
6 Why is English called a 'world language'?
7 What is a 'link language'?
8 How many millions of the 50 million people in Britain speak the 'Queen's English'?
9 How many people in Britain can understand someone who is speaking the 'Queen's English'?

2 Find the adjective.

1 reality (line 1)
2 use (line 7)
3 culture (line 49)

3 Put in the correct preposition.

1 If you want to get the best ☐ a culture, you must learn its language properly.
2 Many people in Britain speak ☐ a regional accent.
3 English can help people communicate ☐ borders.
4 English is used ☐ a billion people every day.

4 Rewrite in your own words. Start like this: *If you …*
Speaking and reading English does not mean losing your own language and your own culture.

5 Find questions for the underlined parts of the sentences.

1 Its grammar is simple.
2 It links people across continents.
3 Three-quarters of all the world's letters are written in it.
4 There are English-language newspapers in Egypt, Argentina and France.
5 English is spoken in every continent.

6 Join the two sentences using a relative pronoun.

1 English is spoken in every continent. Its grammar is simple.
2 India has 70 million English speakers. India has a population of 750 million.
3 English is a mixture of several languages. It is spoken by a thousand million people.

2 WHERE TIME HAS STOOD STILL

There is something different about Lancaster County, Pennsylvania. For 'back-to-nature' lovers it's like a dreamland. The people wear the traditional clothes of 18th Century farmers from South Germany. They drive horse-drawn buggies, not cars, and speak 'Pennsylvania Dutch', an old German dialect they brought with them from Europe – almost three hundred years ago.

The Amish People have changed their way of life as little as possible since they fled to North America. About 90,000 of them live and work in the U.S.A. and Canada in their own small communities. They have no electric lighting, no television or radio, and if a telephone is necessary it must be outside, as far away from the house as possible.

Most Amish People are craftsmen or farmers. While farmers in the U.S.A. have had hard times recently, the Amish have not suffered, although they work their land without electricity or tractors. They are known as the best farmers in America. They have no problems with low market prices because most of what they produce is for their own community. And they needn't worry about rising wages because all their farms are family businesses in which every member of the family works.

The Amish believe that they should have as little contact as possible with the 'English' world, as they call it. Modern technology is a part of that 'English' world, which explains why the Amish get along without it. Their religion controls all areas of life and in the Amish religion it is important to be 'plain'. For example, churches are not 'plain' so the community meets for its religious services in a different house every second Sunday. It's the same with education, so the Amish only learn reading, writing and arithmetic. Apart from songbooks and the Bible they have no books.

For about 20% of the Amish People the way of life of their religious communities becomes too narrow and they leave. Others are thrown out of the community if they break the rules. But there is always a way back for those who wish to take it.

In Florida there is an Amish community where young people can be away from their families for a while. They earn their living by working in the 'English' world. Most of them go back. And although many do leave for ever, the Amish communities are still growing in size.

Exercises

1 Answer these questions on the text.

1 Find six things that make the Amish very different to other Americans.
2 How many Amish people are there and where do they live?
3 When did they first come to America and where from?
4 Give two reasons why Amish farmers have fewer problems than other farmers in the U.S.
5 Why do they call the rest of American society the 'English' world?
6 Why do they not like
a) modern technology b) churches c) too much education?
7 For what reasons do Amish people sometimes leave their community?
8 What happens at the Amish community for young people in Florida?

2 Find words or phrases from the text for these definitions.

1 People who would like to live a more natural life.
2 Three important skills you learn at school.
3 A group of people living in an area who share the same beliefs about God.

3 What are the other forms of these words from the text?

	adjective	comparative	superlative
1	different	▭	▭
2	▭	▭	best
3	young	▭	▭

4 Put the verbs in brackets into the correct tense.

When the tourists *(arrive)*[1] in Lancaster last week they *(be)*[2] surprised to see so many 'plain' people. The Amish men *(stand)*[3] next to their buggies and *(talk)*[4] to each other when the tourists *(get)*[5] out of their bus and *(start)*[6] to take photographs. Of course, they *(hear)*[7] about the Amish and the other religious groups before. But it *(be)*[8] always more difficult to believe something you never *(see)*[9] yourself. Now they *(can)*[10] see them with their own eyes.

5 Put in the right prepositions.

1 The tourists try to speak ▭ the Amish men.
2 The plain people are not interested ▭ getting to know the tourists.
3 They are unhappy ▭ the numbers ▭ tourists who come ▭ Lancaster nowadays.
4 ▭ a while they get ▭ their buggies and drive away.
5 The tourists laugh ▭ them.

6 Translate into German from line 18 'Most Amish people are …' to line 23 'best farmers in America.'

7 Write a short report of about 10 sentences on some of the modern technology your family uses in everyday life. You could write about things used at home, for transport, at school/work. Say how these things make life easier. Give your opinion on them.

3 A SPORT MADE FOR THE BOX

Americans have exported their way of life to the rest of the world with cola and hamburgers, Hollywood and 'Dallas'. In the last few years another side of U.S. culture has started to move 5 across the Atlantic: American football.

The interest in American football could be seen as the success story of a clever marketing campaign. For several years Americans themselves have been losing interest in this tough 10 sport and watching it less on TV. Fewer TV viewers means less advertising income for the major TV networks and that, in turn, leads to less money for the National Football League (NFL) from the TV stations. So the NFL has 15 looked for another market for its product and discovered Europe.

It is important to know that American football is completely dependent on television. Over the last five years the major U.S. TV net- 20 works have paid the NFL millions of dollars for the right to broadcast football games. Without that money the league could not exist. In addition, the rules of the game have also been changed over the years to make it more excit- 25 ing for television viewers.

The sport is also ideal for American television. A one hour game takes about three and a half hours to play because of all the natural breaks in it. The TV companies fill those breaks with advertising. People say that is one reason 30 that soccer has never become very popular in the U.S. It does not have enough natural breaks to allow for adverts, so TV companies are not interested in showing it. Sports that are not shown on television have no chance of becom- 35 ing successful in the U.S.A. The question people are now asking is: When will the U.S. TV companies start trying to change the rules of soccer so that they can fit in more adverts?

The role of television also explains the show- 40 business side of this American sport. A football game is not just a sporting event but hours of entertainment for the whole family, with cheerleaders, marching bands, flashing scoreboards. That is probably why the game has a bright, 45 positive, family image in Great Britain nowadays, although it is really one of the most violent of sports.

Exercises

1 Answer these questions on the text.

1 What is the new American export to Europe?
2 What is the NFL? Give a short description.
3 Why does it need to look for new markets for its sport nowadays?
4 What happens to the NFL if fewer people watch American football on TV?
5 Where does the NFL get a large part of its money from?
6 What has happened to the rules of American football because of TV?
7 Why do the TV stations in the U.S. like to show this sport?
8 What problem do they have with showing soccer?
9 Why is an American football game not just sport? What else happens?
10 What do people think of the sport in Britain?
11 Why is its image not quite right?

2 Find synonyms for these words from the text.

1 game (line 23) 2 soccer (line 31) 3 adverts (line 33)

3 In a complete sentence say what this phrase from the text means in your own words.

clever marketing campaign (lines 7-8)

4 What are the other forms of these verbs from the text?

	present	past simple	past participle
1	means	☐	☐
2	☐	☐	paid
3	takes	☐	☐
4	☐	☐	become

5 What are the plurals of these words from the text?

1 success (line 7) 2 product (line 15) 3 family (line 43)

6 A reporter is interviewing an American football fan. Here are the fan's answers. What were the reporters questions?

R: Have you seen many American football games?
F: Yes, I have. Quite a few.
R: ...[1]?
F: I first came to see one last year.
R: ...[2]?
F: Yes, I come here every two weeks. For every home match.
R: ...[3]?
F: Well, it's very tough. That's one reason I like it.
R: ...[4]?
F: Yes, there are some other reasons. The crowds don't cause any trouble.
R: ...[5]?
F: No, I'd never go to a soccer match. The fans are much too violent.

7 Put in the missing prepositions.

Since a league started ☐[1] Britain, American football has become more and more popular. It has only been going ☐[2] a few years now but already gets lots of fans. They have been showing games ☐[3] TV ☐[4] some time now, too. And ☐[5] the past two seasons we have been able to see the final ☐[6] the American league as well.

8 Write an answer to this part of a letter from an American pen friend.

Tomorrow I'm going to a football game. It's the San Francisco Flyers against the Chicago Bears. It'll be great. The whole family's going and we'll eat popcorn and drink coke and all that sort of thing.
Do you have football in Germany or only soccer? I like soccer but they don't show it much on TV here. What sports do you like watching? I only like team sports, like football or basketball. I don't really play any sport. I know I should do some more but I never seem to get the time. Is it the same with you?

4 MOTORWAY MADNESS

'You want to take some photographs of accidents?' the large policeman asked me. 'Well, if you come out with me on motorway patrol on a wet Friday evening, I'll guarantee you'll get what you're looking for.' I was shocked that he could be so calm about it. But next Friday evening at six p.m., I was sitting beside Police Constable Wilkins in his white and blue patrol car, travelling towards the motorway at the start of an eight-hour patrol. Outside, the rain was falling steadily.

At 18.10, the first call came through on the radio – an accident, involving a car and a lorry. There was already a traffic jam on all three lanes

15 of the motorway. The patrol car moved over on to the emergency lane and accelerated up to 90 mph, blue lights flashing.

The lorry driver was unhurt, but the car driver was trapped inside his car. PC Wilkins 20 called for emergency help by radio. We waited until the recovery truck arrived and freed the driver from his car. 'He was driving too close to the lorry,' the policeman told me. 'The lorry braked and – bang! – that was the end of every- 25 body's journey. Friday evening's always the same. Everybody's in a hurry to get home. Madness.'

At 19.15 we continued our patrol. The commuter traffic had been replaced by the week- 30 enders, people getting away from home for the weekend. They were also in a hurry. Five minutes later, another call came in on the radio. Another accident, ten miles away. Three cars had crashed into each other. One was burning. The driver of the first car told me, 'I was driving 35 along at 70 mph in the fast lane and this car here,' – he pointed at the burning car – 'was trying to overtake me. Suddenly, he hit me and my car skidded. We hit the crash barrier and his car caught fire. I don't know how the third car 40 crashed into him.' 'You see,' said PC Wilkins. 'Show me an accident, and I'll show you a driver in a hurry.' I had seen enough for one evening and said so. 'You can go with the ambulance when it comes,' he said. He said he was sorry he 45 could not drive me himself. He had another six and a half hours to do on patrol.

Exercises

1 Answer these questions about the text.
1 Why did the writer of the text want to go on motorway patrol?
2 When did the policeman agree to take the writer on patrol?
3 What was the writer promised?
4 Which vehicles were involved in the first motorway accident?
5 How did the patrol car get past the traffic jam?
6 How did the policeman help the drivers of the vehicles?
7 What was the cause of the accident?
8 What was the cause of the second accident?
9 What, in the policeman's opinion, is the cause of most accidents?

2 Put the following into direct speech. What did the policeman say?
He said he was sorry he could not drive me himself.

3 Put the following into reported speech.
'You can go with the ambulance when it comes,' he said. (lines 44/45)

4 Find the opposites of the following.
1 brake *(v)*
2 trap *(v)*

5 Put the underlined words into the passive.
1 The recovery truck arrived and freed the driver from his car.
2 Suddenly, he hit me.

6 Translate the following into German.
At 18.10, the first call came through on the radio – an accident, involving a car and a lorry. There was already a traffic jam on all three lanes of the motorway. The patrol car accelerated up to 90 mph, blue lights flashing.

7 Find questions for the underlined words.
1 But next Friday evening at six p.m., I was sitting beside Police Constable Wilkins in his white and blue patrol car.

2 There was already a traffic jam on all three lanes of the motorway.
3 'I was driving along at 70 mph in the fast lane.'
4 PC Wilkins called for emergency help by radio.

8 Rewrite the following in your own words.
The commuter traffic had been replaced by the weekenders, people getting away from home for the weekend.

5 UNDERGROUND LONDON THAT NOBODY KNOWS

The London that Londoners and visitors see is only part of the city. Under the ground there are a hundred miles of ancient rivers. Most of London's smaller rivers were covered more than a hundred years ago because the water in them was so dirty that it was a danger to health.

There are twenty tunnels under the Thames today. There are Tube tunnels, Government tunnels, pipes and sewers. They take away waste water and bring fresh water; they carry people, telephone lines, electricity and gas. The first one, simply called the 'Thames Tunnel' was opened in 1843. Originally a foot tunnel, it soon became a dangerous way of crossing the Thames because it was poorly lit and a favourite place for thieves. At the end of the century it was taken over by the Metropolitan Line as part of the London Tube system. It is still used today.

One of the least-known and strangest train tunnels was built by the Post Office sixty years ago. There are no drivers and no passengers. It is six and a half miles long and runs east to west. The nine foot-wide tunnel connects the Eastern District Post Office in the East End of London with Paddington District Post Office, just north of Hyde Park. In all, it connects seven of London's biggest sorting offices and railway stations. Thirty-four small electric trains transport up to half a ton of letters each on every journey. The trains are fully automatic and normally run at 35 mph and, just like a child's model electric railway, the speed of the trains is governed by the amount of electricity in the rails. To save energy, the stations are higher than the rest of the line. In this way, the speed of the train is automatically reduced when it enters the station and is quickly increased when it leaves. Above the stations there are sorting rooms.

Most of the building work for the tunnel took place between 1923 and 1927. The system has been working since 1927 without any serious problems. Not only the Tube system helped to reduce London's traffic problems; after the Post Office railway opened, a quarter of the Post Office's delivery vans disappeared within a year from London's streets.

Exercises

1 Answer these questions about the text.
1 Why did London make its smaller rivers run underground?
2 Are all the Thames tunnels used for the underground railway? If not, what are they also used for?
3 What was the Thames Tunnel originally used for?
4 What did the Thames Tunnel become just before 1900?
5 Why is the Post Office tunnel described as 'strange'?
6 Why was the Post Office tunnel built?
7 How is the speed of the special trains controlled?
8 What problems has the Post Office railway had?
9 What other system of transport besides the Post Office railway has been good for London's traffic problem?

2 Find opposites of the following.

1	bring (line 10)	3	north (line 25)	5	biggest (line 27)
2	disappeared (line 46)	4	increased (line 37)	6	above (line 38)

3 Ask questions about the underlined parts of the sentences.
1 Most of London's smaller rivers were covered more than a hundred years ago because the water in them was so dirty that it was a danger to health.
2 There are twenty tunnels under the Thames today.
3 At the end of the century it was taken over by the Metropolitan Line.
4 To save energy, the stations are higher than the rest of the line.

4 Find a noun.

1	connects (line 23)	3	dirty (line 6)	4	dangerous (line 14)
2	reduced (line 36)				

5 Translate the following into German.
Most of the building work for the tunnel took place between 1923 and 1927. The system has been working since 1927 without any serious problems. Not only the Tube system helped to reduce London's traffic problems; after the Post Office railway opened, a quarter of the Post Office's delivery vans disappeared within a year from London's streets.

6 Put the correct words in the gaps.
The Post Office tunnel has been working ▭[1] sixty years without any problems. Automatic trains have carried letters ▭[2] 1927. Sixty years ▭[3] seven sorting offices were first connected by the tunnel.

6 THE ELECTRONIC CHURCH

The middle-aged man with glasses, dressed in a dark suit and tie, holds the microphone in his left hand. He waves a bible in his right and shouts into the microphone, attacking communists, Catholics and humanists. He calls them servants of the devil. Supporters sitting at desks on stage shout out 'Amen', 'Glory' or 'Praise the Lord' at the right moments. Then the man dances around the stage. Music starts from somewhere and suddenly he's a Gospel singer. In about 9 million homes all over the US the viewers sit back and enjoy the show. In America even religion is a part of TV entertainment.

In the U.S. there are 200 local religious TV stations, as well as cable and satellite networks, which broadcast religious TV 24 hours a day. In addition, the religious stations buy time for their programmes on general TV networks. Over the past ten years 'Pray TV' has developed into a billion dollar industry.

How can the success of the television preachers be explained? Perhaps by the influence of TV and religion in American life. Nearly all Americans say they are religious and, of course, everybody watches TV. The religious networks have used the showbusiness style of American TV to bring religion into everyone's home. That has been the key to their success.

It is not, however, the main American churches that have enjoyed the greatest success. The top TV preachers are almost all fundamentalist Christians. They all offer their followers a personal, traditional religion with simple answers to the complicated problems of

---

Pray TV (line 19) – Fernsehen zum Beten: eine Anspielung auf 'Pay TV', in Amerika weitverbreitete Münzfernsehgeräte.

fundamentalist Christians (lines 31/32) – protestantische christliche Kirchen, die die Bibel wortwörtlich verstehen.

real life. The money they receive from their followers not only pays for their shows but many other business interests as well.

Sociologist Jeffrey Hadden believes the TV preachers will have even more influence in the future. 'They can get on television more easily than any other interest group. They are going to be part of the biggest social movement in America during the late 20th century.'

But recently financial and moral scandals have hit the religious networks. They have led to bitter fighting amongst the TV preachers. Outsiders say the fight is really only about money. Whether that is true or not, the trouble has certainly worried many followers of the TV preachers. They may not give as much money and support in the future.

Exercises

1 Answer these questions on the text.
1 Who is the man described at the beginning?
2 What sort of TV stations broadcast religious shows?
3 How do the TV preachers get on to national television networks?
4 Name two things about Americans that help the 'electronic church' to become popular.
5 What sort of Christians are most successful on TV?
6 What reasons are given for this?
7 What do the religious networks do with the money they get from their supporters?
8 What problems have the TV preachers had recently?
9 What could be the result of these problems?

2 Are these statements about the text right or wrong? Correct the wrong ones.
1 The TV preacher at the beginning is a Catholic.
2 He does not like communists.
3 He sings as well as preaches.
4 Not many Americans watch the TV preachers.
5 Jeffrey Hadden thinks the TV preachers will become even more popular in the future.
6 The TV preachers are all friends of each other.

3 Find words or phrases from the text which fit these definitions.
1 The opposite of God.
2 Pay to have a programme broadcast on TV.
3 Christians who believe in the bible word for word.
4 Someone who studies society.

4 In your own words, say what this sentence from the text means. 'That has been the key to their success.' (line 28)

5 Put the following into reported speech. Start like this:
Jeffrey Hadden said that ...
'They can get on television more easily than any other interest group. They are going to be part of the biggest social movement in America during the late 20th century.'

6 What are the other forms *(simple present, past participle* or *simple past)* of these verbs from the text?
Bring, give *(simple present)* and hit, led *(past participle)*.

7 Write a short report of about 80-100 words on yourself as a TV viewer. Say how much you watch, how often, which sort of programmes you prefer, whether you prefer videos or cable to ordinary TV, etc.

7 HONG KONG COUNT-DOWN

As a result of the Opium Wars between China and Great Britain, Hong Kong became a British colony in 1842. Hong Kong island and the area on the mainland known as Kowloon were to be British 'for all time'. In 1898 the New Territories, which make up the rest of the colony, were leased for 99 years. On 30 June 1997 this will all change. An agreement between Britain and the People's Republic of China will make the colony of Hong Kong Chinese again. Many people are now asking how this capitalist trade centre and a communist country will be able to live together.

Hong Kong will not, however, immediately become just another Chinese city. The agreement is that its economic system will continue unchanged till 2047. Over the years, and especially since the war, Hong Kong has developed into the biggest trading city in Asia with the third largest stock exchange in the world after London and New York. It is also the world's second largest container port. It makes more toys than any other country and is a big exporter of textiles and plastics. But this economic success would never have been possible against the will of its communist neighbour. The five and a half million residents of the colony, 98% of whom are Chinese, need the mainland for food, water and electricity. Without these this Asian Manhattan, with its international community, could not survive.

At the same time, of course, China needs Hong Kong, which has been its 'window to the West' for many years. A lot of its income of foreign currencies comes through the colony. The Beijing Government itself is very active in Hong Kong in trade, banking and shipping. The advantages to China from Hong Kong's economy are the main reason why it has agreed not to change the system in 1997. However, many Hong Kong Chinese are worried about what will really happen. They fear that their civil rights may be in danger when Beijing takes over. But there is no panic. All sides are trying to prepare themselves for the change. Economic connections are being made stronger. Chinese government officials are speaking of 'One land, two systems'. Only time will tell whether the two systems can really exist side by side for long.

Beijing (line 36) – Peking, Hauptstadt der Volksrepublik China

Exercises

1 Answer these questions on the text.

1 When did Hong Kong become a British colony and why?
2 Hong Kong Island and Kowloon were to be British 'for all time'. How are the New Territories different from them?
3 What will happen to the colony in 1997?
4 What does the agreement between China and Britain say about Hong Kong's economic system?
5 What business does the Chinese government already do in Hong Kong?
6 What are some Hong Kong Chinese afraid will happen after 1997?
7 Explain what 'One land, two systems' will mean for China after 1997.

2 Are these statements right or wrong? Correct the wrong ones.

1 Hong Kong is Asia's most important stock exchange.
2 Only Tokyo is a bigger trade centre in Asia.
3 No country produces more toys than Hong Kong.

4 Hong Kong has no other important export products.
5 Most people living in Hong Kong are British.
6 China and Hong Kong could do well without each other.

3 Find synonyms for these words and phrases from the text.
1 for all time (line 5) 2 immediately (line 14) 3 side by side (line 50)

4 What are the other forms of these adjectives from the text?

	adjective	comparative	superlative
1	▭	▭	largest
2	▭	more (toys)	▭
3	active	▭	▭
4	▭	stronger	▭

5 Use the underlined parts of these answers to find the questions.
1 Hong Kong became a colony of Britain after the Opium Wars.
2 These wars were between China and Britain.
3 Britain leased the New Territories from China 56 years later.
4 In 1997 the colony will become Chinese again.
5 They are not going to change the system because it is good for China, too.

6 Form the adverbs.
1 economic (line 16) 2 active (line 36)

7 Choose the correct word from the two in brackets.
1 Hong Kong is an (extreme/extremely) big trade centre.
2 The agreement between Britain and China could be a big (success/successful).
3 The change will not cause many problems (if/unless) people panic.
4 The Chinese have been in business in Hong Kong (for/since) many years now.
5 Their (decide/decision) to keep the same economic system surprised (many/much) people.
6 (During/While) they are waiting for 1997 both sides are preparing themselves.

8 Write a short report of about 80-100 words on the most important industries in your area. Describe the companies you know and what sort of products they make. Say, if possible, how many people work for them, how many factories/offices they have. Say where they sell the products they make.

8 PACIFIC PARADISE?

The age of the jumbo jet and cheap flights has made Australia an attractive place even for tourists from Europe and North America. One of the sights people come to see is 'the world's largest living organism.' 5

Running 2,000 kilometres along the Queensland coast, the Great Barrier Reef is made up of 700 islands and over 2,000 reefs. It is the only sign of life on Earth that can be seen from the moon. 10

This coral paradise is home to thousands of marine lifeforms; in fact, more different types of fish live on the reef of living coral than have been found in the whole of the Atlantic Ocean. For tourists, diving or just snorkelling on the 15 reef opens up a whole new underwater world of movement and colour. Marine biologists, however, are worried that the tourist boom will cause permanent damage.

'The ecology of the reef is extremely complicated' said one expert, 'and every tourist who comes to explore is an added danger to it.'

There are other dangers, too:

➤ Dugongs, large, shy, plant-eating animals have moved away because of the noise of the many tourist boats. Now many coral reefs are covered with sea grasses which the dugongs used to eat.

➤ Fishermen and divers make money by selling fish and shells. Collecting shells may have terrible results for the ecology of the reef. Indeed, parts of some reefs have already been destroyed.

Other experts say that the history of the reef has always been like this. Parts have died off, new reefs have been formed. What is happening now is no different to changes in the past.

One thing does seem certain, however. More tourists will bring more dangers to the Great Barrier Reef. Part of the reef is already a national park but Australian environmentalists would like to protect a lot more than at present. They say that all the possible dangers to the largest coral reef in the world must be kept under close control, if future generations want to enjoy this underwater paradise.

---

dugong (line 24) – Seekuh, ein großes, pflanzenfressendes Meeressäugetier

Exercises

1 Answer these questions on the text.

1 Why can more people now visit Australia?
2 Where is the Great Barrier Reef? How large is it?
3 What is the reef made of?
4 Why has it been called a 'living organism'?
5 What do the tourists do when they visit the reef?
6 How is the reef compared to the Atlantic?
7 What do marine biologists think will happen if too many tourists come?
8 Do all experts agree about the dangers to the reef?
9 How do environmentalists want to protect the Great Barrier Reef?

2 Are these statements about the text right or wrong? Correct the wrong ones.

1 The Great Barrier Reef can only be seen from underwater.
2 It takes a lot to disturb life on the reef.
3 Coral reefs do not have enough sea grasses for the dugongs, so they have moved away.
4 Collecting shells on the reef is a harmless occupation.

3 Find nouns from these words from the text:

1 selling (lines 29/30) 2 protect (line 42)

4 Find adjectives from these words from the text:

1 danger (line 22) 2 noise (line 25)

5 Find opposites to these words from the text:

1 living (line 5) 2 complicated (lines 20/21)

6 Put the verbs in brackets into the correct tense or choose the right word from the two given.

Dear Joan,

I just *(come back)*[1] from Australia. It *(be)*[2] a wonderful holiday. I *(spend)*[3] two weeks down in Sydney and then *(go)*[4] up to Queensland. I *(have)*[5] beautiful weather for most of my stay but it *(rain)*[6] *(for/since)*[7] the last three days.

In fact it *(still rain)*[8] when my plane *(take off)*[9] for Europe. Of course, I *(have to)*[10] get used to the weather back here now. It is *(terrible/terribly)*[11] cold, isn't it? I *(tell)*[12] you more next week. See you then,

Roger

7 Roger's friend Joan asked him about the Barrier Reef. Here are his answers. What were her questions?

Joan What is the water like, Roger?
Roger Oh, the water's very warm and clear. It has to be for corals.
Joan ...[1]
Roger You have to go by boat out to the reef.
Joan ...[2]
Roger Well, from Cairns it took about two hours.
Joan ...[3]
Roger No, you're not allowed to collect shells. It's a national park, you know.
Joan ...[4]
Roger My shells? Oh, I bought them in a souvenir shop in Cairns.
Joan ...[5]
Roger Oh, I suppose the shop got them from the reef.

8 Translate into German from line 34 'Other experts say ...' to line 42 '... than at present.'

9 What are the advantages and disadvantages that tourists bring to the places they visit? Write about 10 sentences. You could use the following words but you do not have to:
money, economy, culture, prices, destroy, help, increase, behave, understand

9 WHERE DOES ALL THE TRASH GO?

Car ownership has always been a sign of a high standard of living. The U.S.A. has one of the highest rates of car ownership in the world with some families owning two, three or even four cars. An average car only has a life of five to six years. Seven million cars are scrapped in the U.S.A. every year. During its lifetime a car will need at least two, possibly five sets of tires. That makes 8 to 20 old tires every five years for every car-owner in the U.S.A. But what happens to all the old tires?

Used tires are becoming a major problem for U.S. states. The state of Ohio alone has to cope with 15 million tires every year. It has tried to recycle them and burn them but it still has half a million used tires in dumps. Tire dumps are not pretty places. Weeds grow in the holes in the black rubber rings. Rats make their nests under them. Worse, the tires collect rainwater and become ideal places for millions of mosquitoes, which then attack local houses. One dump was struck by lightning and burned for several weeks. Fireman could not control the flames and left the tires to burn.

In addition to the used tire problem, the U.S.A. is faced with 20 million tonnes of waste paper, 48,000 million cans and 26,000 million glass bottles each and every year. At present the U.S.A. produces 133 million tonnes of trash yearly. By the year 2000 this will probably rise to nearly 300 million tonnes.

Trash is made up of waste food, packaging materials, industrial waste and many other things all mixed up together. It is this mixture that makes it hard to recycle trash. 'It's time to change our attitude to trash,' said an expert. 'At present we are wasting millions of tonnes of good materials, just because we mix everything up together and throw it in the garbage can. There is a pollution problem, a financial problem and a waste problem all mixed up together, too. Recycling must be part of the answer. If people sorted waste into food, plastics, metals and paper before they put it into their garbage cans, life would be cheaper and 45 more pleasant for everybody.'

Exercises

1 Answer these questions on the text.

1 How long does an ordinary car usually last?
2 How long does a set of tires usually last?
3 Which three things can happen to tires in Ohio?
4 What are the four biggest problems with tire dumps?
5 What other kinds of trash problems does the U.S.A. have?
6 What mixture makes trash hard to recycle?
7 What should people do better with their trash?
8 What would be the result of sorting the trash?

2 Find the opposites.

1 rise (line 30)
2 hard (line 35)
3 answer (line 43)
4 cheaper (line 45)
5 more pleasant (line 46)

3 Put into reported speech. Start your sentence with the underlined words.
'It's time to change our attitude to trash,' said <u>a senior waste-disposal officer</u>.

4 Find a verb.

1 ownership (line 1)
2 life (line 5)
3 mixture (line 34)

5 Put into the passive. Start with the underlined words.

1 Rats make their <u>nests</u> under them.
2 People should sort <u>waste</u> into food, plastics, metals and paper before they put it into their garbage cans.

6 Ask questions about the underlined parts of the sentences.

1 <u>Seven million cars</u> are scrapped in the U.S.A. every year.
2 Used tires are becoming a major problem <u>for U.S. states</u>.
3 It has tried to <u>recycle them and burn them</u>.
4 Tire dumps are <u>not pretty places</u>.

7 Put in the correct prepositions.

1 Unemployment will probably rise by 100,000 ▭ 3 million.
2 Car-owners are faced ▭ the problem of coping with old tires.
3 New York produces 24,000 tonnes ▭ trash every day.
4 Many people do not know what happens ▭ old vehicles.
5 There are often rats' nests ▭ old tires.

10 LIFE IN A GREENHOUSE

Several times during its history ice has covered large areas of the Earth. Now and again scientists have warned that a new Ice Age could be on its way. But what would happen if the 5 world got warmer instead of colder? That is exactly what is worrying scientists now. One expert painted this picture of the future:

'The polar icecaps will melt and, as a result, the seas will rise, flooding many coastal cities around the world. Nobody will live in New York 10 or Hamburg any more. Even Paris will be flooded. The world's weather will change completely. Tourists will spend their holidays in the Antarctic. Rich farmlands will turn into desert, forests will die, while areas now too cold to produce food will become farmland. Russia, not America, will provide the world with grain. The political and social changes will be huge.'

Does this sound unbelievable? According to many experts this may be a true picture of the world in 50 years' time. They are calling it the 'greenhouse effect'. More and more studies are showing that the Earth is slowly but surely warming up. They also know the causes. The biggest is the increase in the atmosphere of carbon dioxide (CO_2). This gas stops the heat from the sun being reflected from the Earth back into space. It acts in the same way as a greenhouse in which vegetables are grown. The causes of the increase in CO_2 are also clear. It comes especially from the burning of coal and oil in industry and cars. And the forests and oceans of the world can no longer absorb as much CO_2 gas. The cutting down of more and more forests is making the situation worse all the time.

Of course, there are those who do not think the situation is really that bad. They say that studies have not yet proved that there is cause for alarm. 'The history of the Earth has always been one of changes in climate, as the Ice Ages prove,' says one U.S. weather expert.

What can be done to save the world from a catastrophe? Experts say clean, safe alternatives to coal and oil must be found. Tropical forests must not be cut down and a huge replanting programme should be started. If we do not start now, the 'greenhouse effect' could mean the end of human life in 500 to 1,000 years' time.

Exercises

1 Answer these questions on the text.

1 If the world does get warmer what would be the results for
   a) cities by the sea?
   b) the Arctic and the Antarctic?
   c) farming in the U.S.A.?
   d) forests and farmlands?
2 What gas is the main cause of the rise in the Earth's temperature?
3 Why is there more of this gas now?
4 How does it make the Earth warmer?
5 Why is this process called the 'greenhouse effect'?
6 What three things must be done to fight the 'greenhouse effect'?
7 What might happen if nothing is done?

2 Are these statements right or wrong? Correct the wrong ones.

1 The Earth's climate has always been the same.
2 Scientists think the world is getting warmer.
3 All experts agree with these scientists.

3 Find opposites of these words from the text.

1 rich (line 14)
2 cold (line 15)
3 unbelievable (line 19)
4 increase (line 25)
5 clean (line 44)
6 safe (line 44)

4 Put the verbs in brackets into the correct tense.

In the last few years the Earth *(get)*[1] warmer and warmer. The years 1981, 1983 and 1984 *(be)*[2] the hottest ever. Now experts *(warn)*[3] governments that something *(must)*[4] be done soon. If people *(go)*[5] on burning as much coal and oil as at the moment, there *(be)*[6] no human life left on Earth in a few hundred years. But *(listen)*[7] politicians to the warnings?

5 Put in the right prepositions.

1 Carbon dioxide is the cause ☐ the problem.
2 It stops the sun's heat ☐ getting back ☐ space.
3 ☐ the end of the century this could already have terrible results.
4 ☐ the next century many coastal areas could be flooded ☐ the sea.
5 It's a problem that everybody should be thinking ☐.

6 Put this sentence from the text into the passive. Make the underlined words the subject of your sentence.
Several times during its history ice has covered <u>large areas of the Earth</u>.

7 Translate into German from line 30 'The causes of the ...' to line 36 '... worse all the time.'

8 Write a short report of about 80-100 words on an environmental problem you know about. Describe its causes, what results it could have, and what can be done to help the situation.

11 LOOKING FOR MILLIONAIRES

Just imagine it! One morning a letter arrives addressed to you from New York, U.S.A. It happened to Joachim Hartman from Wiesbaden. He received the following letter: 'We have reason to believe that you are the heir to the property of Mr and Mrs Hartman, who died in 1985. Mr and Mrs Hartman left the sum of $50,000 in their New York bank account. Could you please send to this office a copy of your personal identity card or other proof of identity?'

Every year, many dozens of people receive letters like this from a New York firm, *Abandoned Funds Research Co.* This firm specialises in finding the heirs to fortunes. In 1982 thirty lucky people successfully claimed nearly $250,000 left by people who died without leaving wills. Most people received between $5,000 and $6,000 although one person was paid $50,000.

It is estimated that there is approximately $700 million in unclaimed money in New York banks alone. In Californian banks there is another $137 million and $74 million more in the U.S. state of Illinois. In the U.S.A., ownerless money normally passes into the hands of the state after a few years, so that it can be used for public investment until the owner is found. In 1981, New York city received $92 million in this way. Only about 15% of the unclaimed money in the biggest city of the U.S.A. is paid out to claimants in an average year.

Abandoned Funds Research Co. uses a computer to check bank lists and then tries to find possible heirs, not only in the U.S.A. but all over the world. The firm looks for the names of members of the dead person's family and sends letters to the last known address. If they are successful in finding a possible heir, the firm has to prove that he or she has a right to the money. If the firm can prove who is the heir and the bank pays up, *Abandoned Funds Research Co.* demands 15% of the sum of money recovered. Most people are happy to get 85% of a sum of money they did not know even existed.

Exercises

1 Answer these questions about the text.

1 Where did Joachim Hartman's letter come from?
2 Who was the letter sent by?
3 Why was he sent the letter?
4 What was Joachim Hartman asked to do?

5 Why did thirty lucky people receive nearly $250,000 in 1982?
6 Who does the $700 million in New York belong to?
7 What do the states use ownerless money for?
8 How does *Abandoned Funds Research* try to find the heirs to ownerless money?
9 How does the firm earn its money?

2 Find the opposite of the following:
1 possible (line 35) 3 happy (line 44) 5 successfully (line 16)
2 dead (line 37) 4 lucky (line 16)

3 Find a noun/verb.
1 pays (line 42) 3 proof (line 10) 5 happy (line 44)
2 existed (line 46) 4 investment (line 28)

4 Put the sentences into the passive. Start with the underlined words.
1 Every year, many dozens of people receive letters like this.
2 *Abandoned Funds Research Co.* uses a computer to check bank lists.
3 The firm looks for the names of members of the dead person's family.

5 Put the following from the letter to Joachim Hartman into reported speech.
'Could you please send to this office a copy of your personal identity card?'

6 Find synonyms for the following words: approximately, receive.

7 Rewrite the following sentence using 'were successful'.
In 1982 thirty lucky people successfully claimed nearly $250,000.

8 Which part of the text means the same as the following:
... is transferred to ...
... which does not belong to anybody ...

12 SILICON VALLEY – HI-TECH AND POLLUTION

Silicon Valley does not exist. At least, you won't find an official signpost to tell you you've arrived. The name was made up for a number of small towns and villages in Santa Clara County. The area is about 15 by 40 kilometres along the San Francisco Bay in California. The name symbolizes the industries here. Although the first firm connected with silicon chip technology, the *Shockley Transistor Corporation*, was founded as early as 1956, most of the hightechnology firms were set up in the late Seventies. The production of cheap, mass-produced personal home computers caused a massive growth in the industry.

Microchips are made here, but most of the production work is done abroad, in countries where wages are lower; e.g. metal boxes are made in West Germany, chips are mass-produced in Texas and California but are finished and assembled in factories in Taiwan; keyboards come from Ireland and power units from the Far East. The components needed to make an ordinary home computer can travel one million miles before they reach the place where the computer is finally assembled.

Silicon Valley has become a symbol for clean, ultramodern technology, very unlike traditional industries with their noise and their dirt. Salaries can easily reach $100,000 a year. Many of the highest-paid workers are under 25 years old. The legendary *Apple* computer was built in the family garage because the founders, Steve Jobs and Steve Wozniak could not afford a proper workshop. Both had

35 become millionaires by the time they were 30.
The Valley, however, has its negative sides, too. Not all jobs are well-paid. Many production-line workers do not earn much more than in industry elsewhere. In spite of its image,
40 there is pollution in the Valley, too. During the production process for microchips, very toxic chemicals are used. One storage tank in Santa Clara county was found to be leaking toxic waste into the ground water, causing a serious pollution problem. Although computers are 45 generally non-pollutant and in many ways help society to reduce pollution, they can, it seems, also be part of the problem as well as part of the solution.

Exercises

1 Answer these questions about the text.
1 What is 'Silicon Valley'?
2 Which was the first hi-tech company in 'Silicon Valley'?
3 When did most firms arrive there?
4 Why did the computer industry grow?
5 Why is computer production work done outside the U.S.A.?
6 Which computer parts are made in Asia?
7 Why are 'Silicon Valley' industries different from older industries?
8 Is $100,000 the average wage in 'Silicon Valley'? If not, what are wages like?
9 What kind of difficulties exist there?

2 Find the opposites.
1 negative (line 36)
2 well-paid (line 37)
3 problem (line 45)
4 clean (line 27)

3 Put in the right prepositions.
1 Hi-tech is the name that was made ☐ for modern technology.
2 Hi-tech parks are being set ☐ in many parts of Germany.
3 There has been fast growth ☐ hi-tech firms generally.
4 Some computer millionaires are ☐ 25 years old.
5 There is some pollution ☐ the production process for chips.

4 Put in the correct conjunctions.
1 ☐ some computer firms were set up in the '50s and the '60s, most arrived in the '70s.
2 The first *Apple* computer was not built in a proper factory ☐ its builders could not afford one.
3 Components are built in several different countries ☐ they are made into a home computer.

5 Rewrite the following in your own words.
Although computers help society to reduce pollution, they can also be part of the problem as well as part of the solution.

6 Find a noun.
1 symbolizes (line 7)
2 produced (line 12)
3 reduce (line 47)

7 Translate into German.
The Valley, however, has its negative sides, too. Many production-line workers do not earn much more than in industry elsewhere. In spite of its image, there is pollution in the Valley, too. During the production process for microchips, very toxic chemicals are used. One storage tank was found to be leaking toxic waste into the ground water, causing a serious pollution problem.

GRAMMAR

1 Verb tenses – active
2 Questions and negatives
3 Verb tenses – passive
4 Modal verbs
5 Infinitive
6 -ing/-ed form
7 Infinitive/-ing form
8 Relative clauses
9 Conditional
10 Reported speech
11 Adverbs and adverbial clauses
12 Quantifiers
13 Pronouns
14 Comparison
15 Definite and indefinite article
16 Genitive 's/s'/of-phrase

1 Verb tenses – active

p. 12 36 52 152 156

1.1 Simple present

You **like** the cinema.
My sister **prefers** TV.

Grundform des Verbs + *s* in 3. Person Singular

➤ Für allgemeine Wahrheiten, Zustände, Gewohnheiten, wiederkehrende Vorgänge, Meinungen, Gefühle, Sinneswahrnehmungen.

1.2 Present continuous

You'**re sitting** next to me.
She'**s enjoying** a video.

am/are/is ('m/'re/'s) + *ing* Form des Verbs

➤ Vorgänge, die gerade jetzt passieren. Für längere Prozesse und vorübergehende Zustände.

p. 56 152

1.3 Present perfect

I'**ve lived** in London for years.
We'**ve** never **been** to Germany.

have/has + 3. Form des Verbs (*-ed* Form bei regelmäßigen Verben)

➤ Handlungen in der Vergangenheit, deren Wirkung heute noch spürbar ist.
➤ Handlungen in einem noch nicht abgeschlossenen Zeitraum.

1.4 Present perfect continuous

She'**s been travelling** to London since she studied English.

have/has been + *-ing* Form des Verbs

➤ Handlungen, die in der Vergangenheit begannen und bis (oder fast bis) in die Gegenwart andauern. Betonung auf Andauern der Handlung.

PRESENT PERFECT TENSES	GEGENWART
I **have worked** here for six months. She **has been practising** all morning.	Ich **arbeite** hier seit sechs Monaten. Sie **übt** schon den ganzen Vormittag.

p. 26 82 116 152

1.5 Simple past

The police **arrived** at 10 p.m.

Regelmäßige Verben *-ed* Form des Verbs, gleiche Form für alle Personen

➤ Abgeschlossene Ereignisse in der Vergangenheit: oft mit Zeitangaben, die zeigen, daß ein Zeitraum abgeschlossen ist: *ago, last month, yesterday, in 1987.*

1.6 Past continuous

We **were listening** to some music.

was/were + *-ing* Form des Verbs

➤ Handlungen in der Vergangenheit, die noch im Verlauf waren.
➤ Beschreibende Teile von Erzählungen und Berichten.
➤ Oft zusammen mit **simple past**, wenn die Handlung unterbrochen wurde.

86 16

1.7 Past perfect

After I **had written** to the company, they gave me an interview.

had ('d) + 3. Form des Verbs (*-ed* bei regelmäßigen Verben)

➤ Handlungen oder Ereignisse, die vor einem/r anderen Ereignis/Handlung in der Vergangenheit stattfanden. Oft mit Zeitangaben wie *after, before* und in Verbindung mit **simple past**.

42 56

1.8 Will-future

I'**ll see** you after work.

will ('ll) + Grundform des Verbs

➤ Allgemeinste Ausdruckform für das Futur, z. B. für gerade gefaßte Entschlüsse, allgemeine Voraussagen.

1.9 Will-future continuous

It **will be getting** cold in December.

will be + *ing* Form des Verbs

➤ Betont das Andauern einer zukünftigen Handlung. Gewöhnliche, geplante, selbstverständliche Abläufe in der Zukunft.

42

1.10 Going to-future

I'**m going to** visit the USA next summer.

am/are/is going to + Infinitiv des Verbs (ohne *to*)

➤ Aufgrund von bestimmten Vorzeichen Ereignisse in der nahen Zukunft voraussagen. Bezeichnet u. a. Absichten und Pläne.

42 76

1.11 Simple present as future

The train **leaves** at 7.06 p. m.

➤ Für Pläne, Programme u. ä., gewöhnlich mit einer Zeitangabe.

1.12 Present continuous as future

We'**re having** lunch with friends on Saturday.

➤ Für Verabredungen, die kurz bevorstehen.

2 Questions and negatives

12 36 52 156

2.1 Simple present

Do you **work** for a big company?
Does it **sell** its products in Germany?
It **doesn't have** an agent in town.
I **don't think** so, anyway.
Are you a salesman?
He **isn't** the sales manager.

2.2 Present continuous

Are you **looking for** a good training place?
I'**m not finding** it very easy to get one.

56 152

2.3 Present perfect

Has that new cinema **opened** yet?
Have you **seen** the new James Bond film?
I **haven't** ever **seen** one.

2.4 Present perfect continuous

Have you **been waiting** there all this time?
Has it **been raining** long?
They **haven't been speaking** to each other for a week.
She **hasn't been going** to work, either.

26 82

2.5 Simple past

Did she **play** tennis last weekend? I **didn't see** her at the club.
Were you there? Well, I **wasn't** there for long.

2.6 Past continuous

Was he **driving** carefully when it got dark?
Were his lights **working** properly?
He **wasn't concentrating** hard enough and we **weren't watching** the road at all.

86

2.7 Past perfect

Had they **learnt** any useful English before they arrived in New York?
They **hadn't heard** any real English at all.

p. 156
2.8 Will-future

When **shall** we **see** you next weekend?
Will you **be** at Frank's party?
Well, I **won't be** there until quite late.

2.9 Will-future continuous

Will you **be helping** me with the housework tomorrow?
I **won't be getting** home till eight.

p. 42
2.10 Going to-future

Are you **going to come** to the game on Saturday?
I'm not going to watch that useless team again.

p. 16
2.11 Modal verbs

Can I **help** you?
Should we **put** the cake in the kitchen?
We **couldn't find** the street his house was in.

p. 12 26 36
2.12 Questions

HILFS-/MODALVERB	SUBJEKT	VOLLVERB	OBJEKT/ERGÄNZUNG
Do	you	speak	English?
Will	the men	be	here this evening?
Have	we	seen	this film before?
Did	I	tell	you this last time?

➤ Fragen, die man mit *yes/no* beantworten kann, werden durch ein Hilfsverb oder Modalverb eingeleitet.
➤ Fragen, die mit einem Fragewort eingeleitet werden, folgen der gleichen Regel mit einer Ausnahme – wenn das Fragewort das Subjekt des Satzes ist, bleibt die normale Satzgliedstellung erhalten.

SUBJEKT	VERB	OBJEKT/ERGÄNZUNG
Who	comes	to school by bus?
What trains	arrived	late?

p. 12 26 36
2.13 Question words

who	wer	when	wann	how much	wieviel
where	wo	how	wie	what sort of/kind of	was für
why	warum	how often	wie oft	which	welche(r, s, n)

how many (children)	*mit zählbaren Substantiven*	wieviele (Kinder)
how much (sugar)	*mit unzählbaren Substantiven*	wieviel (Zucker)

p. 12 26 36
2.14 Negatives

We **are not (aren't)** coming.
I **haven't** done this before.
They **didn't** miss the bus.
We have **never** been to Scotland.

➤ In Verneinungen wird *n't* oder *not* nach dem Hilfs- bzw. Modalverb eingesetzt.
➤ In den Verlaufsformen **(continuous)** ist das Hilfsverb *be*.
➤ In den Perfektformen **(perfect)** ist das Hilfsverb *have*.
➤ In den einfachen Zeiten **(simple)** wird eine Form von *do* verwendet.
➤ *No, none, nobody, no one, nothing, nowhere, never* können auch verwendet werden, um Aussagen zu verneinen.

p. 76
2.15 Question tags

➤ *Question tags* sind ein Mittel, einen Gesprächspartner zu veranlassen, eine Aussage zu bestätigen.
Sie werden mit dem Hilfs- bzw. Modalverb gebildet, das im Hauptsatz benutzt wird. Falls der Hauptsatz kein Hilfsverb enthält, werden *question tags* mit Formen von *do* gebildet.

POSITIVE SATZAUSSAGE	NEGATIVE QUESTION TAG
You can come to the party, They play tennis in the mornings,	can't you? don't they?
NEGATIVE SATZAUSSAGE	POSITIVE QUESTION TAG
She didn't forget to take the key, The film wasn't as good as we expected,	did she? was it?

3 Verb tenses – passive

p. 92
3.1 Present passive

The businessman **is driven** to work every morning **by** his chauffeur.
At our local cinema the films **are changed** every Friday.

p. 96
3.2 Past passive

The big house **was bought by** the local council.
The windows **were broken by** kids from the area.

p. 96
3.3 Perfect passive

Two people **have been injured** in an accident this morning.
One of them **has been taken** to hospital.

Korrekte Zeit und Form des Verbs *be* + **past participle**

➤ Das Passiv wird im Englischen sehr oft verwendet, vor allem in Berichten über Ereignisse oder Handlungen, bei denen man die Ursache/den Verursacher bzw. den Auslöser nicht kennt oder nicht nennen will.
➤ Wenn man die Ursache oder den Verursacher doch nennen kann oder will, schließt man sie bzw. ihn durch *by (by-agent)* an.
➤ Das Passiv im present, past und perfect kann auch in der Verlaufsform verwendet werden. Simple und continuous form entspricht der im Aktiv.

4 Modal verbs

p. 16
72
92
4.1 can

I **can** see the town from the top of the hill.
Can we take the car tomorrow, dad? – No, you **cannot**.
They **can't** play chess very well yet.

➤ Möglichkeit/Fähigkeit, etwas zu tun.
Um Erlaubnis bitten, Erlaubnis gewähren oder verweigern.

p. 16
72
92
4.2 could

We **could** be home by five with luck. *(könnten)*
They **couldn't** see the road because of the fog. *(konnten)*

➤ Möglichkeit/Fähigkeit, etwas zu tun.

p. 92
122
4.3 may/might

You **may** put the cassette recorder on as long as it's not too loud.
May/might I trouble you for a light?
I **may/might** visit my brother next weekend. I'm not sure yet.
Try and phone him now. He **may/might** be in.

- Um Erlaubnis bitten, Erlaubnis gewähren oder verweigern (höflich).
- Eine Möglichkeit oder bestimmte Absicht (Zukunft/Gegenwart) ausdrücken.

p. 22
72

4.4 must/mustn't/needn't/have to

You **must** do a training course if you want a good job.
You **mustn't** smoke when people are still eating.

- Notwendigkeit ausdrücken. Eindringlicher Vorschlag/Ratschlag, Zwang.
- Die Verneinung *mustn't (must not)* drückt aus, daß etwas **nicht erlaubt** ist.
- 'Nicht müssen' wird im Englischen mit *needn't* oder der Verneinung von *have to* ausgedrückt.

p. 32

4.5 ought to

You **ought to** take off those wet clothes before you catch cold.

- Nachdrückliche Ratschläge und Ermahnungen. Seltener in Fragen und Verneinungen.

p. 42

4.6 shall

I **shall** arrive in time for dinner.
Shall I help you with the cooking?

- Nur erste Person von **will-future** (um über die Zukunft zu sprechen).
- In Fragen, um Hilfe anzubieten oder einen Vorschlag zu machen.

p. 32

4.7 should

They **should ask** everybody in the neighbourhood before they widen the road.
You **shouldn't build** new roads without local support.

- Ratschläge, Ermahnungen erteilen.

5 Infinitive

p. 32

5.1 Verbs + infinitive

He **decided to apply** for the job and then **managed to get** an interview.

Der *infinitive + to* kann nach bestimmten Verben gebraucht werden (mit * markierte Verben können auch von der *-ing form* gefolgt werden):

agree – appear – apply – arrange – ask – begin* – choose – claim – continue* – decide – expect – fail – forget* – hate* – hope – learn – like* – love* – manage – need – offer – plan – prefer* – promise – refuse – remember* – start* – try* – want – wish – would like.

p. 116

5.2 Infinitive construction to show intentions

I went to the Jobcentre **to look for** a job.
Some people were there **in order to apply** for unemployment money.

Mit *in order to + verb* oder nur dem Infinitiv können Absichten ausgedrückt werden.

6 -ing/-ed form

6.1 -ing form

call – cal**ling**
stop – stop**ping**

6.2 -ed form

call – call**ed**
stop – stop**ped**

➤ Ein Endkonsonant nach einfachem, kurzem, betontem Vokal wird verdoppelt.

mak**ing** – mak**ing**

make – mak**ing**
die – d**ying**

➤ Ein stummes End-*e* fällt weg.
➤ *-ie* wird zu *-y*...

agree – agree**d**
change – change**d**
apply – appl**ied**

➤ bei Verben auf *-ee* oder stummes End-*e* wird nur *-d* angefügt.
➤ *-y* wird zu *-i*...

102

6.3 -ing form as noun

Swimming is a very healthy sport.
She did her **training** at weekends.

➤ Als Substantiv kann die *-ing form* Subjekt oder Objekt des Satzes sein.

6.4 -ing form after certain verbs

I **like watching** tennis on TV.

➤ Die *-ing form* kann nach bestimmten Verben gebraucht werden (mit * markierten Verben können auch von dem Infinitiv gefolgt werden):

admit – begin* – continue* – deny – dislike – enjoy – can't face – finish – forget* – hate* – can't help – imagine – like* – love* – don't mind – miss – practise – prefer* – remember* – can't stand – start* – stop – suggest – try*.

106
112

6.5 -ing form after prepositions

By working in a pub on Saturdays he saved enough money for a holiday.
In spite of arriving a little late he managed to get on the plane.

➤ Nach einer Präposition z. B. *at, by, in, of* (außer *to*) folgt die *-ing form* eines Verbs.
➤ Präpositionen können allein (als präpositionale Wendungen) und in Verbindung mit Adjektiven oder Verben vorkommen.

106

6.6 -ing form after set phrases

It's not worth learning English if you are not going to use it.

➤ Nach bestimmten feststehenden Redewendungen folgt die *-ing* Form.

116
162

6.7 -ing forms to shorten sentences

John lived for six years in London, **working** in a factory all the time.
He often sat on the bus, **reading** his newspaper.
He left the big city at last, **returning** to the village he was born in.

➤ Sätze oder Satzteile können mit der *-ing* Form zusammengefaßt werden, wenn die (1) handelnde Person gleich ist, (2) Handlungen gleichzeitig durchgeführt werden, (3) Handlungen direkt nacheinander geschehen. Ferner, um einen Relativsatz zu verkürzen: The teenager who was sitting on the bus was black. – The teenager sitting on the bus was black.

7 Infinitive/-ing form

p. 86 112

7.1 -ing form or infinitive with verbs of perception

We could **hear** them **singing** all afternoon. I **watched** her **go** upstairs.

Nach Verben der Sinneswahrnehmung wie *felt, hear, listen to* etc. findet man oft folgende Konstruktionen:

Objekt + *-ing* Form (Handlungsablauf)	Objekt + Infinitiv ohne *to* (Beendigung einer Handlung)

p. 102

7.2 -ing form or infinitive after certain verbs

She **remembered playing** there as a child. *(Sie erinnerte sich daran, daß sie als Kind dort spielte.)*
She **remembered to buy** some bread when she was in town. *(Sie dachte daran, Brot einzukaufen, als sie in der Stadt war.)*

Nach manchen Verben können beide Formen folgen. Sie können, müssen aber nicht unterschiedliche Bedeutungen haben.

remember, not forget	*-ing Form:* bezieht sich auf die Vergangenheit/ eine vergangene Tätigkeit. *Infinitiv:* bezieht sich auf die Zukunft/ eine bevorstehende Tätigkeit.
begin, continue, like, love, start	beide Formen möglich, kein Bedeutungsunterschied.
would like, would love, would prefer, would hate	nur Infinitiv möglich.
try	*-ing Form:* man tut etwas als Versuch. *Infinitiv:* man tut sein Bestes, um Erfolg zu haben.
stop	*-ing Form:* die Handlung findet nicht mehr statt. *Infinitiv:* zur Begründung, warum jemand eine Handlung beendet hat.

8 Relative clauses

p. 62

8.1 Defining relative clauses

The man **who entered** was tall and dark.
The hat **which was lying on the floor** was too small for him.
The ones **that had arrived earlier** started to eat.

Relativsätze beziehen sich auf ein vorausgehendes Wort und bestimmen es genauer.
Sie werden durch ein Relativpronomen (Subjekt des Nebensatzes) eingeleitet (*who* Personen, *which* Sachen, *that* Personen/Sachen).

➤ Die Information, die ein **bestimmender** Relativsatz enthält, ist notwendig, um den ganzen Satz zu verstehen.

p. 62

8.2 Defining relative clauses without relative pronouns (contact clauses)

The man **(who/that)** they saw was a foreigner.

➤ Das Relativpronomen als **Objekt** kann weggelassen werden, wenn im Relativsatz ein neues Subjekt folgt.

The people **who were laughing** were local residents.

➤ Das Relativpronomen als **Subjekt** kann nicht weggelassen werden.

p. 66
8.3 Non-defining relative clauses

The man, **who had only arrived the night before**, was looking for my uncle.
This funny story, **which I have told many times before**, is really true.

➤ Relativpronomen – nur *who, which* (nicht *that*). Kann nicht weggelassen werden.
➤ Immer vom Hauptsatz durch Kommata getrennt.
➤ Enthält zusätzliche Informationen, die nicht unbedingt notwendig sind, um den Inhalt des ganzen Satzes zu verstehen. Vor allem in formellem Englisch üblich.

p. 66
8.4 Relative clauses with preposition

The man **who they were laughing at** opened his mouth to speak.

In einem Relativsatz wird eine Präposition meist an dieselbe Stelle gesetzt wie im Hauptsatz. Nur in formellem Englisch kommt eine Präposition vor das Relativpronomen.

p. 66
8.5 Relative pronoun whose

My uncle, **whose family had lived in Spain for many years**, spoke to the foreigner in his own language.
The house **whose door was open** was larger than we had expected.

➤ *Whose* (dessen/deren) – für **Personen** und für **Sachen**.

p. 66
8.6 Relative pronoun whom

We knew the girl **whom he was to marry**.

➤ *Whom* – Objektform des Relativpronomens *who*. Heutzutage nur noch in sehr formellem Englisch üblich.

9 Conditional

p. 76
9.1 Conditional 1

If you **arrive** before six, you **will find** the house empty.
Unless we give you a key, you **won't be able to** get in.

if-Satz **present**	Hauptsatz **will-future**

➤ Drückt aus, was geschehen wird, wenn eine Bedingung erfüllt ist.
➤ Die Verneinungsform *if … not* kann durch *unless* ersetzt werden.
➤ Für alle Bedingungssätze (Typ 1-3): der *if*-Satz kann **vor** oder **nach** den Hauptsatz gestellt werden.

p. 122
9.2 Conditional 2

If we **were** rich, we **would fly** to Australia in the winter.
If we **left** in ten minutes, we **would arrive** before dark.

if-Satz **simple past** (*were* in allen Personen)	Hauptsatz *would/could/might* + Infinitiv

➤ Auf die Gegenwart bezogen – unrealistisch, wenn auch theoretisch möglich.
➤ Auf die Zukunft bezogen – die Handlung ist möglich, aber unwahrscheinlich.

p. 126
9.3 Conditional 3

If we **had shown** them the way, they **would have arrived** here by now.

if-Satz **past perfect**	Hauptsatz *would/could/might have* + *-ed*/3. Form des Verbs

➤ Um über eine Handlung in der Vergangenheit zu reden, die zwar nicht passiert ist, die aber hätte geschehen können.

10 Reported speech

p. 132

10.1 Statements and negatives

DIRECT SPEECH	REPORTED SPEECH
'You must get here at six.'	John **says we** must get **there** at six.
'They aren't playing tomorrow.'	He **has told us** that they aren't playing tomorrow.
'I saw you at the cinema yesterday.'	Cindy **said** she **had seen me** at the cinema **the day before**.
'I'll see you at school tomorrow morning.'	She **added** that **she would see me** at school **the next morning**.

➤ Berichten, was jemand gesagt oder geschrieben hat.

➤ Verben des Berichtens sind oft: *say* und *tell*, wobei *tell* immer ein Dativobjekt benötigt, z. B. *tell someone*.

➤ Weitere Verben: *add, agree, answer, be sure, know, remark, think*

➤ Steht das einleitende Verb im **present, present perfect** oder **will-future**, ändert sich die Zeit der direkten Rede in der indirekten Rede nicht.

p. 142

➤ Steht das Verb in der **Vergangenheit** müssen die Zeiten in der indirekten Rede verändert werden:

DIRECT SPEECH		REPORTED SPEECH	
simple present	aren't	weren't	*simple past*
present continuous	is beginning	was beginning	*past continuous*
present perfect	have seen	had seen	*past perfect*
simple past	went	had gone	*past perfect*
past continuous	was watching	had been watching	*past perfect continuous*
going to-future	is going to	was going to	*was/were going to*
will-future	will/'ll	would	*would + infinitive*
	can	could	
	may	might	
	must	had to/must	

➤ Die Modalverben *would, could, should, might, ought to* bleiben unverändert in der indirekten Rede.

p. 142

Adverbien der Zeit und des Ortes sowie Personal- und Possessivpronomen der 1. und 2. Person müssen häufig verändert werden, aber nur, wenn es der Sinn des Satzes verlangt.

DIRECT SPEECH	REPORTED SPEECH
PRONOMEN	
I, you *(sing.)*	he, she
we, you *(plur.)*	they
my, your *(sing.)*	his, her
our, your *(plur.)*	their
ADVERBIEN	
here	there
today	that day
yesterday	the day before
... ago	... before
last week	the week before/the previous week
tomorrow	the next/following day
next week	the following week/a week later

p. 146
10.2 Questions

DIRECT SPEECH	REPORTED SPEECH
'How did you get here?' 'Are you going on holiday this summer?'	He **wanted to know how** I **had got there**. She **asked if** I **was going** on holiday this summer.

➤ Indirekte Fragen werden oft mit Verben wie *ask*, *want to know* oder *wonder* eingeleitet.
➤ Die Verschiebung der Zeiten *(back-shift)* gilt auch für Fragen.
➤ In indirekten Fragen bleibt die Wortstellung von Aussagesätzen erhalten (Subjekt – Prädikat – Objekt).
➤ Bei Fragen mit Fragewörtern verwendet man diese auch in der indirekten Rede.
➤ Bei Fragen ohne Fragewort *(yes-/no-questions)* bildet man die indirekte Frage mit *if* oder *whether* (ob).

11 Adverbs and adverbial clauses

p. 46
11.1 Adverbs (adverbial clauses): formation, use

My father came slow**ly** down the stairs. He usual**ly** ran quick**ly** down them.

ADJECTIVE	slow	quick	usual	happy (alle auf *-y*)
ADVERB	slowly	quickly	usually	happily

➤ Unregelmäßige: *good* – **well**; *fast* – **fast**; *hard* – **hard**
➤ Adverbien und adverbiale Nebensätze sind Wörter oder Satzteile, die beschreiben, **wie, wann** und **wo** Ereignisse stattfinden. Adverbien bestimmen Verben, Adjektive, andere Adverbien oder ganze Sätze näher.

p. 46
11.2 Adverbs of frequency

I **often** play tennis at the club.
The club is **usually** full on Saturdays.

➤ Adverbien der Häufigkeit zeigen an, wie oft etwas passiert.
➤ Stellung: Normalerweise zwischen Subjekt und Verb. Bei Formen von *to be* nach dem Verb.

p. 46
136
11.3 Adverbs of place and time

You can't play tennis just **anywhere**.
I'm playing with some friends **tomorrow**.
We play **inside in winter**.

➤ Adverbien der Zeit und des Ortes zeigen an, **wann** und **wo** etwas geschieht.
➤ Stellung: Meistens am Satzende. Im allgemeinen steht **Ort** vor **Zeit**. Will man die Adverbien besonders betonen, können sie auch am Satzanfang stehen. Wenn zwei Adverbien des gleichen Typs zusammentreffen, steht der genauere Ausdruck vor dem weniger genauen.

She has **already** become a member of the club.
I've **just** had a few lessons with the club trainer.
The club hasn't got a team together **yet**.
Haven't you **ever** had any lessons?

p. 56 ➤ *Already, yet, just, ever* zeigen an, **wann** oder **ob** eine Handlung stattgefunden hat.
➤ Stellung: *already, just* und *ever* meist zwischen der *have*-Form und dem **past participle**; *yet* meistens am Ende des Prädikats.
➤ *Not ever* wird meistens statt *never* in Fragen benutzt.

p. 46
11.4 Adverbs of manner

I put the eggs down on the table **carefully**. **Slowly**, one of them rolled off and broke on the floor.

➤ Adverbien der Art und Weise zeigen an, **wie** etwas geschieht.
➤ Stellung: Normalerweise **nach** dem Hauptverb und **nach** dem Prädikat, aber nicht dazwischen. Seltener auch davor, zwecks Betonung.

136
11.5 Adverbs of degree

It is **extremely** cold today.

➤ Adverbien des Grades verstärken eine Aussage oder schwächen sie ab.
➤ Stellung: Meist unmittelbar **vor** dem Ausdruck, den sie näher bestimmen.

12 Quantifiers

p. 16
126
12.1 all, a few, a little, a lot of, many, most, much, some

➤ Direkt mit einem Substantiv verbunden: *most people, some friends, all Americans, a lot of Germans* usw.
➤ Eine Auswahl dieser Dinge oder Personen mit *of the, of my* usw. verbunden: *most of my friends, some of the disc jockeys, all of the Americans in Frankfurt* usw.

MIT **ZÄHLBAREN** SUBSTANTIVEN	MIT **UNZÄHLBAREN** SUBSTANTIVEN
a few friends, **many** animals	**a little** money, not **much** time

p. 36
12.2 Some, any/some-, any-, every-, no-

Is there **any** tea left?
Yes, there's **some** tea in the pot.
Mmmm! I haven't had **any** tea as good as this for a long time.

Bejahende Sätze *(some)*	Verneinende Sätze/Fragen *(any)*

Nobody will come. I don't know **anyone anywhere** who would want to watch **something** as bad as this.

Folgende Endungen können alle mit *some, any, every* und *no* verwendet werden:

-THING	um über Sachen zu sprechen
-WHERE	um über Orte zu sprechen
-BODY, -ONE	um über Personen zu sprechen

13 Pronouns

p. 16
22
13.1 Personal pronouns

SUBJEKT	I	you	he	she	it	we	you	they
OBJEKT	me	you	him	her	it	us	you	them

p. 32
13.2 One – ones

Which pen would you like? I'll take the blue **one**.
I like red apples but you love the green **ones**.

➤ Anstelle eines Substantivs, um es nicht wiederholen zu müssen.

62
13.3 Possessive adjectives and pronouns

ADJEKTIVE	my	your	his	her	its	our	your	their
PRONOMEN	mine	yours	his	hers	–	ours	yours	theirs

82
13.4 Reflexive pronouns

He found **himself** a good restaurant and had a meal.
The restaurant **itself** was not that good but the food was.

➤ Singular *-self (my/your/her/him/it).*
➤ Plural *-selves (our/your/them).*
➤ Reflexiv – die Aussage bezieht sich auf das Subjekt.
➤ Es kann zur Hervorhebung verwendet werden.
➤ Im Englischen verwendet man die Reflexivpronomen viel seltener als im Deutschen, z. B. sich treffen = *meet*, sich bewegen = *move*, sich erinnern = *remember* usw.

82
13.5 Each other, one another

They looked at **each other**. — Sie sahen einander an.
They loved **one another**. — Sie liebten sich.
He looked at himself in the mirror. — Er sah sich selbst im Spiegel an.

➤ *Each other, one another* – wechselseitige Beziehung
➤ *-self, -selves* – rückbezügliche Beziehung

14 Comparison

26
52
14.1 Comparison of adjectives

REGELMÄSSIG	GRUNDFORM	KOMPARATIV	SUPERLATIV
Einsilbige Adjektive	fast	faster	fastest
Zweisilbige auf -y	happy	happier	happiest
Andere Zweisilbige	useful	more useful	most useful
Länger als zweisilbig	expensive	more expensive	most expensive

➤ Rechtschreibung bei einsilbigen Adjektiven:
big – big**ger** – big**gest** — Ein Konsonant nach kurzem Vokal wird verdoppelt.
late – lat**er** – lat**est** — Ein stummes End-*e* fällt weg.

UNREGELMÄSSIG	GRUNDFORM	KOMPARATIV	SUPERLATIV
	good	better	best
	bad	worse	worst
(nicht zählbar)	much	more	most
(zählbar)	many	more	most
(nicht zählbar)	little *(wenig)*	less	least

26
14.2 Comparison in sentences

Tokyo is **bigger than** London, but Mexico City is the **biggest** of the three.
2.54 cm is **as** long **as** an inch.
New York is **not as** big **as** Shanghai.

GLEICHHEIT	UNGLEICHHEIT	GRÖSSER, SCHNELLER USW. ALS ...
as ... as	not as/so ... as	than (bigger, faster than ...)

p. 52 **14.3 Comparison of adverbs**

REGELMÄSSIGE STEIGERUNG	GRUNDFORM	KOMPARATIV	SUPERLATIV
	slowly carefully quickly	**more** slowly **more** carefully **more** quickly	**most** slowly **most** carefully **most** quickly

ADVERBIEN MIT DER GLEICHEN FORM WIE ADJEKTIVE	fast high early	fast**er** high**er** earl**ier**	fast**est** high**est** earl**iest**

➤ Steigerung wie Adjektive.

UNREGELMÄSSIGE STEIGERUNG	well much/a lot a little badly far	better more less worse farther/further	best most least worst farthest/furthest

15 Definite and indefinite article

p. 112 **15.1 a/an**

My father was **a** mechanic and my mother **an** actress.

➤ Im Gegensatz zum Deutschen braucht man bei **Berufsbezeichnungen** im Englischen den unbestimmten Artikel *a* bzw. *an.*

p. 112 **15.2 the**

The women in the bar all looked at him. He looked at **the** strange tables and chairs they were sitting at.

➤ Wenn man über **bestimmte** Menschen oder Sachen spricht/schreibt, benötigt man *the.*

Music is a wonderful form of art. **The** music **of the 1960s** spoke to a whole generation.

➤ Bei abstrakten Begriffen wie Leben, Tod, Ehrlichkeit, Musik usw. benötigt man einen Artikel nur, wenn man den Begriff näher beschreibt.

p. 66

16 Genitive 's/s'/of-phrase

SINGULAR ('s) The teacher's face was red.	PLURAL (s') The boys' eyes were full of laughter.
OF The name of the ship was Ariadne.	IRREGULAR PLURAL The women's shoes were wet.

➤ Mit dem *s*-Genitiv wird **Besitz** oder **Zugehörigkeit** (Urheberschaft) ausgedrückt (Personen und Tiere). Der Genitiv mit *of* wird eher bei Sachen, selten mit Personen verwendet.

VOCABULARY

1 Wörterverzeichnis – in der Reihenfolge des Auftretens

Englische Vokabel und deutsche Entsprechung sind zweispaltig angeordnet: zum Lernen eine Seite abdecken.

Die Vokabeln der einzelnen Units sind – zur besseren Übersicht – auf jeweils einer getrennten Seite des Anhangs aufgeführt.

Deutsche Übersetzung nur in diesem speziellen Sinnzusammenhang; mehrere Bedeutungen sind möglich. Der Anhang ersetzt nicht die umfassende Übersetzung eines zweisprachigen Wörterbuchs.

Seitenzahl in der Unit; pro Seite ist die Auflistung alphabetisch.

Fast jede Seite enthält Zusatzinformation in einem Kästchen (Grammatikausdrücke, Englisch–Deutsch und Lerntips).

'Leiste' mit Hinweisen zur Lautschrift und Aussprache.

11	**afternoon** ['ɑ:ftə'nu:n]	Nachmittag
12	**reply** [rɪ'plaɪ]	antworten
13	**frequently** ['fri:kwəntlɪ]	häufig
	generally ['dʒenrəlɪ]	im allgemeinen
	kind [kaɪnd]	Art
	normally ['nɔ:məlɪ]	normalerweise
	regularly ['regjʊləlɪ]	regelmäßig
	weekend [wi:k'end]	Wochenende
14	**air** [eə]	Luft

Aussprache von Vokabeln

Lesen Sie jeden Vokabeleintrag mehrmals laut, und prägen Sie sich die Aussprache gut ein. Die Lautschriftbeispiele in der „Fußleiste" helfen Ihnen, die richtige Aussprache zu finden. Wörter, die Sie schwer behalten können, sollten Sie auf ein getrenntes Blatt schreiben.

tʃ	dʒ	ʃ	ʒ	θ	ð
chips	jet	ship	garage	thing	the

2 Wörterverzeichnis – in alphabetischer Reihenfolge

Die Zahl gibt an, auf welcher Seite die Vokabel zum ersten Mal auftaucht.

Vokabeln, die als bekannt vorausgesetzt werden, sind nur mit einem Punkt gekennzeichnet.

140 **add** hinzufügen
173 **in addition** darüber hinaus
• **address**
58 **admire** bewundern
124 **admit** zugeben
50 **adult** erwachsen
121 **advantage** Vorteil
44 **adventure** Abenteuer
• **adverb**
• **adverbial**
24 **advert** Anzeige, Annonce
176 **ancient** alt
64 **angel** Engel
120 **announcement** Durchsage
144 **anti-** gegen
90 **antique** Antiquität
• **antonym**
34 **anybody** (irgend) jemand
34 **anyone** (irgend) jemand
14 **anyway** jedenfalls
34 **not... anywhere**

3 Liste der unregelmäßigen Verben – (irregular verbs)

1. Form (infinitive)
2. Form (past tense)
3. Form (past participle)

Auch regelmäßige Form möglich!

Irregular verbs

1 **be** [i:] *sein* **was** [ɒ], **were** [ɜ:] **been** [i:]		21 **feed** [i:] *füttern* **fed** [e] **fed** [e]
2 **beat** [i:] *schlagen* **beat** [i:] **beaten** [i:]		22 **feel** [i:] *fühlen* **felt** [e] **felt** [e]
3 **become** [ʌ] *werden* **became** [eɪ] **become** [ʌ]		23 **fight** [aɪ] *kämpfen* **fought** [ɔ:] **fought** [ɔ:]
9 **burn** [ɜ:] *brennen* **burnt/ed** [ɜ:] **burnt/ed** [ɜ:]		29 **give** [ɪ] *geben* **gave** [eɪ] **given** [ɪ]

Wörterverzeichnis

in der Reihenfolge des Auftretens (seitenweise alphabetisch)

1 SWITCHED ON

10	**broadcast** ['brɔ:dkɑ:st]	Sendung, Übertragung
	broadcast, broadcast, broadcast ['brɔ:dkɑ:st]	senden, übertragen
	camp [kæmp]	campen
	camper ['kæmpə]	Camper(in)
	capital ['kæpɪtl]	Hauptstadt
	classical ['klæsɪkl]	klassisch
	comedy ['kɒmədɪ]	Komödie
	commercial [kə'mɜ:ʃl]	Werbe(spot)
	company ['kʌmpənɪ]	Gesellschaft
	different ['dɪfrənt]	verschieden
	documentary [dɒkjʊ'mentrɪ]	Dokumentarbericht, -sendung
	entertainment [entə'teɪnmənt]	Unterhaltung
	great [greɪt]	groß, großartig
	guest [gest]	Gast
	hitchhike ['hɪtʃhaɪk]	trampen
	licence ['laɪsns]	Genehmigung
	light [laɪt]	leicht
	main [meɪn]	Haupt-
	maybe ['meɪbi:]	vielleicht
	mix [mɪks]	mischen
	news [nju:z]	Nachrichten (-sendung)
	report [rɪ'pɔ:t]	Bericht
	separate ['seprət]	getrennt
	still [stɪl]	noch
	tent [tent]	Zelt
	unit ['ju:nɪt]	Lektion
	welcome ['welkəm]	willkommen
11	**afternoon** ['ɑ:ftə'nu:n]	Nachmittag
12	**reply** [rɪ'plaɪ]	antworten
13	**frequently** ['fri:kwəntlɪ]	häufig
	generally ['dʒenrəlɪ]	im allgemeinen
	kind [kaɪnd]	Art
	normally ['nɔ:məlɪ]	normalerweise
	regularly ['regjʊləlɪ]	regelmäßig
	weekend [wi:k'end]	Wochenende
14	**air** [eə]	Luft
	on the air	auf Sendung
	a.m. [eɪ'em]	vormittags
	anyway ['enɪweɪ]	jedenfalls
	area ['eərɪə]	Gebiet, Bereich
	around [ə'raʊnd]	herum
	there are around	es gibt etwa
	audience ['ɔ:dɪəns]	Publikum
	because [bɪ'kɒz]	weil
	complicated ['kɒmplɪkeɪtɪd]	kompliziert
	editor ['edɪtə]	Redakteur(in)
	favourite ['feɪvərɪt]	Lieblings-, liebst
	joke [dʒəʊk]	Witz
	organize ['ɔ:gənaɪz]	organisieren
	outside [aʊt'saɪd]	Außen-
	phone-in ['fəʊnɪn]	Telefonstudio
	p.m. [pɪ'em]	nach Mittag
	present [prɪ'zent]	vorstellen, moderieren
	presenter [prɪ'zentə]	Moderator(in)
	prize [praɪz]	Preis, Auszeichnung
	really ['rɪəlɪ]	wirklich
	record [rɪ'kɔ:d]	aufzeichnen
	special ['speʃl]	besondere
	staff [stɑ:f]	Angestellte Personal
	style [staɪl]	Stil
	VHF = very high frequency	UKW
15	**event** [ɪ'vent]	Ereignis
18	**cassette recorder** [kə'set rɪ'kɔ:də]	Kassettenrecorder
	check [tʃek]	überprüfen
	edit ['edɪt]	redigieren
	etc = et cetera	und so weiter
	gap [gæp]	Lücke
	inside [ɪn'saɪd]	innen
	item ['aɪtəm]	Artikel
	pub [pʌb]	Pub, Kneipe

Aussprache von Vokabeln

Lesen Sie jeden Vokabeleintrag mehrmals laut, und prägen Sie sich die Aussprache gut ein. Die Lautschriftbeispiele in der „Fußleiste" helfen Ihnen, die richtige Aussprache zu finden. Wörter, die Sie schwer behalten können, sollten Sie auf ein getrenntes Blatt schreiben.

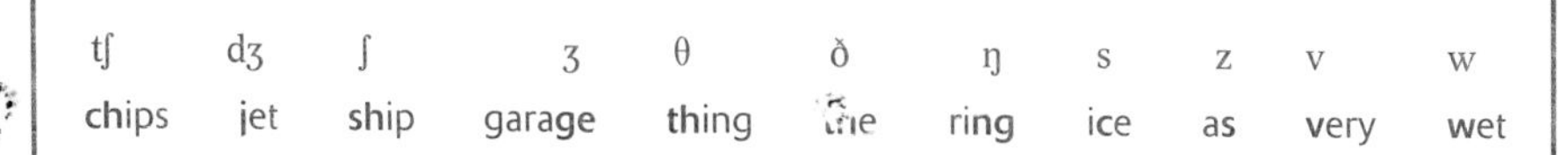

tʃ	dʒ	ʃ	ʒ	θ	ð	ŋ	s	z	v	w
chips	jet	ship	garage	thing	the	ring	ice	as	very	wet

20	**believe** [bɪ'li:v]	glauben
	break [breɪk]	Pause
	busy ['bɪzɪ]	belebt
	change [tʃeɪndʒ]	Wechselgeld
	counter ['kaʊntə]	Theke, Tresen
	customer ['kʌstəmə]	Kunde, Kundin
	duty ['dju:tɪ]	Dienst, Pflicht
	food [fu:d]	Nahrung, Essen
	(French) fries (AE) [frentʃ 'fraɪz]	Pommes frites
	hate [heɪt]	hassen, nicht mögen
	hey [heɪ]	hey
	keep, kept, kept ['ki:p, kept]	(be-)halten
	nobody ['nəʊbədɪ]	niemand
	pay [peɪ]	Bezahlung, Lohn
	pretty ['prɪtɪ]	recht, ziemlich
	serve [s3:v]	bedienen
	shake [ʃeɪk]	Mixgetränk
	shift [ʃɪft]	Schicht
	sure [ʃʊə]	sicher(lich)
	wear, wore, worn [weə, wɔ:, wɔ:n]	tragen (Kleidung)
21	**eggburger** ['egb3:gə]	Hamburger mit Ei
	lunch time ['lʌntʃtaɪm]	Mittagspause
	menu ['menju:]	Speisekarte
	mind [maɪnd]	(etwas) dagegen haben
22	**be able to** ['eɪbl]	können
23	**cleaner** ['kli:nə]	Reinigungspersonal
	enough [ɪ'nʌf]	genug
	touch [tʌtʃ]	berühren
24	**advert** ['ædv3:t]	Anzeige, Annonce
	ago [ə'gəʊ]	vor
	also ['ɔ:lsəʊ]	auch
	chain [tʃeɪn]	Kette
	cheap [tʃi:p]	billig
	expect [ɪk'spekt]	erwarten
	feed, fed, fed [fi:d, fed]	füttern
	fibre ['faɪbə]	Faser
	health [helθ]	Gesundheit
	healthy ['helθɪ]	gesund
	important [ɪm'pɔ:tənt]	wichtig
	industry ['ɪndəstrɪ]	Industrie
	invent [ɪn'vent]	erfinden
	junkfood ['dʒʌŋkfu:d]	Nahrung ohne Nährwert
	natural ['nætʃrəl]	natürlich
	polite [pə'laɪt]	höflich
	popular ['pɒpʊlə]	beliebt
	public ['pʌblɪk]	öffentlich
	quick [kwɪk]	schnell
	reach [ri:tʃ]	erreichen
	reason ['ri:zn]	Grund
	sales [seɪlz]	Umsatz, Verkäufe
	share [ʃeə]	Anteil, Aktie
	success [sək'ses]	Erfolg
	trade union [treɪd 'ju:nɪən]	Gewerkschaft
	world [w3:ld]	Welt
	worth [w3:θ]	wert
25	**describe** [dɪ'skraɪb]	beschreiben
	line [laɪn]	Zeile
27	**less** [les]	weniger
	price [praɪs]	Preis (zu zahlen)
28	**famous** ['feɪməs]	berühmt
	something ['sʌmθɪŋ]	etwas
29	**no-one** ['nəʊ wʌn] **no one**	niemand

Rechtschreibung von Vokabeln

Um Ihre Rechtschreibkenntnisse zu testen, decken Sie am besten die englische Spalte mit einem Blatt Papier zu und schreiben Sie die deutschen Entsprechungen darauf ab. Dann ergänzen Sie diese Liste mit den englischen Vokabeln. Vergleichen Sie die Wörter im Vokabelanhang. Die fehlerhaften Wörter sollten Sie noch einmal richtig ausschreiben.

Words

noun [naʊn]	Substantiv
article ['ɑ:tɪkl]	Artikel
definite article ['defɪnət]	bestimmter Artikel
indefinite article [ɪn'defɪnət]	unbestimmter Artikel
verb [v3:b]	Verb
pronoun ['prəʊnaʊn]	Pronomen
adjective ['ædʒɪktɪv]	Adjektiv
adverb ['ædv3:b]	Adverb
preposition [prepə'zɪʃn]	Präposition
conjunction [kən'dʒʌŋkʃn]	Konjunktion
number ['nʌmbə]	Zahlwort
quantifier ['kwɒntɪfaɪə]	Mengenbezeichnung
word formation [fə'meɪʃn]	Wortbildung
prefix ['pri:fɪks]	Präfix, Vorsilbe
suffix ['sʌfɪks]	Suffix, Nachsilbe
compound ['kɒmpaʊnd]	zusammengesetztes Wort
wordlist ['w3:dlɪst]	Wortliste, Wörterverzeichnis
bold (type) [bəʊld]	fett(er Druck)
in italics [ɪ'tælɪks]	kursiv
normal ['nɔ:ml]	gewöhnlich

i:	ɪ	e	æ	ɑ:	ɒ	ɔ:	ʊ	u:	ʌ	3:	ə
see	sit	ten	bad	arm	got	saw	put	too	cut	bird	about

3 A START IN LIFE

30	**career** [kə'rɪə]	Beruf(sleben)
	certificate [sə'tɪfɪkət]	Zeugnis
	chance [tʃɑ:ns]	Gelegenheit, Möglichkeit, Chance
	decide [dɪ'saɪd]	(sich) entscheiden
	decision [dɪ'sɪʒn]	Entscheidung
	earn [ɜ:n]	verdienen
	education [edʒʊ'keɪʃn]	Erziehung
	employer [ɪm'plɔɪə]	Arbeitgeber
	experience [ɪk'spɪərɪəns]	Erfahrung
	Jobcentre ['dʒɒbsentə]	Arbeitsamt
	may [meɪ]	können
	offer ['ɒfə]	(an)bieten
	officer ['ɒfɪsə]	Beamter, Beamtin
	ought to ['ɔ:tə]	sollte(n)
	remember [rɪ'membə]	daran denken
	scheme [ski:m]	Programm
	school leaver ['sku:l li:və]	Schulabgänger(in)
	skill [skɪl]	Fertigkeit, Fähigkeit
	step [step]	Schritt
	trainee [treɪ'ni:]	Auszubildene(r)
	youth [ju:θ]	Jugend(liche/r)
31	**nearly** ['nɪəlɪ]	nahezu, fast
	shoe [ʃu:]	Schuh
32	**advice** [əd'vaɪs]	Rat(schlag)
	warning ['wɔ:nɪŋ]	Ermahnung, Verbot
33	**employ** [ɪm'plɔɪ]	beschäftigen
	mechanic [mɪ'kænɪk]	Mechaniker(in)
	ordinary ['ɔ:dɪnrɪ]	gewöhnlich
	promise ['prɒmɪs]	versprechen
	replace [rɪ'pleɪs]	ersetzen
	secretary ['sekrətrɪ]	Sekretär(in)
34	**anybody, anyone** [enɪbɒdɪ, 'enɪwʌn]	(irgend) jemand
	not … anywhere ['enɪweə]	nirgends, nirgend wohin
	article ['ɑ:tɪkl]	Artikel
	certainly ['sɜ:tnlɪ]	gewiß
	confident ['kɒnfɪdənt]	selbstsicher
	disgraceful [dɪs'greɪsfʊl]	abscheulich
	dole [dəʊl]	Stempelgeld
	not … either ['aɪðə]	auch nicht
	employee [emplɔɪ'i:]	Angestellte(r)
	government ['gʌvənmənt]	Regierung
	labour ['leɪbə]	Arbeit
	paint [peɪnt]	malen, anstreichen
	(bus) pass [pɑ:s]	Dauerkarte
	slave [sleɪv]	Sklave, Sklavin
	till [tɪl]	Ladenkasse
	type [taɪp]	tippen
	unemployed [ʌnɪm'plɔɪd]	ohne Beschäftigung, arbeitslos
	wages ['weɪdʒɪz]	Lohn
35	**everywhere** ['evrɪweə]	überall (hin)
	idea [aɪ'dɪə]	Idee
	yourself [jɔ:'self]	du/dir selbst
37	**for certain** ['sɜ:tn]	sicher
	clerk [klɑ:k]	Büroangestellte(r)
	hallo [hə'ləʊ]	hallo
	hi [haɪ]	hi
	instead of [ɪn'sted]	(an)statt
	metalworker ['metlwɜ:kə]	Schlosser, Metallarbeiter(in)
	nowhere ['nəʊweə]	nirgends
38	**per** [pɜ:]	pro

Punctuation *(Zeichensetzung)*

full stop ['fʊlstɒp] **period (AE)**	Punkt
comma ['kɒmə]	Komma
colon ['kəʊlən]	Doppelpunkt
semi-colon [semɪ'kəʊlən]	Semikolon
question mark ['kwestʃn mɑ:k]	Fragezeichen
exclamation mark [ekskIə'meɪʃn mɑ:k] **~ point (AE)**	Ausrufezeichen
dash [dæʃ]	Gedankenstrich
hyphen ['haɪfn]	Bindestrich
apostrophe [ə'pɒstrəfɪ]	Apostroph
brackets ['brækɪts]	Klammern
inverted commas [ɪn'vɜ:tɪd 'kɒməz]	Anführungszeichen
asterisk ['æstərɪsk]	Sternchen

Word order *(Satzstellung)*

sentence structure ['sentəns 'strʌktʃə]	Satzstruktur
subject ['sʌbdʒɪkt]	Subjekt
object ['ɒbdʒɪkt]	Objekt
direct ~ ['dɪrekt]	direktes Objekt
indirect ~ ['ɪndɪrekt]	indirektes Objekt
verb [vɜ:b]	Prädikat
adverbial phrase [əd'vɜ:bɪəl freɪz]	Adverbialbestimmung
prepositional phrase [prepə'zɪʃənl freɪz]	präpositionale Bestimmung
complement ['kɒmplɪment]	Ergänzung

tʃ	dʒ	ʃ	ʒ	θ	ð	ŋ	s	z	v	w
chips	jet	ship	garage	thing	the	ring	ice	as	very	wet

40 **bye** [baɪ] tschüß
college [ˈkɒlɪdʒ] College
comfortable [ˈkʌmftəbl] bequem
date [deɪt] Verabredung
decent [ˈdiːsnt] anständig
keen on [kiːn] scharf auf
lovely [ˈlʌvlɪ] herrlich
nor do I [nɔː] ich auch nicht
performance [pəˈfɔːməns] Vorstellung
prefer [prɪˈfɜː] vorziehen
seat [siːt] Sitz
shall [ʃæl] sollen
suggest [səˈdʒest] vorschlagen
thriller [ˈθrɪlə] Reißer
41 **near** [nɪə] in der Nähe, nahe
43 **bored** [bɔːd] gelangweilt
chips [tʃɪps] Pommes frites
lesson [ˈlesn] Lektion
whom [huːm] wen, wem
44 **activity** [ækˈtɪvətɪ] Tätigkeit
adventure [ədˈventʃə] Abenteuer
archery [ˈɑːtʃərɪ] Bogenschießen
barbecue [ˈbɑːbɪkjuː] Grillparty
beach [biːtʃ] Strand
building [ˈbɪldɪŋ] Gebäude
canoe [kəˈnuː] Kanu
canoeist [kəˈnuːɪst] Kanute, Kanufahrer(in)
concentrate on [ˈkɒnsntreɪt] sich konzentrieren auf
control [kənˈtrəʊl] beherrschen
course [kɔːs] Kurs
crafts [krɑːfts] Handarbeiten
direction [dɪˈrekʃn] Anweisung; Richtung(sangabe)
district [ˈdɪstrɪkt] Gebiet
fire [ˈfaɪə] Feuer
flow [fləʊ] fließen
fun [fʌn] Spaß
in general [ˈdʒenrəl] im allgemeinen
include [ɪnˈkluːd] einschließen
indoor [ˈɪndɔː] Innen-
instructor [ɪnˈstrʌktə] Ausbilder(in), Lehrer(in)
insurance [ɪnˈʃʊərəns] Versicherung
map [mæp] Karte
mountain [ˈmaʊntɪn] Berg
orienteering [ɔːrɪenˈtɪərɪŋ] Geländekunde, Kartenlesen
outdoor [ˈaʊtdɔː] im Freien
pine [paɪn] Kiefer
river [ˈrɪvə] Fluß
roll [rəʊl] Rolle; rollen
safety [ˈseɪftɪ] Sicherheit
second [ˈsekənd] Sekunde
set [set] Satz
south [saʊθ] Süden; südlich
suddenly [ˈsʌdnlɪ] plötzlich
surprising [səˈpraɪzɪŋ] überraschend
view [vjuː] Sicht, Ausblick
woods [wʊdz] Wald, Wälder
wool [wʊl] Wolle
workshop [ˈwɜːkʃɒp] Arbeitsgemeinschaft
45 **dictionary** [ˈdɪkʃənrɪ] Wörterbuch
woodworking [ˈwʊdwɜːkɪŋ] Holzbearbeitung
46 **badly** [ˈbædlɪ] schlecht, schlimm
straight [streɪt] gerade, direkt
47 **fit** [fɪt] passen (zu)
sunny [ˈsʌnɪ] sonnig
usual [ˈjuːʒl] gewöhnlich
48 **action** [ˈækʃn] Aktion
careless [ˈkeəlɪs] sorglos
dislike [dɪsˈlaɪk] nicht mögen
mystery [ˈmɪstərɪ] Kriminalfilm
nurse [nɜːs] Krankenpfleger(in)
practical [ˈpræktɪkl] praktisch
probably [ˈprɒbəblɪ] wahrscheinlich
can't stand [stænd] nicht leiden können
sunshine [ˈsʌnʃaɪn] Sonnenschein
unhappy [ʌnˈhæpɪ] unglücklich
unpopular [ʌnˈpɒpjʊlə] unbeliebt
vehicle [ˈviːɪkl] Fahrzeug
yellow [ˈjeləʊ] gelb
49 **north** [nɔːθ] Norden, nördlich

Wiederholen von Vokabeln

Ohne Wiederholung vergessen Sie nach ein paar Tagen die Hälfte der neu gelernten Vokabeln.
Bauen Sie deshalb in gewissen zeitlichen Abständen, z. B. alle 14 Tage, Wiederholungsphasen ein, arbeiten Sie die gelernten Vokabeln nochmals durch und lassen Sie sich abfragen. Es wird dringend abgeraten zu versuchen, alle Vokabeln am letzten Tag vor einem Test zu lernen.

iː	ɪ	e	æ	ɑː	ɒ	ɔː	ʊ	uː	ʌ	ɜː	ə
see	sit	ten	bad	arm	got	saw	put	too	cut	bird	about

5 A LOOK AT BRITAIN

50	**adult** ['ædʌlt]	erwachsen
	alone [ə'ləʊn]	allein
	average ['ævərɪdʒ]	Durchschnitts-
	belong to [bɪ'lɒŋ]	gehören
	both ... and [bəʊθ]	sowohl ... als auch
	central ['sentrəl]	Zentral-
	Christian ['krɪstʃən]	Christ(in)
	colour ['kʌlə]	Farbe
	comprehensive school [kɒmprɪ'hensiv sku:l]	Gesamtschule
	council ['kaʊnsl]	Gemeinde
	cut, cut, cut [kʌt]	schneiden, mähen
	die [daɪ]	sterben
	figure ['fɪgə]	Zahl
	heating ['hi:tɪŋ]	Heizung
	household ['haʊshəʊld]	Haushalt
	housing ['haʊzɪŋ]	Unterkunft
	low [ləʊ]	niedrig
	majority [mə'dʒɒrətɪ]	Mehrheit
	marriage ['mærɪdʒ]	Ehe
	married ['mærɪd]	verheiratet
	member ['membə]	Mitglied
	minority [maɪ'nɒrətɪ]	Minderheit
	mortgage ['mɔ:gɪdʒ]	Hypothek, Darlehen
	non- [nɒn]	nicht-
	nowadays ['naʊədeɪz]	heutzutage
	own [əʊn]	eigen, besitzen
	population [pɒpjʊ'leɪʃn]	Bevölkerung
	punctually ['pʌŋktʃʊəlɪ]	pünktlich
	pupil ['pju:pl]	Schüler(in)
	qualified ['kwɒlɪfaɪd]	qualifiziert
	receive [rɪ'si:v]	empfangen
	rent [rent]	Miete
	rise, rose, risen [raiz, rəʊz, 'rɪzn]	(an)steigen
	schoolchildren ['sku:ltʃɪldrən]	Schulkinder
	set [set]	Apparat, Gerät
	share [ʃeə]	sich teilen (in)
	survey ['sɜ:veɪ]	Erhebung, Umfrage
	unemployment [ʌnɪm'plɔɪmənt]	Arbeitslosigkeit
	wealth [welθ]	Reichtum
	worry ['wʌrɪ]	sich Sorgen machen
51	**neither** ['naɪðə]	keine(r)
	opposite ['ɒpəzɪt]	entgegengesetzt
53	**dive** [daɪv]	tauchen
	either ... or ['aɪðə]	entweder ... oder
	jump [dʒʌmp]	springen
	practise ['præktɪs]	üben
54	**afford** [ə'fɔ:d]	sich leisten können
	available [ə'veɪləbl]	verfügbar
	back [bæk]	zurück
	bedsitter [bed'sɪtə]	möbliertes Zimmer, Wohnschlaf-zimmer
	downstairs [daʊn'steəz]	im Erdgeschoß, unten
	factory ['fæktərɪ]	Fabrik
	freedom ['fri:dəm]	Freiheit
	hostel ['hɒstl]	Heim, Herberge
	proper ['prɒpə]	geeignet
	seaside ['si:saɪd]	Küste
55	**compare** [kəm'peə]	vergleichen
	copy ['kɒpɪ]	übertragen, kopieren
	housework ['haʊswɜ:k]	Hausarbeit
	table ['teɪbl]	Tabelle
58	**admire** [əd'maɪə]	bewundern
	coast [kəʊst]	Küste
	continent ['kɒntɪnənt]	Kontinent
	disagree [dɪsə'gri:]	nicht zustimmen
	discover [dɪ'skʌvə]	entdecken
	discuss [dɪ'skʌs]	besprechen
	divorce [dɪ'vɔ:s]	Scheidung
	grandparents ['grændpeərənts]	Großeltern
	impress [ɪm'pres]	imponieren
	lifestyle ['laɪfstaɪl]	Lebensstil
	unlucky [ʌn'lʌkɪ]	unglücklich
	unusual [ʌn'ju:ʒl]	ungewöhnlich

Adverbs

adverb ['ædvɜ:b]	Adverb
~ of frequency ['fri:kwənsɪ]	Häufigkeitsadverb
~ of place [pleɪs]	Adverb des Ortes
~ of time [taɪm]	Adverb der Zeit
~ of manner ['mænə]	adverbiale Bestimmung der Art und Weise
~ of degree [dɪ'grɪ:]	Gradadverb
adverbial clause [əd'vɜ:bɪəl klɔ:z]	adverbialer Nebensatz
formation [fɔ'meɪʃn]	Bildung
position [pə'zɪʃn]	Stellung
comparison [kəm'pærɪsn]	Steigerung, Vergleich

tʃ	dʒ	ʃ	ʒ	θ	ð	ŋ	s	z	v	w
chips	jet	ship	garage	thing	the	ring	ice	as	very	wet

6 THE SENSIBLE WAY TO TOWN?

60	**bike** [baɪk]	Fahrrad
	cancel ['kænsl]	streichen
	cash [kæʃ]	Bargeld
	cause [kɔ:z]	verursachen
	choice [tʃɔɪs]	Wahl
	commuter [kə'mju:tə]	Pendler(in)
	flash [flæʃ]	Blitz
	model ['mɒdl]	Modell
	park [pɑ:k]	parken
	public transport ['pʌblɪk 'trænspɔ:t]	öffentliche Verkehrsmittel
	salesman ['seɪlzmən]	Verkäufer
	sensible ['sensəbl]	vernünftig
	surprise [sə'praɪz]	Überraschung; überraschen
	timetable ['taɪmteɪbl]	Fahrplan
	traffic jam ['træfɪk dʒæm]	Stau
61	**motorbike** ['məʊtəbaɪk]	Motorrad
	move [mu:v]	(sich) bewegen
63	**even** ['i:vn]	sogar
	kph = kilometres per hour	(km/h)
	motorcyclist ['məʊtəsaɪklɪst]	Motorradfahrer(in)
	Travelcard ['trævlkɑ:d]	Zeitkarte (London)
64	**ambulance** ['æmbjʊləns]	Krankenwagen
	angel ['eɪndʒl]	Engel
	angel of mercy ['mɜ:sɪ]	Schutzengel
	because of [bɪ'kɒz]	wegen
	Chief Inspector [tʃi:f ɪn'spektə]	Chefinspektor
	control [kən'trəʊl]	Kontrolle, Beherrschung
	criticize ['krɪtɪsaɪz]	kritisieren
	cut [kʌt]	Schnittwunde
	danger ['deɪndʒə]	Gefahr
	driving licence ['draɪvɪŋ laɪsns]	Führerschein
	eyewitness ['aɪwɪtnɪs]	Augenzeuge, -zeugin
	first aid [ɜ:d]	Erste Hilfe
	injure ['ɪndʒə]	verletzen
	injury ['ɪndʒərɪ]	Verletzung
	law [lɔ:]	Gesetz
	lose, lost, lost [lu:z, lɒst]	verlieren
	mercy ['mɜ:sɪ]	Gnade
	necessary ['nesəsərɪ]	notwendig
	provisional licence [prə'vɪʒənl laɪsns]	Führerschein auf Probe
	risk [rɪsk]	Risiko
	serious ['sɪərɪəs]	ernsthaft
	swerve [swɜ:v]	ausweichen
	themselves [ðəm'selvz]	sie/ihnen selbst
	while [waɪl]	während (conj)
	whose [hu:z]	dessen, deren
	write-off ['raɪtɒf]	Schrottwert
65	**heading** ['hedɪŋ]	Überschrift
	sergeant ['sɑ:dʒənt]	Wachtmeister
	support [sə'pɔ:t]	unterstützen
67	**middle** ['mɪdl]	Mitte
	separate ['sepəreɪt]	trennen, teilen
68	**below** [bɪ'ləʊ]	unten
	a couple of ['kʌpl]	ein paar
69	**relax** [rɪ'læks]	(sich) entspannen

Vokabelkartei

Viele Schüler arbeiten mit einer Vokabelkartei. Sie hat den Vorteil, daß sich schwer zu merkende Vokabeln leicht aussortieren und gezielt wiederholen lassen. Eine Karteikarte könnte etwa wie folgt aufgebaut sein:

Vorderseite	Rückseite
rich (adj)	*reich*
def?	*having a lot of money*
opp ▶◀	*poor*
syn ▶▶	*wealthy*

Adjectives

adjective ['ædʒɪktɪv]	Adjektiv
positive ['pɒzətɪv]	Grundform
comparative [kəm'pærətɪv]	Komparativ
superlative [su:'pɜ:lətɪv]	Superlativ
comparison [kəm'pærɪsn]	Steigerung, Vergleich
irregular [ɪ'regjʊlə]	unregelmäßig
possessive adjective [pə'zesɪv]	adjektivisch gebrauchtes Possessivpronomen

i:	ɪ	e	æ	ɑ:	ɒ	ɔ:	ʊ	u:	ʌ	ɜ:	ə
see	sit	ten	bad	arm	got	saw	put	too	cut	bird	about

7 THE CHUNNEL

70	**accept** [ək'sept]	annehmen
	billion ['bɪlɪən]	Milliarde (10^9)
	channel ['tʃænl]	Kanal
	cliff [klɪf]	Klippe
	cross [krɒs]	kreuzen, überqueren
	cross-channel ['krɒs tʃænl]	den Kanal überquerend
	crossing ['krɒsɪŋ]	Überfahrt
	daytime ['deɪtaɪm]	Tages-
	deck [dek]	Deck
	decrease [dɪ'kri:s]	verringern
	direct [dɪ'rekt]	direkt
	ferry ['ferɪ]	Fähre
	fixed [fɪkst]	fest
	freight [freɪt]	Güter, Fracht
	hope [həʊp]	hoffen
	however [haʊ'evə]	jedoch
	huge [hju:dʒ]	riesig
	increase [ɪn'kri:s]	zunehmen, steigen
	invade [ɪn'veɪd]	eindringen
	island ['aɪlənd]	Insel
	journey ['dʒɜ:nɪ]	Reise(zeit)
	lane [leɪn]	Fahrspur
	link [lɪŋk]	Verbindung
	(electrically-) lit [ɪ'lektrɪklɪ lɪt]	(elektrisch) erleuchtet
	lorry ['lɒrɪ]	Lkw
	mins = minutes	
	nighttime ['naɪtaɪm]	Nacht-
	oppose [ə'pəʊz]	sich aussprechen gegen, ablehnen
	passenger ['pæsɪndʒə]	Passagier, Fahrgast
	possible ['pɒsəbl]	möglich
	rail [reɪl]	Bahn
	shuttle ['ʃʌtl]	Pendelverkehr
	supporter [sə'pɔ:tə]	Vertreter(in), Verfechter(in)
	terminal ['tɜ:mɪnl]	(End-)Station
	traditionally [trə'dɪʃənəlɪ]	traditionell
	unless [ən'les]	wenn nicht
71	**century** ['sentʃərɪ]	Jahrhundert
	yearly ['jɜ:lɪ]	jährlich
72	**opponent** [ə'pəʊnənt]	Gegner(in)
73	**swimming-pool** ['swɪmɪŋpu:l]	Schwimmbad
74	**affect** [ə'fekt]	betreffen
	against [ə'genst]	gegen
	be allowed to [ə'laʊd]	dürfen
	although [ɔ:l'ðəʊ]	obwohl
	claim [kleɪm]	behaupten
	community [kə'mju:nətɪ]	Gemeinde
	depend (on) [dɪ'pend]	abhängen (von)
	destroy [dɪ'strɔɪ]	zerstören
	disappear ['dɪsə'pɪə]	verschwinden
	disaster [dɪ'zɑ:stə]	Unglück
	fresh [freʃ]	frisch
	gallon ['gælən]	Gallone (4,5 l/ AE 3,8 l)
	ghost [gəʊst]	Geist, Gespenst
	motorway ['məʊtəweɪ]	Autobahn
	mph = miles per hour	
	pollute [pə'lu:t]	verschmutzen
	pollution [pə'lu:ʃn]	(Umwelt-) Verschmutzung
	progress ['prəʊgres]	Fortschritt
	rule [ru:l]	Bestimmung, Verbot
	speed [spi:d]	Geschwindigkeit
	warn [wɔ:n]	warnen, darauf hinweisen
	yard [jɑ:d]	Hof
	railyard	Rangierbahnhof
75	**argument** ['ɑ:gjʊmənt]	Argument
76	**minister** ['mɪnɪstə]	Minister(in)
78	**continue** [kən'tɪnju:]	fortfahren, fortsetzen
	discussion [dɪ'skʌʃn]	Diskussion
	heavy ['hevɪ]	schwer
	hundredweight ['hʌndrədweɪt]	Zentner
	imagine [ɪ'mædʒɪn]	sich vorstellen
	imperial (system) [ɪm'pɪərɪəl]	Maßeinheiten-system in GB
	inch [ɪntʃ]	Zoll
	lb(s) = pound(s)	
	measure ['meʒə]	Maß
	measurement ['meʒəmənt]	Maß
	metric ['metrɪk]	metrisch
	ounce [aʊns]	Unze
	oz = ounce	
	sea [si:]	See, Meer
	skate [skeɪt]	Schlittschuh (laufen)
	ton [tʌn]	Tonne (2240 lb in GB)
	tonne [tʌn]	metrische Tonne (1000 kg)
	tool [tu:l]	Werkzeug
	weigh [weɪ]	wiegen
	weight [weɪt]	Gewicht
	yd = yard [jɑ:d]	Elle (91,4 cm)

tʃ	dʒ	ʃ	ʒ	θ	ð	ŋ	s	z	v	w
chips	jet	ship	garage	thing	the	ring	ice	as	very	wet

8 AMERICAN WAYS OF LIFE

80	**aggressive** [ə'gresɪv]	aggressiv
	altogether [ɔ:ltə'geðə]	gänzlich, überhaupt
	attack [ə'tæk]	Angriff
	Chamber of Commerce ['tʃeɪmbə, 'kɒmɜ:s]	Handelskammer
	congratulate [kən'grætʃʊleɪt]	gratulieren
	create [krɪ'eɪt]	schaffen
	dead-end ['dedend]	ohne Zukunft
	economy [ɪ'kɒnəmɪ]	Wirtschaft
	in favor of (AE) ['feɪvə]	dafür
	herself [hɜ:'self]	(sie/ihr) selbst
	hourly ['aʊəlɪ]	stündlich, Stunden-
	improve [ɪm'pru:v]	verbessern
	inner ['ɪnə]	Innen-
	itself [ɪt'self]	(sich) selbst
	labor (AE) ['leɪbə]	Arbeiter –
	lead, led, led [li:d, led]	führen
	messenger ['mesɪndʒə]	Bote, Botin
	myself [maɪ'self]	(ich/mir/mich) selbst
	politician [pɒlɪ'tɪʃn]	Politiker(in)
	poverty ['pɒvətɪ]	Armut
	retraining [ri:'treɪnɪŋ]	Umschulung
	society [sə'saɪətɪ]	Gesellschaft
	sound [saʊnd]	klingen
	storeroom ['stɔ:ru:m]	Lager
	welfare ['welfeə]	Sozialhilfe
	while [waɪl]	Weile
81	**employment** [ɪm'plɔɪmənt]	Arbeit, Beschäftigung
	fight [faɪt]	Kampf
	right [raɪt]	Recht
	suggestion [sə'dʒestʃən]	Vorschlag
	unfair [ʌn'feə]	ungerecht
82	**himself** [hɪm'self]	(er/ihm/ihn) selbst
	mirror ['mɪrə]	Spiegel
	ourselves [aʊə'selvz]	(uns) selbst
83	**balcony** ['bælkənɪ]	Balkon
	butler ['bʌtlə]	Butler
	civil rights [sɪvl 'raɪts]	Bürgerrechte
	gardener ['gɑ:dnə]	Gärtner(in)
	kill [kɪl]	töten
	Lord [lɔ:d]	Lord
	master ['mɑ:stə]	Herr
	murder ['mɜ:də]	Mord; ermorden
	murderer ['mɜ:dərə]	Mörder
	neighbourhood ['neɪbəhʊd]	Nachbarschaft
	repair [rɪ'peə]	reparieren
	shoot, shot, shot [ʃu:t, ʃɒt]	(er)schießen
	shot [ʃɒt]	Schuß
	speech [spi:tʃ]	Rede
	truth [tru:θ]	Wahrheit
84	**art** [ɑ:t]	Kunst
	artist ['ɑ:tɪst]	Künstler
	attraction [ə'trækʃn]	Anziehung
	beer [bɪə]	Bier
	crowd [kraʊd]	Menschenmenge
	desert ['dezət]	Wüste
	facility [fə'sɪlətɪ]	Einrichtung
	impossible [ɪm'pɒsəbl]	unmöglich
	jewellery ['dʒu:əlrɪ]	Schmuck, Juwelen
	kid [kɪd]	Kind
	launderette [lɔ:n'dret]	Waschsalon
	mama [mə'mɑ:]	Mama
	missile ['mɪsaɪl]	Rakete
	movie ['mu:vɪ]	Kino, Film
	muscle ['mʌsl]	Muskel
	overseas [əʊvə'si:z]	überseeisch
	parking lot ['pɑ:kɪŋ lɒt]	Parkplatz
	proud [praʊd]	stolz
	range [reɪndʒ]	Testgelände
	resort [rɪ'zɔ:t]	Ferien-, z. B. Bade-, Wintersportort
	roller skate ['rəʊlə skeɪt]	Rollschuh
	seafront ['si:frʌnt]	Strand, Küste
	sidewalk ['saɪdwɔ:k]	Bürgersteig
	strange [streɪndʒ]	fremd(artig)
	vendor ['vendə]	Verkäufer(in)
85	**apart (from)** [ə'pɑ:t]	abgesehen (von)
	climate ['klaɪmɪt]	Klima
86	**notice** ['nəʊtɪs]	bemerken
87	**crime** [kraɪm]	Verbrechen
	grow, grew, grown [grəʊ, gru:, grəʊn]	wachsen
	gun [gʌn]	Gewehr, Schußwaffe
	income ['ɪŋkʌm]	Einkommen
	increase ['ɪŋkri:s]	Steigerung
	peace [pi:s]	Frieden
	rest [rest]	Rest
	Snowbelt ['snəʊbelt]	Schneegürtel
	southern ['sʌðən]	Süd-
	state [steɪt]	Staat
	Sunbelt ['sʌnbelt]	Sonnengürtel
	towards [tə'wɔ:dz]	auf ... zu
	war [wɔ:]	Krieg
88	**airport** ['eəpɔ:t]	Flughafen

i:	ɪ	e	æ	ɑ:	ɒ	ɔ:	ʊ	u:	ʌ	ɜ:	ə
see	sit	ten	bad	arm	got	saw	put	too	cut	bird	about

bright [braɪt]	hell
fashion ['fæʃn]	Mode
flight [flaɪt]	Flug
pill [pɪl]	Pille
sneakers ['sni:kəz]	Turnschuhe
suit [su:t]	Anzug
tax [tæks]	Steuer
vacation [və'keɪʃn]	Urlaub
vegetarian [vedʒɪ'teərɪən]	vegetarisch
wine [waɪn]	Wein

9 LONDON PRIDE

90	**antique** [æn'ti:k]	Antiquität
	atmosphere ['ætməsfɪə]	Atmosphäre
	attractive [ə'træktɪv]	attraktiv
	busker ['bʌskə]	Straßensänger(in)
	crazy ['kreɪzɪ]	verrückt
	entertain [entə'teɪn]	unterhalten
	foreign ['fɒrən]	fremd
	luxury ['lʌkʃərɪ]	Luxus
	market ['mɑ:kɪt]	Markt
	musician [mju:'zɪʃn]	Musikant(in), Musiker(in)
	persuade [pə'sweɪd]	überzeugen, -reden
	plenty of ['plentɪ]	viel
	postcard ['pəʊstkɑ:d]	Postkarte
	pride [praɪd]	Stolz
	pull down [pʊl]	niederreißen
	stall [stɔ:l]	Stand
	tropical ['trɒpɪkl]	tropisch
	vegetable ['vedʒtəbl]	Gemüse
	wander ['wɒndə]	schlendern
92	**free** [fri:]	frei
	might [maɪt]	könnte(n)
93	**refuse** [rɪ'fju:z]	ablehnen
94	**beat, beat, beaten** [bi:t, 'bi:tn]	schlagen, überlisten
	bomb [bɒm]	Bombe
	breathe [bri:ð]	atmen
	completely [kəm'pli:tlɪ]	vollständig
	drain [dreɪn]	(Abwasser-)Kanal
	-drawn [drɔ:n]	gezogen
	dummy ['dʌmɪ]	Attrappe
	engine ['endʒɪn]	Lokomotive
	flooding ['flʌdɪŋ]	Überflutung
	force [fɔ:s]	zwingen
	pleasant ['pleznt]	angenehm
	railway ['reɪlweɪ]	Bahn
	rat [ræt]	Ratte
	result [rɪ'zʌlt]	Ergebnis
	rush hour ['rʌʃ aʊə]	Stoßzeit
	shape [ʃeɪp]	Form
	shelter ['ʃeltə]	sich in Sicherheit bringen
	smell [smel]	riechen
	steam [sti:m]	Dampf
	track [træk]	Schiene, Gleis
	tube [tju:b]	U-Bahn
	underground ['ʌndəgraʊnd]	U-Bahn
	waste [weɪst]	Abfall
	waste water	Abwasser
95	**movement** ['mu:vmənt]	Bewegung
	thirsty ['θɜ:stɪ]	durstig
	uncomfortable [ʌn'kʌmftəbl]	unbequem
97	**desk** [desk]	Schalter
	fan [fæn]	Ventilator
	friendly ['frendlɪ]	freundlich
	neighbour ['neɪbə]	Nachbar(in)
98	**construction** [kən'strʌkʃn]	Bau
	overground ['əʊvəgraʊnd]	Hochbahn
	power ['paʊə]	Stärke
	provide [prə'vaɪd]	liefern, (an)bieten
	solve [sɒlv]	lösen
	subway ['sʌbweɪ]	U-Bahn **(AE)**

Clauses

clause [klɔ:z]	Satz(teil)
main ~ [meɪn]	Hauptsatz
sub-clause ['sʌbklɔ:z]	Nebensatz
relative ~ ['relətɪv]	Relativsatz
defining relative ~ [dɪ'faɪnɪŋ]	bestimmender Relativsatz
non-defining relative ~ ['nɒndɪfaɪnɪŋ]	nichtbestimmender Relativsatz
contact ~ ['kɒntækt]	Relativsatz ohne Relativpronomen
adverbial ~ [əd'vɜ:bɪəl]	adverbialer Nebensatz
positive statement ['pɒzətɪv 'steɪtmənt]	bejahender Satz
negative statement ['negətɪv 'steɪtmənt]	verneinender Satz
question tag ['kwestʃn tæg]	bestätigende Rückfrage
set phrase [freɪz]	feststehende Redewendung

tʃ	dʒ	ʃ	ʒ	θ	ð	ŋ	s	z	v	w
chips	jet	ship	garage	thing	the	ring	ice	as	very	wet

10 WORK AND PLAY

100	**barn**	[bɑ:n]	Scheune
	close	[kləʊs]	nahe
	concrete	['kɒŋkri:t]	Beton
	depressing	[dɪ'presɪŋ]	deprimierend
	drug	[drʌg]	Droge
	dry	[draɪ]	trocknen
	fit	[fɪt]	fit
	height	[haɪt]	Höhe
	human	['hju:mən]	menschlich
	ladder	['lædə]	Leiter
	lay, laid, laid	[leɪ, leɪd]	legen
	nurse	[nɜ:s]	pflegen
	patient	['peɪʃnt]	geduldig
	pressure	['preʃə]	Druck
	reed	[ri:d]	Reet
	in spite of	[spaɪt]	trotz
	split, split, split	[splɪt]	teilen
	stick	[stɪk]	Stock
	thatch	[θætʃ]	mit Reet decken
	thatcher	['θætʃə]	Reetdachdecker
	tie	[taɪ]	binden
	ward	[wɔ:d]	(Kranken-)Station
101	**meaning**	['mi:nɪŋ]	Bedeutung
	quality	['kwɒlətɪ]	Qualität
	seem	[si:m]	scheinen
102	**comprehend**	[kɒmprɪ'hend]	verstehen
	govern	['gʌvn]	regieren
	perform	[pə'fɔ:m]	aufführen
103	**agreement**	[ə'gri:mənt]	Vertrag
	description	[dɪ'skrɪpʃn]	Beschreibung
	farmworker	['fɑ:mwɜ:kə]	Landarbeiter(in)
	feeling	['fi:lɪŋ]	Gefühl
	goods	[gʊdz]	Waren
	headline	['hedlaɪn]	Schlagzeile
	injection	[ɪn'dʒekʃn]	Spritze
	old-fashioned	[əʊld'fæʃnd]	altmodisch
	invention	[ɪn'venʃn]	Erfindung
	pleasure	['pleʒə]	Vergnügen
104	**association**	[əsəʊsɪ'eɪʃn]	Verband
	background	['bækgraʊnd]	Herkunft, Hintergrund
	cap	[kæp]	Mütze
	champion	['tʃæmpɪən]	Sieger(in), Meister(in)
	championship	['tʃæmpɪənʃɪp]	Meisterschaft
	chant	[tʃɑ:nt]	singen; Gesang
	cheerleader	['tʃɪəli:də]	Anführer(in) des organisierten Beifalls
	chess	[tʃes]	Schach
	coach	[kəʊtʃ]	Trainer(in)
	confidence	['kɒnfɪdəns]	Selbstvertrauen
	helmet	['helmɪt]	Helm
	kick	[kɪk]	Hochwerfen
	league	[li:g]	Liga
	look forward to	['fɔ:wəd]	sich freuen auf
	mental	['mentl]	geistig
	miner	['maɪnə]	Bergmann
	padding	['pædɪŋ]	Polsterung
	protective	[prə'tektɪv]	Schutz-
	physical	['fɪzɪkl]	(betont) körperlich
	practise	['præktɪs]	üben
	soccer	['sɒkə]	(europäischer) Fußball
	spare time	[speə]	Freizeit
	tights	[taɪts]	Strumpfhosen
	typical	['tɪpɪkl]	typisch
	violence	['vaɪələns]	Gewalt(tätigkeit)
	violent	['vaɪələnt]	gewalttätig
	youngster	['jʌŋstə]	Jugendliche(r)
105	**cheerleading**	['tʃɪəli:dɪŋ]	Beifall organisieren
106	**according to**	[ə'kɔ:dɪŋ]	entsprechend, gemäß
	due to	[dju:]	infolge von
	except (for)	[ɪk'sept]	außer
	mad (about)	[mæd]	verrückt (nach)
	owing to	['əʊɪŋ]	dank
107	**business**	['bɪznɪs]	Geschäft
	pot	[pɒt]	Kanne
	snooker	['snu:kə]	Billard
	thought	[θɔ:t]	Gedanke
	twice	[twaɪs]	zweimal
108	**enquiry**	[ɪn'kwaɪərɪ]	Anfrage
	responsibility	[rɪspɒnsə'bɪlətɪ]	Verantwortung
	thoughtful	['θɔ:tfʊl]	nachdenklich
	whether	['weðə]	ob

Phonetics (Lautlehre)

sound	[saʊnd]	Laut
vowel	['vaʊəl]	Vokal (Selbstlaut)
consonant	['kɒnsənənt]	Konsonant (Mitlaut)
pronunciation	[prənʌnsɪ'eɪʃn]	Aussprache
stress	[stres]	Betonung
intonation	[ɪntə'neɪʃn]	Intonation (Stimmführung)

i:	ɪ	e	æ	ɑ:	ɒ	ɔ:	ʊ	u:	ʌ	ɜ:	ə
see	sit	ten	bad	arm	got	saw	put	too	cut	bird	about

11 LEGEND

110	**arrest** [ə'rest]	verhaften
	autograph ['ɔ:təgrɑ:f]	Autogramm
	bug [bʌg]	belästigen
	candle ['kændl]	Kerze
	doorman ['dɔ:mən]	Portier
	forever [fə'revə]	für immer
	gun-control ['gʌn kəntrəʊl]	Waffenkontrolle
	gunman ['gʌnmən]	Bewaffneter
	guy [gaɪ]	Typ, Bursche, Kerl
	killer ['kɪlə]	Killer
	legend ['ledʒənd]	Legende
	lit [lɪt]	angezündet
	lollipop ['lɒlɪpɒp]	Lutscher
	miss [mɪs]	vermissen
	particular [pə'tɪkjʊlə]	bestimmt
	printworker ['prɪntwɜ:kə]	Drucker(eiarbeiter/in)
	recording studio [rɪ'kɔ:dɪŋ 'stju:dɪəʊ]	Aufnahmestudio
	return [rɪ'tɜ:n]	zurückkehren
	screwball ['skru:bɔ:l]	Wirrkopf
	several ['sevrəl]	einige, mehrere
	shocked [ʃɒkt]	schockiert
	succeed in [sək'si:d]	erfolgreich sein
	waste [weɪst]	Verlust, Vergeudung

Numbers

number ['nʌmbə]	Zahl
singular ['sɪŋgjʊlə]	Einzahl
plural ['plʊərəl]	Mehrzahl
cardinal number ['kɑ:dɪnl]	Kardinalzahl (Grundzahl)
one	ein, eins
two	zwei
three	drei
ordinal number ['ɔ:dɪnl]	Ordinalzahl (Ordnungszahl)
first	erste(r, s)
second	zweite(r, s)
third	dritte(r, s)
fourth	vierte(r, s)
decimal number ['desɪml]	Dezimalzahl
fraction ['frækʃn]	Bruchzahl
percentage [pə'sentɪdʒ]	Prozentzahl
sum [sʌm]	Summe
quantifier ['kwɒntɪfaɪə]	Mengenbezeichnung

2,000 = 2.000
1.5 (one point five) = 1,5
7 a.m. = 7 Uhr
7 p.m. = 19 Uhr

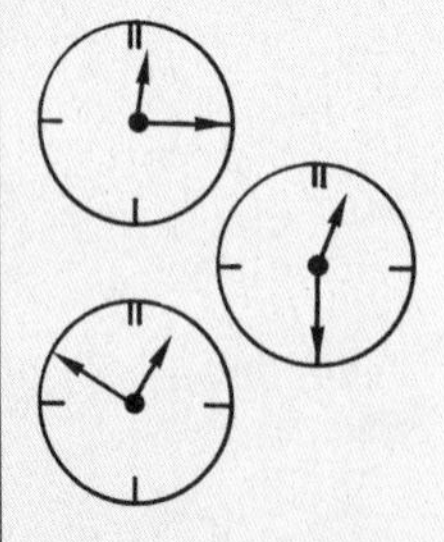

12.15 (quarter past ...) = viertel nach ...
12.30 (half past ...) = halb ...
12.50 (ten to ...) = zehn vor ...

111	**obituary** [ə'bɪtʃʊərɪ]	Todesanzeige
	react [rɪ'ækt]	reagieren
	safe(ly) ['seɪflɪ]	sicher
	unfriendly [ʌn'frendlɪ]	unfreundlich
113	**history** ['hɪstrɪ]	Geschichte
	pleased [pli:zd]	zufrieden
	weekday ['wi:kdeɪ]	Wochentag
114	**ain't** [eɪnt]	= isn't, hasn't
	alive [ə'laɪv]	lebend
	amongst [ə'mʌŋst]	unter
	copper ['kɒpə]	Kupfer
	deny [dɪ'naɪ]	abstreiten
	dream [dri:m]	träumen
	emigrate ['emɪgreɪt]	auswandern
	evidence ['evɪdəns]	Beweis(e)
	immigrant ['ɪmɪgrənt]	Einwanderer, Einwanderin
	industrial [ɪn'dʌstrɪəl]	Industrie-
	meeting ['mi:tɪŋ]	Versammlung, Treffen
	mine [maɪn]	Bergwerk
	mourn [mɔ:n]	trauern
	particularly [pə'tɪkjʊləlɪ]	besonders
	release [rɪ'li:s]	Freilassung
	sentence ['sentəns]	verurteilen; Urteil
	skilled [skɪld]	gelernt
	songwriter ['sɒŋraɪtə]	Liedermacher(in)
	strike [straɪk]	Streik
	tune ['tju:n]	Melodie
	unionization [ju:nɪənaɪ'zeɪʃn]	Organisation in Gewerkschaften
	unskilled [ʌn'skɪld]	ungelernt
115	**lifestory** ['laɪfstɔ:rɪ]	Biographie
117	**moon** [mu:n]	Mond
118	**appear** [ə'pɪə]	erscheinen
	boring ['bɔ:rɪŋ]	langweilig
	charge [tʃɑ:dʒ]	Anklage
	emigrant ['emɪgrənt]	Auswanderer(in)
	emigration [emɪ'greɪʃn]	Auswanderung
	experienced [ɪk'spɪərɪənst]	erfahren
	frame [freɪm]	reinlegen
	immigrate ['ɪmɪgreɪt]	einwandern
	immigration [ɪmɪ'greɪʃn]	Einwanderung
	legendary ['ledʒəndrɪ]	legendär
	mill [mɪl]	Fabrik, (Walz-)Werk
	sad [sæd]	traurig
	successful [sək'sesfʊl]	erfolgreich

tʃ	dʒ	ʃ	ʒ	θ	ð	ŋ	s	z	v	w
chips	jet	ship	garage	thing	the	ring	ice	as	very	wet

12 HEAD IN THE CLOUDS

120	**announcement** [ə'naʊnsmənt]	Durchsage
	belt [belt]	Gürtel
	board [bɔ:d]	Bord
	captain ['kæptɪn]	(Flug-)Kapitän
	cloud [klaʊd]	Wolke
	commercially [kə'mɜ:ʃəlɪ]	kommerziell
	daydream ['deɪdri:m]	Träumerei
	develop [dɪ'veləp]	entwickeln
	development [dɪ'veləpmənt]	Entwicklung
	doubt [daʊt]	Zweifel
	earth [ɜ:θ]	Erde
	fasten ['fɑ:sn]	befestigen
	finally ['faɪnəlɪ]	schließlich
	flight lane ['flaɪt leɪn]	Flugschneise, -korridor
	fuel ['fju:əl]	Treibstoff
	glide [glaɪd]	gleiten (Segelflug)
	hydrogen ['haɪdrədʒən]	Wasserstoff
	landing ['lændɪŋ]	Landung
	liquid ['lɪkwɪd]	flüssig
	manufacturer [mænjʊ'fæktʃərə]	Hersteller(in)
	oxygen ['ɒksɪdʒən]	Sauerstoff
	realistic [rɪə'lɪstɪk]	realistisch
	reality [rɪ'ælətɪ]	Wirklichkeit
	runway ['rʌnweɪ]	Startbahn
	seat belt ['si:t belt]	Sicherheitsgurt
	stage [steɪdʒ]	Phase, Stadium
	supersonic [su:pə'sɒnɪk]	mit Überschall (geschwindigkeit)
	take off [teɪk 'ɒf]	abheben, starten
	take-off ['teɪkɒf]	Start
	technically ['teknɪklɪ]	technisch
121	**advantage** [əd'vɑ:ntɪdʒ]	Vorteil
	smoothly ['smu:ðlɪ]	glatt, ruhig
122	**fare** [feə]	(Flug-)Kosten, Preis
	go sightseeing ['saɪtsi:ɪŋ]	Sehenswürdigkeiten besichtigen
123	**take care of** [keə]	sich kümmern um
	kangaroo [kæŋgə'ru:]	Känguruh
	mark [mɑ:k]	Mark
	be in operation [ɒpə'reɪʃn]	in Betrieb sein
124	**admit** [əd'mɪt]	zugeben
	airfield ['eəfi:ld]	Flugfeld
	airforce ['eəfɔ:s]	Luftwaffe
	airline ['eəlaɪn]	Fluggesellschaft
	amount [ə'maʊnt]	Menge
	brake [breɪk]	(ab)bremsen
	cabin ['kæbɪn]	Kabine
	calm [kɑ:m]	beruhigen
	chute [ʃu:t]	Rutsche
	crash (landing) [kræʃ]	Bruchlandung
	crew [kru:]	Besatzung, Mannschaft
	down [daʊn]	zum Absturz bringen
	emergency [ɪ'mɜ:dʒənsɪ]	Notfall
	(fire) extinguisher [ɪk'stɪŋgwɪʃə]	Feuerlöscher
	fail [feɪl]	aussetzen, versagen
	glider ['glaɪdə]	Segelflugzeug
	glider pilot ['paɪlət]	Segelflieger(in)
	ground staff [stɑ:f]	Bodenpersonal
	instead [ɪn'sted]	statt dessen
	luckily ['lʌkɪlɪ]	glücklicherweise
	manage ['mænɪdʒ]	handhaben, leiten
	minor ['maɪnə]	geringfügig
	mistake [mɪ'steɪk]	Fehler
	mix up [mɪks 'ʌp]	verwechseln
	mix-up ['mɪksʌp]	Durcheinander, Verwechslung
	procedure [prə'si:dʒə]	Verhalten, Maßnahme(n)
	race [reɪs]	rasen
	silent ['saɪlənt]	still
	tyre ['taɪə]	Reifen
125	**damage** ['dæmɪdʒ]	beschädigen
	exactly [ɪg'zæktlɪ]	genau
127	**calm** [kɑ:m]	ruhig
	convenient [kən'vi:nɪənt]	bequem
	difficulty ['dɪfɪkəltɪ]	Schwierigkeit
	motorcycle ['məʊtəsaɪkl]	Motorrad
	rewrite [ri:'raɪt]	umschreiben
128	**aboard** [ə'bɔ:d]	an Bord
	aisle [aɪl]	Gang
	altitude ['æltɪtju:d]	Höhe
	armrest ['ɑ:mrest]	Armlehne
	arrival [ə'raɪvl]	Ankunft
	cruising altitude ['kru:zɪŋ]	Reiseflughöhe
	degree [dɪ'gri:]	Grad
	exit ['eksɪt]	Ausgang
	galley ['gælɪ]	Bordküche
	instruction [ɪn'strʌkʃn]	Anweisung
	mask [mɑ:sk]	Maske
	match [mætʃ]	passen zu, entsprechen
	nonsense ['nɒnsns]	Unsinn
	refreshment [rɪ'freʃmənt]	Erfrischung
	sink, sank, sunk [sɪŋk, sæŋk, sʌŋk]	sinken
	wish [wɪʃ]	wünschen

i:	ɪ	e	æ	ɑ:	ɒ	ɔ:	ʊ	u:	ʌ	ɜ:	ə
see	sit	ten	bad	arm	got	saw	put	too	cut	bird	about

13 DOWNTOWN AND UPTOWN

130	**almost** ['ɔ:lməʊst]	beinahe
	argue ['ɑ:gju:]	darauf hinweisen
	citizen ['sɪtɪzn]	Bürger(in)
	concerned [kən'sɜ:nd]	betroffen
	conflict ['kɒnflɪkt]	Konflikt
	criminal ['krɪmɪnl]	kriminell
	downtown (AE) ['daʊntaʊn]	(im/ins) Stadtzentrum
	gasoline (AE) ['gæsəli:n]	Benzin
	newcomer ['nju:kʌmə]	Neuankömmling
	overcrowding [əʊvə'kraʊdɪŋ]	Überbevölkerung
	political [pə'lɪtɪkl]	politisch
	privacy ['prɪvəsɪ]	Zurückgezogenheit
	renovate ['renəveɪt]	renovieren
	renovation [renə'veɪʃn]	Renovierung
	suburb ['sʌbɜ:b]	Stadtrandsiedlung
	unable [ʌn'eɪbl]	unfähig
	be unable	nicht in der Lage sein
	uptown ['ʌptaʊn]	in den Außenbezirken
131	**attitude** ['ætɪtju:d]	Einstellung, Haltung
	lonely ['ləʊnlɪ]	einsam
	remain [rɪ'meɪn]	bleiben
132	**remark** [rɪ'mɑ:k]	bemerken
133	**connect** [kə'nekt]	verbinden
	continue [kən'tɪnju:]	fortsetzen
	defence (AE defense) [dɪ'fens]	Verteidigung
	move [mu:v]	Bewegung
	report [rɪ'pɔ:t]	berichten
	resident ['rezɪdənt]	Einwohner(in)
	state [steɪt]	feststellen
134	**amenity** [ə'mi:nətɪ]	öffentliche Einrichtung
	blame [bleɪm]	die Schuld geben
	block [blɒk]	(Häuser-)Block
	condominium (AE) [kɒndə'mɪnɪəm]	Eigentumswohnung
	decay [dɪ'keɪ]	verfallen
	definitely ['defɪnətlɪ]	bestimmt
	elementary (AE) [elɪ'mentərɪ]	Grund-
	environmental [ɪnvaɪərən'mentl]	Umwelt-
	extremely [ɪk'stri:mlɪ]	äußerst, außerordentlich
	fancy ['fænsɪ]	Luxus-
	flash of light [flæʃ]	Lichtblick
	grand [grænd]	großartig
	guess [ges] **(AE)**	glauben, vermuten
	hardly ['hɑ:dlɪ]	kaum
	highrise ['haɪraɪz]	Hochhaus
	maintain [meɪn'teɪn]	pflegen
	mixture ['mɪkstʃə]	Mischung
	multi-family unit (AE) [mʌltɪ'fæməlɪ]	Mehrfamilienhaus
	residential [rezɪ'denʃl]	Wohn-
	shame [ʃeɪm]	Schande
	shine, shone, shone [ʃaɪn, ʃɒn]	scheinen
	slum [slʌm]	Elendsviertel
	store [stɔ:] **(AE)**	Laden, Geschäft
	study ['stʌdɪ]	Studie
	suffer (from) ['sʌfə]	leiden (an)
	summit ['sʌmɪt]	Gipfel
	trade [treɪd]	Handel
	turn of the century	Jahrhundertwende
	twin city [twɪn]	Doppelstadt
	uninviting [ʌnɪn'vaɪtɪŋ]	wenig einladend
	zone [zəʊn]	Zone
135	**freeway** ['fri:weɪ] **(AE)**	Schnellstraße
	furthest ['fɜ:ðɪst]	am weitesten
	useful ['ju:sfʊl]	nützlich
136	**afterwards** ['ɑ:ftəwədz]	danach
	detached [dɪ'tætʃt]	freistehend
	duplex (AE) ['dju:pleks]	Zweifamilienhaus
	fairly ['feəlɪ]	ziemlich
	immediately [ɪ'mi:dɪətlɪ]	sofort
	lately ['leɪtlɪ]	kürzlich
	owner-occupied flat ['əʊnə'ɒkjʊpaɪd]	Eigentumswohnung
	semi-detached house [semɪdɪ'tætʃt]	Doppelhaushälfte
137	**library** ['laɪbrərɪ]	Bücherei
	rare [reə]	selten
	waterfall ['wɔ:təfɔ:l]	Wasserfall
	wheat [wi:t]	Weizen
138	**behave** [bɪ'heɪv]	sich (gut) benehmen
	chromium ['krəʊmɪəm]	Chrom
	clue [klu:]	Lösungshilfe, Frage
	coke [kəʊk]	Koks
	crawl [krɔ:l]	kriechen
	crossword puzzle ['krɒswɜ:d pʌzl]	Kreuzworträtsel
	ex- [eks]	ehemalig
	flag [flæg]	Fahne
	graduation [grædʒʊ'eɪʃn]	Diplom

tʃ	dʒ	ʃ	ʒ	θ	ð	ŋ	s	z	v	w
chips	jet	ship	garage	thing	the	ring	ice	as	very	wet

	hand down	überliefern
	hang, hung, hung [hæŋ, hʌŋ]	hängen
	iron ['aɪən]	Eisen
	restlessness ['restlɪsnɪs]	Ruhelosigkeit
	soldier ['səʊldʒə]	Soldat
	steel [sti:l]	Stahl

14 CAN YOU BELIEVE IT?

140	**add** [æd]	hinzufügen
	balloon [bə'lu:n]	Ballon
	borrow ['bɒrəʊ]	borgen
	capsule ['kæpsju:l]	Kapsel
	charity ['tʃærətɪ]	Wohltätigkeit
	daredevil ['deədevl]	Teufelskerl
	devote [dɪ'vəʊt]	widmen
	edition [ɪ'dɪʃn]	Auflage
	face [feɪs]	sich gegenübersehen
	farewell [feə'wel]	Abschied, Lebewohl
	grab [græb]	ergreifen
	heart [hɑ:t]	Herz
	major ['meɪdʒə]	größer
	media ['mi:dɪə]	Medien
	message ['mesɪdʒ]	Botschaft
	publicity [pʌb'lɪsətɪ]	Publizität
	record ['rekɔ:d]	Rekord
	responsible [rɪ'spɒnsəbl]	verantwortlich
	sock [sɒk]	Socke
	thirst [θɜ:st]	Durst
	transatlantic [trænzət'læntɪk]	transatlantisch
	wave [weɪv]	Welle
141	**length** [leŋθ]	Länge
	rescue ['reskju:]	retten
143	**actual** ['æktʃʊəl]	tatsächlich
	arrange [ə'reɪndʒ]	verabreden
	criminal ['krɪmɪnl]	Verbrecher(in)
	hero ['hɪərəʊ]	Held
	hurt, hurt, hurt [hɜ:t]	verletzen
	maths [mæθs]	Mathe
	it doesn't matter ['mætə]	es macht nichts
	previous ['pri:vɪəs]	vorhergehend
	quote [kwəʊt]	Zitat
144	**acceptable** [ək'septəbl]	annehmbar
	anti- [æntɪ]	gegen
	benefit ['benɪfɪt]	Vorteil, Nutzen
	circulation [sɜ:kjʊ'leɪʃn]	Verbreitung, Auflage
	daily ['deɪlɪ]	täglich
	display [dɪ'spleɪ]	Bildschirm
	east [i:st]	(nach) Osten
	effect [ɪ'fekt]	Wirkung
	input ['ɪnpʊt]	Eingabe
	management ['mænɪdʒmənt]	Management
	process ['prəʊses]	Prozeß
	produce [prə'dju:s]	herstellen
	rationalisation [ræʃnəlaɪ'zeɪʃn]	Rationalisierung
	research [rɪ'sɜ:tʃ]	Forschung
	screen [skri:n]	(Bild-)Schirm
	series ['sɪəri:z]	Reihe
	spokesman ['spəʊksmən]	Sprecher
	survive [sə'vaɪv]	überleben
	tremendously [trɪ'mendəslɪ]	ungeheuer, kolossal
145	**print** [prɪnt]	drucken; Druck
	term [tɜ:m]	Ausdruck
147	**cartoon** [kɑ:'tu:n]	Karikatur
	clear [klɪə]	frei
	culture ['kʌltʃə]	Kultur
	gossip ['gɒsɪp]	Klatsch
	insert [ɪn'sɜ:t]	einfügen
	involve [ɪn'vɒlv]	verwickeln
	mainly ['meɪnlɪ]	hauptsächlich
	questionnaire [kwestʃə'neə]	Fragebogen
	research [rɪ'sɜ:tʃ]	recherchieren
	showbusiness ['ʃəʊbɪznɪs]	Showgeschäft
	subscribe (to) [səb'skraɪb]	abonnieren
	treat [tri:t]	behandeln
	treatment ['tri:tmənt]	Behandlung
	unconscious [ʌn'kɒnʃəs]	bewußtlos
	weekly ['wi:klɪ]	wöchentlich
	wonder ['wʌndə]	sich fragen
148	**exam** [ɪg'zæm]	Prüfung
	express [ɪk'spres]	ausdrücken
	fingernail ['fɪngəneɪl]	Fingernagel
	fireman ['faɪəmən]	Feuerwehrmann

time [taɪm]	Zeitabschnitt, Tagesabschnitt
tense [tens]	Zeitform des konjugierten Verbs, z. B. simple present, present perfect, future usw.

i:	ɪ	e	æ	ɑ:	ɒ	ɔ:	ʊ	u:	ʌ	ɜ:	ə
see	sit	ten	bad	arm	got	saw	put	too	cut	bird	about

15 CLEANING UP

150	**ashore** [ə'ʃɔː]	an Land
	breed, bred, bred [briːd, bred]	brüten
	breeding ground	Brutplatz
	cargo ['kɑːgəʊ]	Fracht
	coastline ['kəʊstlaɪn]	Küste
	dump [dʌmp]	Kippe; abladen
	fisherman ['fɪʃəmən]	Fischer
	highly ['haɪlɪ]	hoch
	indeed [ɪn'diːd]	tatsächlich
	interest ['ɪntrəst]	Interesse
	internationally [ɪntə'næʃnəlɪ]	international
	leak [liːk]	sickern
	mess [mes]	Schmutz, Durcheinander
	oil [ɔɪl]	Öl
	oiled [ɔɪld]	ölverschmutzt
	oily ['ɔɪlɪ]	ölig
	ore [ɔː]	Erz
	patrol [pə'trəʊl]	Patrouille
	port [pɔːt]	Hafen
	pump [pʌmp]	pumpen
	recover [rɪ'kʌvə]	bergen
	recovery [rɪ'kʌvərɪ]	Bergung
	rock [rɒk]	Felsen
	rubbish ['rʌbɪʃ]	Müll
	rubbish dump	Müllkippe
	seabed ['siːbed]	Meeresgrund
	seabird ['siːbɜːd]	Seevogel
	seal [siːl]	Seehund
	toxic ['tɒksɪk]	giftig
	wildlife ['waɪldlaɪf]	Tierwelt
	wrecked [rekt]	gescheitert, schiffbrüchig
151	**restore** [rɪ'stɔː]	erneuern, wiederherstellen
152	**passively** ['pæsɪvlɪ]	passiv
153	**can** [kæn]	Büchse, Dose
	snow [snəʊ]	schneien
154	**acre** ['eɪkə]	Morgen (ca. 4.000 qm)
	burn [bɜːn]	brennen
	bush [bʊʃ]	Busch
	in common ['kɒmən]	gemeinsam
	cover (in) ['kʌvə]	bedecken (mit)
	decay [dɪ'keɪ]	Verfall
	disadvantage [dɪsəd'vɑːntɪdʒ]	Nachteil
	engineer [endʒɪ'nɪə]	Ingenieur(in)
	environment [ɪn'vaɪərənmənt]	Umwelt
	go-kart ['gəʊkɑːt]	Gokart
	landscape ['lændskeɪp]	landschaftsgärtnerisch gestalten
	plant [plɑːnt]	Pflanze; pflanzen
	playground ['pleɪgraʊnd]	Spielplatz
	raise [reɪz]	(an)heben
	remind (of) [rɪ'maɪnd]	erinnern (an)
	reserve [rɪ'zɜːv]	Naturschutzgebiet
	rot [rɒt]	Verfall
	soil [sɔɪl]	Erde, Erdboden
	tackle ['tækl]	angehen
	unfortunately [ʌn'fɔːtʃʊnətlɪ]	unglücklicherweise
	untrained [ʌn'treɪnd]	ungelernt
	unused [ʌn'juːzd]	unbenutzt
	wasteland ['weɪstlənd]	Brachland
155	**voluntary** ['vɒləntrɪ]	freiwillig
157	**cause** [kɔːz]	Ursache
	comment ['kɒment]	Kommentar
	disturb [dɪ'stɜːb]	stören
	impolite [ɪmpə'laɪt]	unhöflich
158	**apply (for)** [ə'plaɪ]	(sich) bewerben (um)
	gardening ['gɑːdnɪŋ]	Gartenbau
	landscape gardener	Landschaftsgärtner (-in)
	protect [prə'tekt]	schützen

The Passive

active (voice) ['æktɪv vɔɪs]	Aktiv
the passive ['pæsɪv]	das Passiv
present ~ ['preznt]	~ der Gegenwart
past ~ [pɑːst]	~ der Vergangenheit
present perfect ~ ['preznt 'pɜːfɪkt]	~ des Perfekts
by-agent [baɪ'eɪdʒənt]	Verursacher der Handlung
past participle [pɑːst 'pɑːtɪsɪpl]	Perfektpartizip

Pronouns

pronoun ['prəʊnaʊn]	Pronomen, Fürwort
personal ~ ['pɜːsənl]	Personalpronomen
possessive ~ [pə'zesɪv]	Possessivpronomen
reflexive ~ [rɪ'fleksɪv]	Reflexivpronomen
relative ~ ['relətɪv]	Relativpronomen
demonstrative ~ [dɪ'mɒnstrətɪv]	Demonstrativpronomen
interrogative ~ [ɪntə'rɒgətɪv]	Interrogativpronomen
indefinite ~ [ɪn'defɪnət]	Indefinitpronomen
emphasizing ~ ['emfəsaɪzɪŋ]	verstärkendes Pronomen
reciprocal ~ [rɪ'sɪprəkl]	reziprokes Pronomen
prop-word one ['prɒpwɜːd]	Stützwort one

tʃ	dʒ	ʃ	ʒ	θ	ð	ŋ	s	z	v	w
chips	jet	ship	garage	thing	the	ring	ice	as	very	wet

160 **accounts** [əˈkaʊnts] Buchhaltung
edge [edʒ] Rand
fear [fɪə] Angst
mugging [ˈmʌgɪŋ] Raubüberfall
nervous [ˈnɜːvəs] nervös
noisily [ˈnɔɪzɪlɪ] geräuschvoll
prejudice [ˈpredʒʊdɪs] Vorurteil
purse [pɜːs] **(AE)** Handtasche
raincoat [ˈreɪnkəʊt] Regenmantel
savagely [ˈsævɪdʒlɪ] grausam, brutal
scare [skeə] erschrecken
soul music [səʊl] Soul-Musik
steal, stole, stolen [stiːl, stəʊl, ˈstəʊlən] stehlen
unsafe [ʌnˈseɪf] unsicher
vandalism [ˈvændəlɪzəm] Zerstörungswut
161 **loudly** [ˈlaʊdlɪ] laut
163 **exciting** [ɪkˈsaɪtɪŋ] aufregend
guilty [ˈgɪltɪ] schuldig
wide [waɪd] breit
164 **amusing** [əˈmjuːzɪŋ] amüsant
apparently [əˈpærəntlɪ] anscheinend
applicant [ˈæplɪkənt] Bewerber(in)
application [æplɪˈkeɪʃn] Bewerbung
brains [breɪnz] Verstand, Grips
cattle [ˈkætl] Kühe, Rinder
cope [kəʊp] zurechtkommen
cowherd [ˈkaʊhɜːd] Kuhhirte, -hirtin
dairy [ˈdeərɪ] Molkerei; Milch-
diet [ˈdaɪət] Diät, Futterplan
disease [dɪˈziːz] Krankheit
farming [ˈfɑːmɪŋ] Landwirtschaft-
fatten [ˈfætn] mästen
feed [fiːd] Futter
female [ˈfiːmeɪl] weiblich
financially [faɪˈnænʃəlɪ] finanziell
helpful [ˈhelpfʊl] hilfreich
helpless [ˈhelplɪs] hilflos
herd [hɜːd] Herde
illogical [ɪˈlɒdʒɪkl] unlogisch
improbable [ɪmˈprɒbəbl] unwahrscheinlich
irresponsible [ɪrɪˈspɒnsəbl] unverantwortlich
lighten [ˈlaɪtn] erleichtern
manageress [mænɪdʒəˈres] Managerin
overworked [əʊvəˈwɜːkt] überarbeitet
shovel [ˈʃʌvl] schaufeln
temporary [ˈtemprərɪ] zeitlich
unbelievably [ʌnbɪˈliːvəblɪ] unglaublich
undeniably [ʌndɪˈnaɪəblɪ] unleugbar
underpaid [ʌndəˈpeɪd] unterbezahlt
unliftable [ʌnˈlɪftəbl] nicht anzuheben
unsure [ʌnˈʃʊə] unsicher
wheelbarrow [ˈwiːlbærəʊ] Schubkarre
165 **cow** [kaʊ] Kuh
166 **disunited** [dɪsjuːˈnaɪtɪd] getrennt
liftable [ˈlɪftəbl] anzuhebend
likeable [ˈlaɪkəbl] liebenswert
reliable [rɪˈlaɪəbl] zuverlässig
rely [rɪˈlaɪ] sich verlassen
unhelpful [ʌnˈhelpfʊl] nicht hilfreich
unreasonable [ʌnˈriːznəbl] unvernünftig
167 **actor** [ˈæktə] Schauspieler
actress [ˈæktrɪs] Schauspielerin
chairperson [ˈtʃeəpɜːsn] Vorsitzende(r)
logical [ˈlɒdʒɪkl] logisch
overpriced [əʊvəˈpraɪst] überteuert
saleable [ˈseɪləbl] verkäuflich
sense [sens] Sinn
spokesperson [ˈspəʊkspɜːsn] Sprecher(in)
underfed [ʌndəˈfed] unterernährt
waitress [ˈweɪtrɪs] Kellnerin
168 **imagination** [ɪmædʒɪˈneɪʃn] Phantasie
be prejudiced [ˈpredʒʊdɪst] Vorurteile haben

Verbs

verb [vɜːb] Verb
main ~ [meɪn] Hauptverb
auxiliary ~ [ɔːgˈzɪlɪərɪ] Hilfsverb
modal ~ [ˈməʊdl] Modalverb

defective [dɪˈfektɪv] unvollständig
regular [ˈregjʊlə] regelmäßig
irregular [ɪˈregjʊlə] unregelmäßig
verb of perception [pəˈsepʃn] Verb der Sinneswahrnehmung

infinitive [ɪnˈfɪnətɪv] Grundform
-ing form -ing Form
gerund [ˈdʒerənd] Gerundium

iː	ɪ	e	æ	ɑː	ɒ	ɔː	ʊ	uː	ʌ	ɜː	ə
see	sit	ten	bad	arm	got	saw	put	too	cut	bird	about

READING TEXTS

170	**actually** ['ækʃʊlɪ]	tatsächlich
	border ['bɔ:də]	Grenze
	communicate [kə'mju:nɪkeɪt]	sich verständigen
	cultural ['kʌltʃərəl]	kulturell
	Latin ['lætɪn]	Latein
	native speaker ['neɪtɪv 'spi:kə]	Muttersprachler(in)
171	**arithmetic** [ə'rɪθmətɪk]	Rechnen
	belief [bɪ'li:f]	Glaube
	bible ['baɪbl]	Bibel
	buggy ['bʌgɪ]	leichte, zweirädrige Kutsche
	craftsman ['krɑ:ftsmən]	Handwerker
	dreamland ['dri:mlənd]	Traumland
	electricity [ɪlek'trɪsətɪ]	Elektrizität
	flee, fled, fled [fli:, fled]	fliehen
	narrow ['nærəʊ]	eng
	plain [pleɪn]	schlicht, einfach
	recently ['ri:sntlɪ]	in letzter Zeit
	religious [rɪ'lɪdʒəs]	religiös
	songbook ['sɒŋbʊk]	Gesangbuch
173	**in addition** [ə'dɪʃn]	darüber hinaus
	advertising ['ædvətaɪzɪŋ]	Werbe-; Werbung
	campaign [kəm'peɪn]	Kampagne, Feldzug
	dependent (on) [dɪ'pendənt]	abhängig (von)
	exist [ɪg'zɪst]	existieren
	final ['faɪnl]	Endspiel
	flash [flæʃ]	blinken, aufleuchten
	march [mɑ:tʃ]	marschieren
	market ['mɑ:kɪt]	vermarkten
	network ['netwɜ:k]	Sender
	role [rəʊl]	Rolle
	scoreboard ['skɔ:bɔ:d]	Anzeigetafel
	season ['si:zn]	Spielzeit
	sporting ['spɔ:tɪŋ]	Sport-
	tough [tʌf]	rauh, zäh
	viewer ['vju:ə]	Zuschauer(in)
174	**accelerate** [ək'seləreɪt]	beschleunigen
	bang [bæŋ]	päng, rums
	(crash) barrier ['bærɪə]	Leitplanke
	beside [bɪ'saɪd]	neben
	constable ['kʌnstəbl]	Polizist
	free [fri:]	befreien
	guarantee [gærən'ti:]	garantieren
175	**hurry** ['hʌrɪ]	Eile
	madness ['mædnɪs]	Wahnsinn
	overtake, overtook, overtaken [əʊvə'teɪk, -'tʊk, -'teɪkən]	überholen
	skid [skɪd]	schleudern
	steadily ['stedɪlɪ]	gleichmäßig
	unhurt [ʌn'hɜ:t]	unverletzt
176	**ancient** ['eɪnʃənt]	uralt
	automatic [ɔ:tə'mætɪk]	automatisch
	delivery van [dɪ'lɪvərɪ]	Lieferwagen
	enter ['entə]	einfahren in
	fully ['fʊlɪ]	völlig
	originally [ə'rɪdʒənəlɪ]	ursprünglich
	parcel ['pɑ:sl]	Paket, Päckchen
	pipe [paɪp]	Röhre
	poorly ['pʊəlɪ]	schwach
	reduce [rɪ'dju:s]	verringern
	sewer ['sju:ə]	Abwasserkanal
	simply ['sɪmplɪ]	einfach
	sort [sɔ:t]	sortieren
	van [væn]	Lieferwagen
	within [wɪ'ðɪn]	innerhalb
177	**cable** ['keɪbl]	Kabel
	Catholic ['kæθəlɪk]	katholisch
	devil ['devl]	Teufel
	fundamentalist [fʌndə'mentəlɪst]	Fundamentalist(in)
	glory ['glɔ:rɪ]	Ruhm, Ehre
	gospel ['gɒspl]	Evangelium
	influence ['ɪnflʊəns]	Einfluß
	outsider ['aʊtsaɪdə]	Außenstehende(r)
	praise [preɪz]	loben
	pray [preɪ]	beten
	preach [pri:tʃ]	predigen
	servant ['sɜ:vənt]	Diener(in)
	sociologist [səʊsɪ'ɒlədʒɪst]	Soziologe, Soziologin
	support [sə'pɔ:t]	Unterstützung
	wave [weɪv]	schwenken
179	**banking** ['bæŋkɪŋ]	Bankwesen
	connection [kə'nekʃn]	Verbindung
	container [kən'teɪnə]	Container
	currency ['kʌrənsɪ]	Währung
	economic [i:kə'nɒmɪk]	wirtschaftlich
	extreme [ɪk'stri:m]	außerordentlich
	lease [li:s]	leihen
	mainland ['meɪnlənd]	Festland
	official [ə'fɪʃl]	Beamter, -tin
	prepare [prɪ'peə]	vorbereiten

tʃ	dʒ	ʃ	ʒ	θ	ð	ŋ	s	z	v	w
chips	jet	ship	garage	thing	the	ring	ice	as	very	wet

	shipping ['ʃɪpɪŋ]	Transportwesen
	stock exchange ['stɒk ɪkstʃeɪndʒ]	Effektenbörse (Aktien-, Wertpapier-)
	textiles ['tekstaɪlz]	Textilien
	unchanged [ʌn'tʃeɪndʒd]	unverändert
180	**biologist** [baɪ'ɒlədʒɪst]	Biologe, Biologin
	boom [bu:m]	wirtschaftlicher Aufschwung
	dugong ['du:gɒŋ]	Seekuh
	ecology [ɪ'kɒlədʒɪ]	Ökologie
	environmentalist [ɪnvaɪərən'mentəlɪst]	Umweltschützer(in)
	explore [ɪk'splɔ:]	erforschen
	harmless ['hɑ:mlɪs]	harmlos
	lifeform ['laɪfɔ:m]	Lebensform
	marine [mə'ri:n]	Meeres-
	occupation [ɒkjʊ'peɪʃn]	Beschäftigung
	organism ['ɔ:gənɪzəm]	Organismus
	reef [ri:f]	Riff
	shell [ʃel]	Muschel
	shy [ʃaɪ]	scheu
	snorkel ['snɔ:kəl]	schnorcheln
	suppose [sə'pəʊz]	glauben
	underwater ['ʌndəwɔ:tə]	Unterwasser-
182	**disposal** [dɪ'spəʊzl]	Beseitigung
	flame [fleɪm]	Flamme
	garbage can ['gɑ:bɪdʒ]	Mülleimer
	lifetime ['laɪftaɪm]	Lebenszeit
	lightning ['laɪtnɪŋ]	Blitz
	ownership ['əʊnəʃɪp]	Besitz
	packaging ['pækɪdʒɪŋ]	Verpackung
	rainwater ['reɪnwɔ:tə]	Regenwasser
	rate [reɪt]	Rate, Anteil
	recycle [ri:'saɪkl]	wiederverwerten
	rubber ['rʌbə]	Gummi
	scrap [skræp]	verschrotten
	senior ['si:nɪə]	älterer
	tire (AE)	Reifen
	trash [træʃ]	Abfall, Müll
	weeds [wi:dz]	Wildkräuter
183	**absorb** [əb'sɔ:b]	absorbieren
	carbon dioxide ['kɑ:bən daɪ'ɒksaɪd]	Kohlendioxid
	coastal ['kəʊstl]	Küsten-
	farmland ['fɑ:mlənd]	Acker- und Weideland
	forest ['fɒrɪst]	Wald
	grain [greɪn]	Korn
	greenhouse ['gri:nhaʊs]	Gewächshaus
	icecap ['aɪskæp]	Eisdecke, Gletscher
	melt [melt]	schmelzen
	prove [pru:v]	beweisen
	reflect [rɪ'flekt]	reflektieren
	replant [ri:'plɑ:nt]	wieder bepflanzen
	scientist ['saɪəntɪst]	Wissenschaftler(in)
	unbelievable [ʌnbɪ'li:vəbl]	unglaublich
185	**abandon** [ə'bændən]	verlassen
	account [ə'kaʊnt]	Konto
	approximately [ə'prɒksɪmətlɪ]	annähernd
	claimant ['kleɪmənt]	Anwärter(in)
	demand [dɪ'mɑ:nd]	fordern
	dozen ['dʌzn]	Dutzend
	estimate [estɪ'meɪt]	schätzen
	fortune ['fɔ:tʃu:n]	Vermögen
	funds [fʌndz]	Fonds, Gelder
	heir [eə]	Erbe
	identity [aɪ'dentətɪ]	Identität
	identity card	Personalausweis
	investment [ɪn'vestmənt]	Investition
	ownerless ['əʊnəlɪs]	ohne Besitzer
	proof [pru:f]	Beweis
	property ['prɒpətɪ]	Eigentum
	specialize (in) ['speʃəlaɪz]	(sich) spezialisieren (auf)
	sum [sʌm]	Summe
	transfer [træns'fɜ:]	überweisen
	unclaimed [ʌn'kleɪmd]	nicht beansprucht oder abgehoben
	will [wɪl]	Testament
186	**abroad** [ə'brɔ:d]	im/ins Ausland
	assemble [ə'sembl]	zusammensetzen
	chemical ['kemɪkl]	Chemikalie
	corporation [kɔ:pə'reɪʃn]	(Aktien-)Gesellschaft, Körperschaft, Firma
	dirt [dɜ:t]	Schmutz
	elsewhere [els'weə]	anderswo
	found [faʊnd]	gründen
	growth [grəʊθ]	Wachstum
	hi-tech ['haɪ tek]	Hochtechnologie
	keyboard ['ki:bɔ:d]	Tastatur
	massive ['mæsɪv]	mächtig
	mass-produced [mæs prə'dju:st]	in großen Stückzahlen gefertigt
	non-pollutant [nɒnpə'lu:tənt]	umweltfreundlich
	salary ['sælərɪ]	Gehalt
	signpost ['saɪnpəʊst]	Wegweiser
	silicon ['sɪlɪkən]	Silizium
	solution [sə'lu:ʃn]	Lösung
	storage ['stɔ:rɪdʒ]	Lager
	symbolise ['sɪmbəlaɪz]	symbolisieren
	unlike [ʌn'laɪk]	unähnlich
	valley ['vælɪ]	Tal

i:	ɪ	e	æ	ɑ:	ɒ	ɔ:	ʊ	u:	ʌ	ɜ:	ə
see	sit	ten	bad	arm	got	saw	put	too	cut	bird	about

Wörterverzeichnis

in alphabetischer Reihenfolge

(• = Wörter, die als bekannt vorausgesetzt werden, aber nicht zum Grundwortschatz gehören, d. h. sogenannte *cowboy words* und Grammatikausdrücke)

185 **abandon** verlassen
22 **be able to** können
128 **aboard** an Bord
186 **abroad** im/ins Ausland
183 **absorb** absorbieren
174 **accelerate** beschleunigen
• **accent**
70 **accept** annehmen
144 **acceptable** annehmbar
106 **according to** gemäß, entsprechend
185 **account** Konto
160 **accounts** Buchhaltung
154 **acre** Morgen
48 **action** Aktion
• **active**
44 **activity** Tätigkeit
167 **actor** Schauspieler
167 **actress** Schauspielerin
143 **actual** tatsächlich
170 **actually** tatsächlich
140 **add** hinzufügen
173 **in addition** darüber hinaus
• **address**
58 **admire** bewundern
124 **admit** zugeben
50 **adult** erwachsen
121 **advantage** Vorteil
44 **adventure** Abenteuer
• **adverb**
• **adverbial**
24 **advert** Anzeige, Annonce
173 **advertising** Werbung; Werbe-
32 **advice** Rat(schlag)
74 **affect** betreffen
54 **afford** sich leisten können
11 **afternoon** Nachmittag
136 **afterwards** danach
74 **against** gegen
80 **aggressive** aggressiv
24 **ago** vor
103 **agreement** Vertrag
64 **(first) aid** (Erste) Hilfe
114 **ain't** = isn't, hasn't
14 **air** Luft
124 **airfield** Flugfeld
124 **airforce** Luftwaffe
124 **airline** Fluggesellschaft
88 **airport** Flughafen
128 **aisle** Gang (Flugzeug)
• **alibi**
114 **alive** lebend
74 **be allowed to** dürfen
130 **almost** beinahe
50 **alone** allein
24 **also** auch
• **alternative**
74 **although** obwohl
128 **altitude** Höhe
80 **altogether** gänzlich, überhaupt
14 **a.m.** vormittags
64 **ambulance** Krankenwagen
• **amen**
134 **amenity** öffentliche Einrichtung
114 **amongst** unter
124 **amount** Menge
164 **amusing** amüsant
84 **art** Kunst
34 **article** Artikel
84 **artist** Künstler(in)
150 **ashore** an Land
• **aspect**
186 **assemble** zusammensetzen
104 **association** Verband
90 **atmosphere** Atmosphäre
80 **attack** Angriff
131 **attitude** Einstellung, Haltung

Die angegebenen Übersetzungen sind nur in diesem speziellen Sinnzusammenhang zu sehen. Es sind mehrere Bedeutungen möglich. Die Liste ersetzt nicht die umfassende Übersetzung eines zweisprachigen Wörterbuches.

176 **ancient** alt
64 **angel** Engel
120 **announcement** Durchsage
144 **anti-** gegen
90 **antique** Antiquität
• **antonym**
34 **anybody** (irgend) jemand
34 **anyone** (irgend) jemand
14 **anyway** jedenfalls
34 **not ... anywhere** nirgends, nirgend wohin
85 **apart (from)** abgesehen (von)
• **apartment**
164 **apparently** anscheinend
118 **appear** erscheinen
164 **applicant** Bewerber(in)
164 **application** Bewerbung
158 **apply (for)** (sich) bewerben (um)
185 **approximately** etwa, annähernd, ungefähr
44 **archery** Bogenschießen
14 **area** Gebiet, Bereich
130 **argue** darauf hinweisen
75 **argument** Argument
171 **arithmetic** Rechnen
128 **armrest** Armlehne
14 **around** herum
143 **arrange** verabreden
110 **arrest** verhaften
128 **arrival** Ankunft
84 **attraction** Anziehung
90 **attractive** attraktiv
14 **audience** Publikum
• **audio**
• **auto**
110 **autograph** Autogramm
176 **automatic** automatisch
• **automobile**
54 **available** verfügbar
50 **average** Durchschnitts ...

54 **back** zurück
104 **background** Herkunft, Hintergrund
46 **badly** schlecht, schlimm
83 **balcony** Balkon
140 **balloon** Ballon
• **band**
174 **bang** päng, rums
179 **banking** Bankwesen
44 **barbecue** Grillparty
100 **barn** Scheune
174 **barrier** Leitplanke
• **basis**
• **basketball**
44 **beach** Strand
94 **beat, beat, beaten** schlagen, überlisten
14 **because** weil
64 **because of** wegen
54 **bedsitter** möbliertes Zimmer, Wohnschlafzimmer
84 **beer** Bier
138 **behave** sich (gut) benehmen
171 **belief** Glaube
20 **believe** glauben
50 **belong to** gehören
68 **below** unten
120 **belt** Gürtel
144 **benefit** Vorteil, Nutzen
174 **beside** neben
171 **bible** Bibel
60 **bike** Fahrrad
180 **biologist** Biologe, -gin
• **bitter**
134 **blame** die Schuld geben
134 **block** (Häuser-)Block
120 **board** Bord
• **bold (type)**
94 **bomb** Bombe
180 **boom** wirtschaftlicher Aufschwung
170 **border** Grenze
43 **bored** gelangweilt
118 **boring** langweilig
140 **borrow** borgen
• **boss**
50 **both ... and** sowohl ... als auch
164 **brains** Verstand, Grips
124 **brake** (ab)bremsen
20 **break** (n) Pause
94 **breathe** atmen
150 **breed, bred, bred** brüten
150 **breeding ground** Brutplatz
88 **bright** hell
10 **broadcast** senden, übertragen
• **brochure**
• **brutal**
110 **bug** belästigen
171 **buggy** leichte, zweirädrige Kutsche
44 **building** Gebäude
• **burger**
154 **burn, burnt, burnt** brennen
154 **bush** Busch
107 **business** Geschäft
90 **busker** Straßensänger(in)
83 **butler** Butler
• **by-agent**
40 **bye** tschüß

124 **cabin** Kabine
177 **cable** Kabel
• **café**
127 **calm** (adj) ruhig
124 **calm** (v) beruhigen
10 **camp** campen
173 **campaign** Kampagne, Feldzug
10 **camper** Camper(in)
153 **can** Büchse, Dose

• **canal**
60 **cancel** streichen
10 **candle** Kerze
44 **canoe** Kanu
44 **canoeist** Kanute, Kanufahrer(in)
04 **cap** Mütze
10 **capital** Hauptstadt
• **capitalist**
40 **capsule** Kapsel
20 **captain** (Flug-)Kapitän
83 **carbon dioxide** Kohlendioxid
23 **(take) care of** sich kümmern um
30 **career** Beruf(sleben)
48 **careless** sorglos
50 **cargo** Fracht
• **carnival**
47 **cartoon** Karikatur
60 **cash** Bargeld
18 **cassette recorder** Kassettenrecorder
• **catastrophe**
77 **Catholic** katholisch
64 **cattle** Kühe, Rinder
57 **cause** (n) Ursache
60 **cause** (v) verursachen
• **cent**
• **centimetre**
50 **central** Zentral-
71 **century** Jahrhundert
37 **(for) certain** sicher
34 **certainly** gewiß
30 **certificate** Zeugnis
24 **chain** Kette
67 **chairperson** Vorsitzende(r)
30 **Chamber of Commerce** Handelskammer
04 **champion** Sieger(in), Meister(in)
04 **championship** Meisterschaft
30 **chance** Gelegenheit, Möglichkeit, Chance
20 **change** Wechselgeld
70 **channel** Kanal
04 **chant** singen; Gesang
• **character**
18 **charge** Anklage
40 **charity** Wohltätigkeit
• **chauffeur**
24 **cheap** billig
18 **check** überprüfen
04 **cheerleader** Anführer(in) des organisierten Beifalls
• **cheeseburger**
36 **chemical** Chemikalie
04 **chess** Schach
64 **Chief Inspector** Chefinspektor
43 **chips** (BE) Pommes frites
60 **choice** Wahl
50 **Christian** Christ(in)
38 **chromium** Chrom
24 **chute** Rutsche

144 **circulation** Verbreitung, Auflage
130 **citizen** Bürger(in)
• **city**
83 **civil rights** Bürgerrechte
74 **claim** behaupten
185 **claimant** Anwärter(in)
10 **classical** klassisch
23 **cleaner** Reinigungspersonal
147 **clear** frei
37 **clerk** Büroangestellte(r)
70 **cliff** Klippe
85 **climate** Klima
100 **close** (adj) nahe
120 **cloud** Wolke
• **club**
138 **clue** Lösungshilfe, Frage
104 **coach** Trainer(in)
59 **coast** Küste
183 **coastal** Küsten-
150 **coastline** Küste
• **cockpit**
138 **coke** Koks
40 **college** College
50 **colour** Farbe
10 **comedy** Komödie
40 **comfortable** bequem
• **comma**
157 **comment** Kommentar
10 **commercial** Werbe(spot)
120 **commercially** kommerziell
154 **in common** gemeinsam
170 **communicate** sich verständigen
• **communist**
74 **community** Gemeinde
60 **commuter** Pendler(in)
10 **company** Gesellschaft
• **comparative**
55 **compare** vergleichen
• **comparison**
94 **completely** vollständig
14 **complicated** kompliziert
• **component**
• **composition**
• **compound**
102 **comprehend** verstehen
50 **comprehensive school** Gesamtschule
• **computer**
44 **concentrate (on)** sich konzentrieren (auf)
• **concentration**
130 **concerned** betroffen
• **concert**
100 **concrete** Beton
• **condition**
• **conditional**
134 **condominium** (AE) Eigentumswohnung

104 **confidence** Selbstvertrauen
34 **confident** selbstsicher
130 **conflict** Konflikt
80 **congratulate** gratulieren
• **conjunction**
133 **connect** verbinden
179 **connection** Verbindung
• **conservative**
174 **constable** (BE) Polizist
98 **construction** Bau
• **contact (clause)**
179 **container** Container
58 **continent** Kontinent
133 **continue** fortsetzen
64 **control** (n) Kontrolle, Beherrschung
44 **control** (v) beherrschen
127 **convenient** bequem
• **conversation**
164 **cope** zurechtkommen
• **co-pilot**
114 **copper** Kupfer
55 **copy** übertragen, kopieren
186 **corporation** Firma, (Aktien-)Gesellschaft, Körperschaft
• **correct**
50 **council** Gemeinde
20 **counter** Theke, Tresen
68 **a couple of** ein paar
44 **course** Kurs
154 **cover (in)** bedecken (mit)
165 **cow** Kuh
164 **cowherd** Kuhhirte, -tin
44 **crafts** Handarbeiten
171 **craftsman** Handwerker
124 **crash (landing)** Bruchlandung
138 **crawl** kriechen
90 **crazy** verrückt
80 **create** schaffen
124 **crew** Besatzung, Mannschaft
87 **crime** Verbrechen
130 **criminal** (adj) kriminell
143 **criminal** (n) Verbrecher(in)
64 **criticize** kritisieren
70 **cross** kreuzen, überqueren
70 **cross-channel** den Kanal überquerend
70 **crossing** Überfahrt
138 **crossword puzzle** Kreuzworträtsel
84 **crowd** Menschenmenge
128 **cruising altitude** Reiseflughöhe
170 **cultural** kulturell
147 **culture** Kultur
179 **currency** Währung
20 **customer** Kunde, Kundin

64 **cut** (n) Schnittwunde
50 **cut** (v) schneiden, mähen

144 **daily** täglich
164 **dairy** Molkerei; Milch-
125 **damage** beschädigen
64 **danger** Gefahr
140 **daredevil** Teufelskerl
40 **date** Verabredung
120 **daydream** Träumerei
70 **daytime** Tages-
80 **dead-end** ohne Zukunft
134 **decay** verfallen
40 **decent** anständig
30 **decide** (sich) entscheiden
30 **decision** Entscheidung
70 **deck** Deck
70 **decrease** verringern
• **defective (modal)**
133 **defence** (AE **defense**) Verteidigung
• **define**
• **defining relative clause**
• **definite (article)**
134 **definitely** bestimmt
• **definition**
128 **degree** Grad
176 **delivery van** Lieferwagen
185 **demand** fordern
114 **deny** abstreiten
74 **depend (on)** abhängen (von)
173 **dependent (on)** abhängig (von)
100 **depressing** deprimierend
25 **describe** beschreiben
103 **description** Beschreibung
84 **desert** (n) Wüste
97 **desk** Schalter
74 **destroy** zerstören
136 **detached** freistehend
120 **develop** entwickeln
120 **development** Entwicklung
177 **devil** Teufel
140 **devote** widmen
• **dialect**
45 **dictionary** Wörterbuch
50 **die** sterben
• **diesel**
164 **diet** Diät, Futterplan
10 **different** verschieden
127 **difficulty** Schwierigkeit
70 **direct** direkt
44 **direction** Anweisung; Richtung(sangabe)
186 **dirt** Schmutz
154 **disadvantage** Nachteil
58 **disagree** nicht zustimmen
74 **disappear** verschwinden

74 **disaster** Unglück
• **disc jockey**
• **disco**
58 **discover** entdecken
58 **discuss** besprechen
78 **discussion** Diskussion
164 **disease** Krankheit
34 **disgraceful** abscheulich
48 **dislike** nicht mögen
144 **display** Bildschirm
182 **disposal** Beseitigung
44 **district** Gebiet
157 **disturb** stören
166 **disunited** getrennt
53 **dive** tauchen
58 **divorce** Scheidung
10 **documentary** Dokumentarbericht, -sendung
34 **dole** Stempelgeld
• **dollar**
110 **doorman** Portier
120 **doubt** Zweifel
124 **down** zum Absturz bringen
54 **downstairs** unten, im Erdgeschoß
130 **downtown** (im/ins) Stadtzentrum
185 **dozen** Dutzend
94 **drain** (Abwasser-) Kanal
94 **-drawn** gezogen
114 **dream** träumen
171 **dreamland** Traumland
64 **driving licence** Führerschein
100 **drug** Droge
• **drugstore**
100 **dry** trocken
106 **due to** infolge von
180 **dugong** Seekuh
94 **dummy** Attrappe
150 **dump** Kippe; abladen
136 **duplex** (AE) Zweifamilienhaus
20 **duty** Dienst, Pflicht

30 **earn** verdienen
120 **earth** Erde
144 **east** (nach) Osten
180 **ecology** Ökologie
179 **economic** wirtschaftlich
80 **economy** Wirtschaft
160 **edge** Rand
18 **edit** redigieren
140 **edition** Auflage
14 **editor** Redakteur(in)
30 **education** Erziehung
144 **effect** Wirkung
21 **eggburger** Hamburger mit Ei
34 **not … either** auch nicht
53 **either … or** entweder … oder
• **electric**
70 **electrically-lit** elektrisch erleuchtet
171 **electricity** Elektrizität
• **electronic**
134 **elementary** Grund-
186 **elsewhere** anderswo
124 **emergency** Notfall
118 **emigrant** Auswanderer(in)
114 **emigrate** auswandern
118 **emigration** Auswanderung
33 **employ** beschäftigen
34 **employee** Angestellte(r)
30 **employer** Arbeitgeber
81 **employment** Beschäftigung
• **ending**
• **energy**
94 **engine** Lokomotive
154 **engineer** Ingenieur(in)
23 **enough** genug
108 **enquiry** Anfrage
176 **enter** einfahren in
90 **entertain** unterhalten
10 **entertainment** Unterhaltung
154 **environment** Umwelt
134 **environmental** Umwelt-
180 **environmentalist** Umweltschützer(in)
• **episode**
• **essay**
185 **estimate** schätzen
18 **etc** und so weiter
63 **even** sogar
15 **event** Ereignis
• **everyday**
35 **everywhere** überall(hin)
114 **evidence** Beweis(e)
138 **ex-** ehemalig
125 **exactly** genau
148 **exam** Prüfung
106 **except (for)** außer
163 **exciting** aufregend
173 **exist** existieren
128 **exit** Ausgang
24 **expect** erwarten
30 **experience** Erfahrung
118 **experienced** erfahren
• **experiment**
• **expert**
180 **explore** erforschen
• **export**
148 **express** ausdrücken
• **expression**
124 **(fire) extinguisher** Feuerlöscher
179 **extreme** außerordentlich
134 **extremely** äußerst, außerordentlich
64 **eyewitness** Augenzeuge, -zeugin

140 **face** Gesicht
84 **facility** Einrichtung
54 **factory** Fabrik
124 **fail** aussetzen, versagen
136 **fairly** ziemlich
28 **famous** berühmt
97 **fan** Ventilator
134 **fancy** Luxus-
122 **fare** (Flug-)Kosten, Preis
140 **farewell** Abschied, Lebewohl
164 **farming** Landwirtschaft
183 **farmland** Acker- und Weideland
103 **farmworker** Landarbeiter(in)
88 **fashion** Mode
120 **fasten** befestigen
164 **fatten** mästen
80 **in favor of** (AE) dafür
14 **favourite** Lieblings-, liebste(r, s)
160 **fear** Angst
24 **feed, fed, fed** füttern
164 **feed** (n) Futter
164 **female** weiblich
70 **ferry** Fähre
• **festival**
24 **fibre** Faser
• **fiction**
81 **fight** Kampf
50 **figure** Zahl
173 **final** Endspiel
120 **finally** schließlich
• **financial**
164 **financially** finanziell
148 **fingernail** Fingernagel
44 **fire** Feuer
148 **fireman** Feuerwehrmann
150 **fisherman** Fischer
100 **fit** (adj) fit
47 **fit** (v) passen (zu)
70 **fixed** fest
138 **flag** Fahne
182 **flame** Flamme
60 **flash** (n) Blitz
173 **flash** (v) blinken, aufleuchten
134 **flash of light** Lichtblick
171 **flee, fled, fled** fliehen
88 **flight** Flug
120 **flight lane** Flugschneise, -korridor
94 **flooding** Überflutung
44 **flow** fließen
94 **force** zwingen
90 **foreign** fremd
183 **forest** Wald
110 **forever** für immer
• **form**
• **formal**
• **formation**
185 **fortune** Vermögen
104 **look forward to** sich freuen auf
186 **found** gründen
118 **frame** reinlegen
174 **free** (v) befreien
92 **free** (adj) frei
54 **freedom** Freiheit
135 **freeway** Schnellstraße
70 **freight** Güter, Fracht
• **frequency**
13 **frequently** häufig
74 **fresh** frisch
97 **friendly** freundlich
20 **(French) fries** (AE) Pommes frites
120 **fuel** Treibstoff
176 **fully** völlig
44 **fun** Spaß
185 **funds** Fonds, Gelder
177 **fundamentalist** Fundamentalist(in)
135 **furthest** am weitesten
• **future**

128 **galley** Bordküche
74 **gallon** Gallone
• **gangster**
18 **gap** Lücke
182 **garbage can** Mülleimer
83 **gardener** Gärtner(in)
158 **gardening** Gartenbau
• **gas**
130 **gasoline** (AE) Benzin
44 **in general** im allgemeinen
13 **generally** im allgemeinen
• **generation**
• **gerund**
74 **ghost** Geist, Gespenst
120 **glide** gleiten (Segelflug)
124 **glider** Segelflugzeug
124 **glider (pilot)** Segelflieger(in)
177 **glory** Ruhm, Ehre
154 **go-kart** Gokart
• **golden**
103 **goods** Waren
177 **gospel** Evangelium
147 **gossip** Klatsch
102 **govern** regieren
34 **government** Regierung
140 **grab** ergreifen
138 **graduation** Diplom
183 **grain** Korn
134 **grand** großartig
58 **grandparents** Großeltern
10 **great** groß, großartig
183 **greenhouse** Gewächshaus
• **grill**
124 **ground staff** Bodenpersonal
87 **grow, grew, grown** wachsen
186 **growth** Wachstum
174 **guarantee** garantieren
134 **guess** (AE) glauben, vermuten
10 **guest** Gast
163 **guilty** schuldig
• **guitar**
87 **gun** Gewehr, Schußwaffe
110 **gun-control** Waffenkontrolle

10 **gunman** Bewaffneter
10 **guy** Typ, Bursche, Kerl

37 **hallo** hallo
• **hamburger**
38 **hand down** überliefern
38 **hang, hung, hung** hängen
34 **hardly** kaum
80 **harmless** harmlos
20 **hate** hassen, nicht mögen
65 **heading** Überschrift
03 **headline** Schlagzeile
24 **health** Gesundheit
24 **healthy** gesund
40 **heart** Herz
50 **heating** Heizung
78 **heavy** schwer
00 **height** Höhe
85 **heir** Erbe
04 **helmet** Helm
64 **helpful** hilfreich
64 **helpless** hilflos
64 **herd** Herde
43 **hero** Held
• **herring**
80 **herself** (sie/ihr) selbst
20 **hey** hey
37 **hi** hi
50 **highly** hoch
34 **highrise** Hochhaus
10 **hitchhike** trampen
82 **himself** (er/ihm/ihn) selbst
13 **history** Geschichte
86 **hi-tech** Hochtechnologie
• **hobby**
70 **hope** hoffen
• **horror**
54 **hostel** Heim, Herberge
80 **hourly** stündlich, Stunden-
50 **household** Haushalt
55 **housework** Hausarbeit
50 **housing** Unterkunft
70 **however** jedoch
70 **huge** riesig
00 **human** menschlich
• **humanist**
78 **hundredweight** Zentner
74 **hurry** Eile
43 **hurt, hurt, hurt** verletzen
20 **hydrogen** Wasserstoff
• **hygiene**

83 **icecap** Eisdecke, Gletscher
35 **idea** Idee
85 **identity** Identität
85 **identity card** Personalausweis
• **illegal**
64 **illogical** unlogisch
• **image**
68 **imagination** Phantasie
78 **imagine** sich vorstellen
136 **immediately** sofort
114 **immigrant** Einwanderer, Einwanderin
118 **immigrate** einwandern
118 **immigration** Einwanderung
78 **imperial** Maßeinheitensystem (in GB)
157 **impolite** unhöflich
24 **important** wichtig
84 **impossible** unmöglich
58 **impress** imponieren
164 **improbable** unwahrscheinlich
80 **improve** verbessern
78 **inch** Zoll (Maßeinheit)
44 **include** einschließen
87 **income** Einkommen
70 **increase** (v) steigen, zunehmen
87 **increase** (n) Steigerung
150 **indeed** tatsächlich
• **indefinite (article)**
• **indirect**
44 **indoor** Innen-
114 **industrial** Industrie-
24 **industry** Industrie
• **inflation**
177 **influence** Einfluß
• **informal**
• **information**
103 **injection** Spritze
64 **injure** verletzen
64 **injury** Verletzung
80 **inner** Innen-
144 **input** Eingabe
147 **insert** einfügen
18 **inside** innen
• **inspector**
124 **instead** statt dessen
37 **instead of** (an)statt
128 **instruction** Anweisung
44 **instructor** Lehrer(in), Ausbilder(in)
44 **insurance** Versicherung
• **intention**
• **InterCity**
150 **interest** Interesse
• **international**
150 **internationally** international
• **interview**
70 **invade** eindringen
• **invasion**
24 **invent** erfinden
103 **invention** Erfindung
185 **investment** Investition
147 **involve** verwickeln
138 **iron** Eisen
• **irrelevant**
164 **irresponsible** unverantwortlich
70 **island** Insel
18 **item** Artikel
80 **itself** (sich) selbst

• **jacket**
• **jet**
84 **jewellery** Schmuck, Juwelen
30 **Jobcentre** Arbeitsamt
• **jogging**
14 **joke** Witz
• **journal**
• **journalist**
70 **journey** Reise(zeit)
• **judo**
• **jumbo jet**
53 **jump** springen
24 **junkfood** Nahrung ohne Nährwert

123 **kangaroo** Känguruh
• **karate**
40 **keen (on)** scharf (auf)
20 **keep, kept, kept** (be-)halten
• **ketchup**
186 **keyboard** Tastatur
104 **kick** Hochwerfen
84 **kid** Kind
83 **kill** töten
110 **killer** Killer
• **kilo**
• **kilogramme**
• **kilometre**
13 **kind** Art
63 **kph** kmh

80 **labor** (AE) Arbeit
100 **ladder** Leiter
• **land**
120 **landing** Landung
158 **landscape** (n) Landschaft
154 **landscape** (v) landschaftsgärtnerisch gestalten
70 **lane** Fahrspur
136 **lately** kürzlich
170 **Latin** Latein
84 **launderette** Waschsalon
64 **law** Gesetz
100 **lay, laid, laid** legen
78 **lb** Pfund
80 **lead, led, led** führen
104 **league** Liga
150 **leak** sickern
179 **lease** leihen
30 **(school) leaver** Schulabgänger(in)
• **legal**
110 **legend** Legende
118 **legendary** legendär
141 **length** Länge
27 **less** weniger
43 **lesson** Lektion
• **liberal**
10 **licence** Genehmigung
180 **lifeform** Lebensform
115 **lifestory** Biographie
58 **lifestyle** Lebensstil
182 **lifetime** Lebenszeit
166 **liftable** anzuhebend
10 **light** (adj) leicht
164 **lighten** erleichtern
182 **lightning** Blitz
166 **likeable** liebenswert
25 **line** Zeile
70 **link** Verbindung
120 **liquid** flüssig
70 **lit** erleuchtet
110 **lit** angezündet
• **local**
167 **logical** logisch
110 **lollipop** Lutscher
131 **lonely** einsam
83 **Lord** Lord
70 **lorry** Lkw
64 **lose, lost, lost** verlieren
161 **loudly** laut
40 **lovely** herrlich
50 **low** niedrig
124 **luckily** glücklicherweise
21 **lunch time** Mittagspause
90 **luxury** Luxus

106 **mad (about)** verrückt (nach)
174 **madness** Wahnsinn
10 **main** Haupt-
179 **mainland** Festland
147 **mainly** hauptsächlich
134 **maintain** pflegen
140 **major** größer
50 **majority** Mehrheit
84 **mama** Mama
124 **he managed** es gelang ihm
144 **management** Management
• **manager**
164 **manageress** Managerin
• **manner**
120 **manufacturer** Hersteller(in)
44 **map** Karte
173 **march** marschieren
180 **marine** Meeres-
123 **mark** Mark
90 **market** (n) Markt
173 **market** (v) vermarkten
50 **marriage** Ehe
50 **married** verheiratet
128 **mask** Maske
186 **massive** mächtig
186 **mass-produced** in großen Stückzahlen gefertigt
83 **master** Herr
128 **match** (v) passen zu
• **material**
143 **maths** Mathe
143 **it doesn't matter** es macht nichts
30 **may** können
10 **maybe** vielleicht
101 **meaning** Bedeutung
78 **measure** (n) Maß
78 **measurement** Maß
33 **mechanic** Mechaniker(in)
140 **media** Medien
114 **meeting** Treffen, Versammlung

183 **melt** schmelzen
50 **member** Mitglied
104 **mental** geistig
• **mention**
21 **menu** Speisekarte
64 **mercy** Gnade, Schutz
150 **mess** Schmutz, Durcheinander
140 **message** Botschaft
80 **messenger** Bote, Botin
• **metal**
37 **metalworker** Schlosser, Metallarbeiter(in)
78 **metric** metrisch
• **metropolis**
• **microchip**
• **microphone**
67 **middle** Mitte
92 **might** könnte(n)
118 **mill** Fabrik, (Walz-)Werk
• **millionaire**
21 **mind** (v) (etwas) dagegen haben
114 **mine** (n) Bergwerk
104 **miner** Bergmann
• **mineral**
• **minimum**
76 **minister** Minister(in)
124 **minor** kleiner, leicht
50 **minority** Minderheit
70 **mins** = minutes
82 **mirror** Spiegel
110 **miss** (v) vermissen
84 **missile** Rakete
124 **mistake** Fehler
10 **mix** mischen
134 **mixture** Mischung
124 **mix up** verwechseln
124 **mix-up** Verwechslung, Durcheinander
60 **model** Modell
• **moment**
117 **moon** Mond
• **moped**
• **moral**
50 **mortgage** Hypothek, Darlehen
• **mosquito**
• **motor**
61 **motorbike** Motorrad
127 **motorcycle** Motorrad
63 **motorcyclist** Motorradfahrer(in)
74 **motorway** Autobahn
44 **mountain** Berg
114 **mourn** trauern
61 **move** (v) (sich) bewegen
133 **move** (n) Bewegung
95 **movement** Bewegung
84 **movie** Kino, Film
74 **mph** = miles per hour
160 **mugging** Raubüberfall
134 **multi-family unit** Mehrfamilienhaus
83 **murder** Mord, ermorden
83 **murderer** Mörder
84 **muscle** Muskel
• **museum**

90 **musician** Musiker(in)
80 **myself** (ich/mir/mich) selbst
48 **mystery** Kriminalfilm

171 **narrow** eng
• **national**
170 **native speaker** Muttersprachler(in)
24 **natural** natürlich
• **nature**
41 **near** in der Nähe, nahe
31 **nearly** nahezu, fast
64 **necessary** notwendig
• **negate**
97 **neighbour** Nachbar(in)
83 **neighbourhood** Nachbarschaft
51 **neither** keine(r)
160 **nervous** nervös
• **nest**
173 **network** Sender
• **neutral**
130 **newcomer** Neuankömmling
10 **news** Nachrichten (-sendung)
70 **night-time** Nacht-
20 **nobody** niemand
160 **noisily** geräuschvoll
50 **non-** nicht-
• **non-defining (relative clause)**
186 **non-pollutant** umweltfreundlich
128 **nonsense** Unsinn
40 **nor do I** ich auch nicht
13 **normally** normalerweise
49 **north** Norden, nördlich
86 **notice** (v) bemerken
50 **nowadays** heutzutage
36 **nowhere** nirgends
48 **nurse** (n) Krankenpfleger(in)
100 **nurse** (v) pflegen

111 **obituary** Todesanzeige
• **object**
180 **occupation** Beschäftigung
• **ocean**
30 **offer** (v) (an)bieten
30 **officer** Beamter, Beamtin
179 **official** (n) Beamter, Beamtin
150 **oil** Öl
150 **oiled** ölverschmutzt
150 **oily** ölig
103 **old-fashioned** altmodisch
123 **be in operation** in Betrieb sein
• **opium**
72 **opponent** Gegner(in)
70 **oppose** ablehnen, sich aussprechen gegen
51 **opposite** entgegengesetzt

• **optimism**
• **optimistic**
• **orchestra**
33 **ordinary** gewöhnlich
150 **ore** Erz
180 **organism** Organismus
• **organization**
14 **organize** organisieren
44 **orienteering** Geländekunde, Kartenlesen
• **original**
176 **originally** ursprünglich
30 **ought to** sollte(n)
78 **ounce (oz)** Unze
82 **ourselves** (uns) selbst
44 **outdoor** im Freien
14 **outside** Außen-
177 **outsider** Außenstehende(r)
130 **overcrowding** Überbevölkerung
98 **overground** Hochbahn
84 **overseas** überseeisch
167 **overpriced** überteuert
174 **overtake, overtook, overtaken** überholen
164 **overworked** überarbeitet
106 **owing to** dank
136 **owner-occupied flat** Eigentumswohnung
185 **ownerless** ohne Besitzer
182 **ownership** Besitz
120 **oxygen** Sauerstoff

182 **packaging** Verpackung
104 **padding** Polsterung
34 **paint** (v) malen, anstreichen
• **panic**
• **paradise**
• **paraphrase**
• **paraphrasing**
176 **parcel** Paket, Päckchen
60 **park** parken
84 **parking lot** Parkplatz
• **parliament**
• **participle**
110 **particular** bestimmt
114 **particularly** besonders
34 **(bus) pass** Dauerkarte
70 **passenger** Passagier, Fahrgast
• **passive**
152 **passively** passiv
100 **patient** geduldig
150 **patrol** Patrouille
20 **pay** (n) Bezahlung, Lohn
87 **peace** Frieden
38 **per** pro
• **perception**
102 **perform** aufführen
40 **performance** Vorstellung
• **permanent**
• **permission**
90 **persuade** überzeugen, -reden

14 **phone-in** Telefonstudio
104 **physical** (betont) körperlich
• **picnic**
88 **pill** Pille
• **pilot**
44 **pine** Kiefer
176 **pipe** Röhre
171 **plain** schlicht, einfach
• **plan**
154 **plant** Pflanze; pflanzen
• **plastic**
154 **playground** Spielplatz
94 **pleasant** angenehm
113 **pleased** zufrieden
103 **pleasure** Vergnügen
90 **plenty of** viel
14 **p.m.** nach Mittag
• **polar**
24 **polite** höflich
130 **political** politisch
80 **politician** Politiker(in)
• **politics**
74 **pollute** verschmutzen
74 **pollution** (Umwelt-) Verschmutzung
• **pool**
176 **poorly** schwach
• **popcorn**
24 **popular** beliebt
50 **population** Bevölkerung
150 **port** Hafen
• **position**
• **positive**
• **possessive**
70 **possible** möglich
90 **postcard** Postkarte
• **poster**
107 **pot** Kanne
80 **poverty** Armut
98 **power** Stärke
48 **practical** praktisch
53 **practise** (ein)üben
177 **praise** loben
177 **pray** beten
177 **preach** predigen
• **prediction**
40 **prefer** vorziehen
• **prefix**
160 **prejudice** Vorurteil
168 **be prejudiced** Vorurteile haben
179 **prepare** vorbereiten
• **prepositional phrase**
14 **present** (v) vorstellen, moderieren
14 **presenter** Moderator(in)
• **president**
100 **pressure** Druck
20 **pretty** (adv) ziemlich, recht
143 **previous** vorhergehend
27 **price** Preis (zu zahlen)
90 **pride** Stolz
145 **print** drucken; Druck
110 **printworker** Drucker(eiarbeiter/in)

30 **privacy** Zurückgezogenheit
• **private**
14 **prize** Auszeichnung, Preis
48 **probably** wahrscheinlich
• **problem**
24 **procedure** Verhalten, Maßnahme(n)
44 **process** Prozeß
44 **produce** herstellen
• **product**
• **production**
• **profit**
• **program**
• **programme**
74 **progress** Fortschritt
• **project**
33 **promise** versprechen
85 **proof** Beweis
54 **proper** geeignet
85 **property** Eigentum
58 **protect** schützen
04 **protective** Schutz-
• **protest**
84 **proud** stolz
83 **prove** beweisen
98 **provide** liefern, (an)bieten
64 **provisional (licence)** Führerschein auf Probe
18 **pub** Pub, Kneipe
24 **public** öffentlich
40 **publicity** Publizität
60 **public transport** öffentliche Verkehrsmittel
90 **pull down** niederreißen
• **pullover**
50 **pump** (v) pumpen
50 **punctually** pünktlich
• **punk**
50 **pupil** Schüler(in)
60 **purse** (AE) Handtasche
38 **puzzle** Rätsel

• **qualification**
50 **qualified** qualifiziert
01 **quality** Qualität
47 **questionnaire** Fragebogen
• **question tag**
24 **quick** schnell
• **quiz**
143 **quote** (n) Zitat

124 **race** (v) rasen
70 **rail** Bahn
94 **railway** Bahn
74 **rail yard** Rangierbahnhof
160 **raincoat** Regenmantel
182 **rainwater** Regenwasser
154 **raise** (an)heben
84 **range** Testgelände
94 **rat** Ratte
182 **rate** Rate, Anteil
144 **rationalization** Rationalisierung
24 **reach** erreichen
111 **react** reagieren
• **reaction**
120 **realistic** realistisch
120 **reality** Wirklichkeit
14 **really** wirklich
24 **reason** Grund
50 **receive** empfangen
171 **recently** in letzter Zeit
140 **record** (n) Rekord
14 **record** (v) aufzeichnen
110 **recording studio** Aufnahmestudio
150 **recover** bergen
150 **recovery** Bergung
182 **recycle** wiederverwerten
• **recycling**
176 **reduce** verringern
100 **reed** Reet
180 **reef** Riff
183 **reflect** reflektieren
• **reflexive**
128 **refreshment** Erfrischung
93 **refuse** (v) ablehnen
• **region**
• **regional**
13 **regularly** regelmäßig
• **relative (pronoun)**
69 **relax** (sich) entspannen
114 **release** Freilassung
• **relevant**
166 **reliable** zuverlässig
• **religion**
171 **religious** religiös
166 **rely** sich verlassen
131 **remain** bleiben
132 **remark** (v) bemerken
30 **remember** daran denken
154 **remind (of)** erinnern (an)
130 **renovate** renovieren
130 **renovation** Renovierung
50 **rent** (n) Miete
83 **repair** (v) reparieren
33 **replace** ersetzen
183 **replant** wieder bepflanzen
14 **reply** antworten
10 **report** (n) Bericht
133 **report** (v) berichten
141 **rescue** (v) retten
144 **research** (n) Forschung
147 **research** (v) recherchieren
154 **reserve** Naturschutzgebiet
133 **resident** Einwohner(in)
134 **residential** Wohn-
84 **resort** Ferien-, Badeort
108 **responsibility** Verantwortung
140 **responsible** verantwortlich
87 **rest** (n) Rest
138 **restlessness** Ruhelosigkeit
151 **restore** erneuern, wiederherstellen
94 **result** (n) Ergebnis
80 **retraining** Umschulung
110 **return** (v) zurückkehren
• **revision**
• **revolver**
127 **rewrite** umschreiben
81 **right** (n) Recht
50 **rise, rose, risen** (an)steigen
64 **risk** (n) Risiko
44 **river** Fluß
150 **rock** Felsen
173 **role** Rolle
44 **roll** Rolle; rollen
84 **roller skate** Rollschuh
154 **rot** Verfall
• **route**
• **routine**
182 **rubber** Gummi
150 **rubbish** Müll
150 **rubbish dump** Müllkippe
• **rucksack**
74 **rule** Bestimmung, Verbot
120 **runway** Startbahn
94 **rush hour** Stoßzeit

118 **sad** traurig
111 **safe(ly)** sicher
44 **safety** Sicherheit
186 **salary** Gehalt
167 **saleable** verkäuflich
24 **sales** Umsatz, Verkäufe
60 **salesman** Verkäufer
• **satellite**
160 **savagely** grausam, brutal
• **scandal**
160 **scare** erschrecken
30 **scheme** Programm
50 **schoolchildren** Schulkinder
30 **school leaver** Schulabgänger(in)
• **science fiction**
183 **scientist** Wissenschaftler(in)
173 **scoreboard** Anzeigetafel
182 **scrap** verschrotten
144 **screen** (Bild-)Schirm
110 **screwball** Wirrkopf
78 **sea** See
150 **seabed** Meeresgrund
150 **seabird** Seevogel
84 **seafront** Strand, Küste
150 **seal** Seehund
54 **seaside** Küste
173 **season** Spielzeit
40 **seat** Sitz
120 **seat belt** Sicherheitsgurt
44 **second** (n) Sekunde
33 **secretary** Sekretär(in)
• **section**
101 **seem** scheinen
136 **semi-detached house** Doppelhaushälfte
182 **senior** älterer
167 **sense** Sinn
60 **sensible** vernünftig
114 **sentence** verurteilen; Urteil
67 **separate** (v) trennen, teilen
10 **separate** (adj) getrennt
65 **sergeant** Wachtmeister
144 **series** Reihe
64 **serious** ernsthaft
177 **servant** Diener(in)
20 **serve** bedienen
• **service**
44 **set** (n) Satz
50 **set** (n) Apparat, Gerät
110 **several** einige, mehrere
176 **sewer** Abwasserkanal
20 **shake** (n) Mixgetränk
40 **shall** sollen
134 **shame** Schande
94 **shape** Form
24 **share** (n) Anteil, Aktie
50 **share** (v) sich teilen (in)
180 **shell** Muschel
94 **shelter** (v) sich in Sicherheit bringen
• **sherry**
20 **shift** Schicht
134 **shine, shone, shone** scheinen
179 **shipping** Transportwesen
110 **shocked** schockiert
31 **shoe** Schuh
83 **shoot, shot, shot** (er)schießen
• **shorten**
83 **shot** (n) Schuß
164 **shovel** (v) schaufeln
147 **showbusiness** Showgeschäft
70 **shuttle** Pendelverkehr
180 **shy** scheu
84 **sidewalk** Bürgersteig
122 **(go) sightseeing** Sehenswürdigkeiten besichtigen
186 **signpost** Wegweiser
124 **silent** still
186 **silicon** Silizium
176 **simply** einfach
• **simultaneous**
128 **sink, sank, sunk** sinken
• **situation**
• **size**
78 **skate** (v) Schlittschuh (laufen)
174 **skid** schleudern
30 **skill** Fertigkeit, Fähigkeit
114 **skilled** gelernt
34 **slave** Sklave, Sklavin
134 **slum** Elendsviertel

94 **smell** riechen
• **smog**
121 **smoothly** glatt, ruhig
88 **sneakers** Turnschuhe
180 **snorkel** (v) schnorcheln
153 **snow** (v) schneien
87 **Snowbelt** Schneegürtel
104 **soccer** (europäischer) Fußball
• **social**
80 **society** Gesellschaft
177 **sociologist** Soziologe, Soziologin
140 **sock** Socke
• **sofa**
154 **soil** Erde, Erdboden
138 **soldier** Soldat
186 **solution** Lösung
98 **solve** lösen
28 **something** etwas
171 **songbook** Gesangbuch
114 **songwriter** Liedermacher(in)
176 **sort** (v) sortieren
160 **soul music** Soul-Musik
80 **sound** (v) klingen
44 **south** Süden, südlich
87 **southern** Süd-
• **souvenir**
104 **spare time** Freizeit
14 **special** besondere
185 **specialize (in)** (sich) spezialisieren (auf)
83 **speech** Rede
74 **speed** Geschwindigkeit
100 **in spite of** trotz
100 **split, split, split** teilen
144 **spokesman** Sprecher
167 **spokesperson** Sprecher(in)
173 **sporting** Sport-
• **squash**
14 **staff** Angestellte, Personal
120 **stage** Phase, Stadium
90 **stall** Stand
48 **(can't) stand** nicht leiden können
• **standard**
87 **state** (n) Staat
133 **state** (v) feststellen
174 **steadily** gleichmäßig
160 **steal, stole, stolen** stehlen
94 **steam** Dampf
138 **steel** Stahl
30 **step** Schritt
• **stereo**
• **stewardess**
100 **stick** (n) Stock
10 **still** noch
179 **stock exchange** (Aktien-, Effekten-, Wertpapier-)Börse
186 **storage** Lager
134 **store** (AE) Laden, Geschäft
80 **storeroom** Lager
46 **straight** gerade, direkt
84 **strange** fremd(artig)
114 **strike** (n) Streik
• **structure**
• **student**
• **studio**
134 **study** Studie
14 **style** Stil
• **subject**
147 **subscribe** abonnieren
130 **suburb** Stadtrandsiedlung
98 **subway** (AE) U-Bahn
110 **succeed in** erfolgreich sein
24 **success** Erfolg
118 **successful** erfolgreich
44 **suddenly** plötzlich
134 **suffer (from)** leiden (an)
• **suffix**
40 **suggest** vorschlagen
81 **suggestion** Vorschlag
88 **suit** (n) Anzug
185 **sum** Summe
• **summarize**
134 **summit** Gipfel
87 **Sunbelt** Sonnengürtel
47 **sunny** sonnig
48 **sunshine** Sonnenschein
• **super**
120 **supersonic** mit Überschall(geschwindigkeit)
65 **support** unterstützen
70 **supporter** Vertreter(in), Verfechter(in)
180 **suppose** glauben
20 **sure** sicher(lich)
60 **surprise** (n) Überraschung, überraschen
44 **surprising** überraschend
50 **survey** Erhebung, Umfrage
144 **survive** überleben
64 **swerve** ausweichen
73 **swimming-pool** Schwimmbad
• **symbol**
186 **symbolize** symbolisieren
• **synonym**
• **system**

55 **table** Tabelle
120 **take off** (v) abheben, starten
120 **take-off** (n) Start
• **tank**
• **tanker**
88 **tax** Steuer
120 **technically** technisch
• **technology**
• **teenager**
• **telegram**
• **telegramme**
• **telex**
• **temperature**
164 **temporary** zeitlich
10 **tent** Zelt
145 **term** Ausdruck
70 **terminal** (n) (End-)Station
• **test**
179 **textiles** Textilien
100 **thatch** mit Reet decken
100 **thatcher** Reetdachdecker(in)
• **theater** (US)
• **theatre**
64 **themselves** sich/ihnen selbst
140 **thirst** Durst
95 **thirsty** durstig
107 **thought** Gedanke
108 **thoughtful** nachdenklich
40 **thriller** Reißer
100 **tie** (v) binden
104 **tights** Strumpfhosen
34 **till** Ladenkasse
60 **timetable** Fahrplan
182 **tire** (AE) Reifen
• **toast**
• **toilet**
78 **ton** Tonne
78 **tonne** metrische Tonne
78 **tool** Werkzeug
• **tornado**
23 **touch** berühren
173 **tough** rauh, zäh
• **tour** (n)
• **tourist**
87 **towards** auf ... zu
150 **toxic** giftig
94 **track** Schiene, Gleis
• **tractor**
134 **trade** Handel
24 **trade union** Gewerkschaft
• **traditional**
70 **traditionally** traditionell
60 **traffic jam** Stau
30 **trainee** Auszubildene(r)
140 **transatlantic** transatlantisch
185 **transfer** überweisen
• **transistor**
• **translation**
182 **trash** Abfall, Müll
63 **Travelcard** Zeitkarte (London)
147 **treat** behandeln
147 **treatment** Behandlung
144 **tremendously** ungeheuer, kolossal
• **trend**
90 **tropical** tropisch
83 **truth** Wahrheit
• **T-shirt**
94 **tube** U-Bahn
114 **tune** Melodie
• **tunnel**
134 **turn of the century** Jahrhundertwende
107 **twice** zweimal
134 **twin city** Doppelstadt
34 **type** (v) tippen
104 **typical** typisch
124 **tyre** Reifen

• **ultra-modern**
130 **unable** unfähig
183 **unbelievable** unglaublich
164 **unbelievably** unglaublich
179 **unchanged** unverändert
185 **unclaimed** nicht beansprucht oder abgehoben
95 **uncomfortable** unbequem
147 **unconscious** unbewußt
164 **undeniably** unleugbar
167 **underfed** unterernährt
94 **underground** U-Bahn
164 **underpaid** unterbezahlt
180 **underwater** Unterwasser-
34 **unemployed** ohne Beschäftigung, arbeitslos
50 **unemployment** Arbeitslosigkeit
81 **unfair** ungerecht
154 **unfortunately** unglücklicherweise
111 **unfriendly** unfreundlich
48 **unhappy** unglücklich
166 **unhelpful** nicht hilfreich
174 **unhurt** unverletzt
• **uniform**
134 **uninviting** wenig einladend
24 **union** Gewerkschaft
114 **unionization** Organisation in Gewerkschaften
10 **unit** Lektion
70 **unless** wenn nicht
164 **unliftable** nicht anzuheben
186 **unlike** unähnlich
58 **unlucky** unglücklich
48 **unpopular** unbeliebt
166 **unreasonable** unvernünftig
160 **unsafe** unsicher
114 **unskilled** ungelernt
164 **unsure** unsicher
154 **untrained** ungelernt
154 **unused** unbenutzt
59 **unusual** ungewöhnlich
130 **uptown** in den Außenbezirken
135 **useful** nützlich
47 **usual** gewöhnlich

88 **vacation** Urlaub
186 **valley** Tal
176 **van** Lieferwagen

160 **vandalism** Zerstörungswut
90 **vegetable** Gemüse
88 **vegetarian** vegetarisch
48 **vehicle** Fahrzeug
84 **vendor** Verkäufer(in)
14 **VHF** UKW
• **video(-recorder)**
44 **view** Sicht, Ausblick
173 **viewer** Zuschauer(in)
104 **violence** Gewalt(tätigkeit)
104 **violent** gewalttätig
• **vitamin**
155 **voluntary** freiwillig
• **vowel**

34 **wages** Lohn
• **waggon**
167 **waitress** Kellnerin
• **walkman**
90 **wander** zu Fuß gehen
87 **war** Krieg
100 **ward** (Kranken-)Station
• **warm**
74 **warn** warnen, darauf hinweisen
32 **warning** Ermahnung, Verbot
94 **waste** Abfall
110 **waste** Verlust, Vergeudung
154 **wasteland** Brachland
140 **wave** (n) Welle
177 **wave** (v) schwenken
50 **wealth** Reichtum
20 **wear, wore, worn** tragen (Kleidung)
182 **weeds** Wildkräuter
113 **weekday** Wochentag
13 **weekend** Wochenende
147 **weekly** wöchentlich
78 **weigh** wiegen
78 **weight** Gewicht
10 **welcome** willkommen
80 **welfare** Sozialhilfe
164 **wheelbarrow** Schubkarre
108 **whether** ob
64 **while** (cj) während
80 **while** (n) Weile
43 **whom** wen, wem
64 **whose** dessen, deren
163 **wide** breit
• **wild**
150 **wildlife** Tierwelt
185 **will** (n) Testament
• **wind**
88 **wine** Wein
128 **wish** (v) wünschen
176 **within** innerhalb
147 **wonder** sich fragen
44 **woods** Wald, Wälder
45 **woodworking** Holzbearbeitung
44 **wool** Wolle
• **wordlist**
44 **workshop** Arbeitsgemeinschaft
24 **world** Welt
50 **worry** (v) sich Sorgen machen
24 **worth** wert
150 **wrecked** gescheitert, schiffbrüchig
64 **write-off** Schrottwert

78 **yard** Elle
71 **yearly** jährlich
48 **yellow** gelb
104 **youngster** Jugendliche(r)
35 **yourself** du/dir selbst
30 **youth** Jugendliche(r)

134 **zone** Zone

Grundwortschatz

Diese Liste umfaßt die Vokabeln, die für das Schülerbuch vorausgesetzt werden. Da nicht in allen Fällen Mehrfachbedeutungen in der Übersetzung angegeben werden können, ersetzt diese Liste nicht ein umfassendes zweisprachiges Wörterbuch. Beim Verwenden der Liste als Übersetzungshilfe muß immer der Kontext beachtet werden.

Zahlwörter (one, two, first, second ...), Pronomen (I, you, my, your ...), die Wochentage (Monday, Tuesday, ...) sowie die Monatsnamen (January, February, ...) sind nicht enthalten.

a ein(e)
about über, um
above über
accident Unfall
across (quer) über
act handeln, spielen
adjective Adjektiv
afraid: I'm afraid Angst haben, leider
after nach, nachdem
again wieder
age Alter
aged im Alter von
agree zustimmen, übereinstimmen
all alle(s)
along entlang
already schon, bereits
always immer
am (be) bin (sein)
an ein(e)
and und
angry ärgerlich
animal Tier
another noch ein(e), ein(e) andere(r/-s)
answer Antwort
any irgendein(e/er)
anything irgend etwas
apple Apfel
are (be) bist (sein)
arm Arm
arrive ankommen
as wie, als
ask fragen
at an, in, zu
aunt Tante
away weg

baby Baby
bad schlecht
bag Tasche
bake(r) backen, (Bäcker)
banana Banane
bank Bank
bar Bar
bathroom Badezimmer
be, was/were, been sein, war, gewesen
beautiful schön
become, became, become werden
bed(room) Bett, (Schlafzimmer)
before vor, bevor
begin, began, begun anfangen, beginnen
behind hinter
best beste(r, s)
better besser
between zwischen
bicycle Fahrrad
big groß, dick
bird Vogel
birthday Geburtstag
bit Teil, ein bißchen
black schwarz
blood Blut
blue blau
boat Boot
body Körper
book Buch
born geboren
both beide
bottle Flasche
box Karton, Schachtel
boy Junge
boyfriend Freund (eines Mädchens)
brackets Klammer
bread Brot
break, broke, broken (zer)brechen, kaputt machen
breakfast Frühstück
bring, brought, brought bringen
Britain Großbritannien
British britisch; Brite
brother Bruder
build, built built bauen
bus Bus
but aber
buy, bought, bought kaufen
by: by bus durch, mit dem Bus

cake Kuchen
call rufen, nennen, heißen
camping Zelten
can kann, darf
cannot (can't) kann nicht, darf nicht
car Auto
card Karte
careful vorsichtig
carry tragen
cat Katze
catch, caught, caught fangen
centre Zentrum, Mitte
change ändern, Wechselgeld
cheese Käse
child Kind
children Kinder
chocolate Schokolade
choose, chose, chosen wählen, aussuchen
Christmas Weihnachten
church Kirche
cigarette Zigarette
cinema Kino
class Klasse
clause Satz(teil)
clean adj, v sauber, putzen
clever klug
climb hinaufgehen, klettern
clock Uhr
close adj, v nah, schließen
clothes Kleidung
Co Ko-
coal Kohle
coat Mantel
coffee Kaffee
cold adj, n kalt, Erkältung
collect sammeln
comb n, v Kamm, kämmen
come, came, come kommen
complete ergänzen
comprehension Verständnis
context Zusammenhang
continuous form Verlaufsform
cook n, v Koch, kochen
corner Ecke
cost, cost, cost kosten
could könnte(n), konnte(n)
count zählen
country Land
course: of course natürlich, selbstverständlich
crash n, r Zusammenstoß, zusammenstoßen
cream Sahne
cry n, v Schrei, weinen
cup Tasse
cupboard Schrank

dad Vater
dance n, v Tanz, tanzen
dangerous gefährlich
dark dunkel
day Tag
Dear... Liebe(r, s)...
dialogue Gespräch
difference Unterschied
difficult schwierig
dinner Abendessen
dirty schmutzig
do, did, done tun, machen
doctor Doktor
dog Hund
door Tür
down (nach) unten
dress Kleid
drink, drank, drunk trinken
drive, drove, driven (Auto)fahren
during während

each jede(r, s)
early früh
easy leicht, einfach
eat, ate, eaten essen
else sonst
empty leer
end n, v Ende, beenden
England England
English englisch; Engländer(in)
enjoy gefallen, genießen
especially besonders
European europäisch, Europäer(in)
evening Abend
ever je(mals)
every(-body) (-one), jede(r,s)
every(-thing) alles
exact genau
example Beispiel
exercise Übung
expensive teuer
explain erklären
extra extra
extract n Auszug
eye Auge

face Gesicht
fact Tatsache
fall, fell, fallen fallen
family Familie
far weit
farm(er) Bauernhof (Bauer)
fast schnell
fat dick
father Vater
feel, felt, felt fühlen
feeling Gefühl
feet Füße
few wenige
field Feld
fill füllen
film Film
find, found, found finden
fine gut, schön
finger Finger
finish aufhören, beenden
first erste(r, s), zuerst
fish Fisch
flat Wohnung
flower Blume
fly, flew, flown fliegen
follow folgen
foot(ball) Fuß(ball)
for für
forget, forgot, forgotten vergessen
form Form
friend Freund
from von
front: in front of vor
fruit Frucht, Obst
full voll
funny lustig

game Spiel
garage Garage; Werkstatt
garden Garten
gate Tor
genitive Genitiv
German deutsch; Deutsche(r)
Germany Deutschland
get, got, got erhalten, bekommen, werden
girl Mädchen
girlfriend Freundin
give, gave, given geben
glad froh
glass Glas
go, went, gone/been gehen, fahren
good gut
got (get) bekommen werden (erhalten)
grammar Grammatik
grandfather (-mother) Großvater (-mutter)
grass Gras
green grün
grey grau
ground Boden
group Gruppe
guess raten

hair(-dresser) Haar(e) (Friseur)
half halb
hall Halle, Flur
hand Hand
handbook Handbuch
happen geschehen
happy fröhlich, glücklich
hard hart
hat Hut
have, had, had haben
head Kopf
hear, heard, heard hören
help n, v Hilfe, helfen
here hier, hierher
high hoch
hit, hit, hit schlagen
hold, held, held halten
hole Loch
holiday Ferien
home nach Hause, zu Haus
homework Hausaufgaben
horse Pferd
hospital Krankenhaus
hot warm, heiß
hotel Hotel
hour Stunde
house Haus
how wie
hungry hungrig

ice Eis
if wenn, falls, ob
ill krank
in in
infinitive Infinitiv
input input
intelligent klug
interested interessiert
interesting interessant
into in, hinein
irregular unregelmäßig
is (be) ist (sein)

jeans Jeans
job Beruf, Stelle, Aufgabe
join beitreten, mitgehen
just gerade, nur

key Schlüssel
kitchen Küche
know, knew, know kennen, wissen

lady Dame
lake See
language Sprache
large groß
last adj, v letzte(r, s), dauern
late spät, zu spät
later später
latest letzte(r, s), neueste(r, s)
laugh lachen
learn, learnt/-ed, learnt/-ed lernen
least: at least mindestens, wenigstens
leave, left, left verlassen, abreisen, weggehen
leg Bein
let lassen, zulassen
letter Brief
lie lügen
lie, lay, lain liegen
life Leben
lift n, v Aufzug, heben
light, lit, lit beleuchten

light adj, n hell, leicht, Licht
like mögen, wie
list Liste
listen zuhören
little klein
live leben, wohnen
long lang
look schauen, aussehen
lot: a lot of viel(e)
lots viele
loud laut
love Liebe
lucky Glück haben
lunch Mittagessen

machine Maschine
magazine Zeitschrift
make, made, made machen
man Mann, Mensch
many viele
match Spiel, Match
may dürfen
meal Essen, Mahlzeit
mean, meant, meant bedeuten, meinen
meaning Bedeutung
meat Fleisch
meet, met, met treffen
men Männer
metre Meter
mile Meile
milk Milch
minute Minute
Miss Fräulein
modal (verb) Modal-(verb)
modern modern
money Geld
month Monat
more mehr
morning Morgen, Vormittag
most meiste(r, s)
mother Mutter
Mr Herr
Mrs Frau
much viel
mum Mutter
music Musik
must müssen

name Name
need brauchen
negative negativ
never nie(mals)
new neu
newspaper Zeitung
next nächste(r, s)
nice schön, nett, gut
night Nacht
no nein, kein
noise Lärm, Geräusch
normal normal
not nicht
note Notiz
nothing nichts
noun Substantiv
now jetzt
number Zahl, Nummer

of von, bei, aus
off weg
office Büro
often oft
oh ach!
old alt
on auf, an
once einmal
one ein(e)
only nur
open adj, v offen, öffnen
opinion Meinung
or oder
order bestellen
other andere(r, s)
out aus
over über
own adj, v eigene(r, s), besitzen

page Seite
pair Paar
paper Papier
paragraph Abschnitt
parents Eltern
park Park
part Teil
partner Partner
party Party
pass vorbeigehen, (eine Prüfung) bestehen
passage Gang, Passage
past n, prep Vergangenheit, nach
pay, paid, paid (be)zahlen
pen Stift
people Leute
perfect Perfekt
perhaps vielleicht
person Person
personal persönlich
petrol Benzin
phone n, v Telefon, anrufen
photo(graph) Foto(graf)
phrase Phrase, Satz
piano Klavier
pick (up) wählen (aufheben)
picture Bild
piece Stück
place Ort
plane Flugzeug
plate Teller
play n, v Schauspiel, spielen
please bitte
plural Plural, Mehrzahl
pocket Tasche (Kleidung)
point Punkt
police(-man) (-women) Polizei (Polizist/in)
poor arm
pop Pop
possessive possessiv, besitzanzeigend
post Post
postcard Postkarte, Ansichtskarte
pound Pfund
practice üben
preposition Präposition, Verhältniswort
present adj, n anwesend, Geschenk, Gegenwart
press drücken
pretty hübsch
pronoun Pronomen, Fürwort
pull ziehen
push drücken
put, put, put stellen, legen, befestigen

quantifier Mengenbezeichnung
quarter Viertel
queen Königin
question Frage
quiet ruhig
quite fast, ganz

radio Radio
rain Regen, regnen
rather lieber
read, read, read lesen
real echt
record Schallplatte
red rot
regular regelmäßig
relative Verwandte(r)
restaurant Restaurant
rich reich
ride, rode, ridden reiten, fahren
right richtig, rechts
ring, rang, rung läuten, klingeln
road Straße
roof Dach
room Zimmer
rose n Rose
round rund, um, herum
run, ran, run rennen

safe sicher
sail segeln
same gleiche(r, s), selbe(r, s)
sand Sand
save retten, sparen, speichern
say, said, said sagen
school Schule
Scotland Schottland
second adv, n zweite(r, s), Sekunde
see, saw, seen sehen
sell, sold, sold verkaufen
send, sent, sent schicken, senden
sentence Satz
set, set, set stellen, setzen, legen
sheep Schaf
ship Schiff
shop(ping) Laden (Einkaufen)
short kurz
should soll/en, sollte/n
shout schreien
show, showed, shown/ showed zeigen
shut, shut, shut schließen
side Seite, Rand
sign Schild, Zeichen
silly dumm, blöd
silver Silber
simple einfach
since seit
sing, sang, sung singen
single einzel(n)
singular Singular, Einzahl
sir Herr
sister Schwester
sit, sat, sat sitzen
sky Himmel
sleep, slept, slept schlafen
slow langsam
small klein
smell, smelt/-ed, smelt/-ed riechen
smile n, v Lächeln, lächeln
smoke n, v Rauch, rauchen
so so, in dieser Weise
some(-body) (-one) (-times)(-where) etwas, einige, (jemand) (manchmal) (irgendwo/ hin)
son Sohn
song Lied
soon bald
sorry Entschuldigung
sort Art, Typ
space Platz, Raum
speak, spoke, spoken sprechen
spelling Rechtschreibung
spend, spent, spent verbringen, ausgeben
stairs Treppe
stand, stood, stood stehen
start Anfang
statement Aussage
station Bahnhof
stay bleiben
stone Stein
stop aufhören, Halt
story Geschichte
street Straße
strong stark
stupid dumm, blöd
such solche(r, s)
sugar Zucker
suitcase Koffer
summer Sommer
sun Sonne
superlative Superlativ
supermarket Supermarkt
sweet adj, n süß, Bonbon
swim, swam, swum schwimmen
switch (on/off) n, v Schalter, ein/ausschalten

table Tisch
take, took, taken nehmen
talk reden, sprechen
tall hoch, lang, groß
tape Band
tea Tee
teach, taught, taught unterrichten
teacher Lehrer(in)
team Team
telephone Telefon
television Fernseher
tell, told, told sagen, erzählen
tennis Tennis
tense Zeitform
terrible schrecklich
text Text
than als
thank bedanken
thanks Danke
that adv, conj, pron jene(r, s), daß, das
the der, die, das
then dann
there (is/are) dort, (es gibt)
these diese
thief Dieb
thin dünn
thing Ding, Sache
think, thought, thought denken, meinen
this diese(r, s)
those jene
through durch
throw, threw, thrown werfen
ticket (Fahr)karte
till bis
time Zeit, Mal
tired müde
title Titel
to an, zu, nach, bis
today heute
together zusammen
tomorrow morgen
tonight heute Nacht
too auch, zu
top Spitze, Gipfel
town Stadt
toy Spielzeug
traffic Verkehr
train Zug
translate übersetzen
travel reisen
tree Baum
trip Reise
trouble Ärger
true richtig
try versuchen
turn einbiegen, sich verändern
TV n, v Fernseher(n)

under(lined) unter, unterhalb (unterstrichen
understand, understood, understood verstehen
until bis
up auf, hinauf
use verwenden
usually gewöhnlich

verb Verb, Tätigkeitswort
very sehr
village Dorf
visit n, r Besuch, besuchen
vocabulary Vokabular, Wortschatz
voice Stimme

wait warten
waiter/waitress Kellner(in)
wake, woke/waked, woken/waked aufwachen, wecken
walk laufen, gehen
wall Wand, Mauer
want wollen
warm warm
was (be) war (sein)
wash waschen
watch beobachten, anschauen
water Wasser
way Weg
weather Wetter
week Woche
well adj, interj gut, gesund, also
were (be) waren (sein)
wet naß
what was
wheel Rad
when wann
where wo(hin)
which welche(r, s)
white weiß
who wer
whole ganz
why warum
wife Ehefrau
will werden
win, won, won gewinnen
window Fenster
winter Winter
with(-out) mit (ohne)
woman Frau
wonderful wunderbar
wood Holz, Wald
word Wort
work, n, v Arbeit, arbeiten
worse schlechter
worst am schlechtesten
would würde(n)
write, wrote, written schreiben
wrong falsch

yeah ja, klar
year Jahr
yes ja
yesterday gestern
yet schon, bis jetzt
young jung

Irregular verbs

No.	Infinitive	Past tense	Past participle	German
1	**be** [iː]	**was** [ɒ], were [ɜː]	**been** [iː]	*sein*
2	**beat** [iː]	**beat** [iː]	**beaten** [iː]	*schlagen*
3	**become** [ʌ]	**became** [eɪ]	**become** [ʌ]	*werden*
4	**begin** [ɪ]	**began** [æ]	**begun** [ʌ]	*beginnen*
5	**break** [eɪ]	**broke** [əʊ]	**broken** [əʊ]	*brechen*
6	**breed** [iː]	**bred** [e]	**bred** [e]	*züchten*
7	**bring** [ɪ]	**brought** [ɔː]	**brought** [ɔː]	*bringen*
8	**build** [ɪ]	**built** [ɪ]	**built** [ɪ]	*bauen*
9	**burn** [ɜː]	**burnt/ed** [ɜː]	**burnt/ed** [ɜː]	*brennen*
10	**buy** [aɪ]	**bought** [ɔː]	**bought** [ɔː]	*kaufen*
11	**catch** [æ]	**caught** [ɔː]	**caught** [ɔː]	*fangen*
12	**choose** [uː]	**chose** [əʊ]	**chosen** [əʊ]	*wählen*
13	**come** [ʌ]	**came** [eɪ]	**come** [ʌ]	*kommen*
14	**cost** [ɒ]	**cost** [ɒ]	**cost** [ɒ]	*kosten*
15	**cut** [ʌ]	**cut** [ʌ]	**cut** [ʌ]	*schneiden*
16	**do** [uː]	**did** [ɪ]	**done** [ʌ]	*tun*
17	**drink** [ɪ]	**drank** [æ]	**drunk** [ʌ]	*trinken*
18	**drive** [aɪ]	**drove** [əʊ]	**driven** [ɪ]	*fahren*
19	**eat** [iː]	**ate** [e]	**eaten** [iː]	*essen*
20	**fall** [ɔː]	**fell** [e]	**fallen** [ɔː]	*fallen*
21	**feed** [iː]	**fed** [e]	**fed** [e]	*füttern*
22	**feel** [iː]	**felt** [e]	**felt** [e]	*fühlen*
23	**fight** [aɪ]	**fought** [ɔː]	**fought** [ɔː]	*kämpfen*
24	**find** [aɪ]	**found** [aʊ]	**found** [aʊ]	*finden*
25	**flee** [iː]	**fled** [e]	**fled** [e]	*fliehen*
26	**fly** [aɪ]	**flew** [uː]	**flown** [əʊ]	*fliegen*
27	**forget** [e]	**forgot** [ɒ]	**forgotten** [ɒ]	*vergessen*
28	**get** [e]	**got** [ɒ]	**got** [ɒ]	*bekommen*
29	**give** [ɪ]	**gave** [eɪ]	**given** [ɪ]	*geben*
30	**go** [əʊ]	**went** [e]	**gone** [ɒ]	*gehen*
31	**grow** [əʊ]	**grew** [uː]	**grown** [əʊ]	*wachsen*
32	**hang** [æ]	**hung/hanged** [ʌ]	**hung/hanged** [ʌ]	*hängen*
33	**have** [æ]	**had** [æ]	**had** [æ]	*haben*
34	**hear** [ɪə]	**heard** [ɜː]	**heard** [ɜː]	*hören*
35	**hit** [ɪ]	**hit** [ɪ]	**hit** [ɪ]	*schlagen*
36	**hold** [əʊ]	**held** [e]	**held** [e]	*halten*
37	**hurt** [ɜː]	**hurt** [ɜː]	**hurt** [ɜː]	*verletzen*
38	**keep** [iː]	**kept** [e]	**kept** [e]	*(be)halten*
39	**know** [əʊ]	**knew** [juː]	**known** [əʊ]	*kennen, wissen*
40	**lay** [eɪ]	**laid** [eɪ]	**laid** [eɪ]	*legen*
41	**lead** [iː]	**led** [e]	**led** [e]	*führen*
42	**learn** [ɜː]	**learnt/ed** [ɜː]	**learnt/ed** [ɜː]	*lernen*

iː	ɪ	e	æ	ɒ	ɔː	ʊ	uː	ʌ	ɜː	əʊ	aʊ	aɪ	eɪ	eə	ɪə
see	sit	ten	bad	got	saw	put	too	cut	bird	no	now	I	say	air	ear

43	**leave** [iː] **left** [e] **left** [e]	*(ver)lassen*
44	**let** [e] **let** [e] **let** [e]	*lassen*
45	**lie** [aɪ] **lay** [eɪ] **lain** [eɪ]	*liegen*
46	**lose** [uː] **lost** [ɒ] **lost** [ɒ]	*verlieren*
47	**make** [eɪ] **made** [eɪ] **made** [eɪ]	*machen*
48	**mean** [iː] **meant** [e] **meant** [e]	*meinen, bedeuten*
49	**meet** [iː] **met** [e] **met** [e]	*treffen*
50	**overtake** [eɪ] **overtook** [ʊ] **overtaken** [eɪ]	*überholen*
51	**pay** [eɪ] **paid** [eɪ] **paid** [eɪ]	*zahlen*
52	**put** [ʊ] **put** [ʊ] **put** [ʊ]	*setzen, stellen, legen*
53	**read** [iː] **read** [e] **read** [e]	*lesen*
54	**ride** [aɪ] **rode** [əʊ] **ridden** [ɪ]	*reiten, fahren*
55	**ring** [ɪ] **rang** [æ] **rung** [ʌ]	*läuten*
56	**rise** [aɪ] **rose** [əʊ] **risen** [ɪ]	*steigen*
57	**run** [ʌ] **ran** [æ] **run** [ʌ]	*rennen, laufen*
58	**say** [eɪ] **said** [e] **said** [e]	*sagen*
59	**see** [iː] **saw** [ɔː] **seen** [iː]	*sehen*
60	**sell** [e] **sold** [əʊ] **sold** [əʊ]	*verkaufen*
61	**send** [e] **sent** [e] **sent** [e]	*senden*
62	**set** [e] **set** [e] **set** [e]	*setzen*
63	**shine** [aɪ] **shone** [ɒ] **shone** [ɒ]	*scheinen*
64	**shoot** [uː] **shot** [ɒ] **shot** [ɒ]	*schießen*
65	**show** [əʊ] **showed** [əʊ] **shown/showed** [əʊ]	*zeigen*
66	**shut** [ʌ] **shut** [ʌ] **shut** [ʌ]	*schließen*
67	**sing** [ɪ] **sang** [æ] **sung** [ʌ]	*singen*
68	**sink** [ɪ] **sank** [æ] **sunk** [ʌ]	*sinken*
69	**sit** [ɪ] **sat** [æ] **sat** [æ]	*sitzen*
70	**sleep** [iː] **slept** [e] **slept** [e]	*schlafen*
71	**speak** [iː] **spoke** [əʊ] **spoken** [əʊ]	*sprechen*
72	**spend** [e] **spent** [e] **spent** [e]	*verbringen*
73	**split** [ɪ] **split** [ɪ] **split** [ɪ]	*teilen*
74	**stand** [æ] **stood** [ʊ] **stood** [ʊ]	*stehen*
75	**steal** [iː] **stole** [əʊ] **stolen** [əʊ]	*stehlen*
76	**strike** [aɪ] **struck** [ʌ] **struck** [ʌ]	*schlagen, streiten*
77	**swim** [ɪ] **swam** [æ] **swum** [ʌ]	*schwimmen*
78	**take** [eɪ] **took** [ʊ] **taken** [eɪ]	*nehmen*
79	**teach** [iː] **taught** [ɔː] **taught** [ɔː]	*lehren*
80	**tell** [e] **told** [əʊ] **told** [əʊ]	*erzählen*
81	**think** [ɪ] **thought** [ɔː] **thought** [ɔː]	*denken*
82	**throw** [əʊ] **threw** [uː] **thrown** [əʊ]	*werfen*
83	**understand** [æ] **understood** [ʊ] **understood** [ʊ]	*verstehen*
84	**wake** [eɪ] **woke/waked** [əʊ] **woken/waked** [əʊ]	*aufwachen, wecken*
85	**wear** [eə] **wore** [ɔː] **worn** [ɔː]	*tragen (Kleidung)*
86	**win** [ɪ] **won** [ʌ] **won** [ʌ]	*gewinnen*
87	**write** [aɪ] **wrote** [əʊ] **written** [ɪ]	*schreiben*

iː	ɪ	e	æ	ɒ	ɔː	ʊ	uː	ʌ	ɜː	əʊ	aʊ	aɪ	eɪ	eə	ɪə
see	sit	ten	bad	got	saw	put	too	cut	bird	no	now	I	say	air	ear

QUELLENNACHWEIS

UMSCHLAGFOTO

Zentrale Farbbildagentur GmbH, Düsseldorf

LAYOUT DER LANDESKUNDESEITEN

David Graham at **Hewett Street Studios,** London

ILLUSTRATIONEN/FOTOS

David Graham at **Hewett Street Studios,** London

WEITERE ILLUSTRATIONEN/FOTOS

S. 10: **BBC**, London; **Radio Times**, John Storey, London; S. 11: **BBC**, London; **Radio Trent**; S. 15, 20, 25, 32, 45, 48, 53, 55, 60, 61, 63, 73, 75, 78, 85, 90, 93, 101, 106, 123, 126, 141, 147, 151, 165: Mike Mosedale at **Hewett Street Studios**, London; S. 23: **Michael Staiger**, Berlin; S. 28: **Cornelsen Verlag**, Berlin; S. 30, 34, 35, 164: **Manpower Services Commission** (Crown Copyright); S. 40: **Warner Bros. Film** GmbH, Frankfurt; S. 40, 100, 104, 110, 140, 150: **Topham Picture Library**, London; S. 44: **Network Photographers**, London; **Wales Tourist Board**, Cardiff; S. 64: **Royal Society for the Prevention of Accident** (ROSPA), Birmingham; S. 70: **Channel Tunnel Group** Ltd., London; S. 74: **The Guardian**, London; **Channel Tunnel Group** Ltd., London; S. 84, 129, 130: **Allan Cash Photo Library**, London; S. 94, 114, 154, 155: **BBC Hulton Picture Library**, London; S. 95: **London Regional Transport**, London; S. 96: **The Mansell Collection**, London; S. 98: **British Railways Board**, London; S. 99: **London Regional Transport**, London; S. 103, 148, 158: Graham Humphreys at **Hewett Street Studios**, London; S. 104: **Network Photographers**, London; S. 114, 118: **MCA Music** GmbH, München; S. 114, 115, 168: **Reinhard Schultz**, Berlin; S. 120: **British Aerospace** plc., Hertfordshire; S. 124: **Deutsche Presse Agentur**, Frankfurt; S. 138: **SBK Song Musikverlag**, Frankfurt; S. 154: **Susan Thomas**, Hadlow, Kent; S. 159: **Knight Features**, London.

DANKSAGUNG

Der Verlag bedankt sich für die freundliche Unterstützung bei folgenden Personen/Institutionen: **The Cabinet Office** (Office for the Minister for the Civil Service), London; **The Curator of the House of Commons Library**, London; **The Development Office of Cumbria County Council**; **Allan Cash Photo Library**, London.